GRESHAM'S LAW

THE LIFE AND WORLD OF
QUEEN ELIZABETH I'S BANKER

GRESHAM'S LAW

THE LIFE AND WORLD OF
QUEEN ELIZABETH I'S BANKER

JOHN GUY

P

PROFILE BOOKS

First published in Great Britain in 2019 by
Profile Books Ltd
3 Holford Yard
Bevin Way
London WC1X 9HD
www.profilebooks.com

A CIP catalogue record for this book is available from the British Library.

ISBN 978 1 78816 236 4
eISBN 978 1 78283 541 7

Typeset in Garamond by MacGuru Ltd
Printed and bound in Great Britain by Clays Ltd, Elcograf S.p.A.

FSC
www.fsc.org
MIX
Paper from
responsible sources
FSC® C018072

CONTENTS

Acknowledgements   vii
List of illustrations   x
Abbreviations   xii
Author's note   xvi

Introduction   1
1   Seeds of ambition   9
2   Antwerp   19
3   Trade and domesticity   32
4   Risks and rewards   44
5   A family quarrel   53
6   The wheel of fortune   64
7   Smoke and mirrors   74
8   Regime change   86
9   Gresham's law   95
10 Shifting tides   106
11 New threats and dangers   118
12 A merchant prince   129
13 Royal Exchange   140
14 Into the black   151
15 Marrying off a daughter   162
16 The end of Antwerp   173

17 A golden goodbye   183
18 One last glorious deal?   193
19 A widow's plight   205
20 Gresham College   216
21 Gresham on the stage   227
22 A reputation established   237
    Appendix: The birth date of Thomas Gresham   251

    Notes and references   253
    Index   311

ACKNOWLEDGEMENTS

This book is something of a new departure for me. Commissioned by the Corporation of London and the Mercers' Company through the vehicle of Gresham College for the 500th anniversary of Gresham's birth, I undertook to write it on the understanding that it was always to be a biography rather than an economic history of banking or the Royal Exchange. In easing my passage towards compiling an electronic and photographic database of sources and for other help and assistance, I'm especially grateful to Jane Ruddell, the Mercers' Company historian, and her colleague Donna Marshall, the Company's archivist. Equally supportive were the archivists and staff of the Large Documents Room at the National Archives at Kew, the Archives Générales du Royaume in Brussels, the FelixArchief in Antwerp, the London Metropolitan Archives, the British Library, Lambeth Palace Library, Gonville and Caius College archives, and the art curators of the Rijksmuseum in Amsterdam and the National Portrait Gallery in London, notably Charlotte Bolland. As ever, the staff of Cambridge University Library and the superlative London Library provided exceptional help. For invaluable comments on the draft manuscript, I warmly thank Sir Roderick Floud, Sir Richard Evans, Debby Ounsted, Jane Ruddell, Ian Adamson, Charles O'Brien, Giles Shilson and Michael Mainelli. Any unexpurgated mistakes are my own.

Gresham left behind a vast body of archival material, but much of it is widely scattered and his often eclectic handwriting and orthography mean than some of it is extremely time-consuming to read fully and digest. My greatest debts are to Nigel Ramsay for generously sharing with me many of the Gresham letter transcripts and related notes made by his father, the eminent economic historian G. D. Ramsay, and to Ian Adamson, the leading authority on the early history of Gresham College, who lent me copies of his doctoral dissertation as well as several published articles and unpublished typescripts, and allowed me to cite them. Alan Bryson was sponsored by Gresham College for six months to identify and transcribe a clutch of Gresham letters, mainly of the period of Edward VI and Mary's reigns, and to obtain electronic copies where possible of the entire Gresham letter manuscript corpus. I am most grateful for his contributions. Assistance with the letters enabled me to concentrate during the earlier stages of research on identifying and photographing the very large quantities of financial and legal records, many of them inadequately listed, if listed at all, that contain material relevant to Gresham. Much of this information has never previously been used by historians, and some never previously seen. Its often very technical nature meant that photographing the whole was necessary before decisions could be made as to what was of the highest significance for the biography and what, necessarily, had to be left out.

Fellow scholars, hearing of my work on Gresham, have kindly sent me references or photocopies. Professor Glyn Parry generously gave me several key references to Gresham's debts and Spanish adventure from the voluminous Elizabethan Exchequer Memoranda Rolls (E 159), which he was searching for a project of his own. For help with illustrations, and for generously allowing usage free of reproduction charges, I'm most grateful to the officials of the Rijksmuseum, the Mercers' Company, the London Metropolitan Archives, Cambridge University Library, the Masters of the Bench of the Honourable Society of Gray's Inn, and the Yale Center for British Art, New Haven, Connecticut. Other images were supplied by their copyright owners with their usual speed and efficiency.

I warmly thank Peter Robinson and Natasha Fairweather, my agents, for their encouragement and support. It was Peter who first persuaded me that this was a challenge I could realistically complete. I owe an immense debt to Ed Lake, my editor at Profile, for the speed and sensitivity with which he made helpful suggestions when editing the initial draft of the manuscript and for a number of particularly valuable reflections as to why Gresham still matters and how his story could be thrown open a little more for a wider audience. Fiona Screen did a superb job as copy-editor, and for this I thank her. As ever, I'm grateful to my students at Clare College, Cambridge, for engaging with my views on Gresham and for putting up during their weekly supervisions with our discussions turning round to issues of Tudor trade, banking and royal borrowing more than would usually have been the case.

My wife, the historian Julia Fox, has lived through the last three years in which Gresham has haunted our lives with a degree of tolerance for which I feel decidedly unworthy. Only rarely have her eyes glazed over on the many occasions his name has been mentioned. And at an exceptionally busy time in 2017, when an adaptation of my 2004 biography of Mary queen of Scots was being filmed for the cinema, she bailed me out by heroically sorting and filing transcripts and photocopies of the entire Gresham correspondence in chronological order and making an invaluable crib that I could use to cross-correlate with exchequer documents and other primary sources from the National Archives and elsewhere. She read and commented on every chapter of the book, some several times. Without her love and generosity, I would not have been able to finish a project involving such a large archival sweep in time to meet a submission deadline yoked to a 500th anniversary. For her help and constant support, I can never adequately thank or repay her.

London
5 March 2019

ILLUSTRATIONS

Front endpaper: Plan of Antwerp, *c.*1605; engraving by Pieter van der Heyden, after Lambert van Noort (by permission of the Rijksmuseum, Amsterdam)

Back endpaper: Map of Flanders, showing the principal corridor of Gresham's journeys to and from Antwerp; by an unknown engraver, published by Domenico Zenoi, Venice, 1559 (by permission of the Rijksmuseum, Amsterdam)

Colour plates

Thomas Gresham, *c.*1545; oil on panel by an unknown Netherlandish artist (by permission of the Mercers' Company, London)

A letter from Thomas Gresham to Queen Elizabeth I, relating to money borrowed in Antwerp, 25 February 1559 [1560] (by permission of the National Archives, Kew)

The New Bourse at Antwerp; engraving from L. Guicciardini, *Descrittione ... di tutti i paesi Bassi*, Antwerp, 1588 (by permission of the Syndics of Cambridge University Library)

Gresham's Royal Exchange, *c.*1569, engraving by Frans Hogenberg (by permission of the Rijksmuseum, Amsterdam)

Thomas Gresham's house, 'St Franciscus', in Antwerp (author's photograph)

A ring presented by Thomas Gresham to Richard Lee (© Victoria and Albert Museum, London)

Thomas Gresham, *c.*1563; oil on panel by Anthonis Mor (by permission of the Rijksmuseum, Amsterdam)

Thomas Gresham's wife, Anne Ferneley, *c.*1563; oil on panel, transferred
    to canvas, by Anthonis Mor (by permission of the Rijksmuseum,
    Amsterdam)
The Hof van Liere, the administrative headquarters of the English cloth
    merchants in Antwerp from 1558 (author's photograph)
Gresham College, *c.*1739; engraving by George Vertue (by permission of
    London Metropolitan Archives)
Lord Robert Dudley, wearing the collar of the Order of the Garter; oil
    on panel, attributed to Steven van der Meulen (by permission of the
    Yale Center for British Art, New Haven, Connecticut)
Margaret of Parma; oil on panel, transferred to canvas, by Anthonis Mor
    (John G. Johnson Collection, 1917, Cat. 428, Philadelphia Museum
    of Art)
William I, Prince of Orange; oil on panel by Adriaen Thomasz Key (by
    permission of the Rijksmuseum, Amsterdam)
William Cecil, wearing the collar of the Order of the Garter, *c.*1572; oil
    on panel by an unknown artist (by kind permission of the Masters
    of the Bench of the Honourable Society of Gray's Inn)
Thomas Gresham's tomb in St Helen's church, Bishopsgate, (detail)
    showing his badge of a grasshopper above the knight's helm
    (author's photograph)
Thomas Gresham, *c.*1567; oil on panel by an unknown Netherlandish
    artist (by permission of the Mercers' Company, London)

ABBREVIATIONS

AGR	Archives Générales du Royaume, Brussels
APC	*Acts of the privy council of England*, ed. J. R. Dasent, 46 vols (London, 1890–1964)
Bath MSS	*Calendar of the manuscripts of the Most Honourable The Marquess of Bath*, 5 vols (London, 1904–80)
BIHR	*Bulletin of the Institute of Historical Research*
BL	British Library, London
BM	British Museum, London
CP	Cecil papers (available on microfilm at the BL and Folger Shakespeare Library)
CPR	*Calendar of patent rolls*, ed. H. C. Maxwell-Lyte, R. C. Fowler, C. T. Flower, J. H. Collingridge et al., 71 vols (London, 1891–1974)
CSPF	*Calendar of state papers, foreign*, ed. W. B. Turnbull, J. Stevenson and A. J. Crosby, 25 vols in 28 parts (London, 1861–1950)
CSPSp	*Letters and state papers relating to English affairs preserved principally in the archives of Simancas*, ed. M. A. S. Hume, 4 vols (London, 1892–9)
CSPV	*Calendar of state papers and manuscripts relating to English affairs in the archives and collections of Venice and in other libraries of Northern Italy*, ed. R. Brown, G. Cavendish-Bentinck and H. F. Brown, 38 vols (London, 1864–1947)
CUL	Cambridge University Library
De Castries	*Les sources inédites de l'histoire du Maroc. Première série*, ed. H. de Castries, 3 vols (Paris, 1918–25)

EcHR	*Economic history review*
EHR	*English historical review*
FelixArchief	FelixArchief, Antwerp
Hatfield MSS	Manuscripts of the Most Honourable The Marquis of Salisbury, preserved at Hatfield House
Haynes	*A collection of state papers ... left by William Cecil, Lord Burghley*, ed. S. Haynes (London, 1740)
HEH	Henry E. Huntington Library, San Marino, California
HJ	*Historical journal*
HMC	Historical Manuscripts Commission
JBS	*Journal of British studies*
JEEH	*Journal of European economic history*
JMH	*Journal of modern history*
Lettenhove	*Relations politiques des Pays-Bas et de l'Angleterre sous le règne de Philippe II*, ed. K. de Lettenhove, 11 vols (Brussels, 1882–1900)
Longleat MSS	Manuscripts of the Most Honourable The Marquis of Bath, preserved at Longleat House (available on microfilm at the Institute of Historical Research and CUL)
LMA	London Metropolitan Archives
LP	*Letters and papers, foreign and domestic, of the reign of Henry VIII*, ed. J. S. Brewer, J. Gairdner and R. H. Brodie, 21 vols in 32 parts, and addenda (London, 1862–1932)
LPL	Lambeth Palace Library
MC	Mercers' Company archives
MS	Manuscript
NBS	*The papers of Nathaniel Bacon of Stiffkey*, ed. A. Hassell Smith, G. M. Baker, R. W. Kenny, V. Morgan and others, 5 vols (Norwich, 1979–2000)
Nichols	*The progresses and public processions of Queen Elizabeth ... illustrated with historical notes*, ed. J. Nichols, new edn, 3 vols (London, 1823)
NA	National Archives, London
NPG	National Portrait Gallery, London

ODNB	*The new Oxford dictionary of national biography*, ed. C. Matthew and B. Harrison, 60 vols (Oxford, 2004) and http://www.oxforddnb.com/public/index.html
RO	Record Office
STC	*A short-title catalogue of books printed in England, Scotland and Ireland, and of English books printed abroad*, ed. W. A. Jackson, F. S. Ferguson and K. F. Pantzer, 2nd edn, 3 vols (London, 1976–91)
Teulet	*Papiers d'état, pièces et documents inédits ou peu connu relatifs à l'histoire de l'Écosse*, ed. A. Teulet, 3 vols (Paris, n.d.)
TRHS	*Transactions of the Royal Historical Society*
TRP	*Tudor royal proclamations*, ed. P. Hughes and J. F. Larkin, 3 vols (London, 1964–9)

Manuscripts preserved at NA are quoted by the call number there in use. The descriptions of the classes referred to are as follows:

AO 1	Audit Office, Declared Accounts
C 1	Chancery, Early Chancery Proceedings
C 2	Chancery, Six Clerks' Office, Pleadings, Series I, Elizabeth I to Charles I
C 3	Chancery, Six Clerks' Office, Pleadings, Series II, Elizabeth I to Interregnum
C 24	Chancery, Examiners' Office, Town Depositions
C 33	Chancery, Order and Decree Books
C 54	Chancery, Close Rolls
C 66	Chancery, Patent Rolls
C 78	Chancery, Decree Rolls
C 142	Chancery, *Inquisitiones Post Mortem*, Series II
E 34	Exchequer, Treasury of the Receipt, Records of Loans to the Crown
E 36	Exchequer, Treasury of the Receipt, Miscellaneous Books
E 101	Exchequer, King's Remembrancer, Various Accounts
E 115	Exchequer, King's Remembrancer, Certificates of Residence
E 128	Exchequer, King's Remembrancer, Decrees and Orders Files
E 134	Exchequer, King's Remembrancer, Depositions taken by Commission

E 159	Exchequer, King's Remembrancer, Memoranda Rolls
E 163	Exchequer, King's Remembrancer, Miscellanea of the Exchequer
E 179	Exchequer, King's Remembrancer, Subsidy Rolls
E 210	Exchequer, King's Remembrancer, Deeds, Series D
E 314	Exchequer, Court of Augmentations and Court of General Surveyors, Miscellanea
E 351	Exchequer, Lord Treasurer's Remembrancer and Pipe Offices, Declared Accounts (Pipe Office)
KB 8	King's Bench (Crown Side), Bag of Secrets
LR 9	Office of the Auditors of Land Revenue: Memoranda
PROB 11	Prerogative Court of Canterbury, Registered Copy Wills
SP 1	State Papers, Domestic, Henry VIII, General Series
SP 10	State Papers, Domestic, Edward VI
SP 11	State Papers, Domestic, Mary
SP 12	State Papers, Domestic, Elizabeth
SP 15	State Papers, Domestic, Edward VI–James I, Addenda
SP 40	State Papers, Signet Office, Warrant Books
SP 46	State Papers, Supplementary
SP 68	State Papers, Calais, Edward VI
SP 70	State Papers, Foreign, General Series, Elizabeth
SP 71	State Papers, Foreign, Barbary States
SP 89	State Papers, Foreign, Portugal
STAC 5	Court of Star Chamber, Proceedings, Elizabeth
STAC 8	Court of Star Chamber, Proceedings, James I

AUTHOR'S NOTE

Dates are given in the Old Style Julian Calendar, but the year is assumed to have begun on 1 January, not on Lady Day or the Feast of the Annunciation (25th March), which by custom was the first day of the calendar year in the sixteenth century. The New Style Gregorian Calendar, advancing the date by ten days, was issued in Rome in 1582 and adopted in Italy and by Philip II throughout Spain, Portugal and the New World in October that year. France followed in December, as did much of the Netherlands. The Catholic states of the Holy Roman Empire followed in 1583. England, Scotland, Ireland, Denmark and Sweden retained the old calendar until the 1700s. Where applicable, dates in primary sources using the new Gregorian Calendar are amended to match the Julian Calendar used elsewhere.

Spelling and orthography of primary sources in quotations are given in modernised form. Modern punctuation and capitalisation have also been provided where none exists in the original manuscript.

Units of currency appear, in the case of English coins, in the pre-decimal form in use until 1971. There are twelve pence (12d.) in a shilling (modern 5p or US 7 cents), twenty shillings (20s.) in a pound (£1 or US $1.39), and so on. Of specie commonly in circulation on the Continent, a Flemish stiver was a silver coin worth two Flemish groats or pence. The Carolus guilder or florin of Brabant was a silver coin worth 20 stivers. The ducat meant usually the gold ducat, worth about 42 stivers. The Rhenish florin was a gold guilder, worth about five ducats. The French crown of the sun (named after the sunburst placed above the royal arms) was worth 38 stivers. A pound in Antwerp meant the Flemish pound, made up of 20 shillings, each of 12 groats. Depending on rates of exchange, one Flemish pound could range in value from anything between 15s. or 16s. and 22s. 6d. sterling. No actual pound coins were in circulation: the pound was a unit of reckoning devised by accountants, but one Flemish pound was equivalent to six Carolus guilders.

Modern purchasing equivalents for sixteenth-century sums are given in parenthesis only where it seems helpful to readers. The effects of inflation and huge fluctuations in relative values render accurate conversions intractable. In 2016, the relative wage or income worth of £1 from 1569 was £3,580 using an average earnings index. The relative value of £1 calculated by alternative methods can range from £305 to £112,800 depending on the index used. A further problem is that the vast majority of government loans or foreign exchange deals in this period were fixed in relation to the price of bullion, chiefly silver, which has not adequately kept pace with inflation. I am therefore sticking to the approach adopted in my other books, which provide occasional rough estimates of minimum modern purchasing equivalents to guide readers by multiplying all the numbers by a thousand. I believe this, on average, to yield credible results based on the values of contemporaries.

Sizes of broadcloths and kerseys were regulated by statute. For customs purposes, the taxable unit was the 'short cloth', i.e., the undyed broadcloth: three kerseys counted as equivalent to one of these. The standard broadcloths each measured 26–28 yards by 1¾ yards, and weighed at least 68 lbs. They were transported and sold in packs of ten.

INTRODUCTION

On 31 October 1517, a young, unknown professor of the Bible at the (then) intellectual backwater of the University of Wittenberg in Germany shocked the whole of Europe by posting up Ninety-Five Theses attacking the abuses of the papacy and the medieval Catholic church. Printed in placard form for debate and disputation in densely printed type covering a whole sheet of nearly A3 size, copies of Martin Luther's famous theses had travelled as far as Hamburg within six weeks and London within four months, by which time the first book burnings of the Reformation had begun, swiftly to be followed by people cheerfully killing each other for the sake of religion.

In England, Luther's theses came first into the hands of Thomas More, appointed in March 1518 to be a councillor, then secretary to the young King Henry VIII. Two years before, More, an early advocate of church reform himself, although afterwards a staunch defender of Catholic tradition and a scourge of the earliest Protestants, had sent a landmark book of his own to the printing press. His *Utopia*, published in December 1516, had as its chief protagonist an imaginary ship's captain, Raphael Hythloday, who had travelled to the New World three times with Amerigo Vespucci before obtaining Vespucci's permission to be one of twenty-four men who stayed behind on an idyllic island at the farthest point of the last voyage. Intended to describe a primitive society where the ideals of 'justice' and 'equality' were made possible only by the strict regulation of wealth, More's pioneering work of social theory was also the very first to argue unambiguously that sovereign rulers had a duty to rule more for the welfare of their subjects than to indulge their private passions, such as warfare, amassing treasure and building luxurious palaces.

When Henry recruited More to his service, he urged him to 'first look unto God and after God unto him' – advice More took all too literally. In 1535 he was executed for opposing both the king's break with the papacy and Henry's claim to be the Supreme Head of the English Church under Christ. More's catastrophe coincided with the stratospheric rise of a Putney yeoman and brewhouse keeper's son. Thomas Cromwell was a self-made man who had fought in Italy as a mercenary in his twenties, worked in Florence for the Frescobaldi merchant bank and in Antwerp for the English cloth merchants, besides making a number of visits to Rome in his early thirties while retraining as a lawyer. A revolutionary intelligence of the first order, but also Henry's enforcer who oversaw with ruthless efficiency the king's rigged treason trials and the dissolution of the monasteries, Cromwell put Parliament as well as the king at the apex of the English constitution. His novel conception of a national, parliamentary sovereignty after Henry's break with Rome raced audaciously ahead of his master's absolutist view of kingship. So when Cromwell married the king to the wrong wife, then was caught out nurturing clandestine cells of religious radicals, Henry killed him too.

In 1519, a third Thomas was born. Thomas Gresham, the son of a wealthy merchant-banker friend of both More and Cromwell, was another revolutionary man, if in an entirely different sphere. He cut his teeth smuggling bullion for Henry during the 1540s, before becoming government banker to three Tudor monarchs, notably Elizabeth I, whom he successfully served for some twenty years. Endowed with an uncanny mastery of the intricacies of foreign exchange dealing and of self-preservation in a period of rapid regime change, he made a near-seamless transition from Edward VI's Protestant to Mary I's Catholic, and back to Elizabeth's Protestant regime. A man with an exalted sense of his own worth, he could be devious, perceptive and capable of a rare impertinence when teaching rulers the basic principles of economics. His originality lay mainly in his unswerving commitment to the new market ethos that emerged during the later Renaissance era, as the sharp recovery of population all over Europe after the ravages of the Black Death stimulated a new desire for wealth. He is best known today as the inventor of 'Gresham's law', first expressed in the catchy phrase 'bad money drives out good money'. A nineteenth-century economist, Henry D. MacLeod, retrospectively attributed this insight to him, but Gresham's foresight in this particular quarter is a myth: the 'law' (insofar as it is one) was already well understood in ancient Greece and had been expounded in the 1360s by Nicholas Oresme, bishop of Lisieux in Normandy. Oresme offered this unwritten law of money in advice to Charles V of France, who succeeded to the throne crushed by debt after his predecessors had repeatedly debased the coinage.

As his remarkable career unfolded, Gresham came to understand better than any of his contemporaries how bankers and money markets could hold monarchs to ransom. The reverse had applied during the Hundred Years War (1337–1453) and Wars of the Roses (1455–1485), when rulers imposed extraordinary taxes and levies on merchandise, notably wool and wine, to pay for armies and shipping. Wool merchants bore the brunt of it: during the first half of the fifteenth century, loans were frequently demanded from them, to be repaid from customs receipts or direct taxation and not on favourable terms.

A century later, the costs of warfare had escalated: innovations in weapons manufacture, and the design of fortifications and shipbuilding, combined with the need to recruit large armies of foreign mercenaries to make war an expensive business. In this fast-evolving milieu, Gresham realised how vulnerable credit-hungry sovereign rulers were to market fluctuations. His insights would turn out to be more applicable to relatively small nation-states like post-Reformation England than to the Habsburg empire or Catholic Spain, with their far greater fiscal resources. But by fearlessly informing successive Tudor monarchs and their leading councillors of these new facts of life, Gresham made himself the first high priest of market economics.

Rulers as unbending as Elizabeth did not always appreciate Gresham's messages or his lack of circumspection in delivering them. This was not least as he was several times tempted to spell out his wider philosophy at length, in circuitous, repetitive memos in which he rarely succeeded in getting across the salient points in a concise or polished way. Adopting a sometimes excruciatingly wheedling, nagging style, he would often omit key elements of his argument, failing to spell out what was obvious to him and opaque to everyone else. Generally his thoughts pour out chaotically onto the page just as they occurred to him. His sophisticated grasp of numbers and rates of exchange, unrivalled by other English and most European bankers and merchants, and his sheer virtuosity as a dealmaker were not matched by his communication skills.

To his fellow London citizens, Gresham was something of an anti-hero. A dark wizard where money was concerned, he was ruthless, obsessive, seemingly loveless, a man unperturbed by the bloody religious turmoil of his age other than when it affected the money markets. To us, he can seem something of an enigma. To enter his world is often to feel trapped in a maze of fast trades, dizzyingly complex financial instruments, rigged exchange rates, devilish small print and blatant cronyism. For all his mastery of the exchanges, his methods often reeked of smoke and mirrors, and much of his early city prowess depended on brute force or blackmail. Few of the more nefarious techniques of the New York and London banking world before the crash of 2008 were unknown to him. A Tudor banker's world, admittedly, was almost entirely unregulated: standards were lower, but many of the tricks were the same.

Thomas was the younger son of Sir Richard Gresham, a merchant who made his fortune as much from making personal loans and speculating in land as he did from trade. From an early age, Thomas showed unusual gifts as a linguist. Educated at Cambridge before being apprenticed to his uncle, Sir John Gresham, he climbed up the ladder in the Mercers' Company, establishing himself by his mid-thirties as a force to be reckoned with. To secure working capital, he cynically married Anne Ferneley, widow of William Read, a wealthy merchant who died young. Noted for his tough negotiating skills and punishing routine in the 'bourse' or main credit market at Antwerp, Thomas made himself a second home in that vibrant, diverse city, then the hub of the financial markets and luxury trades north of the Alps. From there, he carved out a very different type of career path to those of his father and uncle, commuting to and from London, making around 120 journeys over the next thirty years.

In 1549, when the boy-king Edward VI was the titular ruler of England, massive crown debts left over from Henry VIII's wars in France coupled with a stroke of good fortune and an unrivalled capacity for self-promotion enabled Gresham to begin his high-flying career as the official government banker. On Edward's early death, he ingeniously made the transition to the new regime of Henry's elder daughter, the Catholic Mary I. Almost miraculously, when the Protestant Elizabeth, Henry's younger daughter, succeeded her in November 1558, Gresham was one of the first to greet her at Hatfield in Hertfordshire. He knelt before her and kissed her hand alongside his new-found friend William Cecil, her long-standing fixer and future chief minister. Cecil was a relentless persuader by all means at his disposal – cordial, devious or quietly brutal – and it would be as much through his mediation as from Elizabeth's personal choice that Gresham found it possible to ingratiate himself and retain his role as government banker.

For the next two decades, Gresham worked hand-in-glove with Elizabeth's leading advisers, chiefly Cecil and later the queen's favourite, Lord Robert Dudley. In these dangerous years, the politics of Europe were transformed by the death of the Holy Roman Emperor, Charles V, and by the onset of bloody religious wars in France and the Spanish Netherlands. When Philip II introduced the Inquisition into the Netherlands, Antwerp descended into chaos and the threat to England's independence from Spain's global empire morphed into cold war. To meet this challenge, Thomas encouraged Elizabeth to borrow from merchants and wealthy individuals in the city of London rather than abroad, so as to reduce, then almost eliminate, her dependence on overseas credit. And yet it would prove to be a slow process of transition, fraught with hazards, imperfectly achieved and carrying with it extraordinary risks.

Gresham sought and won fame through costly building and philanthropic projects he could scarcely afford, notably the Royal Exchange and Gresham College. Desired by a generation of city merchants, the Royal Exchange was London's very own bourse, modelled on Antwerp's in its heyday: a magnificent edifice designed by a Flemish architect and largely built by Flemish workmen. Not content with this, Gresham went on to found Gresham College as an institution of higher learning for Londoners. It opened its doors in 1597, the year after his wife's death, on the site of his grand town house in Bishopsgate.

Some of the raciest passages in this book will come from a fuller investigation of Gresham's private life than anything attempted before. Not only did he seek to short-change his wife and stepsons, he also twice betrayed her by sleeping with other women, the second time with explosive long-term consequences. For all his fabled wealth, he died heavily in debt, leaving his resentful widow to pick up the pieces. He short-changed a future son-in-law on his marriage, his shenanigans provoking the bridegroom's father sourly to complain that Gresham was 'an ill-dealer' and that 'these merchants would never perform their promises when it came to the push'. He short-changed his sister-in-law, granting her an annuity in her hour of need, but failing to keep up regular payments.

To pull off the Royal Exchange, Gresham offered to pay all the construction costs of the new premises if the Corporation of London would purchase and clear a prime site near the junction of Cornhill and Threadneedle Street, more or less directly opposite what is now the Bank of England. He promised to leave the Corporation the building and all its profits outright after his and his wife's death, but failed to deliver in his will, diverting those assets to found his other pet project, Gresham College. He promised money to Cambridge University, then abruptly changed his mind. He even secured a prized burial spot at his local parish church, St Helen's Bishopsgate, by offering an endowment to build a steeple on which he never made good.

To get to grips with Gresham's professional life, I had to reassemble close to 10,000 pages of previously unexploited financial papers and parchments hidden away in the National Archives, British Library, FelixArchief in Antwerp and Archives Générales du Royaume in Brussels. Pride of place goes to some 440 of Thomas's letters now held in libraries and archives in London, New York and Chicago. The letter corpus currently stands at 314 letters from Gresham and 125 to him. Of the 314, 142 have never been printed, apart from some very brief summaries. Gresham's hand is generally neat, but often difficult to read as he favoured unusual letter shapes and wrote phonetically. From his unorthodox spelling, we can infer that he spoke with a thick Norfolk accent just like his father and grandfather.

To unearth the secrets of his private life, I had to look well beyond his journal or 'Day Book' now in the Mercers' Company archives. It was only after sifting through some 450 boxes of unlisted, largely unsorted Chancery depositions and several hundred folios of witness testimony in the court of Star Chamber that I was able to make the crucial discoveries. Taken together, these materials allow Gresham's professional and private lives to be reintegrated on a mutually reinforcing basis. Rarely does a twenty-first-century biographer tackling a major Tudor player have large caches of often entirely virgin sources to work with. Such is my astonishing good fortune with Thomas Gresham, and I hope it will be the reader's too.

SEEDS OF AMBITION

In August 1538, a tallish, dapper, nineteen-year-old Londoner, recently returned from Paris and already fluent in French, was chosen as a guide and interpreter for a party of visiting French noblewomen. Led by Madame de Montreuil, whom Henry VIII was considering as a future fourth queen, the women were making their way home overland from St Andrews in Scotland, where they had been attending James V's wedding to Marie de Guise. Sir Richard Gresham, London's lord mayor, began by feasting them in the City of London's Guildhall, then deputed this same young man to escort them in horse litters to the port of Dover where their ship was waiting.

The young man was none other than Thomas Gresham, Sir Richard's son. As Richard informed Thomas Cromwell, 'My son hath waited upon and doth keep the same company ... to see them well entertained and used by reason of his language'.[1] Stopping in Canterbury to kill time until Henry came in person to bid the visitors farewell, the young Thomas Gresham took the women and the French ambassador to view the shrine of Thomas Becket. They were almost the last people ever to do so: within a month Henry would flatten and despoil it as part of his campaign against the pope, keeping for himself its treasures, which were packed into two chests so large that eight men were needed to carry them away.[2]

Becket's shrine represented everything that had defined medieval England. That made it repugnant to Henry. Here was an archbishop who resisted his king, whom he denounced as a tyrant. Here were pilgrims seeking absolution at the shrine of a saint. Here was huge monastic wealth, accumulated through the veneration of relics of dubious provenance, but with a history of miracles of healing.

Belief was all, and Becket's shrine had to be seen to be believed. On an

elevated marble base decorated with openwork quatrefoils lay an effigy of
the saint, surmounted by columns and crowned by a sculpted cornice on
which rested a wooden reliquary chest. The sides of the chest were plated
with gold and studded with golden baubles, pearls and precious jewels; its
gabled roof was embossed with golden quatrefoils set in a diaper pattern.
Votive gifts would be attached directly to the surface of the chest by waiting
goldsmiths. According to the great Dutch reforming intellectual and satirist Erasmus of Rotterdam, who visited the shrine in about 1512 with his
friend the dean of St Paul's, 'every part glistened, shone and sparkled with
very rare and very large jewels, some of them bigger than a goose's egg'.[3]

Only rarely were pilgrims allowed to examine the relics. But such was
the status of these visitors that the prior of Canterbury made an exception.
He declined to order the lowering of the chest, so that the women could
lift the lid and see Becket's bones inside their iron box. He did, however,
allow them to examine Becket's shattered skull, kept separately for veneration in an iron box in the crypt.[4]

We don't know what Thomas Gresham made of the experience of
seeing one of the most revered holy relics in the whole of Europe on the
eve of its destruction. Did he recognise this as the last glory of medieval
England, glimpsed moments before its obliteration by a Tudor mod-
ernity whose agent he was destined to become? He might, if he had been
gifted with a certain kind of imagination, have seen in Becket's broken
remains a warning about the consequences of setting any authority above
the English crown. This gorgeous memento mori might have carried any
number of salutary messages to Thomas Gresham. He was himself almost
certainly named after Becket, London's patron saint and patron saint of
the Mercers. And yet, despite writing hundreds of letters over the next
forty years, a dozen or more of which refer to earlier experiences, Thomas
never mentions it. Throughout his life he proved immune to most of the
spiritual and many of the political passions that convulsed his contemporaries amid the new world's collisions of royal, religious and commercial
power.

Gresham was born in 1519, most likely at his father's house in Milk
Street, to the north of Cheapside and within a few yards of the Guildhall
(see appendix for evidence of the birth date). After the publication in 1859
of Samuel Smiles's best-selling *Self-help*, which championed hard work
and self-reliance as the key to life's successes, Thomas came to be regarded
by the admiring Victorians as a self-made man. By 1892, this had fuelled

a myth, circulated by an early banking historian, that he was a castaway infant abandoned in a field, discovered by a passer-by whose attention was attracted by the fortuitous chirping of a grasshopper.[5]

The truth is more mundane. His family took its name from the village of Gresham in Norfolk, near Cromer, where their ancestors lived. His great-grandfather, James Gresham, was a lawyer who made his fortune in London and built a fine manor house in Holt, some four miles from Gresham. James was the first member of the family to use a signet seal with a grasshopper design on it.[6] The family adopted the device as their crest around the year 1450: it was a pun on 'Graes Ham' (the Anglo-Saxon form of the name) when spoken in the thickest of Norfolk accents. Thomas's father, Sir Richard, was born at Holt in about 1485, son of one John Gresham, who married money and catapulted the family into another league. As a teenager, Richard was sent to London and apprenticed to a leading wool exporter named John Middleton, who lived and worked in Fenchurch Street.

In or around 1507, Richard went into business in London and Antwerp with the merchant-tailor William Copeland, a slick operator who knew how to profit from the cheap credit available in Antwerp. Together they bought fashionable silks such as velvet, satin and sarsenet at the Brabant fairs, which alongside dyed and high-quality finished woollen cloths and other luxury goods commanded high prices in London.[7] And when Copeland made his will in 1517 and died within a year, Richard carried on with the trade. Some months before he had married Audrey, the daughter of William Lynne, one of the wealthier Northamptonshire gentry, and they went on to have two sons, John and Thomas.

Precisely how much Richard received in Audrey's dowry we are not told, but knowing Richard the settlement would have been generous. By this time he had a lucrative sideline as a money-lender supplying short-term credit to the cash-strapped gentry and nobility. He pulled off a second coup too, using his role as an executor of Copeland's will to engineer a hasty marriage between his brother William and Ellen, Copeland's grieving widow. This way, he kept most of his former partner's business assets in the family.[8]

After Audrey died in December 1522, very possibly in childbirth, Richard wasted no time in remarrying. His second wife, the feisty Isabel, moved into the household in Milk Street and largely brought up Thomas. She would bear Richard two daughters, Christiana (b. 1526) and Elizabeth

(b. 1528), and as the years went by, she would learn to read Thomas's character so well that by the time she came to make her own will in 1565, she
imposed strict limits on what he could do and what he could touch of her
money and possessions if he wished to become one of her beneficiaries.[9]

Isabel was thirty-three when she married Richard Gresham.[10] For
almost 300 years it was claimed she was the daughter of one 'Worpsall'
and widow of 'Mr. Taverson'. In fact we now know she was one Isabel
Worsopp, the aunt of John Worsopp, the richest scrivener (or legal clerk)
in London.[11] Her friends included the prodigiously wealthy London alderman Sir Thomas Leigh, whose substantial benefactions to the Mercers'
Company in his will would include a silver-gilt grace cup with a cover,
bearing the hallmark of 1499. Her nephew owned the Windmill, a ram-
bling old property a short walk from Mercers' Hall in Cheapside, which
was a synagogue until Edward I expelled the Jews from England in 1290.
Now it boasted 'shops, cellars, solars, stables and appurtenances', along with
a wine tavern.[12] Litigation records and her will suggest that Isabel may have
inherited several family properties. How many may never be known.[13]

It scarcely matters. Richard's business career had taken an upward
leap, and Thomas experienced wealth and luxury as a child. When the
eighteen-year-old Henry VIII succeeded to the throne in 1509, he was
determined to make a great splash. By 1512 or so he was running short of
funds and Richard began cautiously lending him money and supplying
him with luxury items on credit. Before long he was leasing ships, either
from the king or to him, for the transport of goods and munitions from as
far away as Crete and North Africa.

As time went by, one of Richard's specialities became arms dealing for
the king. Henry was determined to claim the French throne and recover
the territories in northern France that were briefly occupied by Henry V
after the battle of Agincourt. Richard financed his military preparations
using a mixture of short-term borrowing in Antwerp and special licences
from the king to export large quantities of unfinished English broadcloths
and kerseys (shorter, coarser woollen fabrics) without paying the usual
customs duties. As early as 1515, he was hiring a royal ship, the *Mary George*,
to sail past the Strait of Gibraltar to purchase naval equipment for Henry.
Two years later he returned to collect several tons of ships' cables valued at
£656 per hundredweight (over £656,000 in modern values).[14]

But the keys to mercantile success in Tudor London were always flexibility and diversification. Richard's most profitable opportunity came in

1520, shortly after the rendezvous between Henry and Francis I of France known as the 'Field of Cloth of Gold', held in the so-called 'Golden Valley' between the towns of Guisnes and Ardres, near Calais. Inspired by the fabulous European textiles and tapestries that had been displayed at this meeting of powers, Henry and his acquisitive chief minister, Cardinal Wolsey, increasingly turned to Richard to supply them with the truly magnificent Flemish-woven tapestries they sought for their palaces and houses.

At first, Richard purchased off-the-peg tapestries on biblical themes for Wolsey's new palace of Hampton Court. Soon, though, he would be measuring up chambers and buying stock for Henry and Wolsey from the leading tapestry suppliers at the great Whitsun fair at Antwerp. His appetite stimulated, Henry began commissioning Richard to procure large, bespoke tapestry sets on selected biblical and classical themes, made at vast cost to his specific sizes and requirements, many woven with solid gold or silver thread so that they shimmered in candlelight.[15]

So useful did Thomas's father become to the king that the family was barely affected when Henry dismissed Wolsey in October 1529 for failing to obtain him his first divorce. It would not be long before Richard had built up an equally close rapport with Wolsey's successor, Thomas Cromwell, whom he would have met in Antwerp in about 1512. The Greshams always possessed an enviable ability to ingratiate themselves with those in power, whoever they were, and to distance themselves from scandal.

Meanwhile, the boy had to be educated. A London merchant's son normally began his schooling around the age of six. Quite possibly Thomas was first sent to the 'alphabet' school run by the Mercers' Company in their chapel, where he would have learned his ABC and the elements of Latin grammar. By 1528, when he was nine, he can be found with sixteen other scholars at St Paul's School, normally located in the cloisters of St Paul's cathedral, though plague forced it, for fifteen or sixteen weeks of that year, to migrate to the country house of the high master, John Rightwise, in Stepney.[16] Thomas's father, or perhaps his stepmother, Isabel, then arranged for him to attend Gonville Hall in Cambridge. It was one of the smaller, older colleges of the university, to all intents and purposes a boarding school of twenty-five to thirty boys and young men, many of whom were monks or training to be priests or monks. Besides taking students in their late teens or early twenties, Gonville Hall was unique among Cambridge colleges in admitting boys as young as eleven or twelve, who paid for their rooms and meals, dined at the fellows' table and paid tuition fees directly to their teachers.[17] These students were known as 'pensioners'.

Thomas arrived in Cambridge in October 1530 at the age of eleven. The college's bursar first billed him (in arrears) for his living costs the following April: he was charged four shillings, and the same again in October 1531. Misplaced for over a century, the handwritten 'indentures for audit' recording these charges were rediscovered in 2016.[18] They identify the much older pensioners by whom Thomas was mentored and alongside whom he studied, notably Richard Taverner, then in his mid-twenties, and William Gonnell, in his mid-forties.

Taverner supported Luther: he was the kind of radical denounced by religious traditionalists as a 'hot gospeller'. A brilliant linguist and translator, Taverner had been recruited by Wolsey for his new Oxford college, then expelled as a suspected heretic. Soon he would be contributing to Henry's propaganda for his marriage to Anne Boleyn and assisting Cromwell as a publicist. Later in his career he went on to write a policy paper attacking the 'insatiable vice of usury', while defending the ready availability of credit as beneficial to society. One imagines that this document would have delighted Thomas were he ever to have seen it.[19]

Gonnell represented an older generation. He was a protégé of Erasmus of Rotterdam, who had attacked papal and monastic abuses and taught Greek and scripture in Cambridge, but condemned Luther for his heresies. Thomas More, an honorary member of the Mercers' Company, had chosen Gonnell as a tutor for his own children and may well have recommended him to Sir Richard Gresham. More's father, a distinguished judge, was one of Richard and Isabel Gresham's nearest neighbours in Milk Street, and Richard once overestimated his own influence with More by trying to bribe him to swing a lawsuit in his favour, sending him 'a fair gilt cup'. In response, he received an embarrassing rebuff. Since the cup's 'legal' worth derived purely from its scrap value, More gave Richard an uglier, more valuable cup in return. By making the swap, he refused the bribe, rebuked the donor and kept a prized piece.[20]

After eighteen months at Gonville Hall, Thomas disappears from the college's records: the presumption must be that his father had earmarked him for the family business. The young Gresham, on the other hand, was eager to make his own way. London's merchants had from very early times been divided into organisations known as 'guilds' or 'fraternities', meaning brotherly associations of a particular trade, usually under the protection of some saint.[21] They were commonly known as 'mysteries', from the Latin word 'ministerium' or the French 'mestier', signifying a trade or occupation. Most importantly, members of these guilds who had completed their apprenticeships were entitled to become freemen of London, giving them privileges and the right to own property in the City. A proportion then went on to become liverymen, which gave them the right to participate in civic elections and run for public office. As the son of a liveryman of the Mercers' Company, Thomas could easily have become a freeman by birth, without serving an apprenticeship. But that was never his way, and most London merchants shared his opinion. As he reflected afterwards, 'Albeit my father Sir Richard Gresham, being a wise man, knew [that] although I was free by his copy, it was to no purpose except I were bound apprentice to the same, whereby to come by the experience and to the knowledge of all kinds of merchandise.'[22]

Thomas was apprenticed to his uncle, John Gresham, who initiated him into the textiles business, while his father taught him some of the secrets of exchange dealing in Lombard Street and Antwerp. By orders introduced in 1449 and 1479, the length of an apprenticeship had been extended from seven to ten years. Claims that Richard secured a place for his son at Gray's Inn so that he could learn the rudiments of commercial law are unfounded. No entry for young Thomas appears in the admissions registers of the inn, and it would have been highly unusual for any student to be admitted there in the 1530s without first undertaking at least two years of study at one of the neighbouring inns of chancery where beginners were trained.[23]

What Richard planned for his son, however, clearly involved a mastery of foreign languages as well as trade. In Cambridge, the teaching was in Latin and for some of the more advanced students Greek. At Gonville Hall Thomas would have acquired a solid grounding in Latin grammar and the study of rhetoric, with a basic knowledge of logic, the classics and history and some acquaintance with moral philosophy. Now it was time for him to become fluent in French and Flemish. He would in time acquire an expert understanding of Italian, a good working knowledge of German and a smattering of Spanish.[24]

We do not know when precisely Thomas left for the University of Paris but by the spring of 1538 he was finishing a stint at the highly selective Collège de Calvi, founded in 1271 and often known as the 'little Sorbonne'.[25] For at least part of his time there, his tutor was an Englishman named Dr John Bekinsaw.[26] When Thomas returned to London in June 1538, he was carrying 'a corporas case' (a silver or enamelled box in which the sacrament of the altar might be placed) for one of Bekinsaw's patrons. His instructions were to deliver it to a tavern called 'the Hanging Leg' in Cheapside to await collection.[27]

Depending on how long he was away, he would have found great changes on his return. The Mercers' Company elected his father as their master in July 1532. He served for a year, and was picked again in 1538 and 1548. In 1531 he was elected sheriff of London – this perhaps a year or two before Thomas left for Paris – and was chosen as mayor for 1537–8.

As a holder of high office, Richard was successful but divisive. The Mercers' Company, which numbered some eighty liveried members, was split between those who opposed and those who supported Henry VIII's revolutionary changes in the 1530s, seeing them as the beginning of a new world. Disquiet flared up when it became apparent that the reformers' careers were being secretly nurtured from inside and outside the royal court by Cromwell and the new archbishop of Canterbury, Thomas Cranmer.

Richard's links to Cromwell and Cranmer were close. He provided Cranmer with credit, breaking the habit of a lifetime by allowing him extra time for repayment, and assisted Cromwell by collecting some of his outstanding debts and by sitting on two of his commissions for trumped-up treason trials; Sir Geoffrey Pole and Sir Nicholas Carew were both sentenced to death partly thanks to Richard, although Pole escaped his fate by turning king's evidence.[28] Cromwell had, in fact, quietly rigged the 1537 mayoral election that Richard won. Without his intervention, another candidate would almost certainly have been chosen.[29] To repay the favour, hearing of Cromwell's wish to remove the images of saints from the rood loft and side altars of St Paul's, Richard at once summoned the dean, and went himself the very same night to supervise the iconoclasm, returning the next morning to check that all had been done.[30]

Once Thomas was home from Paris, his father gradually took a back seat to focus on his dealings on the exchange markets, leaving Thomas and his uncle, Sir John, to manage the textiles and luxury goods side of the family's business. The numbers of broadcloths and kerseys shipped to Antwerp under Richard's name stayed largely unchanged as these years passed. The firm was still the largest shipper out of London, but Sir John was now in charge.[31] Then Richard diversified again, this time speculating heavily in land after Henry dissolved the monasteries. Between 1538 and

1540, Richard purchased properties in Norfolk, Suffolk, Hertfordshire, Kent and several other counties, splitting many into smaller parcels for resale. His richest pickings were at Fountains Abbey in Yorkshire, where the estates yielded a return of £998 annually (over £1 million in modern values). In October 1540, after protracted negotiations with Henry and Cromwell, he paid £7,000 for the abbey church, steeple and churchyard and some 6,000 acres: the title deeds ran to nine large vellum sheets. His first action as the new owner was to strip the monastic buildings of lead and bells.[32]

When Thomas reappears in the records, it is to act as a guide and interpreter for Madame de Montreuil's party. He performed similar duties in December 1539, when he served in the retinue of Sir William Fitzwilliam, the lord admiral, sent over to Calais to accompany Anne of Cleves on the final stages of her journey to London for her brief, ill-fated marriage to the king.[33] Delayed in Calais by the lack of favourable winds, the German-speaking Anne arrived in Dover at the very end of the month. Plans had been drawn up for her reception, with welcome parties stationed at various stages along her route to Greenwich. Too impatient to wait, Henry decided to visit her, incognito, at Rochester Castle in Kent. The plan backfired; he arrived to find her watching a bull-baiting through the window, so engrossed that she paid no attention when an obese stranger in disguise approached her and offered her a gift.[34]

Thomas's marriage to Anne Ferneley, the elder daughter of Suffolk-born merchant William Ferneley and his wife Agnes Daundy of Ipswich, was to last considerably longer than Henry's to Anne of Cleves. The couple tied the knot in 1544 and were yoked together for the next thirty-five years, parted only by Thomas's death. They would have many ups and downs, largely owing to the way their marriage had come about. Quite simply, Thomas married Ferneley for her money. She was a strong-willed woman, several years older and recently widowed.[35] Her first husband was William Read, a wealthy Mercer who dealt extensively in textiles in Norwich and East Anglia before transferring his business to London. At the time of his death he lived with his family in St Lawrence Jewry's parish, no more than 500 or so yards from the Greshams.

Although married for only five or six years by the time William Read fell sick and died, Anne Ferneley had two sons. Perhaps unwisely, Read had named Richard Gresham as one of the supervisors of his estate.[36] Seizing this opportunity, Richard engineered the marriage of the now twenty-five-year-old Thomas to Anne to help meet his son's need for capital.

Thomas's marriage was followed by his promotion within the Mercers' Company. As a liveryman, he was allowed to trade entirely on his own account, to open his own shops and take on apprentices. This important event in Gresham's life came just a year after his admission to the freedom of the Company (only roughly half the freemen could expect to reach the livery). We know his marriage preceded his elevation, and not the other way round, thanks to a newly discovered entry in the handwritten Mercers' Acts of Court. Dated 17 December 1544, it explains:

> Thomas Gresham, Mercer, son of Sir Richard Gresham, knight and alderman of London, for divers good considerations [the] company especially moving, which is apparent & known and also for that he hath married the late wife of William Read, Mercer, deceased, is by the worshipful aldermen, wardens & assistants at this present quarter day assembled, nominated, admitted & appointed to be received into the last livery of 'pewcke' [the 'pewcke' is the famous maroon or dark blueish-brown gown of the Mercers' Company], he to come in at Easter next coming, and to pay the ordinary charges thereof which of right & of old accustomed have been paid.[37]

Thomas celebrated the dual achievements of his marriage and admission as a liveryman in a revealing fashion. While in Antwerp on business, he commissioned a portrait of himself.[38] Oil portraiture on wooden panels was already a well-established genre in Antwerp, but this example was the first of its kind for an ordinary Englishman. Whereas merchants' portraits until that point had shown the sitter's head and upper body alone, this one was full-length, a format then still normally reserved for people of royal descent.[39]

What initially strikes the viewer is Thomas's swagger. He stands slightly at an angle, with one foot edging towards us out of the painting's frame and his shoulders pulled back. His left hand rests on his waist, the thumb tucked casually into his doublet. The unknown Flemish artist carefully depicts his sitter's high cheekbones, long straight nose, short dark hair, thin beard and moustache, but also brilliantly captures how far Gresham imagined himself to be a merchant prince in waiting.

Just as striking is his attire. On each hand he wears a ring, and in his right hand he holds a pair of Spanish leather gloves, a mark of high status. His black cap, doublet and gown are made of fine silk, an expensive fabric and the costliest colour to dye. Despite some paint damage, we can still glimpse how both doublet and gown were embroidered with a leaf pattern, maybe an ivy motif. This was clearly a sitter well acquainted with the rules for the etiquette of dress as set out in Baldassare Castiglione's *Il libro del cortegiano* or 'Book of the courtier', first published in Venice in 1528. Gresham most likely encountered it in the French translation of 1537 during his stay in Paris, where the book was all the rage. As Castiglione advised, a man of taste should generally dress soberly: 'I think black is more suitable for garments than any other colour is; and if it is not black, let it at least be somewhat dark.'[40]

The background to the painting is plain and stark: a bare stone wall of brown and grey, sepulchral in tone and partly in shadow, darkened further by the young man's shadow. On the pale painted tiles of the pavement near his right foot, a human skull with its gaping eye sockets rests on its side, casting more shadow. Whoever the artist was, he was familiar with the Netherlandish trick of counterpointing the bravura of the successful merchant with symbols of mortality and references to spiritual concerns and the afterlife. The ivy motif is itself such an emblem, its evergreen quality suggestive of the soul's immortality.

On either side of the panel, inscriptions identify the young merchant and his recent life events. To the left is written '1544 / Thomas Gresham / 26', followed by Gresham's unique proprietary merchant's mark; to the right 'AG / Love, Serve and Obey / TG'. His merchant's mark and the date, placed exactly where such marks were conventionally positioned in relation to the top and sides of notarially attested contracts and other commercial documents in the archives in Antwerp, extol Thomas's new-found status as a liveryman. As to '26', now that we know the portrait was intended to emblazon events culminating in the twilight days of 1544, it follows that it must have been commissioned and completed in 1545, but with the symbolic date '1544' put on it, by which time Gresham was indeed aged 26.

The other inscription, 'AG / Love, Serve and Obey / TG', clearly memorialises his marriage to Ferneley, but is one of the oddest things about the painting. While it suggests this is, at least in part, a marriage portrait, unlike almost all other Tudor examples of this type, it shows only the bridegroom. Could it have been part of a diptych, as so many other Tudor marriage portraits were?

It appears not. The detailed 'Note Books' of the eminent eighteenth-century art connoisseur George Vertue, now in the British Library, together with a recent examination of the Gresham painting with a high-resolution microscope, put it beyond all doubt that the relatively flat, two-dimensional sides of the painting where the inscriptions are placed are not the product of a botched restoration. The painting looked this way in 1731, when Vertue first described it.[41] In addition, had a companion portrait of Ferneley existed, the composition would have required Thomas's portrait to have been painted with him facing in the opposite direction. In a Tudor portrait diptych, the convention is for the husband to occupy the so-called 'position of power' with his wife to his left, but the position of Gresham's shadow precludes this. There never was a 'lost' companion portrait of Anne Ferneley. Instead, the words 'Love, Serve and Obey' inscribed on the painting find their true meaning as a promise from Ferneley to Gresham, as he believed she had spoken them to him on their wedding day.[42]

This would not be Thomas's last act of presumption in their long, troubled marriage.

ANTWERP

Situated near the sea on a bend in the Scheldt river, Antwerp was a cosmopolitan city with convenient onward river networks, free markets for luxury goods and ready finance.[1] In 1491, the Holy Roman Emperor, Maximilian I, and Philip the Handsome, duke of Burgundy, had granted the city an exclusive right to sell Italian alum, a crystalline sulphate widely used as a fixer of dyes for wool, silk and linen fabrics, and in the manufacture of cosmetics and cheap candles. In 1496, a peace treaty between Henry VII of England and Duke Philip established Antwerp and Bergen-op-Zoom as the principal markets for English cloth on the Continent. In 1498, the king of Portugal made Antwerp the sole northern European outlet for exports of pepper and spices from Asia. By 1500, it was the commercial capital of northern Europe.

Where merchants and money were to be found, artists followed. Soon painters, sculptors, printers, engravers and mapmakers were exhibiting their wares and attracting outsiders to the city. Purchasers from all across Brabant, Flanders and the northern Netherlands would travel to buy altarpieces and paintings, reliquaries, carved panels of saints or scenes from scripture. Since at least 1490, several popes had sent their agents to purchase tapestries and paintings for their palaces and houses, shipped to their destinations in sacks of wool for protection.[2]

Antwerp had wrested its primacy in the European world economy from Venice; now it was one of the great focal points of the world. Spaniards, Germans, Englishmen, Portuguese (notably Jews fleeing the Inquisition), Italians (especially from Florence, Lucca and Genoa), Greeks and Armenians could be found there, and sometimes Turks and black Africans too. Whereas most other cities closed their doors to outsiders through the power of their monopolistic guilds, Antwerp welcomed them and promoted their crafts: leatherworkers from Spain, glass blowers from Venice, tapestry weavers from Brussels and print makers from Germany all set up workshops there. It was the autonomy of Antwerp's markets that allowed merchants to trade between sovereign jurisdictions with a freedom hitherto unknown.

Antwerp's population was fast approaching some 84,000 in 1544, compared with London's 80,000 or so. Paris had more than 100,000 inhabitants and Naples, Venice and Milan each around 100,000. These were huge numbers compared with other English towns. Outside London, the largest cities and towns were Norwich, Bristol, Exeter, York, Coventry, Salisbury and King's Lynn, none of which had a population greater than 12,000. Exeter, York and Salisbury had 8,000 each, and King's Lynn 4,500. In our mind's eye, we may well imagine London to have been the central prop of the Anglo-Netherlandish commercial axis, but in reality this was not the case. For the wealthier consumers of Norfolk and Suffolk, or even Yorkshire coastal towns, it was faster and better to send an intermediary to a market in Antwerp with a shopping list than to ride to London.

The harbour in Antwerp was the most up-to-date of its day. It had an excellent wharf at which sizeable ships could dock and a great loading crane, served by members of a special guild who were in the service of the town and wore its livery. This guild was one of several employed in unloading ships and wagons. One of the earliest things Thomas Gresham would have noticed on his first arrival was builders at work. In 1541 a great fire had consumed both sides of the Maalderijstraat, burning down many houses. Elsewhere, new quays and inland canals were under construction to enable goods to be transported over most of the city, some with wharfs attached, and new walls and fortifications were taking shape, some of which were pierced with triumphal arches in the classical style.

Although far from poor himself, Gresham must have been struck by the wealth of many of the citizens. Notarial documents in the city's archives, many relating to the making of wills or obtaining probate, include inventories recording the contents of typical merchants' houses. These included linen sheets, mattresses and bed hangings; tapestries, embroidered tablecloths, cushions and carpets; paintings and other artworks usually on religious themes, such as the story of Isaac and Rebecca; chandeliers and silver candlesticks; quantities of fine jewellery and chains of gold. Wardrobes would be crammed with clothes of silk, satin, sarsenet and camlet (a fashionable mixture of wool and silk). Bedrooms and some living rooms would contain an ivory crucifix or perhaps a portable altar. Domestic items of copper and iron would be plentiful in kitchens and sculleries – all itemised down to cauldrons and 'pissepots'.[3] When in 1520 the German artist Albrecht Dürer visited Antwerp, many of his admirers gave him presents, often in return for drawings or engravings. The checklist of gifts he received included a piece of white coral, a cedarwood rosary, a plaited hat of alder-bark from southern India, three oil portraits on panel, a pair of Spanish leather gloves, some Portuguese and French wines, sweet-meats including sugar-candy, porcelain from China, a coconut, a Turkish whip, a dish of oysters, barrels of capers and olives, and a parrot.[4]

In a good year, 2,500 ships transported 250,000 tons of merchandise into the port of Antwerp, four times as much as came to London. And given London's relative proximity to the Scheldt estuary across the North Sea, there was every incentive for England's exports to be sold there. By the time Gresham arrived on the scene, some 100,000 cloths a year were being shipped out of London to Antwerp, of which almost 3,000 belonged to different members of the Gresham clan.[5]

Antwerp was busiest during the months of the Brabant fairs, when it positively teemed with life. Around a hundred Englishmen lived there permanently, but the numbers arriving for shorter periods could be six times higher. The Pentecost fair began on the second Sunday before Whitsun, usually from about 25 April to 13 June. The St Bavo's fair began in late August. Only thirty miles away at Bergen-op-Zoom were the 'Pasche' (or Easter) fair and the 'Cold' fair (*Coudemarkt*).

Every year on Maundy Thursday, the commercial cycle opened with the Pasche fair, followed by the greatest of all these fairs at Whitsun, which coincided with the arrival of large grain shipments from the Baltic and of massive wagon trains carrying silk, fustians, linen, silver and copper from Italy and southern Germany. After the harvest was gathered in, the St Bavo's fair started the autumn season and ran to early October, followed with scarcely a break by the Cold fair, which began in late October and lasted a month.

The English merchants used all four fairs to set up their stalls and market their wares. Their busiest weeks fell between Easter and Whitsun, which coincided with the arrival of fresh consignments of broadcloths and kerseys; the Cold fair was usually considered a good time to sell other types of goods, including lead or tin. Ships sailed from London, a fortnight or so before each fair, and once their cargoes were unloaded the English held their 'show days'. Despite agreements between the authorities of Antwerp and Bergen-op-Zoom that their fairs should not compete, as time went by those at Antwerp eclipsed their rivals, and in 1534 the Bergen magistrates complained that the prolongation of the Antwerp fairs was putting their merchants out of business. In the 1490s, Antwerp's Church of Our Lady, whose churchyard stood a mere stone's throw from the market-place, still rented nearly all of its stalls for the duration of the fairs only, but by 1547, some 95 per cent of the church's trade-related income was accounted for by permanent leases of shops, stalls and storage units.[6]

The market-place was the city's largest and most accessible commercial space, but it was not the hub of trade in the city. In 1407, English cloth merchants trading in the Netherlands had united to form the Company of Merchant Adventurers. They secured a house in the Wolstraat, along with warehouses, cranes and weighing-houses, situated between the quays and the market-place. The Company's offices were housed there until 1558, when the Merchant Adventurers moved to a more spacious building, the Hof van Liere in Prinsstraat, an impressive brick structure not unlike a small Cambridge college. Built by the Antwerp patrician Van Liere family during the early 1500s, it boasted a small outer courtyard and an inner quadrangle and is now part of the University of Antwerp.

The Merchant Adventurers were the only Englishmen entitled to ship woollen cloths to the Netherlands. Among these cloth merchants, the most influential were from London, and preeminent among them was the Mercers' Company. It was Thomas Becket, patron saint of the Mercers, who became the patron saint of all the Adventurers, and the Mercers took the lead in London as well as in Antwerp. Around half of the Merchant Adventurers were Mercers; the other half belonged to other livery companies. Of 129 merchants whom we know to have been exporting cloths from London in 1514, at least 43 were definitely Mercers and the actual number was probably around 60. The overlap was such that, when in London, the Adventurers operated out of Mercers' Hall. The Mercers' clerk minuted their proceedings in the Mercers' Acts of Court, and any funds accumulated by the Adventurers at London were locked away in a chest kept at Mercers' Hall. In the absence of the Governor of the Merchant Adventurers, 'the Wardens of the Mercery' were empowered to act as his deputies. When Thomas Gresham was admitted as a liveryman of the Mercers' Company in December 1544, he was automatically enrolled as a member of the Company of Merchant Adventurers. In this sense, the full-length portrait he commissioned of himself shortly afterwards was as much a memorialisation of his trading status in Antwerp as it was of his marriage and admission as a liveryman.[7]

As the cloth trade boomed in the 1520s, the dates by which merchants or their factors were required to pay for their purchases after the Antwerp and Bergen-op-Zoom fairs became a matter of great importance. Credit was dear and scarce except at fair time, and by far the largest part of the bankers' and financiers' business in loans and capital finance was transacted during the fairs, with repayments running from one to the next or rolled over until subsequent fairs. Where transactions not linked to the sale of goods were concerned, Antwerp firmly consolidated its position as northern Europe's premier credit market in 1540, when a decree of Charles V, Holy Roman Emperor, king of Spain and ruler of the Netherlands, legalised the charging of fair interest on commercial loans. In England, it was only in 1571 that Parliament made commercial contracts bearing a rate of interest below 10 per cent unambiguously lawful.[8] Usury, until then a crime condemned by the church and the law, encompassed any loan involving fees or charges, pushing many bankers and merchants into the black economy. In much early Italian Renaissance art, special places were reserved in hell for usurers and sodomites, who were lumped together in Dante's *Inferno* as the worst kind of reprobates, possibly for reasons of anti-Semitism. Charles's move proved to be liberating, making Antwerp the epicentre of the European money markets for the next forty years, surpassing Augsburg, Genoa, Florence and Lyon.[9]

By the time he began his independent business career as a liveryman of the Mercers' Company and as a Merchant Adventurer in 1544, Thomas Gresham had most likely visited Antwerp several times, and he had definitely been to Brussels. When he acted as a guide and translator for Madame de Montreuil and her entourage in 1538, his father, Sir Richard, had urged Thomas Cromwell to find his son a government post. 'Where I have moved your good lordship for my son to be the king's servant', he wrote, 'it may please you to prefer him to the same at this time of your being in Dover'.[10]

Exactly when this preferment came about is unknown, but on 25 February 1540 Sir Thomas Wyatt, the celebrated poet and one of Henry VIII's roving diplomats, wrote to the king from Brussels telling him that 'Mr Parker, Mr Blunt and Mr Gresham', the king's servants, were in this city 'about the provision'.[11] When Wyatt briefed Cromwell from Ghent on 2

April, he mentioned Thomas again: he had brought letters of exchange from his father to Wyatt, who informed Cromwell that he thought Sir Richard would hear shortly from his son that 'I have done him some pleasure in these parts'.[12] Since the business affairs of the Gresham clan meant travelling regularly between England and Antwerp and sometimes Brussels, both Thomas's father and uncle John, or their trusted agents, had served as royal couriers. It was natural that Thomas should do the same, and from there it would be a small step from simply carrying letters to and fro for the king to helping to transport something far more sensitive.[13]

The lion's share of Thomas's career over the next thirty years would be devoted to Antwerp. He made around 120 journeys there, 70 in under 10 years, his stays varying in length from a few days or weeks to three or four months and several times up to twelve.[14] In the earlier years of their marriage, Anne Ferneley sometimes accompanied him. Only once, however, did she consent to a stay exceeding six months. Many of these crossings were extremely hazardous and on more than one occasion Gresham's ship required a naval escort.[15] Quite apart from the threat of attacks by French pirates, ships were vulnerable to shifting sands, high winds and treacherous seas.

Thomas, who suffered badly from sea-sickness, never found these journeys easy.[16] Some ten years after his marriage when he was shipping home some of his and his wife's furniture, clothes and personal effects, he lost everything in a gale. Writing to privy councillors, he bewailed,

> As I was sealing of the letter enclosed herein, I received a letter out of Flanders, whereby I understand that as well my plate, household stuff and apparel of myself and my wife, which I had sent and prepared into Antwerp to serve me in time of my service there, by casualty of weather coming from Antwerp, is all lost. And now God help poor Gresham.[17]

For all the risks, he made his sea crossings directly to Antwerp whenever possible. Only when circumstances required, usually in times of international crisis, did he go by way of Calais or Dunkirk. On these occasions, it was critical to have at least two passports and the right permissions to cross frontiers.[18]

At first Thomas devoted his efforts almost entirely to the lucrative trade in cloth and consumer goods; then slowly but surely he came to be bewitched by the Antwerp exchange, where substantial profits could be made purely from astute currency deals. Trading was concentrated in the New Bourse built at the city's expense, a rectangular, arcaded courtyard 180 feet long and 140 feet wide. Late Gothic in style, the New Bourse had opened in 1531, replacing a smaller one founded in 1469 which was laid out in the shape of an abbey cloister. An inscription over its entrance proclaimed that the New Bourse was for all nations (unlike the bourse at Bruges, which had been frequented mainly by Italians). By 1540, it included, above its covered walks, an upper storey crammed with a hundred or so boutique-sized retail outlets, which famously were tenanted by dealers in fine art and luxury goods, including paintings, tapestries, gold and silverware, diamonds, silk and Turkish carpets.[19]

Each working day, summoned by a bell, merchants from all over Europe crowded into the New Bourse for an hour or so, once in the morning and once in late afternoon. An Antwerp citizen claimed that 5,000 people congregated at these sessions, 'some of whom had to stand outside halfway into the street, not to talk or to hear the news, but only to do business'.[20] Thomas would have noticed the obvious contrast with Lombard Street in London, where merchants were forced to do business in the open air despite the rain and the noise of passing carts and horse traffic.

On their visits to the bourse, merchants invariably checked the notices attached to the board, recording rates of exchange. Thomas would learn to do this, and more, several times a day: 'there is never a bourse', he would later boast, 'but I have a note what money is taken up by exchange, as well by the strangers as by Englishmen'.[21] In this way, he would become a master of fluctuating rates, which he quickly perceived as the key to commercial success or failure.

Deals on the floor of the bourse were usually sealed with a handshake, then confirmed later in writing before local notaries. But before striking them, prudent merchants also caught up on the news. It is scarcely to exaggerate to say that the New Bourse in Antwerp functioned as a sort of early-modern world brain, a great database of information to be ignored at a merchant's peril. 'It was a wonderful thing to see such a great coming together of so many people and nations', observed the Florentine Lodovico Guicciardini in 1567. 'Since there is always such a mass of strangers, there are always new tidings from all over the world.'[22] For those committing hundreds or potentially thousands (millions in modern values) of pounds of working capital to commercial ventures, intelligence of international affairs, peace and war, plague and famine, drought and flood, and cases of bankruptcy or clashes over religion between Catholics and Protestants was critical, because such disorders could quickly affect market rates. Rising rates could ruin merchants who needed to borrow money to buy wares, just as they could line the pockets of lenders. Rates could also have a direct effect on prices. Cheap money opened up the prospect of increased sales and lower prices; dear money had the opposite effects.

Paper money did not yet exist as a circulating medium. Coins were made from either gold or silver, their worth defined by their weight and fineness. Knowledge of which types were in circulation, how finely minted they were and whether their face value differed from their intrinsic value as bullion was crucial.[23] So was information about who else was seeking to borrow money. A mere whisper that Charles V was seeking to raise large sums could throw the entire market into overdrive. Coins from the mints of a dozen or more countries and cities circulated in Antwerp and it was critical for traders like Gresham to understand their relative weights and values.[24]

Wherever there was money, there were fraudsters. Bankers and governments constantly worried over what they called 'clipped coin' – coins with small pieces clipped away by fraudsters who would melt down the stolen metal for sale, then return the coins to circulation. This blatant example of 'bad money' led the Antwerp authorities to devise a scheme for the official valuation of certain coins called 'valued' or 'permission' money. It was held at a premium varying from a quarter of 1 per cent up to 2 or perhaps 3 per cent at times of extreme market pressure.[25] In a century of an exclusively bimetallic coinage, this ensured that such funds would in every case be worth their face value, and it would not be long before Gresham would be stipulating to those who borrowed from him that they should repay him in permission money.

As Thomas gained experience and rose to a position of trust in the government's service, it would be increasingly through his letters that much of the most sensitive commercial intelligence and reports of unexpected swings in northern European politics would find their way to London. By the spring of 1543, all the gossip was of harvest failure, rising prices, the outbreak of plague and, finally, the imminent threat of a renewal of war between England and France. Since Charles V's election as Holy Roman Emperor in 1519, Henry VIII had periodically intervened in the wider ongoing Franco-Habsburg contest, begun in earnest after Charles's forces defeated a French army outside Pavia, near Milan, in 1525, and briefly held

Francis I of France a captive in Madrid. Now once more, Henry was building up his stocks of arms and ammunition, this time ready to aid Charles against Francis. To this end, his agents were busily scouring the German roads and villages to raise mercenary forces from the ranks of the poor and unemployed.

Already in his mid-fifties and walking only with the aid of a staff – his chest circumference had ballooned to fifty-seven inches and his waistline to fifty-four – Henry was in a belligerent mood. In June, his ambassador in Brussels handed Thomas Gresham licences from Mary of Hungary, Charles's younger sister and regent of the Netherlands, to purchase and export to London vast quantities of gunpowder and of saltpetre (or potassium nitrate), the critical element for making gunpowder, ready for the king's campaign.[26]

In July 1544, Henry set out for Calais with his army, sailing on a ship trimmed with sails of cloth of gold. Calais, still garrisoned by the English and the last remnant of Henry V's continental possessions, was an important transit port and trading gateway into Europe, and the presence of a field army there was bad news for merchants. Once his forces had disembarked, however, Henry, struggling to mount his courser, occupied the surrounding area, then led his troops to the town and port of Boulogne, which he besieged in characteristic style, directing his operations at a safe distance from a small wooden temporary palace with its interior walls painted to imitate marble.[27] After his gunners laid a mine under the castle and exploded it, Henry entered the town in triumph and then returned home, handing over the command to others.

But to secure Boulogne, its captors were forced to dig in and build costly fortifications. The war became ruinously expensive. Deserted by his ally Charles V on the very same day as he captured Boulogne, Henry was forced to fight on alone. In 1544–5, he spent a stupendous £1.3 million. With his cash reserves exhausted, he had a hole in his budget of around £1 million (over £1 billion in modern values), even allowing for taxes. He plugged it partly by debasing the coinage, partly by selling off the remainder of the confiscated monastic lands, and partly by borrowing.

First, he raised the prices of gold and silver bullion by royal proclamation, then reduced the fineness of the coinage by replacing some of the precious metal content with cheap alloy, while keeping the face value the same. Between June 1544 and April 1546, the weight of pure metal per £1 sterling in newly minted silver coins more than halved from 116 to 51 grams, and dropped from 12 to 10 grams in gold coins. Henry creamed off the profits of this debasement.

Next, he sold ex-monastic lands, lead, bell metal and other assets in large parcels. Land sales of £165,000 per annum in 1543–4 rose to £240,000 over the next twelve months, while the king's enormous stock of surplus lead, amounting to 12,500 tons, was taken off his hands by two enterprising Spanish merchants who insisted on part-payment in alum. Henry found himself saddled with 300 tons of alum rotting in a Thameside warehouse, since England only consumed 40 tons a year.[28]

Still facing a cash shortfall and unable to raise additional taxes in Parliament as his sovereign authority only took him so far, the king turned to borrowing. Henry sent instructions to Stephen Vaughan, his chief financial agent in the Netherlands, to raise loans approaching £200,000 in Antwerp. The money had to be delivered to the treasurer of Calais, Sir Edward Wotton, who had the unenviable task of mustering and paying the king's mercenaries. In May 1544, Vaughan was reported as attempting to borrow £25,000 a month, and he hit trouble immediately. Credit in Antwerp was scarce and interest rates as high as 12–14 per cent. Henry's chief ally in the war, Charles V, was also seeking funds there, leading Mary of Hungary to complain of Vaughan's activities. Almost immediately, Vaughan discovered that his guarantors, the Buonvisi family of Lucca, had temporarily suspended their operations, so his letters of credit were useless.[29]

It took Vaughan almost a year to agree a loan of £31,800, by which time the mercenaries were demanding payment of four months' wages 'or they will not serve'.[30] 'It is a busy piece of work', he complained, 'to pass through the hands of so ravenous merchants as I shall have had to do with all this town for the said [ex]change, who in every corner lay baits to charge me with interest.'[31] Now the challenge was how to deliver the funds to Wotton in Calais. That's where the Greshams would come in.

It was Italian merchants who invented the all-purpose financial instrument needed to borrow or move money where it was needed without incurring the risks and expenses of shipping cash. Known as the 'bill of exchange', it required the party that wished to remit money and the intended recipient to be at one trade centre, and their factors or agents to be at another. Signed by both parties on receipt of the loan, the bill was an instruction from the borrower to his agent, requiring him to reimburse the lender for the value received at a specified date and place,

and at a stipulated rate of exchange agreed by both sides. The rate would
be expressed at both places as a variable number of coins of one currency
against a fixed amount of another. The rate of exchange would have been
agreed in advance in proportion to the spot or current market rate, and
to the amount of interest payable. (The amount specified for repayment
in the bill of exchange would exclude brokerage fees, which were payable
separately.) It was usual to send two copies of the bill by separate couriers,
so as to avoid loss or delays and thus minimise risk.[32]

Charles, however, had introduced a close surveillance of the posts on
the outbreak of war and issued a decree to catch out those moving larger
quantities of funds by bills of exchange to other markets. For breaching
this decree, the Italian banker Gasparo Ducci of Pistoia, a colourful character from whom Vaughan attempted to borrow 200,000 ducats, would
later be called to account in Brussels: when the authorities finally caught
up with him, they raided his offices and impounded sealed packages containing remittances for Lyon. Ducci would be imprisoned on charges of
usury and monopoly.[33]

If, though, the funds raised by Vaughan had to be delivered to Calais
in cash, it was also obvious they had to be smuggled across the French
frontier and travel through a war zone. Not only that, finding coins in the
correct currencies caused Vaughan many a headache, since Charles refused
to allow certain currencies, notably gold coins from his own mints, to be
exported and ordered random checks on merchants travelling in and out
of his dominions. In enforcing these rules, the authorities were impres-
sively vigilant: to help evade them, Vaughan secured multiple permits to
export different amounts in a variety of different currencies, but it all took
time.[34]

Back in London, Sir Thomas Wriothesley, a leading privy councillor, called in the Greshams to advise how best to move the money to
Calais. Not only could their discretion be relied upon, their expertise in
all matters of commerce was unrivalled. When 'made privy to the purpose'
by Wriothesley, Sir John Gresham cautioned that when moving large
amounts of cash, the sea route from Antwerp was riskier than transporting the money by land, even though, in this instance, the final stage of the
journey after Gravelines involved crossing a war zone. He offered to take
the problem off Wriothesley's hands by sending a trusted person to 'buy
wares and convey them in wagons to Calais'. Henry's loan money would
then be carefully split into batches and hidden inside the bundles of wares

'with a portion of the money in each'. Sir John added, intriguingly, that this was 'as merchants do daily'.[35] Such subterfuge was doubly necessary, as Vaughan had been unable to avoid accepting a portion of the money in the very same gold crowns that Charles had banned from export.

The trusted individual Sir John had in mind was his 'brother's son', his nephew Thomas. To him now fell the risky task of conveying cash amounting to over £31,000 (worth over £31 million today) for the mercenaries in twenty-five large bags, which he was to deliver personally to Wotton.[36] Never had Thomas undertaken anything so crucial or so alarming. He was, in effect, in charge of smuggling a fortune that did not belong to him across Charles's dominions, coupled with the added threat of travelling through hostile territory once he reached France. The route was dangerous: bandits and deserting soldiers haunted the roads, especially after dark. There was always the chance of an ambush by enemy troops. And he knew how much his own future depended on getting the money through safely. The irascible Henry was never one to forgive or to forget failure, especially where such a large sum was involved.

But Thomas was never a coward. Armed with instructions from his father and uncle, and carrying letters to Vaughan, he set off from London to Antwerp.[37] On 9 October 1545, Vaughan handed him the money, and he left for Calais the next day.[38] Gresham was lucky. The journey, in the event, took him less than a month. Not even a heavy shower is recorded to show that his carts were briefly mired in the mud. But the experience brought him face to face with several other problems he would later encounter when working for the government.

One of those was getting paid. After totting up his expenses – even at this early stage Thomas was obsessed by the smallest amounts of money and reckoned his accounts down to the last penny – he claimed the expedition had cost him £28 18s. od. (some £29,000 in modern values).[39] He was about to have first-hand experience of how hard it could be, and how long it would take, to recoup anything from the crown. On 11 June 1546, Vaughan informed the privy council that Gresham 'hath entreated me that his charges may be put to my accounts and that I may allow him, which I will do, if so it please you'.[40] Six weeks later, Henry's councillors finally issued the warrant that allowed Thomas to seek payment from the treasurer of the king's chamber.[41]

Nevertheless, this was Gresham's first significant breakthrough and would prove to be a valuable lesson learned. Suddenly he could dream of repositioning himself from the relatively mundane world of the successful cloth trader and assistant to his father and uncle to that of the government's banker, even of one day perhaps becoming heir apparent to Vaughan in Antwerp. All he needed was time and opportunity.

— 3 —

TRADE AND
DOMESTICITY

For a few weeks or months after their wedding, Thomas Gresham and
Anne Ferneley lived in Sir Richard Gresham's house in Milk Street,
where Thomas had been born and brought up. This was a prime area of the
city, where properties came equipped with cellars and warehousing space,
ideal for merchants.[1] Tax records for 1544–5 suggest, however, that while
Thomas and Anne were briefly there in 1544, they were already planning
to move to Basinghall Street and had done so by the time their taxes were
paid a year later.[2]

While not perhaps quite as prestigious as Milk Street, this was still a
desirable area. For a man like Thomas, status mattered, and where one lived
in London was as important to him as it would be today to an upwardly
mobile city banker. It became part of what he was and wished to become.
Basinghall Street ran south from the city wall at its upper end to the Guildhall. To reach Mercers' Hall, Thomas would only need to walk towards
Catte (or 'Ketton') Street, cross the road and continue along Ironmonger
Lane as far as Cheapside. Along the way, he would pass Blackwell Hall,
London's wholesale cloth market founded in 1397 by Sir Richard ('Dick')
Whittington. City freemen and some privileged foreigners, such as the
merchants of the German Hanseatic League, bought much of their stock
there, although more astute traders like the Greshams rarely did. They
knew how to cut out the middlemen, and preferred, where possible, to buy
directly from country suppliers. Typically Gresham would send his senior
apprentice or another trusted agent on a late winter or very early spring
round trip of Norfolk, Suffolk, Worcestershire and other cloth-producing
areas to negotiate quantities and prices ahead of new stock arriving.

Thomas's accounts show that he bought the lease of his Basinghall
Street home from the executors of Anne Ferneley's late husband, William

Read. This is so, even though Read and his wife had actually lived closer to Milk Street until shortly before his death.[3] Were they planning a move? Or perhaps Read wanted an investment property or more warehouse space; whichever it was, Read had instructed his executors to sell the lease to the highest bidder, along with much of the building's contents, and to divide up the profits among his nephews and nieces.[4] Gresham agreed to pay an annual rent of £66 13s. 4d., and sure enough, his accounts explain that his rent was owed 'to William Read's brothers' and sisters' children', so he honoured Read's conditions.[5] A year or so later, Sir Richard Gresham would take over the lease of a neighbouring property, previously leased to Elizabeth, widow of Sir James Yarford, another wealthy Mercer and city alderman. Richard finally gained entry in the summer of 1548. As this property consisted of 'a great mansion place and garden, with the five tenements adjoining', it is possible that the Gresham clan gradually relocated much of its business to Basinghall Street, although Thomas's father and stepmother kept on their house in Milk Street.[6]

Thomas's house served as his office, shop and warehouse rolled into one. Once he and Anne had settled in, he buckled down to work. Always a fast learner, he quickly leapfrogged over his elder brother John, who would secure his place in the Mercers' Company by right of birth. Lacking ambition for anything much beyond a life of luxury paid for by the hard work of others, John refused to immerse himself in mundane matters of trade. He toyed for a while with the idea of becoming a lawyer, did his preliminary training and secured entry to Lincoln's Inn where he got into a fight; but he never qualified as a barrister.[7]

Not that life at Basinghall Street was always work. The whole household appears to have joined in the celebrations when Thomas's uncle, Sir John Gresham, was lord mayor in 1547–8, and to pass the long winter evenings during the twelve days of Christmas, Thomas hired minstrels to entertain everyone.[8] One pastime he habitually enjoyed in these early years was gambling at cards or dice for comparatively large stakes: advances of cash for this purpose and for settling gambling debts pepper his accounts, typically at the level of £1–2 each, amounts very similar to those Henry VIII bet on cards. Once Thomas bet on a game called 'bank notes'. How many players were needed and how the game worked is unknown, but one would love to think it involved paper money transactions or bills of credit, like an early precursor of Monopoly.[9]

Thomas was regularly in Antwerp in these first years of marriage.

He made several visits a year there, and Anne Ferneley sometimes accompanied him. When he was absent, his establishment at Basinghall Street varied in size depending on the needs of the business. Apart from Ferneley and those of her relatives who had come to stay, it routinely included Thomas Bradshaw, Gresham's senior apprentice; John Elyot, one of the late William Read's factors mentioned in his will; Robert Berney, one of Read's nephews and apprentices who would shortly become Thomas's factor in Antwerp; and several personal and household servants, a number of whom had also worked for Read.[10] In 1547, Gresham would take William Bendlowes and Edmond Hogan as his new apprentices. The Norfolk-born Hogan spoke fluent French, Spanish and German, and would be admitted as a freeman of the Mercers' Company in 1557. He ended up as Gresham's longest-serving, most loyal factor: Thomas, many years later, praised him as 'a man of great credit and service'.[11]

At first, both of Thomas's stepsons, William and Richard, Anne Ferneley's children by her first marriage to William Read, stayed in Basinghall Street. But around the age of five or six, Richard, the younger of the pair, was separated from his mother and sent to board in the country with Ralph Radcliffe, who was paid £10 a year for his tuition and keep. This arrangement sprang from the will of Richard's late father, who specified that his younger son was to be brought up at the discretion of his uncle, Augustine Steward, a former mayor of Norwich. Steward's name crops up several times in Gresham's accounts, not least because he was a leading light in the Baltic trade with the port of Yarmouth.

William, Richard's elder brother, was also placed in the care of a guardian, but in this case the person chosen was Thomas's brother-in-law, Nicholas Bacon, a brilliant young lawyer to whom the family would become intimately tied later in life. Bacon was the husband of Anne Ferneley's sister Jane, and the couple would have six children together. Evidently, though, Bacon decided that it was in young William's best interests to remain with his mother and Thomas. Almost certainly this was because, while Bacon then worked in London as a government lawyer, his main home was eighty miles away in Suffolk and he could not yet afford a London property of his own. To save time and money, he moved in at Basinghall Street. He had his own set of rooms there, for which William Ferneley, Anne's father, ordered a bedstead while Thomas was away on one of his business trips.[12]

On 26 April 1546, Thomas began keeping a journal or 'Day Book' as a principal record of his accounts.[13] It continues until July 1552 when it appears to end abruptly, and the layout and organisation of its 200 densely written folios suggest that he started it at a moment when he had taken over running much of the family business. The journal's entries are terse and often uninformative. To the uninitiated, they seem to add little to Gresham's story. A closer examination, however, reveals much about his life and dealings in these early years.

From the very first page, what most strikes the reader is how far Thomas was attempting to put into practice some of the latest continental approaches to reckoning and accounting. His journal is the earliest example from anywhere in the British Isles of double-entry bookkeeping. Other instances can be found of ledgers using a double-entry format, but they are not examples of complete double-entry bookkeeping. The rules had been set out in 1494 by a Tuscan author, Luca Pacioli, in an influential treatise, published in Venice.[14] We can be fairly confident that Thomas had never seen this: his information came from Antwerp, where an Italian crib was in circulation. A Flemish edition of this crib by Jan Ympyn Christoffels was translated into French in 1543, entitled *Nouvelle instruction et remonstration de la tres excellente science du livre de compte*.[15] When Thomas sat down to lay out the title page of his new journal, he did so on almost the same pattern and in the same words as Jan Ympyn.[16] Improved tracking of credits and debits apart, the great advantage to a merchant of keeping ledgers in this new format was that they could be produced as evidence in the civic courts in Antwerp. Judges accepted them as reliable as they contained sufficient information to be properly audited.

When Gresham was away or too busy, which was much of the time, Thomas Bradshaw kept the journal up to date. From its 6,572 entries, we get a fairly rounded picture of the firm's contribution to overall English trade. By 1546–7 England's exports centred chiefly on unfinished cloths, wool, leather, tin, lead, iron and salt-fish. Imports were dominated by silk, satin, linen, canvas, flax, pepper, sugar, dried fruits, wine (especially French claret and sweet white wines from Spain and the Canaries), oil, wax and alum. Exports specifically to Antwerp mainly comprised broadcloths, kerseys, tin and lead. Imports included German and Italian metallurgical goods, pepper from Asia, sugar, silks, fustians, taffeta, raw materials like madder root (needed for its reddish-purple dye), hops, Baltic timber, pitch and cordage.[17]

England's trade transformed when the country became a prime

exporter not of raw wool but of unfinished cloths; this process had begun in the fourteenth century and was complete by the end of the fifteenth. Exports of broadcloths and kerseys, which came in standard sizes regulated by legislation, totalled around 82,000 per annum in the last six years of Henry VII's reign and had grown to 120,000 or so in 1546–7. Wool exports, meanwhile, fell by 1546–7 to a fraction of what they had been in the 1360s. In the fifty years after 1500, the cloth trade grew in volume by 150 per cent, and it was through Antwerp that English cloth reached its consumers in Germany, eastern Europe, Italy and the Levant. Correspondingly, it was from Antwerp that nearly all imports came to London.[18]

Gresham's journal proves that large shipments of unfinished woollen cloths, tin and lead dominated his contribution to exports.[19] He consigned 1,025 cloths to Antwerp in 1545, rising to a peak of 1,654 in the spring of 1548 despite the onset of more adverse market conditions. Cloths could be sent in as many as twenty separate vessels to split the risk as insurance was expensive and tricky to arrange, costing as much as 3 per cent of the cargo's valuation.[20] Tin was in high demand, largely for making bronze artillery: once unloaded at Antwerp, shipments would be consigned for onward sale to Spain, Italy and the Mediterranean. Supplies came almost entirely from Cornwall. In July 1546, Thomas sent John Elyot there on a buying spree, and the result was that Gresham shipped tin to Antwerp valued at over £2,500 (over £2.5 million in modern values).[21]

Lead, too, was always in demand. Vast quantities of the metal were consumed in central Europe for the manufacture of cannon and as a refining agent for the extraction of silver from argentiferous copper. In a single deal in 1549, Gresham consigned 596 'pieces' weighing a total of 200 'fothers' (roughly 195 tons) to Stephen Vaughan for onward resale, optimistically valued at £2,400. To shift the load, he finally accepted payment in three instalments and offered a discount of £400, making the price per ton £10 5s. 0d.[22] A drastic change would later take place, when the focus of international silver production shifted to the Americas, but this was still to come.

Finally, Gresham ran a major sideline in the export of woad, a plant which when crushed and soaked in water was used in Antwerp as a cheap blue dye for cloth, although as the solution weakened, it could be used to obtain various shades of green instead. In its most concentrated form woad proved to be an excellent preparatory treatment for cloth later to be re-dyed black, but in suitable distillations could also be used for colours such as violet, russet and tawny. In just one of many deals brokered by Thomas's uncle, 300 bales of woad were shipped, weighing 453 hundred-weight, or 23 tons, at an agreed price of £589.[23]

As to Gresham's imports in these early years, he began by specialising in luxury goods and fashionable fabrics such as satin, damask and Genoese velvet which were sold directly out of his warehouse, but soon diversified into bales of cotton and fine jewels, notably diamonds. He also dealt regularly in armaments, shipped in 'vats' and destined for important private clients whose retinues had been conscripted to assist in the defence of Boulogne. Edward Lee, archbishop of York, bought sufficient weapons and armour from Gresham to equip seven light cavalrymen.[24]

In October 1546, when Thomas was in Antwerp and Anne was three or four months pregnant, her father, William Ferneley, moved in at Basing-hall Street. He did not have far to come: he already owned property nearby, something which may have enticed Anne to this part of the city in the first place. His main family home was in West Creeting in Suffolk, where his wife Agnes preferred to live. Arriving in Thomas's counting-house, he first paid the rent, then purchased a large number of items of furniture and other household supplies, all billed to Thomas. These included a table and several cupboards and chests; several linen presses and bedsteads, one to be placed 'over the hall'; a settle and 'foot puff'; a moulding board (for kneading dough); a fireback and large stocks of coal, logs and kindling ready for the onset of winter. For the business, Ferneley bought a 'great beam' or scales for weighing bales of cloth or woad along with 'shop chests'. Finally, he ordered a lead cistern, presumably a water tank, and took 800 lbs of the metal from Thomas's warehouse either to mend a roof or to enable plumbers to tap into a nearby conduit to secure a private water supply for the house or warehouse.[25]

Thomas returned home in late January or February 1547, travelling via Calais and Dover, ready for his wife's lying-in. Between 19 and 26 March, their only child, a son, was born, but the delivery may have been difficult, because Gresham had to call in two different physicians. First was the distinguished Robert Recorde, author of *The urinal of physick*, a treatise on the traditional topic of diagnosis from urine, and then came the much younger Christopher Langton, the manuscript of whose *A very brief treatise, orderly declaring the principal parts of physick* was already at the printer's.[26] Thomas paid Recorde five shillings for his services, and Langton around the same, but in his case for two separate visits. Possibly

Langton was the more effective practitioner, as Thomas would call upon his services later in life.[27]

Gresham's son was named Richard after his paternal grandfather. Thomas found a nurse for him, and in May provided 3 yards of silk say (a light, warm woollen fabric resembling serge) to be made up as clothing, along with money for a fine new gown for his elder stepbrother, to be made by one of Anne Ferneley's relatives on her mother's side.[28]

Among Gresham's trading activities, his journal reveals a large number of exchange transactions, a sphere in which he would increasingly specialise.

On those occasions when he wished to repatriate the profits of his sales in Antwerp rather than purchase wares or make loans to other merchants, one of several methods could be followed. The most obvious, but riskiest, was physically to move the cash. But continuing restrictions on the export of gold and silver coins from Antwerp severely limited this practice. Instead, funds were remitted through the use of bills of exchange. Gresham could acquire pounds sterling in London by selling bills of exchange on Lombard Street to be repaid in Antwerp by his factor, Berney, in Flemish currency one month later, using the firm's cash surplus there.

Alternatively, Berney could lend money in Antwerp, buying bills of exchange to be repaid to Gresham in London in sterling. Bills of exchange were also used to supply Berney with liquid capital when cash was short or when he needed bridging finance. Berney simply borrowed the amounts he needed in Antwerp, to be repaid later by Gresham in London. Care was needed, and not just because exchange rates fluctuated.

Although many of these transactions were intended to be no more than straightforward money transfers, they involved third parties and contained all the basic elements of a loan. Costs could rise and margins fall because of brokerage fees or because lenders contrived to skim off a percentage. It would not take Thomas long to see that behind these risks lay opportunities to make large profits if he could fully master the tricks of the trade. Circumstances could arise in which it might even be more profitable to dispense with his merchant activities altogether, and to specialise in currency exchange dealings and money transfers. Already it may have been a gleam in his eye to build a new family banking business in Lombard Street at the sign of the grasshopper.

So far, Thomas had chiefly observed his father's and uncle's business methods, but now he began to pay more serious attention to those of their friend and associate Antonio Buonvisi of Lucca, one of Europe's most successful merchant bankers. In the early 1500s, the only bankers worthy of the name in London were Italian. Of these, the Frescobaldi of Florence, one of the foremost financial dynasties in Europe, were the most important. They enjoyed Henry VIII's confidence to such an extent that he employed them to act as his agents in paying large subsidies to the Emperor Maximilian I during his early wars, in which matter they failed him. In the ensuing debacle, the Frescobaldi went bankrupt, which threatened other Italian firms and triggered major change.[29]

After the failure of the Frescobaldi in 1518, the most important banking house in London was that of the Buonvisi. With branches in London, Antwerp and Lyon as well as Lucca itself, the mighty Buonvisi bank did a large volume of business with the Greshams and their fellow Mercers. A lifelong friend of Sir Thomas More, to whom he had sent gifts of beer, white wine and stewed meat while More was a prisoner in the Tower after clashing fatally with Henry VIII, Antonio Buonvisi even worshipped at the Mercers' Chapel in Cheapside, where the Lucchese merchants had a side-chapel to which he had made several important benefactions, notably a finely embroidered gold chasuble, now at Stonyhurst College in Lancashire.

Antonio was the second son of the great banking patriarch Benedetto Buonvisi, whose family papers can still be seen in the archives in Lucca. Sent as a boy in the 1490s to London to learn the business, he had made a conscious decision after the death of his father and elder brother to take over the family's commercial operations there.[30] Tax returns show that this branch of the firm was highly profitable; Antonio had long been one of the richest foreign merchants in the city.[31] His house was the great Crosby Place in Bishopsgate, one of the tallest, grandest houses in the older part of town, and with one of the largest walled gardens – it was at Crosby Place that Richard III had lodged in 1483 as he plotted to usurp the throne.

From Buonvisi and his staff, Thomas sought to learn what had given their firm a technical mastery of their trade. These were the skills of bank lending, borrowing and foreign exchange dealing, and of making very considerable profits from the ability to move money quickly from one market or currency to another when differing relative values offered significant margins. It can be no coincidence that Thomas began putting out feelers to Buonvisi's employees, especially Germin di Ciolo, or 'Germain Cioll' as he was more commonly known. Born and bred in Kentish Town, the

illegitimate son of a Pisan merchant, Cioll was already rising high in the
firm and by 1549 would rank second in the hierarchy as Antonio's chief
factor and deputy.[32]

It was doubtless as much from talking to Cioll as from reading text-
books that Thomas had decided to introduce the latest accountancy
standards into his firm. For Gresham, practical experience always trumped
theory. His newly begun journal, however, did not enable him to work out
his trading profits with any degree of accuracy, despite its use of double-
entry bookkeeping. The most he could hope for was to gain a general
impression.

We can look over his shoulder as he wrestled with this conundrum.
In April 1547, he attempted to balance the profits from two of his trading
accounts against cash withdrawals and the costs of merchandise, and
realised he had made a small loss of £74 7s. 4d.[33] The deficiency was attrib-
utable to his muddling up his personal and household expenditure with
his business accounts. In this, Gresham was most unusual. The other three
English merchants whose account books survive for this period did not
confuse professional and personal spending to anything like the same
degree. Later in the year, Gresham tried for an hour or two to calculate
his profits from some recent sales of velvet, tin and armaments. He had no
great success, but modern economic experts armed with laptops believe
that his profits that year were as high as 25 per cent, and 15 per cent annually when averaged over five years.[34]

Just as observing his Italian friends helped to hone Thomas's business
skills and prepare him for his future career, he probably learned how to
dress for the city more by observing Antonio Buonvisi and his factors than
from reading Castiglione. His journal and letters show that he did not
simply wear black: individual fabrics mattered to him, which he selected
according to the season. In spring and summer, as in his portrait commissioned after securing the Mercers' livery, he wore gowns and doublets of
black satin; in winter of woollen cloth lined with satin or fur. His caps
were of black satin all year round. His hose, also black, were of woollen
cloth lined with satin. His nightgowns were made of camlet. His shirts
were white, taken from stock in his shop or warehouse. And like Katherine
Parr, Henry's last queen, Thomas had something of a shoe fetish. He had
four to six bespoke pairs made for him every year. In 1547, he ordered five
pairs of shoes for himself, and thirty-one pairs for his employees – with a
discount for ordering in bulk. He gave his factors and servants presents of

cloth, notably 3 yards of tawny satin to John Elyot for a jerkin. He even gave them buttons and thread, to be taken with the cloth to a tailor who would make up the clothes.[35]

Gifts of cloth to others of his acquaintance included 2 yards of satin to Armagil Waad, a fluent linguist and government official at Calais, as well as up-and-coming administrator about to be promoted as one of the four clerks of the privy council.[36] In making such gestures, Thomas cultivated what would later become a formidable talent for calculating just how valuable or inexpensive a gift needed to be to assure the precise levels of service or favour he expected in return.

Outside of his immediate circle, Thomas maintained a careful series of distinctions. He did not give presents to his fellow Mercers or customers, although he did lend them modest sums of money. He gave imported silks, no more than 3 or 4 yards each, as sweeteners to his country cloth suppliers. He frequently made small gifts to officials and tax collectors in London, Antwerp and Calais to grease their palms. An early beneficiary was William Clifton, the chief customs official at Dover, the sort of man every merchant hoped to have in his pocket. Clifton handled some of Thomas's customs dues for him, usually on imported silks, hopefully assessing exactly the right amount of duty and no more, and preferably less. In return, Thomas sent him and his wife gifts that included cloth and four silver bowls worth £17.

In choosing what to give, Thomas showed a keen social awareness. He sent a purse of money only to craftsmen such as plumbers, tailors, carpenters or scriveners, and gave cash tips or gratuities only to low-level employees of the dockyards or customs houses, such as searchers, porters and waiters. Often, simply plying minor customs officials with copious quantities of beer or wine would do the trick. As he later quipped in a scribbled postscript, '[I write] in haste from Calais, half drunk, half sober with drinking with the searchers at Gravelines'.[37]

Gresham's journal shows that he supplied several members of his extended family with cloth and imported luxury goods, and some of these transactions were gifts. Among those receiving regular gifts of cloth were his brother-in-law and guardian of his elder stepson, Nicholas Bacon. Several times a year, Bacon would draw down cloth from Thomas's warehouse to give to his wife. As a practising lawyer, he assisted from time to time in his brother-in-law's business.[38] He also played an important role as one of two trustees appointed by the will of the late William Read to keep a watchful eye on the Norfolk and Suffolk manors that Thomas's stepsons would inherit when they reached their age of majority.[39]

Gresham, however, had his own plans for these lands. Crucially, the bulk of Read's extensive estates had been owned during his lifetime jointly with Anne Ferneley and, apart from a number of very small properties, they were destined to pass to Thomas's stepsons only on her death. Anne had a life estate in these lands, of which Thomas meant to take full advantage. After the marriage, he systematically took over the day-to-day administration of Read's properties. By the standards of the day he was entitled to do so, and that was valid in law. Whether it was entirely wise is another matter. His attitude was certainly unlike that of most other London merchants, who tended to consider their wives as business partners. Whereas the small print of Ferneley's first husband's will suggests that he had treated her very much as an equal, Gresham kept her on the sidelines. The shock she would have received on her remarriage may have been considerable, not to mention the financial loss to her sons. Among the properties she held in trust for them were the valuable manors of Beccles in Suffolk and West Bradenham in Norfolk, each in excess of 1,500 acres. Thomas indiscriminately amalgamated the profits of these lands with his own sources of income and business profits.[40]

In one respect, Thomas did play fair. From the rents he received, he paid for his stepsons' upbringing and out-of-pocket expenses. The surpluses, on the other hand, he kept for himself. There is absolutely no sign in his accounts that he invested any of these not inconsiderable funds on his stepsons' behalf or thought to account for them separately.

Over time, Gresham's domestic arrangements would begin to create a number of anxieties. His journal entries raise the suspicion that his father-in-law, William Ferneley, began helping himself to expensive cloths from Thomas's warehouse, not to mention inappropriately generous quantities of Malmsey wine. During 1547, moreover, several of Anne's other relatives joined her at Basinghall Street, staying for varying lengths of time. There was also the fact that William Read's will had left Thomas saddled with ongoing smaller payments to no fewer than forty-eight of his wife's extended family for the rest of their lives.[41]

It seems unlikely that such concerns were serious at that point. The only visible hint of discord arises in Gresham's journal entry for 12 November 1547, where he agrees to make a single final payment to his father-in-law 'for the clearing of all accounts from the beginning of the world till this day'.[42] Thereafter, William Ferneley retired from his London business and returned to his wife in West Creeting. Instead of her parents coming to visit her in London, from now on Anne Ferneley rode down to Suffolk, often on her own, taking one or other of her sons with her. But Thomas needed to be careful if he did not wish to antagonise his wife.[43]

RISKS AND REWARDS

On the afternoon of 27 January 1547, the fifty-five-year-old Henry VIII lay slipping in and out of consciousness in a specially manufactured bed designed to cope with his gargantuan size and weight. The end approaching, Archbishop Cranmer was sent for. By the time he arrived, Henry had lost his speech, and he died shortly after midnight. His death sent Thomas Gresham's career into the doldrums for almost four years.

Edward would be king, but in scarcely more than name, for Edward Seymour, earl of Hertford and the young king's uncle, meant to seize power as lord protector. In this, he would be greatly assisted by his side-kick, Sir William Paget, who had risen from the post of Henry's secretary to a position of influence.[1] Their plan had an appealing logic: Edward was intelligent and precocious, but by any measure he was too young to rule unaided. The privy council had already been meeting for several weeks at Hertford's house in the Strand. Now they met for greater secrecy at the Tower, which is where, on 1 February 1547, they first appointed Hertford to be lord protector; then, on 12 March, they confirmed him in the role without limitation.[2]

To pull off this coup, Hertford and Paget used barefaced sleaze, handing out lands and titles like confetti. Among the beneficiaries, Hertford made himself duke of Somerset and Paget received a barony. For all that, in under two years the new lord protector would alienate the very men who had catapulted him into his new position. Not only would he make critical decisions about the economy and the introduction of a new Protestant Prayer Book that many fellow councillors considered to be ill-judged or incomplete, he went on to ruin the country's finances by invading and occupying Scotland and renewing the war in France. The result was crown insolvency.

For Thomas Gresham, these were years of supreme frustration and uncertainty. A prey to rapidly moving political events, he had to watch and wait while (as it seemed to him) economic insanity was all about him. Although Henry had spent £2.1 million (over £2.1 billion in modern values) on warfare between 1544 and his death, his land sales and profits from currency debasements meant that his accumulated deficit was no more than £350,000, of which only £75,000 had been borrowed abroad. The fiscal system could just about have coped, had not Somerset's new war expenditure run up a further deficit of £1.3 million over the next five years. Within a year of Somerset taking power, the government's debt in Antwerp had mushroomed to almost £240,000.[3]

With Somerset in control, Gresham had little choice but to watch from the sidelines. Any hopes he may have nursed of succeeding Stephen Vaughan as the government's banker were emphatically dashed. When Vaughan had stepped back from the post in 1545, Henry VIII had appointed William Damsell to the role. Thomas and his uncle, Sir John Gresham, would continue to be allowed minor supporting duties, undertaking tasks similar to those Thomas had performed in 1544–5, but they were forced to account to Damsell. And there was every reason why Damsell could be expected to succeed. An even-tempered, honest man with an Oxford education and good friends in the Mercers' Company of which he was himself a member, Damsell did not have the drawbacks of some of the more irresponsible or dishonest members of Somerset's kitchen cabinet.[4] He was also exceptionally lucky. For just over two years after Henry's death, interest rates on the Antwerp bourse fell from around 12 per cent to an all-time low of 9 per cent. Damsell could, initially at least, be left largely to his own devices, with instructions to negotiate additional loans while at the same time rolling over the crown's existing debt at costs usually no more than 2 per cent above base interest rates.[5] In this, he had no real need of the Greshams.

The trouble began when Somerset sought to bridge the widening deficit in the government's finances chiefly by fresh asset sales or land confiscations, and by further currency debasements. Beginning in the spring of 1547, lands worth over £14,000 a year were sold off to eager purchasers, often at heavy discounts. Next, and in the face of considerable opposition, Somerset wheedled Parliament into approving legislation dissolving so-called 'chantries', where individual clergy or teams of clergy prayed for the souls in purgatory of wealthy donors. After forbidding requiem masses and attacking the 'superstition' of the doctrine of purgatory as part of his and Cranmer's religious reforms, the lord protector seized these chantry properties, stripping them of lead and bell metal and selling their lands. He then sent out commissioners with orders to take a census of the wealth of all 8,500 parish churches.

Somerset finally ordered fresh currency debasements. In a series of proclamations beginning in April 1548, he called in for re-coinage the shillings (called 'testons') Henry VIII had issued in the opening round of his own currency debasements, which contained a higher proportion of pure silver (up to 75 per cent) than other coins. Over the next eighteen months, these coins were melted down and converted into a variety of new low-denomination ones, but at below half of their earlier fineness, giving the crown a massive cut. In an effort to restore confidence, Somerset ordered the minting of some new gold sovereigns. The quality of these gold coins was almost exactly the same as the old, but such were the suspicions he had aroused that London's merchants prided themselves on never taking them.[6]

By the spring of 1549, the cloth trade was gripped by a severe recession, leaving Antwerp flooded with unsold English cloths. A contraction of the domestic market as inflation soared on account of the debasements was mainly to blame: prices rose by almost half. But the trade depression was also partly caused by a contraction in the wider northern European market as interest rates rose steeply. As a consequence, fewer merchants were buying silks and luxury goods for sale in London, preferring to wait for rates to change back in their favour. Some waited too long. As the depression intensified, they went bankrupt.

Political instability added to the mix. By July 1549, Somerset faced 'stirs' and revolts in much of the southern half of the country, notably in East Anglia and the south-western counties. And as Damsell warned him at the climax of these insurrections, bankers hate uncertainty. Some protests led to serious violence. In Norfolk, the insurgents left their camp on Mousehold Heath to occupy Norwich, where houses were ransacked and leading citizens were held to ransom, among them Augustine Steward, guardian and uncle of young Richard Read, Anne Ferneley's younger son by her first marriage. To restore order, the privy council would be forced to hire Italian and German mercenaries. With this news hitting the Antwerp bourse like a lightning bolt, Damsell warned Somerset that he might be unable to raise the new loan of £100,000 he needed to pay these troops – or if he could, it would be at a punitive interest rate.[7]

Thomas Gresham was only too well aware of the potential for fiscal chaos. Travelling overland from Calais to Antwerp in April 1549, he took a detour to Brussels, which led him to complain that the exchange rate was unusually poor and to advise one of his clients who wanted tapestries that he would do better to seek them out on the second-hand market in England.[8]

In early May, deciding that this might be a good moment to unsettle Damsell and preferably oust him, Thomas made his opening bid to take over as the government's banker. His timing seemed apposite, for it was just as Damsell was beginning to flounder. Somerset's instructions were that Damsell should continue to prolong existing crown debts at the same higher interest rates, but he was to take up fresh loans at only slightly above average rates and then smuggle as much bullion as possible to London to convert into coins at a profit. In the fast-deteriorating conditions in Antwerp, it was an impossible brief. With interest rates rising as high as 14 per cent, Damsell failed to roll over one of Somerset's larger loans: 167,200 Carolus guilders (around £25,330 sterling), borrowed in 1547.[9] The lender, Lazarus Tucher, a Nuremberg banker who had made his home in Antwerp where he cornered a large part of the pepper market, demanded repayment. Only then was he willing to consider a new loan, and as one of Charles V's most important creditors, he refused to co-operate in the illegal export of bullion or coin. To settle the crown's debt to Tucher, Damsell had to turn to Erasmus Schetz, a friend and patron of Erasmus of Rotterdam and the founder of an Antwerp banking dynasty well known to Gresham. Born at Maastricht, Schetz financed zinc mines in Limburg and copper mines in Germany, and had lent money to both Charles V and Henry VIII.[10]

Once Tucher was repaid, Damsell successfully secured from him a fresh loan of 150,000 Carolus guilders. But he quickly fell foul of the privy council for his failure to persuade Tucher to accept repayment, when it fell due, in unsold kerseys, lead or bell metal rather than cash. Worse still, Tucher had only been willing to lend again in the first place on condition that the loan was paid out in goods, but paid back in cash, whereas Somerset understandably wanted it the other way around. Damsell had been hit by a double blow: not only was rolling over debts a costly affair when interest rates were rising, but also borrowers known to be in urgent need of fresh loans would often be obliged to take them wholly or partly from the lender in the form of overpriced jewels or other luxury goods, thereby making the real interest rate far higher than the nominal one. Conversely, borrowers who wished to repay their loans in goods could be forced by their creditors to accept ridiculously low valuations.[11]

Gresham was never slow to put himself forward and dirty tricks were well within the capacity of his clan. When Thomas was only a child in August 1528, an Augsburg merchant, Joachim Höchstetter, had quarrelled violently with Sir Richard and Sir John Gresham over a deal to purchase grain, mercury and vermilion.[12] Höchstetter gained the support of Cromwell and Henry VIII, but the Greshams had their revenge. Insidiously spreading rumours of Höchstetter's imminent insolvency, they ruined his credit all over Europe. Soon he was indeed bankrupt.[13] With a not dissimilar purpose and deep irony, Thomas informed Somerset on 9 May 1549 of his role as one of Damsell's 'friends' in remitting the proceeds of the official government banker's latest borrowings to London. In his first letter sent directly to Somerset, written from Calais, he nonchalantly explained how he was smuggling consignments worth up to £6,000 out of Antwerp via Calais on Damsell's behalf by packing them inside bales of silk and taffeta. The main purpose of his letter was to make it clear to Somerset that to help out his country in its hour of need, Gresham had personally funded several shipments on his own credit, for which he hoped to be fairly reimbursed.[14]

Unfortunately, things went awry when Gresham was hauled to account by customs officials at Dover who would not allow his bales to 'pass unseen but with much ado'. Then, 'both the customer and the searcher did follow my chest to London with no small bruit, which if the thing were known in these parts would be to my utter undoing for ever'. Boldly, Thomas appealed for Somerset's help in dealing with these tiresome underlings to prevent future mishaps, at the same time offering to take over from Damsell in supplying bullion worth up to £13,000–14,000 annually.[15]

Within a week, Damsell was the recipient of a sharp letter of rebuke. What Gresham had failed to foresee was that the privy council would be shocked at the price paid for the smuggled bullion: oblivious to market forces, they believed it had been far too high. The result was that they accused Damsell of embezzlement, and their investigations drew in Gresham too.[16]

Damsell defended himself by blaming Thomas for the price paid, obliging Gresham to write again to Somerset. His letter no longer survives, but its contents can be worked out from the council's response. He offered a credible defence of the purchase price, but as his account differed from Damsell's, the councillors became even more suspicious. The result was that Somerset reimbursed Thomas at a rate well below cost. In total, Gresham lost £460 (over £460,000 in modern values). He complained, 'if the like were to do again, I would not do it for the gain of £2,000, except my lord's grace commands me to the contrary'.[17]

Gresham's attempt to muscle in on Damsell's business had backfired. He learned to take care in future never fully to enlighten privy councillors as to his working methods, or provide them with ammunition to turn against him. Rarely would he again risk his own money on the government's behalf without a good reason. Even then, he would try to clear things with someone in authority first.[18] But, for all the hard lessons he learned, on this occasion Gresham escaped relatively unscathed. No charges of embezzlement were brought against him. Now he just had to wait until Somerset himself overreached himself and was replaced.

Sure enough, the moment came. John Dudley, earl of Warwick, regarded Somerset as a fatal threat to effective government. Rumours were rife that Somerset planned to invite the earl and the marquis of Northampton to a banquet where he would cut off their heads. Warwick launched a pre-emptive strike. On 11 October 1549, he had Somerset arrested and committed to the custody of twelve yeomen of the guard. Somerset was supplanted by Warwick, who took the titles of duke of Northumberland and lord president of the council, shunning that of lord protector.

The newly promoted Northumberland may have been something of a maverick, but once in power he had the good sense to extricate England from any risk of engagement in the concluding phases of the wider Franco-Habsburg struggle that had erupted again after the accession of Henry II of France in 1547. Peace was made with both France and Scotland, ending Somerset's ruinously expensive wars. After that, the council's new leader aimed to put the country's finances back on course.

This was to prove Gresham's big chance. During most summers when he was back in England, Thomas holidayed for a few days or weeks in August at his father's country properties at Ringshall in Suffolk or Intwood in Norfolk. On the night of 23 August 1549, by sheer good fortune, Northumberland was Gresham's guest at Intwood while the duke was on his way to put down the East Anglian revolts on Mousehold Heath. What exactly passed between them on that fateful evening, no one will ever know, but after their brief encounter, Thomas would only have to wait for Damsell to make a serious mistake.

Edward, meanwhile, was fast turning into a teenage know-it-all. Had he lived to a full age he might have become a mirror image of his father, but without the subtlety. Somerset, who hardly noticed that the boy was growing up at all, had made the mistake of leaving him feeling that he was more of a prisoner than a king. Northumberland saw that he was impatient to rule and, on finishing his schooling at the age of fifteen, would most likely insist on choosing his own advisers.

To point Edward in the right direction, Northumberland arranged for one of the clerks of the privy council, William Thomas, to induct him into the mysteries of drafting state papers and policy documents, and contrived that he shadow meetings of the privy council by writing mock agendas and even minutes. Mock council meetings may even have been staged. Many of these policy papers or agenda items related to the crown's finances, the coinage or the need for an English 'mart' or bourse 'where round [i.e., substantial] sums of money might be of them borrowed that haunt the mart'.[19] These were all topics in which the adolescent king took a keen interest. Northumberland saw that a strategy of appearing to tutor Edward in kingship was the way to safeguard his own long-term position.[20] Especially where religion was concerned, the wily duke judged Edward's passion for radical reform to be more than a passing whim, so he gave Cranmer a free hand to revise the half-baked liturgy approved by Somerset in favour of a new fully Protestant Prayer Book.

While waiting for his opportunity to oust Damsell, Thomas Gresham prepared himself for his new career by investing more of his capital in loans or mortgages to courtiers rather than tying up too much money in trade at a time when markets were so difficult to read. He and Anne Ferneley also moved from Basinghall Street to the more prestigious Catte Street, taking a house once owned by John Abbot, a wealthy fifteenth-century silk merchant and public benefactor who had bequeathed it to the Mercers.[21]

Finally, the moment arrived that Thomas had been waiting for. In the course of 1550, the accrued debt with interest run up by Somerset rose to a record high of £350,000, and relations between Damsell and his political masters dramatically worsened to the point where privy councillors decided that they could do a better job themselves.[22] One outstanding loan from the house of Fugger, the leading south German banking firm based in Augsburg but with offices in Antwerp, amounted to 328,000 Carolus guilders and was due for repayment on 15 August.[23]

By then, the crown's annual revenue barely exceeded £168,150 and the exchequer was empty. Even assuming Northumberland could raise sufficient funds, Somerset's currency debasements had played havoc. Gold coins, whose intrinsic value was least diminished, were nowhere to be found, bagged up by goldsmiths and illegally exported to France where they were openly used in trade or else melted down in clandestine forges. As Sir John Mason, writing from Dieppe, warned fellow privy councillors, 'the common opinion of the merchants is that the baseness of your money will at length leave no gold within the realm, cry you the same never so high or make you never so great restraints for the keeping thereof'.[24]

By the skin of his teeth, Damsell renewed the Fugger loan at what the privy council, still detached from reality, assumed to be a punitive interest rate of 12 per cent. His downfall followed a further rolling over of debts with the same banking firm in March 1551 at nominal rates seemingly as low as 8 per cent. The catch lay in the small print, which required huge quantities of surplus fustian and jewellery to be purchased as part of the deal. Edward took a keen interest in this transaction. His diary reported the high price of the bullion to be supplied by the Fugger firm, and noted that the jewellery he was obliged to buy included 'a very fair jewel [of] four rubies, marvellous big, one orient and great diamond, and one great pearl'. No interest was due on this jewellery, but as the price agreed was £30,000 (over £30 million today) and £18,000 for the fustian, some idea of the drawbacks of the bargain can be gained. It was a deal on which Gresham did not hesitate to cast scorn.[25]

No sooner was it signed and sealed than Northumberland – determined to regain control over a dire economic situation – resorted to drastic measures. Digging out the reports of Somerset's commissioners sent out to inventory the wealth of the parish churches, he ordered church plate, bell metal and other valuables to be seized, 'forasmuch as the king's majesty had need presently of a mass of money'.[26] From this squalid exercise, some £30,700 would eventually be received. Anything of value was taken, apart from linen and communion vessels. Gold and silver plate was melted down for coin; jewels ripped from liturgical vestments were stored in coffers or sold. The gold and silver plate from St George's Chapel, Windsor, where the Knights of the Garter held their annual procession and feast, was included in the haul. In the royal library jewels and precious metals were even stripped off the bindings of the books.[27]

Increasingly desperate, and only days after Damsell had contracted to buy the fustian and jewellery, Northumberland called on Thomas Gresham

to handle some of the council's less urgent financial business.[28] And on 6
April 1551, the privy council sent Damsell a brusque letter informing him
that he was dismissed from the post of government banker 'by reason of
his slackness'.[29] He was to be allowed six months to tidy up his affairs, and
was then to return to London.[30] Thomas would be appointed in his place.

As Gresham later somewhat smugly recalled, Northumberland had
organised a beauty contest of leading merchants in the London–Antwerp
trade, probably in March, to see who would be best qualified to be Damsell's successor. 'I was sent for unto the council,' he explained, 'and brought
by them afore the king's majesty, to know my opinion, as they had many
other merchants, what way, with least charge, his majesty might grow out
of debt.'[31] What precisely he said while delivering his pitch we don't know.
The events of the next two years were to prove, however, that the ideas
Gresham is likely to have floated to Edward and his councillors marked a
dramatic departure from anything attempted by Damsell or his predeces-
sor, Stephen Vaughan. By the sheer audacity of the various schemes and
'devices' to which he and Northumberland would shortly give practical
effect, he showed himself to be thinking on another level entirely.

A FAMILY QUARREL

One of the more unusual attributes of the wider Gresham clan was that, though they could work together in their business affairs, their personal relationships with each other frequently descended into feuding and mistrust, generally over money. The prickly Richard Gresham calculated friendships in pounds, shillings and pence, and had never indulged his children for all his wealth. Perhaps Thomas's knack for knowing almost to the penny how much was apt as gifts or bribes was a talent inherited from his father. Or perhaps it was merely the lack of affection that explains why he seems to have gained satisfaction only from his mastery of figures and fluctuating rates of exchange. It may also explain why he seems to have felt a powerful need to prove himself, even when success had been achieved.

On 21 February 1549 Sir Richard Gresham died in his bed at his home in Milk Street with a nurse propping up his head and shoulders, and his family at his bedside. A formal note in the front of Thomas's journal recorded the death, which occurred between the hours of three and four o'clock in the afternoon.[1] It was preceded by the administration of the last rites by a priest named Thomas Stephen, a short dinner attended by all the family and some close friends, the vigil, and the reading of the will twice over by Richard's lawyer. From this and the corresponding entry in the Mercers' Acts of Court, one would never have guessed that anything untoward was about to occur.[2] Indeed, it is only the discovery of a hundred or so closely written pages of legal testimony that makes it possible to consider this decidedly macabre episode now.[3]

That his father died one of the most hated men in London was hardly Thomas's fault. Popular opinion had turned against Richard Gresham after Henry VIII's death – for his willing cooperation in Thomas Cromwell's

iconoclasm, for his multiple purchases of ex-monastic lands and for his
relentless pursuit of his debtors, whom he was happy to reduce to penury.[4]
Shortly before his death, Richard's confessor had urged him for the sake
of his immortal soul to make restitution to 'certain widows for certain
injuries he had done them'.[5] Richard said he had already made amends,
but the complaints persisted, and Thomas would shortly be forced to pay
out compensation from his father's estate to 'the widow Constance for a
recompense of putting her out of her house'.[6]

Such grievances would have a bearing on two costly and distracting
lawsuits Thomas now had to fight in the court of Chancery. The first was
provoked by his feckless elder brother, John. Disgruntled over his share of
the disposition of Richard's assets in his will, John now set out to exploit
their father's reputation as a greedy extortioner and cruel parent. Bad
blood had existed between father and son for many years. According to
William Southwood, a goldsmith and near neighbour in Milk Street, John
would deliberately set out to taunt his father as they travelled together,
playing silly pranks on him and showing an arrogant lack of respect. More
than once, Richard had remarked that his younger son Thomas 'was at
all times diligent', whereas John 'was proud, untrustworthy and a nature
wherein was no grace'.[7]

The storm broke shortly after John duped a young Yorkshire heiress,
Frances Thwaites, into marrying him. Ever short of cash and too idle to
work, he promptly sold some of his wife's lands, claiming them as his own.
Richard, who had spent his whole life accumulating family property, could
not abide the notion of selling any of it. As Thomas's stepmother, Isabel,
testified under oath, Richard tore a strip off his elder son at a meeting at a
house in Bethnal Green on the eastern outskirts of London, rebuking him
for selling his wife's lands and for 'consuming of his living so prodigally'.[8]
Smouldering with rage, Richard decided to revoke his existing will and
make a new one, removing John as an executor and greatly reducing his
share of the inheritance. Thomas would get the lion's share other than a
portion reserved to Isabel. And to make sure no mistakes were made, he
would hire the finest legal minds to prevent John challenging the new will
or dissipating what lesser property was bequeathed to him.[9]

When begged by his brother, Thomas's uncle, Sir John Gresham, not
to exclude his elder son from the roll-call of his executors while putting
Thomas in charge, Richard refused, saying, 'I will in no wise assent thereto.'
In a moment of fury shortly before his death, he even proposed to his

lawyer, Thomas Atkyns of Lincoln's Inn, that he should arrange to lease out the lands to be given to John for twenty-one years, preventing any sales during that period, and forcing John to live on the rents alone. In the end, he merely settled for a clause insisting that if John predeceased his younger brother, then Thomas would inherit both their shares.[10]

John, in retaliation, threatened his father, saying, 'Tie it as sure as you can, and yet there be many ways to loose as to bind, and think you to have your will performed where kings' and princes' wills be broken?' Later, in a violent confrontation with his whole family, he accused his dying father of cheating him and called his uncle a 'churl' for supporting his brother's tough line. Finally, after the revised will was read for the last time and his father was too ill to speak and had to communicate by hand gestures, John declared the whole document to be a fake, an assertion he duly went on to make the basis of his complaint in court. 'The said will,' he repeatedly maintained, 'was a forged will, and so he would prove it.' John persisted in the allegation despite the opinion of four eminent lawyers, two of them judges, who examined the will and pronounced it to be good.[11] The case came before the court of Chancery in July 1549, after the lord chancellor agreed to issue writs of subpoena to summon those involved and hear their testimony.

Thomas was an eyewitness to everything that happened in the last days of his father's life: he had carefully observed the comings and goings of the lawyers as his father made successive amendments to the will. He knew that by the final revision, the document had gone through no fewer than sixteen drafts. He also knew he had to be careful, since litigation was always a risky business, and it now fell to him to secure probate of the will and to steer the executors and bankroll their expenses until these could be claimed back from the estate. His task was made more complicated in that his father's will was, in fact, two separate documents: one exclusively for his lands, the other chiefly for goods, but with some last-minute alterations to the will of lands tacked on to the will of goods.[12]

Within three months of Sir Richard's death, Thomas would successfully obtain a grant of probate of the will of goods, but was left to fight his elder brother in the court of Chancery over the will of lands. To win, he would need to gather sworn testimony from his stepmother, his uncle, his two half-sisters Christiana and Elizabeth, the priest, the goldsmith, Atkyns the lawyer and his clerk, along with several other witnesses to the disputed will of lands, including his father's nurse.

After many days of searching, Thomas tracked down Atkyns's clerk – one Richard Damser. It had been Damser who, on the day of Richard Gresham's death, had undertaken the final reading of both parts of the will after Atkyns was taken ill. And it was Damser whom Thomas would now bludgeon into delivering the killer facts he needed to win his case.

A decidedly reluctant witness, the terrified clerk came into court and swore on oath that Thomas's elder brother had offered him money and other inducements if he would say that the will in its final shape was the result of a conspiracy. Damser confessed to several meetings with the younger John Gresham's barrister, John Lyster of Gray's Inn, once over breakfast in Aldermanbury near Cheapside, once in the Temple Church and once in the yard at Lincoln's Inn, before finally meeting John himself among the crowd in the great watching chamber at Whitehall Palace. There, John had allegedly grasped Damser's hand and offered him 'great rewards and fellowship' if he would perjure himself. 'And he said his father's will was [the] shamefullest thing that ever was done, for he said that his father was noted to be a mighty man in his lifetime, but in the said will, he said, he proved himself a fool.'[13]

The younger John Gresham screamed foul on hearing this testimony. So was Damser lying? The question has to remain open, but in March 1550, the court of Chancery decided in Thomas's favour. By order of the master of the rolls, the court granted probate and ordered Sir Richard's will of lands to be enrolled in its records to be of 'perpetual memory', a verdict from which there could be no further appeal other than to Parliament. In achieving this result, Thomas miraculously avoided giving an affidavit in court himself, but he paid all the lawyers' bills and steered the litigation firmly from the rear. Not only did he retain four of the most distinguished advocates practising at the bar for months on end, he also paid a handsome sum to a fifth for four separate judicial applications to the lord chancellor.[14]

Thomas's journal or 'Day Book' also shows he made a mysterious payment to the king's attorney-general, Henry Bradshaw, for undisclosed services.[15] Quite possibly Gresham was attempting to persuade Bradshaw to consider putting his elder brother on trial in the court of Star Chamber for incitement to perjury, an undeveloped area of the criminal law with which only this highest court in the land was prepared to grapple. (Star Chamber, abolished in 1641, was the king's privy council sitting judicially to hear legal cases.) Why else would Thomas initiate this contact in what otherwise was a purely civil dispute?

Whether or not that was Gresham's intention, he had barely two years' respite before his half-sister Christiana entered the fray. Shortly after the death of her unmarried sister, Elizabeth, who fell mortally ill in late February or early March 1552 and died at the early age of twenty-four, she appealed to the lord chancellor to issue a writ in the court of Chancery against her brother. The writ was granted on 1 April, after which Thomas found himself travelling home from Antwerp to defend himself in court once more.[16]

Unlike her father, Elizabeth had died before she could send for a lawyer and instead 'declared' her will verbally on her deathbed before witnesses. Hearing of her death, Thomas promptly sent his lawyers scurrying off to the archbishop of Canterbury's probate court to seek letters of administration, enabling him to settle all her affairs. Within days, Christiana was complaining that he or his agents had abused that trust. She had more than enough money behind her to hold him to account, because four years earlier she had married the up-and-coming Sir John Thynne, steward of the Duke of Somerset.

At first at least, Thomas heartily approved. As a wedding present to Christiana, Thomas had sent a gold ring set with a ruby, valued at over £13 (in excess of £13,000 today), and in the early months of her marriage, he pulled out all the stops in Antwerp and Brussels to seek out suitable gifts and household luxuries for the couple – large quantities of coverlets, velvets and a cheaper green twilled woollen fabric commonly used for wall hangings, along with solid silver tableware, jewellery, andirons, tapestries and French wines.[17] In return, he asked Thynne to intercede with Somerset at the time of his ill-fated bullion deal with William Damsell. After that help failed to materialise, a distinct cooling of relations can be observed.[18]

Christiana's grievance, however, related as much to the way her father had settled his estate as to the way Thomas now proposed to administer Elizabeth's. Working furiously through the night to incorporate Sir Richard's last-minute changes of mind concerning his lands into the will of goods, the lawyer made a mistake. This had very much affected Elizabeth: since she lacked a husband, she needed her bequests to live on.

Keen to exonerate himself, Atkyns, Sir Richard's lawyer, explained in court that besides her original grant of an equal share with her siblings of those of Sir Richard's chattels not assigned to his widow, he had been asked to assign Elizabeth a half-share of the manor and parsonage of Nunkeeling and the parsonage of Swine in Yorkshire, both granted to Sir Richard by

Henry VIII at the time of his purchase of the lands of Fountains Abbey.[19]
He had done so, but when the will was read for the last time after the
changes were in place, Christiana and her husband protested that these
properties 'were not so much of value by a great sum as the said Sir Richard
was determined to give her'. There was another row, in the course of which
Christiana's husband approached the foot of Sir Richard's bed and 'cried
with a loud voice' to him to remedy this wrong to his daughter Elizabeth.
By this time Sir Richard was already slipping into unconsciousness. He
turned away, 'not speaking, but did rattle in the throat'. In tears, Christiana
blurted out to her husband, 'Let us trouble him no more, we will help her
otherwise.'[20]

They did, offering Elizabeth a home with them, which she gratefully
accepted. When she came to make her own final bequests, she particularly
thanked them, and left all her worldly possessions to them, 'who hath been
very good unto me this four years'.[21]

But the question was, how were her debts and her bequests to her two
faithful servants to be settled? Clearly, Thomas was refusing to pay them,
claiming that she had left insufficient cash. As no evidence exists that her
debts exceeded £100 and the cost of her small legacies could never have
reasonably amounted to more than £20–30, it surely has to be reckoned an
extraordinary act of meanness. In a letter now lost (its contents are known
from Thomas's reply), Christiana told Thomas that she believed him to be
her enemy, 'avaricious, and one that only looketh to singular profit without
respect of persons'.[22] Coming from a sibling, this was a devastating indictment. But Thomas, it seems, was unmoved by Christiana's pleas, or by her
argument that a portion of the future income of Elizabeth's properties
might be used to meet her obligations. That option Thomas ruled out,
since Sir Richard's will, in its final draft, had assigned the reversion of those
lands to his elder son, John, should Elizabeth die still unwed. And John,
predictably, offered no concessions.

How the deadlock was resolved we do not know, as the final records
are lost. Possibly Christiana funded her sister's outstanding liabilities in the
end; there is no hint in the Thynne family papers to suggest that Thomas
changed his mind. Perhaps the case was settled out of court, enabling
him to avoid giving evidence on oath. In a self-serving exculpation of his
actions, he protested his 'assured friendship' to Christiana, accusing her
of 'rash judgement towards me, whom nature moveth me to love because
you are my sister', and insisting that her opinion of him was shaped by

'those persons whose poisoned tongues have stirred this discord'. To this, he received no reply.[23]

At least Thomas could throw himself into his work. It seems that it was only when he was part of the cut and thrust of the bourse in Antwerp that he was able to flourish. During the winter of 1551–2, a few months after he had been called in by the privy council to replace William Damsell as the crown's financial agent in Antwerp, Thomas took the decision to move his entire base of operations temporarily to that city. As he later explained, 'I not only left the realm with my wife and family, my occupation and whole trade of living, for the space of two years, but also posted in that time forty times on the king's sending, at the least, from Antwerp to the Court'.[24]

Travelling to and fro between Antwerp and London so many times in such a short period, even allowing for Gresham's customary hyperbole, was a remarkable feat. With them on their outward crossing, Thomas and Anne Ferneley took a significant portion of their furniture and personal effects, their gold and silver plate and many of Anne's clothes.[25] And before they departed, the upwardly mobile Thomas decided to sell or perhaps lease out his house in Catte Street, and buy another in Lombard Street, the heart of the city's financial district, where a skeleton staff could live and conduct the business he needed done there. In our imagination at least, perhaps, we can finally see him nailing up his sign of the grasshopper by the entrance to the courtyard before he left for Deptford or Dover to board his ship.

A majority of Thomas's employees moved with the family and their servants to the Antwerp office. The one notable exception was Gresham's recently promoted factor, Robert Berney, who left the firm to found his own business. To serve as his factor in Antwerp, Thomas appointed one of his most experienced apprentices, the thirty-five-year-old Richard Clough. A garrulous Welshman with a genius for writing brilliantly observed newsletters, Clough was a Denbigh glover's son who, as a boy, had moved to Chester as a chorister. Seemingly lacking sufficient opportunities for his talents, he made his way as an adolescent to London, then allegedly went on a pilgrimage to Jerusalem in his late twenties. On his return in about 1545, he was apprenticed to Gresham, but chose not to seek the freedom of the Mercers' Company until 1560, and he would never apply for the livery to enable him to start up on his own.[26] Instead, he preferred to work for Thomas, presenting himself in his letters as a loyal and reliable deputy fulfilling his master's wishes, rather than as a man willing to take risks or fly high on his own account.

To replace Berney in London, heading up the firm's now much reduced office in Lombard Street, Thomas chose John Elyot, whom he soon relied on to handle large transactions involving bills of exchange.[27] Assisting Elyot was an Italian, Francesco di Tomasso, who at the time of the Antwerp move had worked for the firm for two and a half years and whose chief task from this point onwards was to deliver the company's confidential paperwork to and from its branches. In absolutely refusing to rely on intermediaries and always insisting on using his own post, Thomas followed the example of the great Jakob Fugger (d. 1525), once principal banker to the Holy Roman Emperor Maximilian I and later the young Charles V, who had pioneered this system. Fugger's network of couriers filed reports about the state of trade and commerce which the firm had printed in Augsburg and distributed to clients in the form of a primitive newspaper.

Also rising steadily in the firm was Edmond Hogan, who had now served Thomas for four years. He travelled to Antwerp with the others, but Thomas soon sent him to Seville in Spain to exploit more nimbly the opportunities created by the steadily increasing quantities of bullion arriving there from the New World and to assist Thomas's uncle, Sir John, with his trading ventures in Crete and Greece. One of Hogan's first acts on arriving in Seville was to purchase a pair of long silk stockings for Thomas to present to the young Edward VI, as these were a great rarity in northern Europe and so far unobtainable in London.[28]

Of Gresham's other staff joining him in Antwerp, two people given unusually trusted and confidential roles were William Bendlowes, who had also worked for Thomas for four years, and John Spritewell, a relatively new member of the team. Bendlowes was put in charge of coffering up and transporting consignments of bullion and armaments during their often illicit passage to London via Calais and Dover. He was assisted by Spritewell, whom Gresham went on to praise in 1555, 'for that he can speak all kinds of languages, and [is] a Calais-man born, who is a very painful [i.e., painstaking] man and a man to be trusted in all matters of charge, having had the trial of him these five years'.[29]

On their arrival in Antwerp, the Greshams lodged in the spacious house of Gaspar Schetz. The eldest son of the banker Erasmus Schetz, Gaspar had a profitable sideline shipping metalware to Africa and would shortly succeed Lazarus Tucher and Gasparo Ducci as Charles V's principal

factor in Brussels. He had so far done much of his business with the house
of Fugger, now headed up by Anton Fugger, Jakob's nephew, who had
taken over the direction of the firm at the age of thirty-two. But Schetz
had also begun trading with Gresham and advanced him several loans. A
letter Thomas wrote in November 1552 suggests that Gaspar had been his
friend for some eight years and that he stayed at his house many times.
Schetz had performed several favours for him, most recently introducing
him to the regent of the Netherlands, Mary of Hungary, and vouching for
him as 'a man of honesty and credit to be trusted ... knowing me to be a
right honest man'.[30]

Gaspar, who in 1550 had succeeded his father Erasmus as head of
the family's operations, was the wealthiest of four brothers. He and his
younger siblings Melchior, Balthazar and Conrad – Gaspar, Melchior
and Balthazar were named after the Magi in the New Testament – were of
German origin, but born and bred Flemish. Directed by their father, the
firm had entered the first division of European banking houses, but could
not yet quite rival the Fugger or the Tucher. Besides his business achievements, Gaspar, following in his father's footsteps, was a scholar who wrote
Latin verses and collected coins. He and Gresham shared a love of art, and
each knew the Antwerp-based Christopher Plantin and Abraham Ortels
(in Latin 'Ortelius'), the first a master-printer, the other arguably Europe's
most acclaimed cartographer. It cannot be a coincidence to find Richard
Clough supplying Ortels with crucial information on the topography of
Anglesey.[31]

How Anne Ferneley reacted to what was to become the longest of
her stays in Antwerp is hard to read. She was already well acquainted with
Melchior Schetz, who had first lodged with the Greshams at Basinghall
Street in 1546, then made several subsequent visits. Thomas had supported
Melchior in a number of ways, providing him or his servants with credit,
quantities of silk and crimson or black satin, and hiring horses for him.
As worthy gifts for Melchior and Balthazar, Gresham had his tailor make
coats of Genoese velvet, lined with silk. In return, the brothers and their
father sent two large solid silver-gilt bowls, weighing 84 ounces, as gifts to
Anne Ferneley.[32] But whether Thomas's wife wanted to entertain long-stay
visitors seems unlikely, nor can we imagine she would have much enjoyed
living for more than a few weeks as Gaspar Schetz's guest. She had by now
built a comfortable life for herself in London, frequently riding out to
attend the christenings of her friends' children and to visit her family.[33]

Anne had kept vigil with her husband at her father-in-law's bedside during his final hours of life, but she appears to have said nothing at all, nor was she prepared to give evidence in either of the Chancery lawsuits her husband was obliged to defend. Scrutiny of the ledger entries in Thomas's 'Day Book' suggests that tensions were rising in their marriage, chiefly from the cynical and imperious way Thomas had taken control of his wife's money and the properties left to her and her two sons in her first husband's will. She clearly adored her son Richard by her second marriage, but she was just as attached to her two sons by her first, whereas Thomas saw them and their future inheritance merely as a source of revenue.

Ledger entries are notoriously unpromising sources from which to tease out relationships, but one thing cries out from the densely packed information in Thomas's journal: unlike the other three English merchants whose account books survive for this period, he included in his business accounts the most diverse matters, down to the last butcher's bill or payment for beer, wine, horse feed or minor repair works.[34] For Thomas Gresham, it would seem, private or family life did not exist as a concept. Most obviously, he gave Ferneley no allowance for the running of the household and allowed her little discretion over spending: everything had to be ordered through the business, where it was muddled up with professional purchases and accounted for as a debit against the profits of the sales of commodities or exchange deals. The Greshams clearly lived well – the accounts include purchases of delicacies such as sturgeon, boxes of biscuits and sugar-coated preserved fruits and marzipan treats known as 'comfits' – but how far these were Thomas's choices rather than his wife's is impossible to say.[35]

As to Ferneley's personal spending, her expenditure on clothes and even on the smallest gifts or minor out-of-pocket expenses, such as riding charges, all had to be set down by Thomas Bradshaw, Gresham's senior apprentice. Cash was issued to her from Gresham's counting-house in relatively modest amounts at a time, and her access to velvet, silk, satin and cotton from stock in the shop or warehouse to make frocks or gowns, once again just a few yards at a time, was carefully recorded. Even the precise value of the two silver bowls she received as gifts from the Schetz was reckoned up – £28 – and entered into the ledger accounts, where it was credited as income received by the business.[36]

This, at least, was emphatically unusual. As Luca Pacioli's original treatise on the subject of double accounting had made plain, all merchants who were adopting this system were supposed to keep a record of their ordinary household expenses. These could include 'expenses for grains, wine, wood, oil, salt, meat, shoes, hats, stockings, cloths, tips, expenses for tailors, barbers, bakers, cleaners, kitchen utensils, vases, glasses, casks, etc.'[37] But according to Pacioli, these costs were to be entered into the journal under a separate heading, otherwise it would be impossible to work out with any degree of accuracy the annual trading profit or loss made by the business.

By ignoring these rules, Gresham created an accounting system that appears to have served no useful administrative purpose other than to ensure that he kept full control over the household and personal expenditure incurred by his wife and employees. And to a woman of spirit with a taste for pearls who had been accustomed during her first marriage to having and spending her own money, this must have begun to jar.

THE WHEEL OF
FORTUNE

When John Dudley, duke of Northumberland, assumed control as the lord president of Edward VI's privy council, Thomas Gresham's career took off in earnest. With a cool intelligence of the type close to Gresham's heart, Northumberland had been a protégé of Thomas Cromwell, but survived his patron's fall. His talents, notably his rudimentary grasp of basic economics, were to refashion the conduct of government during the second half of Edward's minority. A decided oddball who rejected theory in favour of practical solutions, Northumberland shunned the controversies of the Reformation and was as blunt and brisk in his conversation as Gresham.

So far the duke had restored peace at home and abroad and given Archbishop Cranmer a relatively free hand to begin overhauling the Protestant Prayer Book that Somerset had botched. Now he proposed to do what he could to restore the country's finances. It is more than possible that, in pursuing this aim, he was acting on the basis of the advice Gresham had tendered during the course of the beauty contest to replace William Damsell.

Top of the list was the problem of Henry VIII and Somerset's coinage debasements. Eager to provide an effective solution, but without fully considering the implications of the move he was about to make, on 30 April 1551 Northumberland suddenly announced by royal proclamation that the value of the worst of the debased coins would be cried down by a quarter with effect from 1 August next, so as to better reflect their true metallic worth. There was logic behind this decision, but by giving three months' advance warning the duke caused chaos, immediately triggering price rises as sellers would no longer accept these inferior coins in payment for goods at face value, whereas buyers expected to spend such coins as they had in their possession as quickly as possible. In an effort to resolve the problem, on 8 July Dudley brought the devaluation into immediate effect. He might have got away with it, too, had he not, six weeks later, devalued these same coins over again, this time by a third. The result was a near-suspension of all trade, nudging dozens of merchants into bankruptcy.[1]

The duke changed tack, repurchasing as much of the debased currency as the regime could afford and replacing it with newly minted fine coins. The weight of pure metal per £1 sterling was fixed at 114.5 grams for silver coins and 10 grams for gold coins, in both cases only slightly less than in 1544. This held out the prospect of a long-term solution. Unfortunately, the duke lacked sufficient funds to buy out all the bad money and so offered an unacceptably low price to merchants and goldsmiths for their cash reserves.[2]

Next, Northumberland appointed a series of royal commissions to review the whole field of government expenditure. Cuts were ordered, especially in food and drink in the royal household, where expenditure had spiralled out of control. Sir Walter Mildmay, a thirty-year-old Cambridge graduate and an eagle-eyed Mercer's son with a special talent for auditing and accounting, was in the vanguard of these reforms. Not only did he supervise the work of the commissioners, he also drafted much of their final report. Intriguingly, he was no stranger to Gresham, who had given him a gold mourning ring to mark the death of his father, Sir Richard.[3]

Northumberland's most urgent objective in these years was to avert government insolvency. As Edward noted in one of his shadow 'state papers' in 1552, his foreign debt was still running at £200,000 (more than £200 million in modern values), but his liquid assets were only £134,000. He had bales of fustian left over from Damsell's ill-fated deal with the Fugger firm, valued at £14,000, but these could not easily be sold as the market was swamped.[4]

Edward's paper was carefully annotated by an official who would soon not just be working closely with Gresham, but would build up a degree of trust and familiarity with him that would endure for the rest of Thomas's life. Sir William Cecil was a thirty-year-old Cambridge graduate. A workaholic who was at his desk every day at 6 a.m., he was short and wiry with a thin face and grey eyes. Cecil had served as one of Somerset's private secretaries and was now third secretary of state. He would soon prove himself as devastatingly effective in the council chamber as Gresham was in the bourse. Already recruited by the future Elizabeth I as her backstairs fixer, Cecil was Northumberland's right-hand man in financial affairs.

Arriving in Antwerp in May 1552, Thomas was under instructions from Northumberland to repay a loan of £14,000 to Anton Fugger, then negotiate terms for the redemption of other loans totalling £123,000, and to do so partly by rolling over the government's existing debt. He successfully repaid £77,500 in two instalments, then borrowed 60,000 Carolus guilders from Lazarus Tucher (around £8,800 at the prevailing exchange rate) at 14 per cent interest.

After closing this deal, Gresham repaid £5,400 due to Gaspar Schetz, then borrowed £14,000 more from him, another £24,000 or so from Fugger and some smaller amounts from other lenders. In August, two of Somerset's loans totalling £56,000 fell due, which Thomas was instructed to roll over if he could. He secured an offer of £52,000 at a rate of 12 per cent for a year to prolong these debts, but only if he took up part of the money in the shape of jewels priced at £8,000 and a diamond priced at £1,000. Alternatively, Fugger would take over the debt, but the quid pro quo was that Gresham would have to purchase yet more bales of overvalued fustian. Caught in a vice, Thomas recommended the deal which required the privy council to purchase the jewels: the problem was getting those in power to agree with him.[5]

Now Gresham came to rue his attacks on Damsell for buying overpriced wares. For with the purchase of jewels at high retail prices again on the table and with little by way of a viable alternative, he was in exactly the same spot. His excuse was that when Stephen Vaughan had held the post in Henry VIII's reign, he too had been forced to purchase such miscellaneous items as jewels, copper, gunpowder and fustian. But Thomas's protests fell on deaf ears.[6]

With a clash of wills with the privy council looming, Thomas briefly returned to London to thrash out the matter, arriving in early August 1552.[7] Northumberland was then away in the country with the king, and in his absence the privy council refused to act as Gresham recommended. Instead, the councillors decided that no deal was better than a bad deal: the king's overseas debts would have to be repaid if they could not be prolonged, but only when the money could be found. Until then, his creditors would have to wait.

To Gresham, who understood the way credit and exchange markets worked better than anyone of his generation, this approach was disastrous. In a series of anguished letters, he explained that if the government defaulted, it would be impossible to raise loans again for many years at reasonable rates. 'Your grace', he pleaded in an anxious appeal to Northumberland, sent on 21 August after his return to Antwerp, 'must have a consideration and an earnest respect thereunto, for truly, my poor opinion is better it were for the king's majesty to lose as much money as he [possesses] as his credit should be touched in this matter.'[8] And he gave the duke a stark warning: 'the world is wonderfully altered here by reason of these wars' (he referred to the latest round of the Franco–Habsburg dynastic struggle between the gout-stricken Charles V and Henry II of France) that 'hath made a marvellous scarcity of money'.[9]

A 'wonderfully altered' world required a more imaginative and daring approach, and Thomas had one. His first, most critical piece of advice was that he should begin systematically to try and rig the Antwerp currency market to England's advantage. He knew that timing in markets was crucial, and that rates of exchange changed daily or even hourly. Hence his proposals involved subtly strengthening the sterling rate of exchange at the precise moments he was making ready to redeem in sterling the government's debts repayable in Flemish pounds. If Northumberland would entrust him with a regular monthly or weekly float, he would use it to fund a myriad of smaller transactions in different currencies that would swing the fluctuating rates of exchange in his favour. 'And for the accomplishment of the same,' he explained, 'my request shall be to his majesty and you, to appoint me out weekly £1,200 or £1,300 to be secretly received [at] one man's hands so that it may be kept secret and that I may thereunto trust, and that I may [make] my receiving thereof assuredly.'[10] Should these weekly funds arrive, Gresham declared,

> I shall so use this m[atter] here in this town of Antwerp that every day I shall be sure to take up £200 or £300 sterling by exchange. And this doing, it shall not be perceived nor not be no occasion to make the exchange fall. For th[at] it shall be taken up in my name. And so by [these] means in working by deliberation and time, the me[rchants'] turn also shall be served, as also this should bring all merchants out of suspicion.[11]

Never one to hide his light under a bushel and elated by the sheer audacity of his proposal, Gresham boasted that, if given such a float and left to his own devices, he could secure the best possible rates and deals, and even pay off completely the crown's debt in Antwerp within two years.

Gresham's second, even bolder piece of advice to Northumberland was that he should take a leaf out of the book of the late Jakob Fugger and attempt to corner the European market in a major commodity. Fugger, the supreme example of a banker who made up his own rules, using his great wealth to cross frontiers and act autonomously of sovereign powers, had sought to monopolise the supply of silver from Tyrol and copper from Hungary. In 1487, Jakob had advanced the sum of 23,627 florins to Siegmund, archduke of Tyrol, who in spite of his rich mining assets was always short of money. He received as security a mortgage on the best of the Schwartz silver mines, under which, if the loan were not redeemed in a timely manner, the silver due from the mines to the archduke should be handed over. Then, in 1488, Jakob advanced another 150,000 florins to the archduke, and until this debt was paid, the whole of the silver production of these mines became the property of the Fugger bank at a very low price. Next, Jakob turned his fertile brain to the Hungarian copper market. Beginning to trade there in 1495, he was soon able largely to monopolise the ore extracted from the large copper mines in Neusohl (now Banská Bystrica in central Slovakia). The Fugger firm built its own smelting facility near Arnoldstein in north-east Germany to refine the copper and traded it quite mercilessly at monopoly prices.[12]

The plan Gresham now proposed to Northumberland was that he should create an English monopoly in lead, in effect nationalising the whole of the English trade in the metal and prohibiting its export for five years other than through a state-controlled outlet. From this, Thomas expected relatively fast profits. Thanks to years of over-supply, English lead was relatively cheap in Europe. Stocks were high, because Somerset's dissolution of the chantries, and Northumberland's own confiscations of bell metal from parish churches, meant that fresh supplies had added to the considerable quantities still remaining in the hands of those who had profited from Henry VIII's dissolution of the monasteries. Precedents existed for the government to impose stiff controls over the metal market. In 1542, Henry had persuaded Parliament to pass a bill forbidding the export of brass, copper, bell metal or anything else 'meet for making of guns'. One of Somerset's proclamations in 1547 reiterated the prohibition, and in 1549 Parliament renewed and reinforced Henry's legislation by increasing the penalties levied on offenders.[13]

Gresham had dealt in large quantities of lead himself as recently as 1549. He knew that prices were dropping, and that the metal was selling in Antwerp for around £8 per ton in Flemish currency. But he also saw an opportunity, as he knew that quantities as large as 300–400 tons at a time could be purchased in Hull for as little as £6 13s. 4d. Here was what he called 'a goodly matter'. If Northumberland was prepared to issue an unusually draconian proclamation, forbidding the export of lead other than through a centralised state-controlled outlet on pain of death or forfeiture of all property, then not only could the English merchants be forced to cut their prices further, but the onward selling price in Antwerp could be artificially inflated by regulating the flow of supplies. 'And this doing', Gresham concluded, 'the king's majesty shall [be] for a great profit … and by these means your grace shall receive much honour and all those that are now of his council in keeping his money within his realm, as also bringing him out of debt that his late father and the late duke of Somerset brought him into'.[14]

Within a month of these proposals landing on Northumberland's desk, the scheme to corner the market in lead would be rejected as too risky and extreme. In particular, Gresham's idea that the death penalty was an appropriate way to enforce a state-controlled trading monopoly shows how divorced from political reality he could occasionally become. However, where the provision of a cash float to help him rig the exchange market in Antwerp was concerned, he emerged triumphant. This plan seemed not only feasible to Northumberland, but also highly attractive – provided it worked.

The privy council instructed Gresham to roll over the now overdue loans as fast as he could, backed by a cash float of £1,200 every week that would allow him to get the best possible rates of exchange. The arrangement led to the unfolding of one of the classic methods that Thomas would use for the rest of his career in his attempts to manipulate foreign exchange markets. Armed with a float, he would every day send seemingly unconnected merchant friends, or else his servants, to buy or sell quantities of sterling ranging from £20 to £500 shortly before he planned to close one of his larger credit deals or make loan repayments, gradually raising or reducing the value of sterling in the direction that best suited him. He did not mention any profits gained from trading by such ingenious methods on his own account.

Coming to Gresham's aid was a more fundamental economic swing. The central European silver mining industry was on the cusp of a sharp decline, caused by the arrival in Spain of New World bullion.[15] As the mines of central Europe gradually reduced production, the price of silver climbed on the Antwerp exchange, for which, as yet, the arrival of the treasure fleets in Seville did not fully compensate. The opportunities were there for those like Gresham and his uncle, who understood the workings of the bourse.

Whereas many of Somerset's loans had been contracted in Flemish pounds at rates of exchange as unfavourable to the crown as 16 Flemish shillings to the pound sterling, Thomas was now sometimes able to repay them at up to 22 Flemish shillings to the pound. And by siphoning off the unused portions of the sterling balances he received for debt servicing, he managed to reduce the government's debts in Antwerp by almost half in barely nine months, a breathtaking feat.[16]

He trumpeted this dark wizardry as if he had turned water into wine. And much of the credit must be his, because by beguiling several major creditors into rolling over loans at their originally agreed exchange rates, he was able to repay them later at the new. It couldn't last. By November 1552, privy councillors were wrestling with debts at home amounting to £108,800 on top of those owed abroad.[17] They instructed Edmund Peckham, the treasurer of the mint, to stop making weekly payments to Thomas for his float, a financially illiterate move given Gresham's recent run of success. As the minutes of the council meeting record, 'that manner of exchange is not profitable for the king's majesty, and that nevertheless [Gresham] may make exchange of the same that he hath already received'.[18]

Thomas would be forced into a fresh round of negotiations with Northumberland. Along the way, he came up with an ingenious scheme that would gradually evolve into his master plan for the next fifteen years. His float could to all intents and purposes be recreated at no cost to the government if the privy council compelled English merchants engaged in the Anglo-Brabant trade to make substantial short-term loans to the crown whether they liked it or not. Northumberland and Cecil tried a dry run of this approach ahead of the 'Cold' fair at Bergen-op-Zoom in October 1552. With three loans amounting to £48,000 due for repayment in Antwerp and only £14,000 already in hand, they successfully extorted £30,000 from the merchants, who were afterwards repaid from the sale of the confiscated chantry lands. This left Thomas with only a relatively small shortfall to juggle.[19]

Now he outlined a more refined version of his thinking in a series of memos to Northumberland. These memos equate to a dummy's guide to his new, more proactive approach to government borrowing.

The council, he began, would need first to place a temporary 'stop' on all English merchant ships sailing for each of the Brabant fairs when they were fully loaded and ready to go. Then, either Gresham or the council's agents would inform these merchants individually that loans were to be exacted from each of them – the highest they could be forced to agree to – at rates set in proportion to the quantities of cloth in each ship's hold. Such loans were to be individually assessed in sterling amounts, but were payable directly to Gresham in Antwerp at certain future dates in Flemish pounds, and at rigged exchange rates he imposed on the merchants, so that, independently, he could use their money to roll over or repay crown debts and take advantage of spikes in market rates.

The merchants' loans would be repayable in London after two or three months, in sterling, and with minimal interest, once more at rates fixed by Gresham. To tie in the merchants and ensure no defaults, all new government loans were to be taken up on the joint security of the king's bonds and those of the city of London. And to make quite sure that the scheme would succeed, Gresham did not hesitate to blackmail his fellow merchants into staying away from the foreign exchange markets in the weeks while he was trading, making it plain that he had spies who told him about the sums which they, as well as foreigners, took up by exchange.[20]

Needless to say, this enraged the merchants, sparking a quarrel between Gresham and his uncle, who accused him of treachery and of being little better than a government lackey. As Thomas warned Northumberland, 'I have spoken with my uncle, Sir John Gresham, whom hath not a little stormed with me for the setting of the price of the exchange, and sayeth that it lies in me now to do the merchants of this realm pleasure, to the increase of my poor name among the merchants for ever'.[21]

Thomas brushed aside his uncle's outburst. The poacher in him became a gamekeeper after he accepted the job of government banker. And this was only the beginning. When his fellow merchants read the devilish small print of their lending agreements, they had yet another nasty surprise: as newly fledged credit providers to the government, they were to pay their loans to Gresham in Antwerp only in so-called 'valued' or 'permission' money, which, since it was independently weighed and assayed, would ensure that the funds borrowed would in every case be worth their face value.[22] It is clear from his successive memos that Thomas knew not only which currencies the privy council should accept or reject, but even which individual coins.

On the more positive side, there were some immediate gains for the merchants in the arrangements Gresham had been proposing: that was the genius of his whole scheme. One was the certainty that their loans would be repaid in London in sterling at known dates and rates, and without brokerage fees or commissions. Another bonus was that the merchants, in return for their loans, were all but promised more generous export licences for their cloths. The privy council kept a lever over the merchants by retaining the licensing system; but on the merchants' side, the concession opened the way to an unprecedentedly free trade in cloths if sufficient demand existed.[23]

Finally, Gresham lobbied the privy council to revoke forever the privileges of the wealthy merchants of the Hanseatic League in favour of the English Merchant Adventurers. Over the greater part of the Middle Ages, the trading of the Hanseatic towns had dominated northern Europe, affecting everything the English did, or failed to do, in the Baltic and North Sea. A vast configuration of around 200 towns and cities extending from Novgorod in the extreme east towards Bruges in the west, and dominated at its centre by Hamburg and Lübeck, the League's members had enjoyed extensive rights in London since 1474, when Edward IV gave them far-reaching concessions. These they had promised to reciprocate, though in fact they never did. As a result, certified Hanse merchants paid only 3d. poundage on goods they brought into London, as against the shilling paid by native Englishmen, while on each cloth exported they paid only 9d. tax as compared with the 1s. 2d. due from the Merchant Adventurers. That unfair advantage enabled the Hanse merchants to undercut the English in every possible way. If left unchecked, Gresham complained that it 'would have undone your whole realm, and your merchants of the same.'[24]

Already Northumberland had set about correcting this imbalance. On 24 February 1552, he had ordered the Germans to produce their 'records, writings, charters, treaties, depositions of witnesses and other evidences and proofs' before the privy council, which ruled that they were 'void by the laws of this realm'. Out of five reasons given, the most explicit was that the Hanse merchants had abused their privileges by trading in London in the commodities of many countries other than their own and by defrauding the crown of its legitimate customs' duties. As a punishment, their concessions were revoked.[25]

The Hanseatic League retaliated, convening a congress at Lübeck the following November. Northumberland sent a letter in Edward's name, offering to discuss a settlement if the League sent an embassy to London. During the early months of 1552, envoys and messages sped from one Hanse town to another, but back in London, Gresham continued to lobby Northumberland to hold fast. He had located documents which, he said, proved 'what sedition [*sic*] and false persons these new men of the Hanse are'.[26] From his own, narrower perspective, it was essential for the duke to maintain the pressure on the League if the English merchants were to help supply Thomas's float in Antwerp.

Within seven months of Northumberland and Cecil's first dry run, the system Thomas had described in his memos would be fully operational. The English merchants duly handed over to him in Antwerp at the agreed dates their funds in Flemish pounds, and were shocked to discover that Gresham reckoned these as future credits for repayment in London using exchange rates even more predatory than those his critics expected. Thomas had to stretch his margins to the limit, since his claims for his ability to manipulate the sterling exchange rate were characteristically inflated.[27] Too many other speculators were already in the bourse, trying their hands at the same game, not to mention genuine merchants who needed the exchange for their trade.[28]

Despite such limitations, Gresham had achieved something truly remarkable, transforming almost at a stroke the privy council's ability to repay or roll over outstanding loans. As the government's credit rating rose correspondingly, Thomas, by the late spring of 1553, could report offers of fresh loans at an interest rate of 12 per cent, whereas Charles V was forced to pay 16 per cent. If Gresham's hyperbole is to be believed, 'these great counters that hath the great banks of money [in Antwerp] doth daily pray to me, by their friends, as to help them lend out their money to the king's majesty'.[29]

Then, out of the blue, the wheel of fortune dramatically shifted again.

SMOKE AND MIRRORS

In January 1553, the duke of Northumberland fell ill. As he told Sir William Cecil, 'I burn as hot as fire. So did I yesterday'. He was also suffering from 'a wonderful great pain in the nether part of my belly'.[1] Shortly afterwards, Edward caught a feverish cold. It would not have mattered, had he not contracted a virulent attack of measles the previous year. With his immune system still gravely weakened by the measles, he developed either bronchial pneumonia or tuberculosis (both are possible, but his symptoms better matched pneumonia). Advised that he might die, the teenager became convinced that his half-sisters, Mary and Elizabeth, should be excluded from the succession, despite their rights as laid down by their father's dynastic settlement.

His motives were chiefly religious. Already a convert to radical Protestantism, Edward did not trust either of his siblings not to reverse or water down Archbishop Cranmer's more drastic reforms. He had also convinced himself that both women were legally barred from inheriting the crown as each had been declared illegitimate by their father's Parliaments. The upshot, after several drafts, was his 'Device for the succession', which 'devised' the crown to the sixteen-year-old Lady Jane Grey, the eldest daughter of Henry VIII's niece, Frances, duchess of Suffolk. Should Jane die, her sister Katherine was to take the throne. Should Katherine die, her younger sister Mary was to succeed. A Protestant who had received an education fit for a queen and who corresponded with several leaders of the Swiss Reformation, Jane had recently married Northumberland's fourth son, Guildford Dudley, another eager Protestant and Edward's protégé.[2]

Edward died on 6 July 1553, leaving a hiatus while Northumberland, still very unwell and slower than usual to react, took control of the Tower and the royal treasury in support of Jane's claim. On the 10th, the heralds proclaimed Jane queen and she moved into the royal apartments at the Tower. Her brief reign ended abruptly nine days later, when Mary raised her forces and led a swift and effective counter-coup.

By late July, a majority of privy councillors not directly linked by ties of blood or allegiance to Northumberland had disowned him, enabling Mary to enter London in triumph. Jane, stripped of the crown jewels and her canopy of state, was escorted from the royal apartments and put under house arrest within the Tower. Northumberland was tried and executed. Jane was initially allowed a reprieve, but then the Protestant Sir Thomas Wyatt led a revolt from Kent early in 1554 that reached the gates of London, and in the resulting crackdowns she was executed with her husband.

Just five days before Edward breathed his last on 6 July 1553, Thomas Gresham was granted large parcels of ex-monastic land secured for him by Northumberland and Cecil. These would form the cornerstone of much of his later landed wealth.[3] In the nick of time he secured his deeds of title to estates and rectories in Westacre, Custhorpe, Great and Little Walsingham, Lakenham, Stiffkey and a dozen other Norfolk villages, worth over £4,000 if managed efficiently (over £4 million today), and yielding a total annual return of £200 (over £200,000). It was a splendid reward for his services: for the first time, he could envisage himself equalling or exceeding the landed wealth of his father or uncle. All he had to do for his new properties was pay a reserved rent of £52 6s. to the crown for the rest of his life.[4]

But with the Catholic Queen Mary enthroned in London, Northumberland's old allies, in particular Cecil, were desperately covering their tracks.[5] Gresham was of course seriously compromised by his close connections to the duke; to make matters worse he had just negotiated a fresh round of loans from the Schetz, the Fugger and others, totalling £62,000, partly using his own credit, which Mary might disavow.[6] His apprehension was compounded by the sinking of the ship in which he sent home much of his plate and household goods because his wife, Anne Ferneley, had decided to return to London.[7]

These were anxious months for 'poor Gresham', as he described himself.[8] He had yoked his career to a politician whom Mary had loathed even before she came to suspect him as the hidden hand behind Edward's 'Device for the succession'. She could be generous: Catholic or kinship connections were crucial in her view of the world. So in a bid to hold on to his position, Gresham sought to reconnect with Antonio Buonvisi of Lucca, one of the new queen's favourite Italians.

Always a devout Catholic, Buonvisi had fled into exile in Leuven in 1549 fearing attack by jealous Protestants eager to seize his wealth. A year later, his house, Crosby Place in Bishopsgate, was impounded and handed over with all its contents to Thomas Darcy, one of the chief gentlemen of Edward's privy chamber.[9] With Mary to help him, Buonvisi had Darcy evicted, but was himself too old and frail to return to London. In October 1553, he entrusted what remained of this branch of the firm to his deputy, Germain Cioll, with orders to report to his nephew Alessandro Buonvisi, who now ran its branches in Antwerp and Marseille.

Seizing their opportunity, Thomas and his uncle joined forces to persuade Sir John's eighteen-year-old daughter Cecily to marry the thirty-four-year-old Cioll.[10] On 20 January 1554, the bride left her father's house in Basinghall Street and the wedding took place at the nearby church of St Michael's, binding Cioll into the family network.[11] This enabled Thomas to connect with Alessandro. Before long the pair would be working together.[12]

It was a small step forward, but it still wasn't clear how far Thomas's career could be salvaged with Mary in power. His nerves must have calmed somewhat when Mary allowed Cecil to go free after an awkward interview, although she dismissed him from the privy council.[13] Gresham must have wondered if his brother-in-law, the lawyer Sir Nicholas Bacon, might be able to pull strings for him as he had tried to do for Cecil. Sir Nicholas's first wife, Jane, Anne Ferneley's sister, had died while the Greshams were in Antwerp, and he had recently married Anne Cooke, one of Mary's trusted gentlewomen of the privy chamber and Cecil's sister-in-law. But Cooke was an ardent Protestant, which limited the leverage she could exert.

Instead, Thomas clawed his way back up the ladder with help of a man who may well have been a kinsman of his stepmother Isabel's friend, the wealthy Mercer and London alderman Sir Thomas Leigh.[14] This was Sir John Leigh, a loyal Catholic who had gone into exile in Antwerp and Rome while Edward was on the throne. As Thomas later informed Cecil, 'for verily, sir, [he] was the man that preserved me when Queen Mary came to the crown, for the which I do account myself bound unto him during my life'.[15] We can only speculate about how Leigh may have met Gresham on the continent and urged Mary to overlook his intimate links to Northumberland, perhaps because he might prove useful.[16] Leigh certainly found him useful in 1560, as he can be found borrowing one of Gresham's confidential couriers to transmit his letters to and from England.[17]

However it was that Leigh came to his aid, Gresham would soon be able to regain much of his old position. Although dogmatically Catholic, Mary came to tolerate Thomas for her own ends. He seemingly experienced no qualms of conscience in adapting himself to suit the new regime.

But at first, he had to go back to where he had been at the beginning of Edward's reign, when William Damsell had been crown agent, and play second fiddle to a lesser man. Mary chose the staunchly Catholic Christopher Dauntsey to represent her in Antwerp. Until Dauntsey made a serious mistake, Thomas once again had to bide his time.

While kicking his heels, Gresham resumed his old trade, buying 308 cloths in London in the summer of 1553 for sale at the Cold fair at Bergen-op-Zoom.[18] Then, as early as November, Dauntsey made a disastrous bargain with Lazarus Tucher to borrow 113,000 Carolus guilders (around £17,120) in Antwerp for a year at an interest rate of 13 per cent, and indicated his acceptance of another 113,000 at the end of the month. As it happened money was available that week on the bourse at 11 or 12 per cent, and Dauntsey's nominal 13 per cent, moreover, turned into a real rate of 14 when Tucher postponed delivery of the first tranche of the loan for a month.

The privy council's reaction was immediate. Within days, Gresham was back in Antwerp with orders to annul Dauntsey's contract and to borrow at 11 or 12 per cent. He arrived on the 17th at 8 p.m., and twice over the ensuing week met an aggrieved Tucher, who was not at all amused by Thomas's claim that Dauntsey lacked authority to deal at such a high rate. He answered stiffly 'that he had concluded a bargain, and he looked to have his bargain kept'.[19]

As news of the impasse spread, what most troubled Gresham was that alternative lenders were now not afraid to demand interest rates as high as 15 per cent. As he warned the privy council, 'they would burst out and say, "Think you that we do not know that the queen's majesty gives Lazarus Tucher thirteen percent for an eleven-month [loan] ... and is not our money as good as his?"'[20] Worse, rumours of the possible repudiation of the deal were adversely affecting the queen's and the London merchants' credit, as Dauntsey's agreement with Tucher was secured on their joint guarantees.

As Thomas continued, Tucher 'is a very extreme man and very open mouthed'. On reflection, he advised the privy council that, 'considering how far Dauntsey hath passed in the matter and that it should touch the queen's credit … it is most meet [for] this bargain to take place'. Once that was settled, Gresham further advised the councillors that they should borrow no more for at least three months. By then, the dust would have settled and lower rates could be obtained. Best of all, Dauntsey was dismissed and Thomas appointed in his place.[21]

Although never acknowledging her mistake, Mary was gratifyingly generous, thanking Gresham before the Christmas festivities in 1553 for his foresight and diligence and instructing him to borrow another £100,000 as soon as he reasonably could, at a rate of up to 12 per cent.[22] She needed money because she had decided to marry. As England's first queen regnant, the pressure was on her from the outset. She knew she had a lawful right to rule, but as Henry VIII had predicted as early as 1532 when he first contemplated an outright break with Rome, a woman ruler in a dynastic monarchy would need to find a husband if the dynasty was to outlast her.[23] Always loyal to her beloved mother, the Spanish princess Katherine of Aragon, Mary was determined to marry Philip of Spain, son and heir of her cousin, Charles V. By marrying early in her reign, she hoped to quiet those who opposed female rule on principle, while her desire for children, unfulfilled in the event, was an important signal that she took her duty as a dynastic monarch seriously.

Overjoyed at the prospect of adding England to the Spanish empire, Philip ditched his plans to marry the Infanta of Portugal and accepted Mary's proposal. His attitude soured somewhat as word of Parliament's terms for the marriage emerged – in particular, he was not to take any children the couple might have out of the country or embroil Mary in wars against France – but by then he had alienated the Portuguese and it was too late to turn back. Luckily for Mary, Philip did not meet her before agreeing to the union. Although still only thirty-seven, she appeared to be twenty years older. According to a modern medical expert, she suffered from a prolactinoma, a non-cancerous tumour of the pituitary gland. This results in too much of a hormone called prolactin in the blood, triggering amenorrhoea in the earlier stages with later symptoms including migraines, vomiting, depression and loss of vision.[24] In private Philip mocked his new bride, calling her an elderly spinster and nicknaming her his aunt.[25]

Their wedding was celebrated at Winchester Cathedral on St James's Day 1554 (25 July). According to the marriage treaties, Philip was not to exercise rights of patronage independently of his wife, but almost as soon as he landed at Southampton, he was accorded precedence. Official documents styled the monarchs: 'Philip and Mary, by the grace of God, King and Queen of England, France, Naples, Jerusalem and Ireland; Defenders of the Faith; Princes of Spain and Sicily; Archdukes of Austria; Dukes of Milan, Burgundy and Brabant; Counts of Habsburg, Flanders and Tyrol'.[26]

In Antwerp, rumours of Mary's impending nuptials seeped out over the winter of 1553–4, further stimulating Gresham's ambition. With Charles V severely affected by gout and preparing to abdicate in favour of his son, Thomas saw himself working closely with the future head of a global empire. In Brussels, the regent Mary of Hungary held the reins of power, which Philip was anxious to seize. His game plan at this point was to rule the northern European portion of his inheritance personally, and appoint regents or councils to govern in Spain and the New World.

One of Philip's obsessions was finance, and just a few weeks after he made his triumphal entry into London, a long procession of carts trundled out of the courtyard at Whitehall Palace, crammed to the brim 'with wedges of gold and silver to the Tower to be coined'.[27] Philip had shipped the bullion from Spain to pay for his large Spanish entourage: it was quickly turned into £40,500 sterling. By the time this was done, Thomas was already in Spain, engaged in one of the most brazen and perilous of his many schemes to make easy money for the government and himself.

The idea of raising funds in Antwerp and collecting them in cash in Spain had first been pitched to Gresham six months before Mary's marriage by a syndicate of Genoese merchants.[28] The loan would be for 300,000 ducats, around £86,000 sterling (more than £86 million today), for a year, and was repayable at the rate of 6s. 5d. to the ducat in Flemish money (around 5s. 11½d. sterling), 'which in my opinion', he said, 'is one of the profitablest bargains if it takes place that can be made'.

Gresham believed that he could clear a profit of up to 15 per cent on the transaction, even after interest and costs were deducted.[29] On account of their exceptionally high silver content, *reales* (the basic Spanish silver coin valued at between 6½d. and 7d. depending on the exchange rate) were worth between 12 and 20 per cent more than their face value when taken out of Castile and melted down.[30] The privy council was desperate for bullion; it had just authorised an experimental minting of gold and silver coins at more or less the same higher standard set by Northumberland in 1551, but until fresh supplies could be found at a reasonable price there could be no prospect of a wider restoration of the coinage, given the prohibitive costs of recalling and re-minting the entire quantity of bad money in circulation.[31]

Already thinking along these lines, Thomas had rented a house in Antwerp for £26 a year (its exact location is unknown). There, like an illicit cannabis farmer in the twenty-first century, he began using the outbuildings to operate an unlicensed forge. As he gleefully informed the privy council, 'I have made a furnace and have all things ready for the same within my house to melt down all such Spanish *reales* as I shall receive, and to make it bullion ... which will be more easier [*sic*] to pack and carry than the coin'.[32]

So far, Gresham had illegally smuggled 5,864 lbs of silver bullion to London, melted down from Spanish *reales* he had taken up from those in unofficial circulation in Antwerp, along with a modest supply of French and Burgundian gold crowns amounting to around £12,000. By plying the local inspectors with food and drink he had evaded Charles V's strict customs controls.[33] Unfortunately, interest rates were on the rise. In May 1554 they stood at 14 per cent, and would peak within three months at 18 per cent, which meant that borrowing costs were rising faster than at any time for a decade.[34] If he could cut the nominal rate to a lower real amount by taking up, melting down and re-minting Spanish *reales* in larger quantities, that was something seriously to consider.

Reluctantly, Thomas had to decline the initial Genoese offer: controls over the export of currency from mainland Spain were even more stringent than those prevailing in the Spanish Netherlands, and for a deal of the size proposed by the Genoese, the quantities of cash involved would have made detection inevitable. But when Mary's wedding date was fixed, everything changed. Now Philip was to be king of England and all Thomas would need would be for Mary to intercede with him to obtain the necessary export licences and passports.

In the end, Thomas borrowed 300,750 ducats from the Antwerp syndicate of Anton Fugger and Gaspar Schetz. The money was to be given him in Castile, where he could collect it in Spanish currency, roughly half at the May fair in Medina del Campo and the balance at the June fair in Villalón. The bargain was sealed in April 1554 by bills of exchange for repayment between seven months and a year later.[35] As Thomas jotted down with suitable exactitude in a previously unidentified private notebook covering this venture and a variety of others during Mary's reign, he now owed the syndicate £97,878 10s. 0d. in Flemish money, or £89,598 8s. 0d. sterling.[36]

On 21 April, Gresham also bought a large jewel from Schetz on behalf of the queen 'of the fashion of an eagle, very richly set with diamonds on the head and on both sides', for which he paid £1,166.[37] This was almost certainly a double-headed imperial eagle, the badge of Charles V, and the jewel was perhaps intended as a wedding gift for Philip or for display as a table decoration at their wedding banquet. Certainly, tapestries showing the double-headed eagle with texts in Castilian and Latin, with Charles's arms and personal mottos embroidered in gold thread along the borders, were on prominent show at the banquet. Before setting out for Spain, Gresham handed over the jewel to Mary personally at St James's Palace, and arranged for royal navy ships to transport the coffers containing the borrowed money back to England.[38]

Leaving the faithful John Elyot to manage his affairs in Antwerp, Thomas sailed from Plymouth shortly after 10 June, heading for the fairs at Medina del Campo and Villalón. He took his trusted assistant, John Spritewell, and arranged to meet his newly promoted Spanish factor, Edmond Hogan, on his arrival.[39]

The trouble started when they reached the fairs and discovered that their plan to withdraw so vast an amount of local currency in just a few days was likely to cause a bank run.[40] If Gresham had done his homework, he would have realised that for some years there had been an acute short-age of cash in the area, which had already provoked bitter complaints. The May fair at Medina del Campo had been postponed on this account in 1543 and 1553, and the 1554 fair was a shadow of its former self.[41]

On entering the banks in Medina del Campo and Villalón, Gresham and Hogan pursued 'by all means and ways with great diligence to be paid out of the banks in ready money'. They were only able to withdraw less than two-thirds of what they were owed, and so had to negotiate fresh bills of exchange for the balance. These were payable in October and Novem-ber, partly at the nearby fair of Medina de Rioseco, close to Valladolid, and partly in Seville, almost 350 miles away.

At Medina de Rioseco, Thomas was in luck. He could withdraw more than half their missing funds in local currency, chiefly *reales*. Unfor-tunately in Seville, Gresham and Hogan encountered more problems. Two prominent bankers, Juan Iñiguez and Octaviano de Negrón, who were in partnership together, declared themselves bankrupt and went into hiding, and since Gresham had already presented his bills of exchange at the counter of their bank and had them entered into the ledger, he had no remedy against the owners, since 'by the law and custom of Spain' he was himself liable for the loss.[42]

By the end of November 1554, Gresham was becoming seriously alarmed at his lack of progress, but all he could do was wait. 'For now there is no other way to help this matter,' he warned the privy council, 'considering the [treasure] ships be not come from the Indies [i.e., New World], which be here looked for daily.'[43] By fair means or foul, he or Hogan later recovered much of the missing money (the suspicion is that Hogan hired thugs to track down the defaulters), but still ended up short. Along the way they ran into serious difficulties with their passports, and the pressure they exerted drove two more bankers into insolvency.[44]

Thomas successfully shipped home the bulk of the cash, tightly packed into 130 wooden cases, in two large consignments, one from the harbour at Seville and the rest from the Biscay port of Laredo. Transport of the cases overland within Spain on the backs of mules cost a stupendous £2,360 (over £2.3 million today), and making ready the queen's ships cost £350. Overall, Gresham and Hogan ran up bank charges in excess of £1,000; brokerage fees of £200; legal fees totalling £150; John Spritewell's expenses came to £640; and so on. While the money was being moved, some of the cases broke open and cash to the value of £75 was lost, for which Gresham was allowed to reclaim only £2.[45]

Returning to London early in January 1555, Gresham claimed to have handed over a grand total of £80,454 in Spanish coins to the under-treasurer of the mint.[46] But as he had a habit of rendering his official accounts in Flemish pounds when it suited him, rather than in sterling, this figure dropped to £73,626 sterling at the prevailing rate of exchange. The sterling figure is tucked away in his notebook.[47]

For all the ostensible advantages of the venture, it is unlikely that it ever made a profit. In fact, the whole episode reeks of smoke and mirrors. In both his notebook and official accounts, Thomas claimed to have held back from the mint £11,718 as a part-repayment for the queen's creditors, but since she owed £89,598 sterling to the investors in the Antwerp syndicate, he had actually made a loss. He might have made a small profit if all the Spanish coins he deposited in the mint had been coined into sterling, but only £17,592 worth of conversion can be accounted for in the mint records. With the first instalments of the debt to the syndicate already due when Gresham's cases of cash were unloaded from his ships, most of them were very likely removed from the mint almost as soon as they had been paid in, and were shipped over to Antwerp with the money still in *reales*. They would have been worth considerably more than their face value there, but full profits could not be achieved without re-minting.[48]

Also on the debit side of the ledger, Thomas had disbursed £4,253 in costs and charges of which around £750 (over £0.75 million in modern values) were his own – to be quite sure of repayment, he had already helped himself to that amount out of the cash he collected in Spain. Mary had granted him an allowance of ten shillings a day for his 'food and entertainment' in Spain, this seemingly on top of her regular allowance of twenty shillings a day, which on an annualised basis came to rather more than she paid her privy councillors. She also promised him a bonus of crown land worth £131 a year.[49]

From its inception to its completion, Gresham's Spanish adventure took over a year. During this time, he only confessed in a letter to missing his family once, and even then, somewhat heartlessly: his concern was chiefly that his wife would be worrying about her 'substance' once the final reckoning of his accounts had been made.[50] He was allowed very little time to see them before Mary ordered him over to Antwerp again. He would later complain, very likely with some exaggeration, that during the time he worked for her she sent him back and forth thirty-two times.

Luckily for Thomas, market conditions had improved by the time he reached the bourse in April 1555. Interest rates had fallen back to 12 per cent, enabling him to repeat the triumph he had achieved in the closing months of Edward's reign: refinancing old borrowing at the new, lower interest rates, then using the savings in interest payments to pay down debt. Over the next twenty or so months he would once more cut overall foreign debt by more than half, from around £225,000 to £100,000.[51]

To pull off this feat, he needed to recreate a float, which once more he fuelled from a series of short-term loans extorted from the London cloth merchants. Not only did the float aid in the refinancing of old borrowing, it enabled Thomas to resume his trick of attempting to nudge the sterling exchange rate in the direction he wanted it to go by dealing regularly in smaller sums. When rendering his official accounts in July 1557, he boasted that 'by his wisdom and diligence' he had made profits totalling £11,426 in this way, which he put towards further loan redemption. This time, he had proved his doubters wrong.[52]

Yet, in both London and Antwerp after his return from Spain, Thomas would have found a changing world. In Antwerp in May 1555, he heard the exhilarating news that Mary had safely given birth to a son and heir. Mary of Hungary ordered the bells of the Church of Our Lady to ring out 'to give all men to understand that the news was true'.[53] Unfortunately, it wasn't: Mary's was a pseudo-pregnancy, complete with a swelling of the breasts and lactation, possibly triggered by her prolactinoma.

Next came the abdication of Charles V in favour of his son, which took place in the royal palace in Brussels in October and which Gresham personally witnessed. Philip fell on his knees and kissed his father's hand, then, in Spanish, asked his spokesman to give an acceptance speech on his behalf as he knew no Flemish. In the set-piece oration that followed, Philip promised to strive for the good of all his subjects.[54] That was more fake news: when Charles retired to the monastery of Yuste, taking with him the finest collection of paintings by Titian the world has ever seen, the balance of power with Spain tilted sharply. At first Philip sought to rule the Netherlands from Brussels, but as the months and years passed, he decided to absorb them into the wider Spanish empire. The result would be an insurgency that turned into a bloody religious war.

While in London, Philip took Reginald Pole under his wing. Pole was Mary's choice as archbishop of Canterbury and a cardinal, who had reconciled the kingdom to the papacy; Philip made him one of his own special advisers on English affairs. On Pole's advice, Mary began to reopen several of the religious houses dissolved by her father, beginning with Westminster Abbey and the royal friaries of Greenwich and Syon. And at Pole's urging, she talked of forcing her wealthier subjects to give back to the church the monastic and chantry lands they had 'unlawfully' acquired. Against Philip's advice, she encouraged a reluctant Pole to create the equivalent of a Spanish Inquisition. Soon, with the encouragement of some Spanish Dominicans who had travelled to London with Philip, Pole would begin roasting Protestants at the stake for heresy.

The mood among the merchant community was anxious. Many, among them Gresham's factor in Antwerp, Richard Clough, were eager converts to the reformers. Thomas, on the other hand, sought to avoid engagement in religious controversy. His personal faith since the closing years of Henry VIII's reign may well have swung towards the reformers and would come to crystallise as his familiarity with men like Cecil blossomed, but since he never, ever talked about religion in his letters or to those around him, we do not really know.[55] Like Cecil and the future Elizabeth I, he was wary of disclosing his true opinions during Mary's reign.

In the summer of 1555, Cecil almost certainly paid a call on Gresham while travelling in Flanders and Brabant. At the very least, he purchased Flemish currency from him.[56] But whereas there were moments when it suited Cecil, and indeed Mary herself, that those who supported the Protestant cause should leave the country or live quietly in obscurity, Gresham's ideals and actions were driven by commerce, not by faith. As he told Mary's councillors in a rare moment of candour, 'it is a small matter to bring the queen in debt, but the greatest matter will be to be to bring her out again ... whereof I have thought good to advertise you, for that this exchange ruleth all things'.[57] Judging by his surviving correspondence, nothing interested him more than the kaleidoscopic fluctuations of rates and margins on the Antwerp bourse and Lombard Street. He was a compulsive dealer, a driven man where money or profit was at stake, 'which verily', he reminded the privy council, 'is one of the chiefest points in our common weal you ought most to look unto'.[58]

Almost as his parting shot to politicians in Mary's reign, he set out in words his guiding philosophy of life. 'As the exchange is the chiefest thing that eats out all princes and all men that use it to the impoverishment of a whole realm, so being looked unto, it is the most profitablest [*sic*] and beneficial matter for the queen's majesty for the wealth of her realm that can be devised by the wit of man.'[59]

Suitably decoded, this was a stark warning. In a new age of extreme market volatility, the delicacy of the balance of power between, on the one hand, sovereign authority, and on the other, the newly emerged and semi-autonomous mercantile world, would mean that entire regimes could stand or fall on the strength of their credit ratings. At the same time, the warning was intended as a signal to England's governors that Thomas Gresham was one of the nation's greatest assets, whether a Catholic or a Protestant sat on the throne. He, and he alone, understood how the markets operated.

If, however, he thought he had heard the last about his Spanish venture, he would turn out to be very much mistaken.

REGIME CHANGE

On 23 October 1556, after an illness of almost two years, Thomas's uncle Sir John Gresham died of what was said to be a 'malignant fever'.[1] Two days later he was buried at the nearby church of St Michael's with all the pomp and heraldry due a man of his station. The church and the neighbouring streets were hung with thick black taffeta. The great hearse of wax on which the coffin rested in the chancel was decorated with 'a standard and a pennon of arms and a coat armour of damask', a helmet, target and sword, mantles and a crest. Displayed on the walls of the church were a further 120 'pencels' and 144 escutcheons. (Pennons were swallow-tailed flags attached to the head of a standard or lance. A target was a light round shield or buckler. Mantles were added decorations to coats of arms or crests, which often surmounted the helmet. Pencels were little pennons or flags adorned with armorial badges. Escutcheons were heraldic shields.) Twelve 'great long wax torches' illuminated the coffin and 144 more 'great staff torches' and hundreds of smaller candles blazed out light around the nave. In solemn procession, sixty poor men and forty poor women walked carrying lighted torches. All were dressed in gowns of black, paid for by Sir John before his death and ordered to be delivered 'ready made' by the tailor in time for the funeral.[2]

The next day, everyone returned for no fewer than three sung masses. After the third, which was the requiem mass and the longest, Dr Nicholas Harpsfield, archdeacon of Canterbury, preached a sermon. The choice of preacher was the deceased's, reflecting the extent of his Catholicism and not just a politic move. By the time Sir John put the final touches to his will, Harpsfield was winning a reputation as one of the most vigorous of Mary's heresy-hunters. Appointed by Cardinal Pole as his agent and vicar-general, Harpsfield made contact with the party of Spanish Dominicans who had arrived with Philip of Spain. They knew all about how to force suspects to confess, recant or face the consequences, and soon Harpsfield would be sweeping through the city's churches in search of Protestants.

Sir John had appointed his widow, Lady Katherine, and eldest son as his executors, then carefully divided up the bulk of his lands and goods between them and his other children and grandchildren. Thomas, now considered to be wealthy enough on his own account and perhaps never fully reconciled to his uncle after their argument over his dummy's guide to crown borrowing, was left only £20. (He and Anne Ferneley also received gold rings and black mourning gowns to wear at the funeral.) Sir John, however, appointed Thomas to be one of the overseers of his estate with specific instructions to chivvy along the executors 'to bring in my inventory of all my goods, jewels and plate into the council chamber before my lord mayor and his brethren, and in no wise to drive or prolong the time as we have done [with] my brother, Sir Richard Gresham'.[3]

Another family quarrel now broke out, which like the first one ended up in the court of Chancery and resulted in embarrassing legal testimony. Witnesses told how Sir John had paid £220 (over £220,000 in modern values) to Sir William Paulet, marquis of Winchester, to buy the wardship of William Uvedale, an underage heir to a large landed fortune. Without a thought, Sir John then married off his unfortunate daughter Ellyn to the feckless youth, who slept with her for a while before getting bored and sending her weeping back to her father. There was a suggestion that the reluctant bridegroom had done this in revenge for Sir John's plunder of his inheritance.

Thomas knew not to get too deeply involved in the dispute. He was not a principal beneficiary of his uncle's will, and in any case he was too busy ingratiating himself with Queen Mary and her husband. As it turned out, the case disappeared from the court records once the witness testimony was placed on the public file. Since Uvedale took back his now wealthier wife and the couple ended their days yoked together in Hampshire, the probability is that Sir John's executors had bought him off at the expense of Sir John's estate.

With the lawsuit against Sir John's executors ongoing until the following summer, Thomas spent the winter of 1555–6 in London. As a New Year's gift to Mary he presented a roll of fine Holland linen, 40 feet long, in a case of black leather, receiving in return a silver-gilt jug weighing 16½ ounces. At the same time, Sir John Leigh, who had stepped in to salvage

Gresham's career after Edward VI's death, gave the queen a Catholic primer, bound in purple velvet and richly decorated with gold wire and embroidery. He also received a silver-gilt jug, but one weighing only 15 ounces.[4]

Such fine distinctions mattered: Mary's gift to Thomas signalled her satisfaction with his services. And she went on, more or less, to keep her promise that she would reward him with crown land worth £131. It took the shape of a reversion of estates in Great Massingham in Norfolk, along with the manor and rectory of Langham and other lands in Great and Little Walsingham, Narford and elsewhere in the same county, yielding annual receipts of £163. The snag was that Thomas had to pay £647 into the exchequer to purchase the lands, and then wait for the deaths of the current grantees. But it was well worth it: Mary sold him the lands for a knock-down price. Not only were Thomas's new acquisitions almost as extensive as those Northumberland had granted him, they were in many cases adjacent to properties he already owned, so increasing their value to him. When managed effectively, they would earn him about £200 a year in rents.[5]

After Sir John's death, the House of Gresham ceased to exist as a wider family firm, and from now on relied almost entirely on Thomas doing solo deals, with in-house support services provided by his factors and assistants. Richard Clough and John Spritewell continued in their posts in Antwerp, Edmond Hogan shuttled between Antwerp and Spain, and Richard Candeler, a Norfolk-born relative of one of Sir John's nieces, took over from John Elyot as Thomas's factor in Lombard Street. Candeler was assisted by Anthony Stringer, another of Gresham's servants since his earliest days in Basinghall Street, who also held a post in the court of Augmentations, dealing with the sales of ex-monastic lands.[6]

Richard Candeler's younger brother, Thomas, Sir John Gresham's last apprentice, also joined the firm, as did Thomas Dutton, one of Clough's kinsmen who deputised for him in Antwerp. Without Sir John to put a brake on his betrayals of confidential city and commercial information to the privy council, Thomas's relations with his fellow merchants would sharply deteriorate. It would not be long before he was sending startlingly frank briefings to individual privy councillors, advising them precisely how to turn the screws on the merchants to encourage them to deliver cheap short-term loans.

By mid-February 1556, Gresham was back in Antwerp for three

months, where once more he set about repaying or rolling over government loans and securing fresh ones to meet the costs of Mary's rising expenditure on clothes, hospitality and renovations at her palaces. He successfully rolled over one loan of £40,000, but had greater difficulty renewing another of £30,000 and had to split what should have been a relatively easy debt of £10,450 into twenty or so smaller portions before another year's credit could be guaranteed. Interest rates were rising again: to secure just £15,000, Thomas had to agree to take out six-monthly contracts with rates in excess of 15 per cent on an annualised basis. And to obtain even that rate, he had to risk his own credit for a month, as he was bold enough to point out to Mary. In the end, he successfully completed this round of borrowing by raising £6,000 in the city of London by so-called 'imprest', meaning to all intents and purposes a forced loan, repayable without interest. Wealthy merchants were sent writs of privy seal from Mary, ordering them to lend her £100 each on pain of retribution.[7]

The renewal of hostilities with France in the spring of 1557 brought on an urgent need for the government to borrow heavily. In London, opposition to the war became painfully visible in March, when Philip returned from Brussels to seek the privy council's agreement to send English forces to fight alongside Spanish and Flemish troops in northern France. Only after pressure from Mary herself was the highly unpopular decision to enter the war finally taken. Hostilities were declared on 7 June, and at first the campaign went well. The English contingent arrived in August just in time to see Philip's troops win a triumphant victory at the siege of St Quentin. At home, however, a very different battle raged over the costs and dangers incurred. Mutual trust between Philip and the privy council collapsed after the king's final departure in July. The greatest humiliation of the reign, the loss of Calais, would follow on 1 January 1558, when the winter cold was so intense that the marshes surrounding the town froze solid, enabling the duke of Guise to lead 27,000 French troops with their artillery across the ice and breach the walls.

As soon as war had been declared, the privy council ordered Gresham with all speed to raise new and substantial loans. It was an almost impossible task: over-expansion of credit and the unsustainable levels of debt incurred by the Spanish-Habsburg monarchy had led Philip to declare bankruptcy. In Spain, the council of finance issued a moratorium on debt repayments, cynically justified by reference to the canon law of usury. In the Netherlands, the banks were close to breaking: Philip's debt to the

Fugger alone was in the region of 1.5 million ducats. To pay his troops, he
diverted two cargoes of New World silver which he had earmarked for
debt and interest repayments: their value was at least 570,000 ducats. After
the victory at St Quentin, Anton Fugger made a series of desperate pleas
to Philip to allow this money to be used for at least partial redemption of
his loans, but his appeal went unheeded.[8]

Before Thomas could get to grips with these dire events, he had to
cope with an audit by the very same marquis of Winchester who had sold
Sir John Gresham the wardship of William Uvedale. A survivor from Northumberland's regime, Winchester was Mary's lord treasurer, the titular
head of the exchequer and the privy council's most senior financial officer.
A plodding, mistrustful mind, but someone whom it was unwise to cross,
he believed Thomas Gresham to be a spiv and a fraud.[9] Not long after
Thomas had smuggled £12,000 in French and Burgundian gold crowns
across the Channel by bribing the customs officials, Winchester had called
in his accounts to be audited. Now he did so again, deeply suspicious of
Thomas's expenses and other claims incurred during his Spanish venture.[10]

A rigorous investigation revealed that, over the previous three years,
Thomas had received just over £160,000 in cash from Mary's coffers to
repay loans; had borrowed £112,000 in cash or by bills of exchange in
Antwerp or London; and had taken up £89,598 by way of loans on his
mission to Spain.[11] Winchester's forensic accounting team included the
eagle-eyed Sir Walter Mildmay, and what he unearthed was that, after costs
and expenses were allowed for, Gresham's account was seriously in the red.
He owed the queen £4,892 (around £5 million in modern values); this
Thomas acknowledged and agreed to repay.

In addition, the lord treasurer's team identified the shortfall from the
funds Thomas had collected in Spanish currency in Castile and Seville.
Gresham had reckoned it to be the equivalent of £1,173 in Flemish pounds,
a figure initially accepted, but now reassessed as closer to the larger sum
of £1,811 sterling.[12] Winchester bound Thomas in legal obligations with
stiff penalty clauses: either he or Edmond Hogan must recover the missing
funds from Spain, or else produce documents signed and sealed by Spanish
notaries and court officials to prove that the cash had been lost through the
unavoidable bankruptcies of those bankers and merchants who had been
due to pay it. Failing that, Thomas must reimburse the exchequer from his
own pocket.[13]

The audit completed, Gresham set out for Brussels with instructions to find new loans to support the English forces in France. Using his connections to Emmanuel Philibert, duke of Savoy and the new regent of the Netherlands, he at last secured an interview with Philip himself, who offered his backing. On St George's Day in 1558 (23 April), as Thomas informed Mary, 'I saw the king's majesty in right good health, thanks be given to God ... in his robes, and the duke of Savoy with him, which feast was very honourably and solemnly kept by his majesty with all his nobles and gentlemen about him'.[14] Things went downhill from there. Gresham's attempts to bribe large numbers of his merchant friends to borrow or repay small sums on specific dates to cause sudden market spikes in his favour failed miserably and he faced the prospect of paying interest rates as high as 16 per cent.

Ordered by the privy council to pay no more than 14 per cent, Thomas turned in desperation to Germain Cioll, his cousin Cecily's husband, now Alessandro Buonvisi's factor at the Antwerp branch of the Buonvisi bank. Gresham sought to borrow £200,000 in two instalments of £100,000.[15] For a while, it did not look promising. As the count of Feria, Philip's captain of the guard, cuttingly reported, Gresham 'has not succeeded in raising more than £10,000. I do not know how this can be possible ... he deserves that your majesty have him punished'.[16] At the lower rate of interest he was authorised to pay, the money had to be gathered in dribs and drabs, so tight was credit on the bourse.[17] At last, though, thanks to Cioll's assistance as an intermediary, Thomas managed to raise loans amounting to some £185,000.

In June 1558, Mary allowed Thomas leave to visit his wife and family for one month.[18] Before setting out for home, he undertook a series of deals to purchase munitions and other supplies for the English forces in France. Earlier commissions had required him to obtain 788 barrels of gunpowder, 28,220 lbs of saltpetre and 55,000 lbs of serpentine powder for firing muskets, along with 1,132 sets of light cavalry equipment, 829 pieces of armour, 300 steel helmets and 400 daggers.[19] Now he was to work with Alessandro Buonvisi 'as the queen's special deputies and factors' to obtain fresh inventories including 3,500 muskets, 10,000 handguns, 100,000 lbs of saltpetre, 3,000 pieces of armour, 3,000 iron helmets and 8,000 lances and pikes. To assist Gresham in exporting this vast arsenal, Philip granted him passports, but Thomas still had trouble with the port authorities in Antwerp, who for some unknown reason held back 324 barrels of gunpowder, 8,000 pikes and 8,900 handguns.[20]

When he returned to London at the beginning of July, Gresham faced a set of problems of a more personal nature. Already in his late thirties, he was going through a bad patch with Anne Ferneley. While left to his own devices in Antwerp, he had fathered an illegitimate daughter, Anne, by an Englishwoman named Winifred.[21] She may have been single at the time of their affair, in which case he promptly married her off to Clough's assistant, Thomas Dutton, as soon as she became pregnant. Or she may already have been Dutton's wife, in which case the cuckolded husband decided his interest (and presumably profit) lay in not making a fuss. So-called 'Antwerp wives' – or 'bed kin' as they were more explicitly known – were commonly encountered among married and unmarried English merchants living abroad.[22] Their expectation was to be kept in some style, and for positions to be found for their children. Seductions of single women were considered to be venial sins, but adultery with a factor's or other employee's wife was a serious breach of mercantile etiquette. Just what Ferneley thought of her husband's infidelity can only be imagined, but she was willing to take his child into her household, and one day she would be pulling all the levers at her disposal to marry her off, using her own family connections to hush up the affair. For her, reputation mattered at least as much as money.

In the event, Thomas stayed in London for three months. Not until 1 October 1558 did he prepare to make his way back to Antwerp, after Mary issued instructions 'to repair with convenient speed to our dearest lord and husband the king, and after delivery of such letters as he shall receive from hence for that purpose, he shall sue to his highness in our name for his good favour and licence to provide and carry thence into England such sums of money as followeth'. The amount specified was £100,000, which he was to arrange to borrow for a year. Not listed in his written instructions was a personal request Mary made when she interviewed Thomas on the eve of his departure. He was to deliver Philip a ring, which she pulled from her finger.[23]

Thomas tracked Philip down to the town of Auxi-le-Château near Abbeville, where he was camped beside the castle with his forces. Having secured his approval both for the loan and for the export of much of it as bullion, Thomas learned that peace negotiations were about to begin with France at the abbey of Cercamp, a short distance away.[24] By this time, Mary was seriously ill. All had not been well for some time in her health and her marriage. Philip had placed all his hopes on the birth of a child and had little sympathy for his wife's anxieties: when he had returned abruptly to Brussels after her first pseudo-pregnancy, she felt deserted and had harangued his portrait before pulling it off the wall of her privy chamber and kicking it out of the room. A second pseudo-pregnancy in the spring of 1558 was made worse by Mary's migraines and other ailments, and in the late summer she suffered a bout of fever, most likely linked to an influenza epidemic that killed thousands. She may have realised she was mortally ill when she asked Gresham to deliver the ring.[25]

On hearing that Mary's health was failing, Philip sent the count of Feria to London to salvage whatever Spanish interests he could. Mary's sister, Elizabeth, was by then at Brocket Hall in Hertfordshire, some two and a half miles to the north of Hatfield. From this base, her cofferer, Thomas Parry, a relative of William Cecil, was coordinating her campaign to secure the throne. Mary died in the early morning of 17 November 1558; Cardinal Pole followed her to the grave a few hours later, which seemed to the Protestants an act of divine providence.

As Feria quickly discovered when he reached Brocket Hall, the new regime would be Protestant. Elizabeth, he informed Philip, was 'a very vain and clever woman ... thoroughly schooled in the manner in which her father conducted his affairs, and I am very much afraid that she will not be well-disposed in matters of religion'. He concluded, 'I see her inclined to govern through men who are believed to be heretics and I am told that all the women around her definitely are.'[26]

Somehow – perhaps from Cecil – Gresham had found out almost every detail of Elizabeth's succession planning, and so knew to wait on her from the outset of her reign. The very moment the news of Mary's death broke in Antwerp, he raced back to London and, without pausing for breath, set out for Hatfield, where he galloped, mud-spattered, into the courtyard on Sunday, 20 November, just in time for Elizabeth's first council meeting of her reign, when he was reappointed as government banker. That he was expected is proved by a previously unremarked note by Cecil, whom the twenty-five-year-old queen quickly made her secretary of state and chief minister. Dated 18 November, it gnomically read: 'Thomas Gresham for matters', an aide-mémoire possibly to be linked to another note Cecil made on the previous day, declaring his intention to impose a temporary ban on foreign exchange transactions that might result in gold or silver coinage being taken out of the country.[27]

As Gresham was not a privy councillor, his presence at Hatfield is not recorded in the official council register, but he described the scene himself in letters to Parry and Cecil, written some time afterwards. At his interview with Elizabeth on 20 November, 'when I took this great charge upon me', he says, she 'promised me by the faith of a queen that she would not only keep one ear shut to hear me, but also, if I did her no other service than I had done to King Edward her brother and Queen Mary her sister, she would give me as much as ever both they did'. She promised him, he added, that his rewards should take the form of grants of land, 'and thereupon, her majesty gave me her hand to kiss it; and I accepted this great charge again'.[28]

Thomas quickly learned that the new queen needed 'a mass of money' – £20,000 to meet the costs of her coronation, along with an eye-watering £100,000 for further stocks of munitions, but these sums did not include what was needed to redeem or roll over the government's existing foreign debts.

The result was that Elizabeth and Cecil gave Thomas his instructions: over the next nine months or so, he was to increase the government's level of borrowing as far as possible, while at the same time continuing to service an accumulated debt that had soared to £336,000 on account of the war. To do this, as Gresham later informed Cecil, he was forced to take up money in 'divers and sundry ways'. In Antwerp, he borrowed £60,758 sterling from a syndicate led by Lazarus Tucher and Paul van Dalle, the owner of vast sugar plantations on the Canary Islands from which he organised the dispatch of whole harvests for his refineries at home. On Lombard Street, Thomas took up offers from whoever was willing to make them, putting his own credit on the line, 'sometimes for £1,000, £40,000, £30,000, £25,000 and £20,000 at divers times'.[29]

On the continent there would be regime change too. In August 1559, Philip II and his entourage left the Netherlands permanently for Spain. The result would be a shift of political power from Brussels to Madrid: from now on there would be a resident English ambassador in Madrid and a Spanish ambassador in London. English diplomatic representation in Brussels would be maintained at a lower level, and the job would be given to Gresham, who would combine it with his role as Elizabeth's banker.[30]

Emboldened by the promotion, it would not be long before Gresham overreached. For one thing, he mistakenly believed that his relationship with Philip would survive Mary's death; his letters show how rapidly he was disabused of that idea. More seriously, for all his long experience in the service of the Tudor monarchs, he had yet to get the measure of the new queen.

— 9 —

GRESHAM'S LAW

Towards the end of 1558, Thomas Gresham sent Elizabeth a famous memo in which he summarised all he claimed to have done since he had first worked with the duke of Northumberland as government banker. Written in a blunt, brisk, matter-of-fact style entirely devoid of courtly polish, it began by trumpeting what Thomas considered to have been the greatest achievements of his career so far, then went on to offer the new queen his opinions as to how she should order her finances. In giving her this advice, no alternatives or options were ever mentioned. Gresham, in every instance, had only one thing to say about how she ought to act: there was his way or there was the wrong way.[1]

Thomas believed his achievements had been to reduce significantly the levels of government borrowing abroad at various points under Northumberland and Mary; to coerce his fellow English merchants into making loans on favourable terms; to raise the value of sterling on the exchanges; and finally, to 'practise' with Northumberland to revoke the privileges of the Hanseatic League. As to how the country had got into its fiscal predicament, the whole sorry saga, as Gresham explained in surprisingly unvarnished language, had followed from her father's catastrophic decisions. 'It may please your majesty to understand,' he began, 'that the first occasion of the fall of the exchange did grow by the king's majesty, your late father, in abasing his coin from six ounces fine to three ounces fine … Secondly, by reason of his wars, the king's majesty fell into great debt in Flanders.'

As to Elizabeth's own economic policies, highest on Gresham's list of priorities was to return the value of sterling to the levels it had attained in Henry VIII's reign before the debasement of the currency. 'And it please your majesty,' he declared in a hastily written, barely grammatical passage, 'to restore this your realm into such estate as heretofore it hath been; first, your highness hath none other ways but when time and opportunity serveth to bring your base money into fine [*sic*] of eleven ounces fine, and so gold after the [same] rate.' Next, the Hanseatic merchants should never be restored 'to their usurped privileges'. Gresham urged Elizabeth to 'come in as small debt as you can beyond [the] seas'. Finally, to cut the Gordian knot, she should 'keep [up] your credit, and especially with your own merchants, for it is they [who] must stand by you at all events in your necessity'.[2]

To reinforce his argument, Thomas, on 1 March 1559, wrote a supporting paper, this time addressed to Cecil. When read with his earlier memo to the queen, the two documents amount to a manifesto for how Elizabeth's government could free itself from dependency on the international money markets and achieve relatively safe and easy access to credit even in the most turbulent of times.[3]

Thomas advised Cecil that the privy council should once again force London merchants engaged in the Anglo-Brabant trade to lend to the crown; while negotiations with them were pending, the merchants must accept punitive restrictions on their ability to cut their own foreign exchange deals. 'Considering', he explained, 'how much it doth import the queen's credit, of force she must use her merchants ... her highness shall have good opportunity both to bargain and to bring them to what price her majesty and you shall think most convenient, as the like proof was made in King Edward her late brother's time.'[4]

Once again, a temporary 'stop' would have to be placed on the merchant ships to prevent them sailing when they were ready to depart. But whereas up until now, the English merchants had been given notice of the government's intention to borrow from them for just a few weeks or months at a time to replenish Gresham's float, now their loans were to be closer to genuine credit provision, lasting for up to a year or maybe more. And to pre-empt evasion, 'this matter must be kept secret, that it may not come to the merchants' knowledge that you do intend to use them; and to lay sure, wait when their last day of shipping shall be.'[5]

Such operations would need to be streamlined. Currently they were too makeshift, too visible to the other credit-brokers on the Antwerp bourse. What's more, they were basically unfair, as those merchants most able to resist would pay the least. Some existing elements were to stay the same: loans should continue to be assessed in sterling, but would still be payable to Gresham in Antwerp in Flemish pounds, and at predatory exchange rates he determined in advance. But instead of Thomas valuing the merchants' cargoes individually and then haggling with each owner to assess the level of loan required, now the privy council was to make blanket assessments on a formula-driven basis, using the official customs records.

To guarantee that the required total amount would be forthcoming, Cecil was to send for the lord mayor of London and city grandees at the beginning of each cycle, and tell them straight that

> the queen's majesty is indebted in Flanders for no small sum, for the which you, my lord mayor and the city, do stand bound for the repayment thereof ... And for the accomplishment of the [same], the queen's majesty doth require at your hands to pay in Flanders 20 shillings sterling upon every cloth that is now shipped, after the rate of 25 shillings Flemish for the pound sterling.

This was at a time when, on Gresham's own admission, the true market rate was 22 shillings Flemish to the pound 'as the exchange now goes in Lombard Street'.[6]

Thomas could readily predict the reaction of his fellow merchants to such demands. 'They will grant nothing till that they have assembled the company together', but 'having all their goods in the queen's power, there is no doubt but that her majesty shall bring them to bargain at such reasonable price as you and the rest of my lords [of the privy council] shall think convenient'.[7] Some flexibility should be allowed in setting the rigged rate of exchange to be imposed on the merchants, but on no account was it to drop below a premium of 2 per cent to the true market rate 'or else they [i.e., the merchants] do no service, but for their own lucre and gain'.

On top of that, Gresham advised, 'whatsoever bargain you do conclude with the merchants, to remember especially that they do pay their money in "valued" money, otherwise termed "permission" money [i.e., the coins had to be been independently valued and assayed], for that the queen is bound to pay it [in Antwerp] in valued money, which may not in no wise be forgotten'. The reason, he reminded Cecil, was that, currently, the market premium for 'valued' money had rocketed to an unprecedented 3 or 4 per cent, 'such is the scarcity thereof'.[8]

In other words, Gresham put to the queen and Cecil something that, if only they chose to adopt it, could be judged a revolutionary new model.

His biggest idea was to shift from now onwards a far greater share of the burden for financing the crown's borrowing requirement away from the more expensive credit markets of Europe and towards London, where the merchants would be required to lend the government money for as long as a year at a time, rather than just a few weeks or months.

Gresham's advice was driven by his failing confidence in his ability to manipulate the exchange markets. Market conditions were changing as the balance of power in Europe shifted south to Madrid, where supplies of silver bullion were arriving from the New World in ever-increasing quantities.[9] For this reason, it made sense to switch as much government borrowing as possible to the city of London, where loans and repayments would both be in sterling and pressure on the lenders could be exerted.[10]

Generally speaking, Gresham took a mercantilist view of economics, meaning that he defined the country's prosperity chiefly in relation to its ability to amass bullion by achieving a favourable balance of trade. One of his chief tenets, repeated many times, was that, where possible, the rate of sterling exchange ought to be kept high. As he hammered home to Elizabeth in his famous memo, 'the exchange is the chiefest and richest thing only above all other to restore your majesty and your realm to fine gold and silver, and is the mean[s] that makes all foreign commodities and your own commodities with all kinds of victuals good cheap, and likewise keeps your fine gold and silver within your realm'.[11]

But, of course, the exchanges in 1558–9 were being used both to transfer funds to and from Antwerp and to raise short-term loans which were borrowed in Flemish pounds. Nudging the exchange rate higher, from Gresham's perspective, had only to be done at moments when the government did *not* need to borrow abroad. As long as Elizabeth still wanted to transfer the proceeds of loans from Antwerp to London, she wished, quite naturally, to receive the maximum quantity of pounds sterling for her borrowed Flemish currency, at which times a low rate of exchange was preferable to a high one.[12] Only when large repayments of outstanding loans were due was a higher than average rate in the crown's interests.[13]

Inevitably, the merchants were in shock when the full impact of Gresham's latest plans dawned on them. As Thomas warned Cecil,

> they do now cry all out upon me for the raising of the money, which
> is not material (and with your good help) I shall make them all either

speak better or worse of me, considering the great trust that her majesty hath committed unto me, for as they be good members of the commonwealth, so [they] be the very worst if they be not looked unto.[14]

But the protests grew vehement, and it would not be long before Thomas shifted his ground, taking up a position that was, in minor respects, more conciliatory, and yet in all its crucial aspects markedly more adversarial. By way of concessions, he urged privy councillors to grant the merchants licences permitting them to ship as many broadcloths to the Brabant fairs as they wished despite the old statutory ban, 'and to let them suffer another way'.[15]

On the other hand, Gresham insisted that no further concessions were to be made until a definite offer of funds had been made by the city, failing which the privy council was 'still to keep their ships and goods in arrest'. 'Sir,' said Thomas, addressing on this occasion both Cecil and Sir Thomas Parry, Elizabeth's cofferer, 'if you enter upon this matter, you may in no wise relent by no persuasion of the merchants, whereby you may keep them in fear and good order, for otherwise if they get the bridle you shall never rule them.'[16] Thomas even dared to recommend raising the prospect of the temporary seizure of the merchants' goods if they refused to cooperate. If they continued to demur, they were to be threatened with bankruptcy and the loss of all their money.[17]

Treating the merchants roughly, Gresham concluded, was the only way to bring them into line. 'This putting forth to them in choler, and in due time, will fear them all, lest the queen's majesty should taste the profit thereof, which doubtless will bring them to what reasonable bargain the queen's majesty can devise'.[18]

Far from signing off on this scheme, however, the privy council took fright. For the moment at least, they heeded the merchants' protests, forcing Thomas to borrow £5,000 on Lombard Street, then take up in Antwerp the rest of the loans the government needed in 1559.[19]

Seemingly unfazed by the rebuff, Gresham turned his attention to the restoration of the currency to its pre-debasement levels. As he urged the queen, she should understand that his efforts to manipulate the value of sterling in her favour would always be largely frustrated unless – expensive as it would be – she now resolved to finish what Northumberland and Mary had begun: calling in all the bad money still in circulation and re-minting it to something approaching its original higher standard. That would be the only way to replace sterling's value as a currency in which credit-brokers would be keen to trade.[20]

Cecil knew only too well the obstacles the government would need to overcome before a general restoration of the coinage could be attempted. Until a restoration was completed, though, every single coin would continue to have to be independently examined and assayed when sterling amounts were borrowed or repaid in 'valued' or 'permission' money on Lombard Street or in Antwerp. Thomas was quite vehement on this point. For as both men were well aware from preliminary work done by Sir Walter Mildmay and others, the aggregate value of fine currency then in circulation was reliably put at somewhere around £440,000, whereas the total amount of bad money exceeded £1.1 million (over £1.1 billion today).[21]

This time, Thomas's lobbying was successful. Preparations for a general re-coinage began in the spring of 1559, when the queen appointed a royal commission led by Cecil, Parry and Mildmay to investigate 'the present state of the mint, what standards of gold and silver are now kept and by what officers and orders they are executed'. The commissioners were to estimate 'how much base coin has been made in the mints since the first debasement of the coinage, with the diversity of standards from the highest to the lowest', and then 'devise' the new standards of gold and silver coin, 'both in weight and fineness', to be adopted.[22]

Gresham was by this time in Antwerp and therefore not himself a commissioner. Nevertheless, he was consulted from the start, advising Cecil chiefly on the logistical problems to be overcome. To melt down and re-strike this quantity of currency required technology of a type presently unknown in the Tower mints, where coins were individually manufactured by stamping the hot metal with a die and hammer.

Once the commissioners had received their instructions, Cecil, who spoke good French but no German, set about recruiting a Frenchman, Eloy Mestrelle, to build the necessary equipment. Mestrelle, who had learned his trade at the Moulin de Monnais, the French royal mint at Versailles, was the inventor of a system able to strike coins by mill rather than by hand. Despite serious reservations in the privy council about putting a foreigner in charge of mass-manufacturing English coins, Cecil hired him on 29 June 1560. He found Mestrelle a house close to the Tower, 'for the safe keeping of the Frenchman and setting up of his engines, as also for that he should [en]grave and work in the court'.[23] Mestrelle's mechanically produced coins would later command a premium for their rarity value.

Shakespeare refers to them in *The Merry Wives of Windsor* as being sold as upmarket gaming counters.[24]

On the very day that Mestrelle joined Cecil's team, Gresham was in Antwerp recruiting a group of German metallurgists under the direction of the banker Daniel Wohlstadt to assist with the re-coinage. As he told Parry, 'it may like you to understand that I sent you my last of the 25th of this present, wherein I sent you the particulars of Daniel Wohlstadt's demand for the refining of our base money, assuring you that the men be honest and substantial enough for the performance of the same'.[25] The arrangement reached was that Wohlstadt's men would refine 60,000 lbs of debased silver currency per month, to a fineness of what ended up as 115 grams of pure metal per £1 sterling, not far short of the level in 1544.[26]

In July, Wohlstadt arrived in England, clutching a letter of recommendation from Gresham in which he declared, 'the enterprise is of great importance, and the sooner it is put in ure [i.e., practice], the more honour and profit it will be to the queen's majesty and the realm'.[27] In November, the Germans found sureties to the extent of £30,000 for their contract, signed on the last day of the month.[28] These were not the only metallurgists involved in the re-coinage. The Fugger firm put in a tender, 'advertised by Mr Gresham's letters ... touching the refining of the base moneys now current in England', and some English refiners were also used on the grounds that they submitted the cheapest bid.[29] But, on Gresham's advice, Wohlstadt's firm was awarded the lion's share of the work.

In a rare act of fiscal audacity led by Cecil and Parry on 27 September 1560, the privy council called down the whole of the debased currency to a fraction below its true bullion value, and almost immediately the Tower mints began issuing new coins.[30] Next, the value of all the principal foreign gold coins in unofficial circulation was reduced, and a year later all foreign coins other than French, Flemish or Burgundian gold crowns were demonetised other than as bullion – this encouraged merchants finally to release such stocks of pre-debasement currency as they had been hoarding, besides forcing everyone else to exchange bad money for the newly minted coins.[31]

In the absence of better sources, the process of re-coinage can best be traced in the work done by Eloy Mestrelle's team. In November 1560, his machinery started production: the first silver coins he manufactured were the shilling, groat and half-groat. During the spring of 1561, he began to strike some gold half-pound and crown coins, and later half-crowns. In

July following, Elizabeth made a special visit to the Tower mints as part of Cecil's publicity for the new coinage. She arrived by river at 10 a.m., leaving at 5 p.m. on horseback with the sword of state carried before her.[32] In October, Mestrelle's newly milled coins were officially assayed, together with those made with a die and hammer by the Germans and English. After that, some of the older silver denominations were dropped in favour of new denominations of 6d., 3d., 1½d. and ¾d. More than three-quarters of Mestrelle's final output was in sixpences, and he produced a significant number of threepenny pieces.[33]

In November 1561, Cecil had the new denominations proclaimed as legal tender, and to commemorate the queen's visit to the mints, Mestrelle presented her with a medallion embossed with a portrait of herself, for which she gave him a pension of £25. Taking just a little over a year to complete, the re-coinage had resulted in some £1.2 million of bad money being melted down, refined and re-minted.[34]

The government's profit after the deduction of costs was in the region of £50,000, largely achieved by the simple expedient of re-minting less bullion than was called in and retaining the surplus.[35] Apart from the queen's Protestant religious settlement of 1559, this did more than any other single measure to secure the stability of the early Elizabethan state, and for his part in it Gresham would later be credited with inventing 'Gresham's law' – usually expressed in the catchy phrase 'bad money drives out good money'. According to Henry Dunning MacLeod, a Victorian economist, writing in 1857: 'At last, Sir Thomas Gresham explained to Queen Elizabeth that allowing base and degraded coin to circulate along with good coin *caused* it to disappear; that bad coin and good coin cannot circulate together; but that the bad coin invariably and necessarily drives out good coin from circulation, and alone remains current.' For this achievement, historians feted his legacy.[36]

Unfortunately, MacLeod possessed what has rightly been called a clairvoyant's talent for reading into a text what is not there. In none of his letters or memos does Gresham express a rule in precisely these terms: his mantras are that coinage debasements cause the value of sterling to fall on the foreign exchanges with the result that all the fine gold is conveyed out of the realm, and that as a consequence of good and bad coinage circulating together, the market premium for 'valued' or 'permission' money steadily increases to unsustainable levels, further raising 'real' borrowing costs.[37]

In any case, the principle that when in a bimetallic coinage two moneys of an equivalent face value, but an unequal bullion one, are placed at the same time, side by side, as currency of the realm, the inferior or less valued will drive the better or more valued from circulation was well known to the dramatist Aristophanes in ancient Athens, who cited it in his comedy *The frogs*. Set out more fully by Nicolas Oresme, bishop of Lisieux, in a treatise written for Charles V of France that had entered the royal library at the Louvre by 1373, the thesis was most systematically expounded by Nicolaus Copernicus, the Polish-born astronomer and mathematician, in the early sixteenth century.

'Gold or silver,' explained Copernicus, 'marked with an imprint, constitutes the money which serves to determine the price of things that are bought and sold, according to the laws established by the state or the prince.' He then went on to highlight how 'if it does not do to introduce a new and good money while the old is bad and continues to circulate, a much greater error is committed by introducing alongside of an old currency, a new currency of less value; this latter does not merely depreciate the old, it drives it away, so to speak, by main force.'[38]

Attempts to pin down Gresham's defining contribution to early-Elizabethan monetary theory are further complicated by the attempts of a leading twentieth-century historian, Raymond de Roover, to attribute to him the sole authorship of a controversial economic dossier, the so-called 'Memorandum of Exchange'.[39] Almost certainly put together between Elizabeth's accession and September 1560, then copied out by hand at a number of later dates, the dossier is divided into three main sections. These discuss the various stages by which the English coinage had been debased: first, from Henry VIII's later years to the middle of Edward VI's reign; second, 'the amended [i.e. re-minted] coinage of gold and silver' begun by Northumberland and continued during Mary's reign; and thirdly and most specifically, the differing ways in which Elizabeth might now intervene to raise the rate of exchange on the international money markets in favour of the pound sterling.[40]

Superficially, Gresham's ideas could well have set the frame for the dossier, but the work is unlikely to be his. No extant copy is in his handwriting, and much of its argument is clumsy and repetitive. In particular, its author's obsession is a belief in a 'natural' rate of exchange based on mint par, meaning the rate should be fixed solely by reference to the gold or silver content of the specific coins in use, whereas Gresham considered the rise and fall of the pound on the foreign exchanges to be the most logical thing in the world; it was subject, after all, to manipulation by master dealers like himself.[41]

The one place where the dossier most obviously builds on Gresham's ideas is where it asks for the creation of a government-funded equalisation (or stabilisation) fund to help solve the problem of sudden, short-term fluctuations on the exchanges. According to these crucial few paragraphs, the value of the pound sterling can, artificially, be supported 'by turning a mass of the queen's treasure upon the exchange by her highness's factor and making England the lord of the exchange', both on Lombard Street and 'beyond sea also'.[42]

After Gresham had persuaded the duke of Northumberland in 1552 to send him a float of £1,200 every week to exploit market spikes, he established just such a fund.[43] When the arrangement was stopped, Thomas recreated his float at the expense of the London merchants, who during the next six years periodically delivered large dollops of cash in Antwerp on temporary loan at negligible interest rates. In 1558–9, however, Gresham's emphasis changed, and he proposed to shift more of the burden for financing the government's borrowing requirement directly to the city of London. After that, the idea of an equalisation fund was never given another serious trial until it was revived to try to prop up the value of sterling after the First World War.[44] On that occasion, it didn't work.

Intriguingly, an almost identical proposal would resurface in the report of another early Elizabethan financial commission, appointed in November 1564. The commissioners were chaired by the lord treasurer, the marquis of Winchester, the same man who had ordered Gresham's accounts to be audited after his ill-fated Spanish venture. Their suggestion was that the queen should set up 'a bank of money of £10,000 or more in her factor's hands [i.e., Gresham's] at Antwerp' to prop up the sterling exchange rate as and when required. The author of their final report, which was completed in February 1565, was Sir Francis Knollys, the favoured husband of one of the queen's Boleyn cousins and a known friend to Thomas.[45]

Whether Gresham gave evidence to Winchester's commission is unknown, but it's possible; he was near London for the entire time the commissioners were sitting. Even if he did not give evidence, he could easily have advised Knollys privately in a document that no longer survives.[46]

Beyond this, we can only speculate as to what precisely Gresham said or thought on the topic of monetary theory. He was *par excellence* a dealer, and a compulsive one, not a theorist – a practical man who could see an opportunity whenever he believed it stared him in the face, and who acted accordingly.

SHIFTING TIDES

Shortly before Christmas 1559, Elizabeth knighted Gresham, partly in recognition of his services so far, but chiefly to give him an appropriate standing in Brussels now that she had asked him to take responsibility for English diplomatic representation there. For a man of Gresham's background, a knighthood was a signal honour, normally reserved for those city liverymen who had stood for public office, served for many years as aldermen and achieved the positions of sheriff or lord mayor. Thomas's father, Sir Richard, and uncle, Sir John, had both secured their knighthoods on election to these offices, but only when Richard was forty-six and his brother forty-five or so. Thomas was just forty.

Once in receipt of a knighthood, a city grandee was expected to play a leading role, often informally, in the government of the city. He might sit on civic commissions such as for tax collection, and on juries or as assistants to the assize judges in legal cases in the Guildhall affecting the crown's interests. Thomas went on occasionally to serve as the foreman of a jury while he was in London, but otherwise his idea of knighthood had little to do with fulfilling civic tasks. Instead, he saw himself more grandly as combining the roles of career diplomat and special economic adviser to the queen. It was never wise to make these sort of presumptions where Elizabeth was concerned.

She was at least unambiguous as to the nature and extent of Gresham's quasi-ambassadorial duties. On returning to Spain, Philip II had appointed his half-sister, Margaret of Parma, Charles V's illegitimate daughter, as the new regent of the Netherlands. Now fully accredited to her court, Thomas was 'to repair to the said regent and communicate with her all such matters as hereafter shall be committed to your charge'.[1] Should his diplomacy run into glitches, he was to seek the advice of Sir Thomas Chaloner, the

English ambassador to Ferdinand I of Austria, Charles's successor as Holy Roman Emperor. Elizabeth had sent Chaloner to Brussels to sound out Margaret of Parma's chief adviser, Antoine Perrenot de Granvelle, bishop of Arras, about Anglo-Netherlandish affairs and future Spanish intentions. She intended to reassign him to Philip's court in Madrid just as soon as Gresham was able to assume his new role.

A day or so after knighting Thomas, Elizabeth wrote off two-thirds of the shortfall of funds he had failed to collect in Castile and Seville during his Spanish adventure in Mary I's reign.[2] Lord Treasurer Winchester had assessed the debt at £1,811 sterling, although it was now said to be £1,847, possibly the result of a late payment charge. Of this amount, the queen 'pardoned and requited' £1,200, which she said Thomas should receive 'as our gift and reward, without prest [i.e., deduction] or other charge to be set upon him'.[3] This capped his loss at £647 (worth over £647,000 today), which he was ordered to pay to the exchequer by instalments over the next three years.

It was not much of a favour: at great trouble and expense, Gresham and Edmond Hogan, assisted by another of Thomas's apprentices, John Gerbridge, had finally obtained witness statements signed and sealed by notaries and court officials in Seville and Valladolid to prove that £1,200 of the missing money had been lost through bankruptcies.[4] As even Winchester had agreed that such a sum could be written off, provided Gresham produced the necessary supporting evidence, all Elizabeth had done for Thomas was to allow him to repay the outstanding balance by instalments.

Once Gresham had his diplomatic credentials, Cecil warned him to expect extended periods of residence on the continent. To this end, Thomas was to be paid additional expenses of £200 over three years 'for the hire of a house in Antwerp ... for his abiding there with his family and household', along with all necessary costs and riding charges arising from his need to commute between Antwerp and Brussels on diplomatic affairs and travel between Antwerp and London to report to Cecil and the queen.[5]

Unusually, Gresham was to be allowed to take his wife, Anne Ferneley, with him at the queen's expense. Anticipating that she might stay for the full length of his commission, he had very recently purchased his own Antwerp house. Its previous owner was Ruy Mendez, a rich Portuguese merchant, who had bought the property six years before from the widow of a member of the Tucher banking family. His deed of sale to Thomas described the property as 'a mansion called St Franciscus, with outbuild-ings, a courtyard, a summer house, stables, and a well, with two other houses next to the mansion which have been incorporated and now make up one mansion'. The house is now no. 43 in the Lange Nieuwstraat.[6]

In 1560, Richard Clough, Gresham's factor, bought a house in the Keizerstraat. Possibly he expected Anne Ferneley to arrive and need the space he occupied at St Franciscus. But Ferneley was either unable or unwilling to make the journey. Most likely her husband's infidelity with Winifred Dutton still rankled with her. If the wounds were still sore, it may well explain why Thomas, for once, now appealed so solicitously to Elizabeth 'to be a comfort unto my poor wife in this my absence in the service of your majesty'.[7] It was a rare gesture of affection, though how sincerely it was felt we cannot tell.

Thomas left London for Brussels late in January 1560, and in a letter to Cecil, dated 5 February, Chaloner reported that Margaret of Parma had granted Gresham and himself an audience. 'After I had,' he explained, 'as well touching myself, as touching the said Sir Thomas Gresham, used to her certain words of office and compliment, as [to] me seemed meetest [i.e., fittest] to the purpose, and he also the like, we both, I assure you, had such good words of answer, and with such good countenance from her, as we rested therewith well satisfied.' The smooth talk over, added Chaloner, 'Sir Thomas Gresham maketh such haste away (as I cannot blame him) for the queen's majesty's affairs – being a jewel for trust, wit and diligent endeavour – I must needs finish this scribbled letter.'[8]

Gresham had reason enough to hurry. Although a peace settlement at Cateau-Cambrésis in April 1559 had ended the long Franco-Habsburg war that had embroiled Mary and lost England its continental foothold in Calais, a fresh crisis was fast taking shape. It centred on Scotland, where a group of rebel Protestant lords – at least one of them would shortly be in Cecil's pay – declared the Catholic Marie de Guise to be suspended from the regency.

Marie was the mother of the seventeen-year-old Mary queen of Scots, who had married the Dauphin of France, now the young King Francis II. Her regency was supported by French forces of occupation, and Cecil's spies informed him that Marie's Guise relatives intended to send another 15,000 crack troops to Scotland to restore her to power. Cecil consid-ered the Guise party in France to be Elizabeth's greatest adversaries: he believed them to be the instigators and intended beneficiaries of a Catholic conspiracy to depose and kill her. He had felt this way since 1558, when Mary's uncle, the Cardinal of Lorraine, had ordered the heraldic arms of England to be emblazoned with those of France and Scotland on all the plate and furniture belonging to the household of the King-Dauphin and Queen-Dauphine.[9]

In December 1559, Cecil had persuaded a reluctant Elizabeth to send a naval force to the Firth of Forth to prevent the French from landing reinforcements. With war with France on the horizon, the queen handed Thomas a large munitions order and instructed him to borrow £200,000 (over £200 million today) for a year without delay at an interest rate 'as low as ye can bring it'. Of this money, all was to be coffered up and shipped to London, 'saving some part thereof to the quantity of £7,000 or £8,000 to be by exchange, made to certain parts in Almain [i.e., Germany] towards the sea coast, and in Lower Saxony, for the pressing of Almains and conducting them over those seas into this realm'.[10]

Borrowing, and then transporting, such a huge volume of cash would require a concerted effort and could prove to be the riskiest task Thomas had attempted since smuggling funds from Antwerp to Calais during Henry VIII's last years. Negotiating for the hire of German mercenaries was no mean feat either, as it involved despatching agents to scour the highways and poorer villages across the frontier for unemployed soldiers or raw recruits willing to serve abroad for wages.

The difficulties Gresham faced in supplying sufficient credit and munitions to Elizabeth in early 1560 can hardly be exaggerated. As fear at the threat the Guises posed to peace gripped the citizens of Antwerp, and especially its merchants, Thomas found he had to cope with 'the great scarcity of money that is now in this place', caused as much by wider international developments as by the immediate crisis.[11] Once Philip II returned permanently to Spain, the Spanish crown secured its funds chiefly from dealings on the Sevillian–Genoese financial axis. The result was that the Antwerp bourse underwent a major transformation. The city's prosperity now rested as much on old-fashioned trade as it did on financial services. Banks were reluctant to lend, and if they did, were exacting hefty interest rates.

It was thus something of a coup that Thomas was able fairly quickly to cobble together £128,449 in Flemish money from fifteen lenders, of whom the most significant were Lazarus Tucher and his brother Anton.[12] Now he had to ship it to London, using old passports secured from Philip II while he was still king of England. On 25 February, Gresham advised Elizabeth:

It may understand your most excellent majesty, that for the better
proof to your highness for the conveyance of such bullion and gold
as I shall provide for you, I have sent you this letter ... being no small
comfort unto me that I have obtained to the knowledge thereof for
the better conveyance of your treasure, which thing must be kept as
secretly as your majesty can devise. For if it should be known or perceived in Flanders, it were as much as my life and goods were worth,
besides the loss that your highness should sustain thereby.[13]

On 8 March, Thomas warned Cecil about the angry rumours circulating against him among the Antwerp citizens, who claimed, not perhaps
without reason in view of the amounts of cash he was said to be smuggling abroad, that he wanted to reduce them to poverty. 'The great bruit
that runs upon me among the merchants and the commons of this town,'
he said, '[is] that I will rob them of all their fine gold and fine silver; by
the reason whereof, I will assure you, I am half afraid to go abroad, but
[meaning except] only at the hours of the bourse time.'[14]

On 29 March, a treaty was signed at Berwick between Cecil's emis-
saries and the Scots: the rebel lords were to have full military assistance
in their campaign to oust occupying French forces.[15] In a memo written
late at night on 12 April, Cecil urged Elizabeth 'to send an express man to
Thomas Gresham to confer with him for the state of the queen's treasure,
powder and such like'.[16]

Thomas, meanwhile, borrowed more money, exploited fluctuating
rates on the bourse, wheeling and dealing to secure the funds the privy
council needed, and organised multiple shipments of munitions.[17] These
increasingly were smuggled illegally, as Gresham's passports from Philip
II were now passing their expiry dates. In case his letters home were intercepted, Thomas began using the words 'velvet', 'silk', 'damask' and 'satin' to
indicate purchases of gunpowder and other armaments.[18] When it became
too hazardous to continue to ship munitions from Antwerp, he moved his
consignments to Hamburg, sending one of his factors to supervise their
despatch, ordering him 'to hire for me four good ships, well equipped with
crew and ordnance', and then load and despatch the cargoes to the value of
£2,000 or £3,000 in each ship.[19]

Gresham pulled wires in Antwerp and Brussels, feasting and bribing
government officials in the hope of obtaining inside information to
prevent his ships being searched.[20] Bribes of multifarious kinds became

The young Thomas Gresham by an unknown Netherlandish artist. Commissioned in 1545, the portrait displays the symbolic date of '1544' (see pp. 16–17, 22–3 & 250)

A letter from Thomas Gresham to Elizabeth I, informing her that he was secretly sending her £128,449, borrowed from fifteen Antwerp bankers, 25 February 1559 [1560]

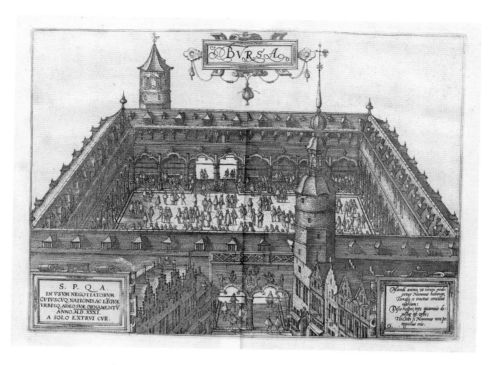

The New Bourse at Antwerp in an engraving of 1588

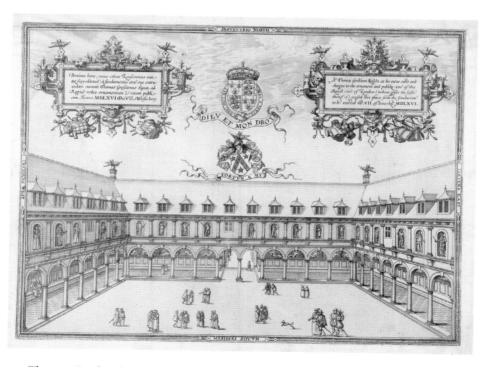

Thomas Gresham's Royal Exchange in an engraving by Frans Hogenberg, c.1569

Thomas Gresham's house, 'St Franciscus', in Antwerp, now no. 43 in the Lange Nieuwstraat

A ring presented by Thomas Gresham to Richard Lee: the oval bezel is engraved with Lee's coat of arms, and an enamelled green grasshopper is on the inside

Thomas Gresham, c.1563, by Anthonis Mor (see pp. 140–41)

Anne Ferneley (Thomas Gresham's wife), c.1563, by Anthonis Mor (see pp. 140–42)

The Hof van Liere, the administrative headquarters of the English cloth merchants in Antwerp from 1558

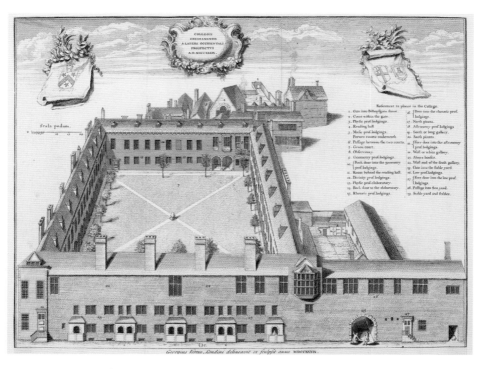

Gresham College in an engraving by George Vertue, c.1739

Lord Robert Dudley, wearing the collar of the Order of the Garter, attributed to Steven van der Meulen

Margaret of Parma, regent of the Netherlands, by Anthonis Mor

William I, Prince of Orange, by Adriaen Thomasz Key

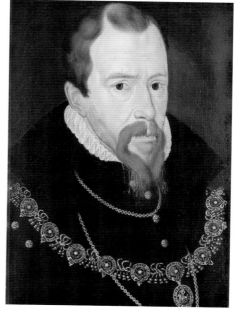

William Cecil, wearing the collar of the Order of the Garter, c.1572, by an unknown artist

Thomas Gresham's tomb in St Helen's church, Bishopsgate, showing his badge of a grasshopper above the knight's helm (detail)

Thomas Gresham, c.1567; one of two duplicate portraits by unknown Netherlandish artists working in the same studio (see pp. 165–6)

second nature to him: he saw them purely as an investment. His classic statement on the topic came in a letter to Cecil, discussing the shipping of munitions, in which he justified his bribes to the Antwerp customs' clerks, saying 'well fares that penny given that saves one hundred'.[21]

Using his diplomatic credentials, Thomas also sought to win over Margaret of Parma, who was deeply troubled at the threat posed by Guise policy in Scotland. Should France annex Scotland or the British Isles, the Netherlands would be vulnerable to attack. She had already sent word to her brother, Philip II, that while she held no brief for the heretic Elizabeth, it was more than doubtful that the Netherlanders could hold their own against a resurgent France.[22]

With so much to do and so little time in which to do it, Thomas tried an experiment in managerial delegation. It occurred to him that, from now on, he might personally handle only the most crucial stages involved in clinching deals, delegating their completion to his trusted Antwerp deputy, Richard Clough. The perfect opportunity arose in May 1560, after Thomas successfully settled in principle the arrangements for a loan of up to 400,000 thalers (over £100 million in modern values) with Hans Keck, the agent of Herzog Christoph Albrecht, count of Mansfeld. The amount finally agreed on was 300,000 thalers. Once Gresham believed the deal had been safely set up, he sent Clough to Saxony to conclude it.[23] So confident was he that Clough would accomplish this with flying colours, he warmly commended him to Cecil, describing him as someone who 'hath taken great pains in the queen's majesty's service in my absence since her highness came to the crown, whom hath right well deserved some consideration at her majesty's hands'.[24]

Whether in Brussels, Antwerp or London, Gresham knew how to put himself about. Once comfortably settled into his new dual role as banker and diplomat, he began making gifts of gold chains or grasshopper rings, carefully chosen by weight and value, to those he wished to cultivate. One such ring was given to Sir Richard Lee, a land surveyor, fortifications expert and protégé of Cecil, who handled large amounts of government money and may have got to know Thomas when he visited Antwerp to inspect the progress of the city's new walls and fortifications.[25]

In Antwerp and Brussels, Gresham turned his network of contacts into the equivalent of a private office. Besides his factors and servants there, he had informers in Holland, Zeeland, Friesland, Hamburg, Emden, Bremen and Dunkirk.[26] When he heard that a force of 20,000 infantry and 5,000 cavalry sought to march from Gelderland through Brabant and into Flanders, he instantly sent a servant, armed with fifty gold crowns, to investigate.[27] In Spain, Edmond Hogan continued to act for him.[28] His brother, Robert, a fluent Italian and Spanish speaker, was a roving spy, variously serving Gresham, Cecil and Nicholas Throckmorton, Elizabeth's ambassador to France.[29] Of such men, Thomas wrote that 'it is most convenient for the queen's majesty to have daily advertisements' and with agents like these scattered across Europe, 'nothing can stir but that her highness is assured to have good advertisements'.[30]

Gresham's trump card was his long-standing friendship with the banker Gaspar Schetz, whose younger brother Melchior had lodged with him and Ferneley several times in Basinghall Street in and after 1546. Gaspar, finally rising to a point in his career where his family firm could rival the Fugger and the Tucher, had become Philip II's factor in the Netherlands shortly before the Spanish ruler left for Madrid, and was now a leading figure in Margaret of Parma's administration. Melchior, for his part, served almost continuously for a decade as Antwerp's city treasurer and an alderman. Gresham regularly received invaluable political and commercial intelligence from them both, so he obtained Elizabeth's permission to present Gaspar with a gold chain worth 500 gold crowns.[31] Along with the gift came a story, one that reveals some of Thomas's more dubious methods.

In October 1559, just as Gresham had been due to roll over government debts of £95,000 before returning to London for Christmas, he had given Gaspar a bribe of 600 crowns. This was to enlist him to persuade Margaret of Parma to limit the premium that could be charged for making certain payments in 'valued' or 'permission' money on the Antwerp bourse to a maximum of 1 per cent. At a time when the unregulated market rate was nudging 3 per cent, this saved Thomas £2,000.[32] The gold chain was by way of a bonus for delivering on the favour.

Now back in Antwerp and Brussels, Thomas wanted Schetz to have another reward, this time for a decree allowing debts in Antwerp to be automatically rolled over for up to three months beyond their contracted settlement date at a fixed interest rate of 2½ per cent (annualised at 10 per cent, or some 3 or 4 per cent below market rates). As Gresham advised Cecil, if Schetz was to be kept on side, he needed not only regular sweeteners, but also a handwritten letter of thanks from the queen, 'in respect of this worthy service'. A refresher of 'at least 500 crowns more' would make an excellent start: favours had to be reciprocated – it was the way of the world.[33]

In the end, the Protestants triumphed in Scotland, although this was due more to Philip II's cautious diplomacy in Paris than to Cecil's military aid. When Marie de Guise died of a severe attack of dropsy in June 1560, the final obstacle to a truce was removed and on 6 July the treaty of Edinburgh was signed. Ostensibly a coda to the treaty of Cateau-Cambrésis, the accord was in reality a fresh one. By its terms, France recognised Elizabeth to be the rightful queen of England. French forces of occupation were to evacuate Scotland without delay, and their forts and garrisons were to be razed to the ground. Scotland was to be ruled by a council of Protestant nobles for as long as Mary queen of Scots was an absentee ruler. Finally, the treaty bound Mary to ratify and fulfil all of its conditions, failing which England would have the right to intervene in Scotland to protect the Protestant religion and keep the French out of the country.

Breathing a sigh of relief now the pressure seemed to be off, Gresham returned to London for what he imagined would be a well-earned summer break. By now, he had been elected upper warden of the Mercers' Company, the most senior official after the master. And in a belief that he might indulge himself after the signing of the treaty of Edinburgh, he decided somewhat overconfidently to invite the queen to be guest of honour at the annual Mercers' supper. It was extraordinarily rare for a monarch to attend city guild functions. Henry VIII and his third queen, Jane Seymour, had attended the Midsummer Watch at Mercers' Hall while Sir John Allen was lord mayor in 1536, but that was the only recent precedent. It would be a glittering accolade for Thomas if she accepted, and he would play a starring role in the ceremonies. After the supper, according to ancient custom, the wardens would go into the parlour beside the hall in front of the guests and put garlands on their heads. They would proceed to the middle of the hall and stand while their new master was chosen, after which it would be Thomas's turn as upper warden to go up to the assistant wardens and hold his garland above each man's head, before laying it in front of the man he had picked to succeed him.[34]

On the morning of Sunday, 21 July, word spread like wildfire through the city – it was said to be 'in every man's mouth plain' – that Elizabeth would indeed deign 'with all her ladies and nobility to be present at the Mercers' supper to see the order thereof and the choosing of the wardens then at that supper used and accustomed'. The date was set for the following evening, 'for as much as that the supper for the company and their guests should be on the morrow, being Monday at night, and Mary Mag-dalene's day'.[35]

On Sunday afternoon, Gresham heard the news that Mansfeld's deal had gone sour. With a debt of £150,000 due to be rolled over or repaid on 10 August, it had never crossed his mind that these German funds would fail to materialise. Alas, Clough was not a driven man like Thomas, and had let him down. Arriving safely in Germany, he had allowed himself to be richly wined and dined, not to mention disarmed by the gift of an expen-sive 'standing cup' of silver gilt.[36] The main task he bungled by allowing Mansfeld to prevaricate until the option on the loan had expired. Clough had not appreciated the degree to which Mansfeld lacked cash himself, and acted on behalf of a syndicate of lenders. His inability to complete the deal landed Gresham in a hole. Never again would Thomas delegate major strategic responsibilities to Clough, instead leaving him in his comfort zone, handling purely operational matters.[37]

'I shall have much ado,' Gresham later warned Sir Thomas Parry, 'to content the queen's majesty's creditors by the reason of the great scarcity of money.'[38] Elizabeth, meanwhile, was furious. Later on the afternoon of Sunday 21st, she sent a messenger to Mercers' Hall, saying that she could no longer attend the supper the next evening, but would come instead on the following Thursday. As a result, gargantuan supplies of fresh salmon and venison ordered for the supper had to be given away.

Later the same night, however, when the food was gone, Gresham received another message saying she would not attend at all.[39] Instead, she would send a delegation of courtiers, headed by Thomas's scourge, the marquis of Winchester, to attend the supper at its original time on Monday. Fresh supplies of food had to be ordered at the shortest of notice, giving Gresham what can only be interpreted as a severe slap on the wrists. The snub was the more pointed because the principal costs for replacing the food were to be expressly billed to him. As the relevant entry in the Mercers' Acts of Court explains, he was to be 'spoken [to] withal', and 'the most part' of the extra charges added to his account.[40]

Elizabeth then left for Richmond, to begin her summer progress in Surrey and Hampshire, ending with a stay at Basing House, Winchester's palatial mansion near Basingstoke.[41] By 2 August, Gresham had the answer to Clough's failure to procure the money from Mansfeld, but it was not a pleasant one. To satisfy the queen's creditors, privy councillors would have to extort a loan of £60,000 sterling from the London merchants without

delay, putting into practice Gresham's scheme of the previous year for shifting the burden for financing the government's borrowing requirement to
the city of London whether the merchants liked it or not.

In a detailed letter of advice, Gresham told Parry how to proceed.
Once the merchants had agreed with the privy council how much they
were going to lend, they were to pay it in Antwerp in Flemish currency.[42]
To achieve this result, it was essential that a 'stop' was placed at once on the
cloth fleet, preventing it from sailing. Unfortunately, by the time the council's orders reached the leaders of the Merchant Adventurers at Mercers'
Hall, the fleet had already sailed for the St Bavo's fair at Antwerp; and
with no loan concluded, Gresham was forced to rush back to Antwerp to
bargain with the disgruntled merchants before they sold their cloths.

On 28 August, Elizabeth sent Gresham an unusually formal letter
that contained a stinging rebuke:

> Where order was given ... that the ships freighted with the cloths of
> our merchants, this present month of August, should have been stayed
> until we might have concluded some bargain with them ... so it is, by
> negligence of such in whom the trust was reposed, they be departed to
> the number of 34,000 cloths, and no bargain concluded.[43]

Cecil, attempting to calm troubled waters, proposed a cooling-off
period. This, retorted Elizabeth peremptorily, 'we cannot allow'.[44] A ruler
who sought, wherever possible, never to shoulder the blame for unpopular decisions, always preferring to work through her subordinates, whose
actions she could disavow whenever she chose, she was dismayed that
things had reached this sorry state. It was not so much that she minded
writing dismissively to Gresham: he was, to a large extent, an insider and
would have to take his medicine. But she was compelled to write just as
forcefully to John Fitzwilliams, the Antwerp-based Deputy Governor of
the Merchant Adventurers, to impress on him that terms for a £60,000
loan had to be agreed upon without further delay.[45]

After considerable anguish on both sides, Thomas had to accept delivery of the money in two instalments of £30,000, payable at a fixed rate of
23s. 4d. Flemish to £1 sterling, yielding far less in Flemish currency than
he had originally demanded.[46] However, the loan was to be reimbursed in
London in sterling after two months at a rate of 25s. Flemish to £1 sterling when the current spot rate on Lombard Street was only around 22s.

6d.[47] That meant Gresham received less money than he felt he needed in Antwerp, but had to pay it back in London at a rate favourable to himself rather than the merchants. The deal left no one satisfied, but it did help to rescue Gresham from default.

Could there have been more to the queen's sudden irritation with Thomas than just her reaction to the loss of Mansfeld's money? For some months, Thomas had been straying into territory which Elizabeth regarded as strictly taboo. He had first started to drop broad hints to her as to when and whom she should marry in October 1559. He began cautiously, telling Cecil, 'I can no more write [to] you in this but the will of God and her majesty be fulfilled', but he went on in the same letter to urge Elizabeth to marry one of Ferdinand I's sons, 'for he is noble born. And in the marrying of him we are sure to have peace with these two great princes, I mean the king of Spain and the French king'.[48] More precisely, he meant that Elizabeth should marry the Archduke Charles, Ferdinand's third surviving son. Low-key negotiations were shortly to begin to this effect, but the prospects of success were not high. Elizabeth was doing so little at the time to conceal her romantic feelings for her dashing young master of the horse, Lord Robert Dudley, the duke of Northumberland's fifth son, that bets were taken on the streets of London that he would divorce his wife to be free to marry her.[49]

Undeterred, Gresham carried on, reporting from Antwerp in May 1560 that anyone who understood international affairs knew that Charles was the man for her.[50] Oblivious to the silence with which his advice was received, he tried again in June. By then, Ferdinand had recalled his ambassador, George von Helfenstein, whom he had sent to London to lobby for the match. On landing in Antwerp on his way back to Brussels to brief Margaret of Parma, Helfenstein met Gresham, to whom he expressed a well-founded belief 'that the queen's majesty is not minded to marry'. Thomas should have paid attention. Instead he wrote to Parry, recommending the marriage afresh.[51]

Faced with continued silence, Thomas tried again. He reminded Parry a fortnight later:

> The emperor's son is noble born, and in marrying of that nobleman she [i.e., Elizabeth] is sure to live in peace and to be allied to all the great princes in Christendom, which is here wished of all her friends, as well Protestants as papists. Wherein the will of God and her majesty

be fulfilled, and bless her highness to take a husband for the stay of succession to the great comfort of her majesty and of all her subjects.[52]

By the time Gresham returned to London after the treaty of Edinburgh, all the signs were that his strident advocacy for Charles was becoming tiresome. Exactly what Elizabeth thought of his meddling we do not know, as she never committed her thoughts on the matter directly to paper. But by his dogged persistence he had brought a different aspect of his character to her attention. She may have given him a diplomatic role in Brussels, but if he thought from their encounters so far that he was in a position to advise her on her personal life or to discuss it with her councillors behind her back, he was extremely naïve. From her perspective, he was unquestionably valuable to her, but she was astute enough to see that he could well be vulnerable to delusions of grandeur.

NEW THREATS
AND DANGERS

In October 1560, fate struck Thomas Gresham a cruel blow. Somewhere near Antwerp, he suffered a serious riding accident while rushing about on the queen's affairs. One of his spies in north Germany, John Brigandine, wrote to him on the 12th: 'I am very sorry for your fall from your horse, in so much [as] I was once in mind to have seen you.'[1]

The leg was broken, possibly crushed, and Gresham described himself as lame for the rest of his life. Four months after the accident, Elizabeth dictated a letter in which she showed a degree of sympathy, albeit with an eye to her own affairs, telling him, 'We trust after this prolongation of this February [1561] debt, your leg will be able to carry you a shipboard to return to us, where, both for your recovery, and for intelligence of your doings, we shall be glad to see you'.[2] As much as six years later, Thomas would excuse himself from a meeting with Cecil at the very last moment, claiming 'my wretched leg would not suffer me'.[3] When the pain then did not subside, he had to cancel another of their meetings, saying 'as yet I cannot get my leg whole, which must come only with rest, as my surgeons informeth me'.[4]

Like Henry VIII after a serious jousting accident in 1536, Thomas could have contracted osteomyelitis: bone fragments left behind after the leg was set may have become infected. Increasingly desperate, he called in a surgeon called 'Dirricke', 'who hath brought my leg to some good pass now that the bones be come out, and sayeth that he will heal it very shortly'.[5] But alas he never did.

Thomas soldiered on. By this time, the worst of the political crisis caused by the loss of the count of Mansfeld's funds was over. With £30,000 immediately available to Gresham from the London merchants and a second tranche of £30,000 due in March 1561, he only needed to raise some fifty-four additional smaller loans on the Antwerp bourse to be able to hold off Elizabeth's creditors until the following November. Other city merchants lent £13,000 and Elizabeth repaid a quarter of her foreign debts from ready cash in the exchequer. But even after these loan redemptions, she still owed £247,000 abroad. Less happily for Gresham, a quarrel he provoked with the Merchant Adventurers over how much of their £60,000 was to come interest-free if lent for more than six months and how much would earn interest at something more or less approaching commercial rates had to be deflected by Lord Treasurer Winchester and Cecil. Gresham lost the argument, and it was a lesson he would need to bear in mind for the future.[6]

Gresham's agents in Hamburg, meanwhile, continued to ship large quantities of munitions to London, including saltpetre, gunpowder, hand-guns, pike heads and bowstaves, hidden in beer barrels or wicker baskets to evade the customs officials and searchers. The privy council was taking no chances where the country's defences were at stake. Cecil, in particu-lar, wanted England to be able to defend itself should war resume on the Continent or begin within the British Isles. To increase bullion stocks at the Tower and the mint, meanwhile, Gresham purchased and smuggled out of Antwerp as many Spanish gold coins as he could lay his hands on.[7]

In June or July 1561, Gresham was allowed to return to London to rest his leg. He was definitely home by 27 July, when he presented Cecil with despatches from Elizabeth's ambassador in Germany and from Richard Clough, bringing intelligence of troop movements, new links forged between the French and German Protestants and the impending marriage in Leipzig of Anna of Saxony to Prince William of Orange, one of the more popular and articulate nobles at Margaret of Parma's court in Brussels.[8]

Very possibly, Thomas spent much of August with Anne Ferneley and their son Richard, now fourteen, visiting their Norfolk estates as he had liked to do in Edward VI's reign, but no correspondence survives to document this. A hiatus exists in the sources, not least as Thomas had long ceased keeping a personal journal or 'Day Book' from which his domestic activities can be traced.[9] Equally uncertain is the whereabouts of the now adolescent William and Richard Read, Ferneley's sons by her first mar-riage. The younger boy, Richard, was still under the authority of his uncle, Augustine Steward, and so was most likely living in the parish of St Peter Hungate, Norwich, where Steward made his home.[10] Whether William was still with his mother or had gone to live with his guardian, Nicholas

Bacon, is also unknown. What is certain is both would shortly be of age, and able to inherit a small number of the Norfolk and Suffolk manors left to them in their father's will – but the bulk, especially of Richard's lands, would still be held in trust by their mother for the rest of her life. And to the profits of these Thomas always stuck like glue.[11]

Ferneley had by now apparently forgiven her unfaithful husband for his affair with Winifred Dutton. Evidence of a thaw in their relations comes in the shape of Gresham's gratitude several times expressed to Cecil or Parry 'for your gentleness showed to my poor wife, whom likewise would gladly have me at home', and for 'the gentle entertainment you gave to my poor wife, who I do right well know molests you daily for my coming home, such is the fondness of women'.[12]

Probably in the summer of 1561, Gresham also had to settle some of the affairs of his elder brother, John, who had died of unknown causes while Thomas had been in Antwerp. Ending his days in Bethnal Green, possibly in property owned by their stepmother, Isabel, John's profligacy in life meant that he died heavily in debt. He had long since sold or mortgaged what was left of the lands brought to him by his marriage to the heiress Frances Thwaites, and had leased out – in exchange for large upfront premiums, but low rents – many of those somewhat grudgingly left to him by his father, which he was unable to sell. Those estates, including Intwood in Norfolk, now passed to Thomas: the upshot was that the widowed Frances was left in relative penury.[13]

To provide for his sister-in-law in her time of need, Thomas granted her an annuity of £133 6s. 8d., which was to be her main financial support for the rest of her life. Guaranteed by a recognisance of £1,333 enrolled in the court of Chancery that would be forfeit to Frances or her heirs if Thomas allowed his payments to fall into arrears, it was a gesture that seemingly gives the lie to his half-sister Christiana's claim that he was 'avaricious, and one that only looketh to [his] singular profit without respect of persons'.[14] Towards the end of Gresham's life, though, several payments to Frances were made late or not made at all, a neglect to be compounded by Anne Ferneley, causing considerable grief and hardship to Frances.[15]

His summer break over, Gresham was back in Antwerp by 2 September, where he found himself genuinely stymied. With repayments of £90,000 or so falling due to Elizabeth's creditors in November, he was unable to raise sufficient cash or fresh loans to prolong the debts: for once his fabled alchemy failed him, and he was forced, humiliatingly, to seek a bailout from his scourge, the marquis of Winchester.[16] 'My lord,' he grovelled, 'as here is great scarcity of money, so here is now as little credit to be had by the reason of great and notable bankrupts that of late hath chanced here and daily will be more and more and more as the saying is.' His shortfall, he said, was £20,000, and he needed it urgently in cash 'for the preserving of the queen's majesty's honour and credit. For that here is no money to be had upon interest at any price, such misery is here at this present'.[17]

The exodus of credit stemmed from Philip II's declaration of bankruptcy, first announced in 1557. By the summer of 1561, the council of finance in Madrid had resumed making regular payments again, but only after it had issued creditors with *juros* or state securities carrying much lower rates of interest to those originally agreed and which compounded for capital repayments at hefty discounts to the outstanding amounts. Of Gresham's more important contacts, Andreas Lixhalls was among several bankers forced into liquidation. Lazarus Tucher survived, but withdrew from the market completely. As to the house of Fugger, Anton Fugger had died in September 1560, leaving the firm in the hands of his eldest nephew, Hans Jakob Fugger.[18] According to Gresham, Philip II owed the Fugger bank 'at least £1,000,000' (over £1 billion in modern values), 'which is a piteous case that ever was heard of'.[19]

On 6 September, Thomas wrote again to Winchester, reiterating his plea for a bailout and assuring him that Elizabeth could win herself a lasting reputation for creditworthiness if only he would remit sufficient funds.[20] This was true, but Gresham also had a personal interest in securing a large cash sum at this precise moment. He had spent £2,542 on various items for the queen 'that your lordship promised me at my departure should be presently paid', and nothing had been received. He had also laid out £5,000 from his own money to repay an earlier debt, for which he had Cecil's warrant, but was still not reimbursed. As he complained, Winchester had several times promised him repayment, but although 'my factor Candeler hath daily called upon him for it', he had 'not received a penny of it'.[21]

Winchester did relent and remitted the cash, but he also called in Gresham's accounts for auditing once more, still persuaded that the queen's factor was a spiv and a fraud. Suspicious that he might be secretly skimming a percentage off the amounts he raised in loans, the wary lord treasurer was notably sceptical of Thomas's bills for brokerage fees, living costs, riding charges and a whole raft of miscellaneous expenses, including bribes and 'rewards' and money spent on 'feastings', shipping costs and customs fees.

Among the more sensitive items soon to catch the attention of Winchester's auditors was a mysterious shortfall of £1,000 between funds marked as 'taken up' and 'received' in Antwerp, a bill of over £6,000 for Gresham's brokerage fees 'as also postage and my diets for the space of fifteen months', and hefty 'entertainment' costs for Gaspar Schetz and others.[22] A neatly written statement of account dated June 1560, somewhat in the nature of a smoking gun, showed that Thomas charged 1 per cent for brokerage on top of his allowance of twenty shillings a day for 'diets', with interest on top, an amount considerably larger than the true costs. This meant that for as little as a fortnight's worth of deals if the capital sums were large enough, his personal whack in brokerage and interest combined could rise as high as 4,901 Carolus guilders (worth over £715,000 today).[23]

Just as after Gresham's Spanish venture in Mary I's reign, the heavy lifting in Winchester's audit was undertaken by Sir Walter Mildmay, now chancellor of the exchequer and Winchester's deputy, who worked alongside Cecil and Sir Francis Knollys.[24] They quickly established that Elizabeth had allowed Thomas twenty shillings a day for 'diets' while in Antwerp, and a reduced allowance of 13s. 4d. a day while he was in London on the queen's business, but that no explicit approval had been granted for payment of brokerage fees since she came to the throne.

Despite this, Gresham had submitted an inflated claim for brokerage costs, along with a bill of twenty shillings a day for his *per diems* regardless of his location.[25] To exonerate himself, he pulled strings with Cecil. The audited version of his accounts shows that, for his activities over a three-year period, he would finally be allowed £3,646 for diets, riding and other miscellaneous charges, £2,408 for customs fees, a generous £6,083 for shipping, carriage and other freight charges, plus £195 for 'rewards' and bribes other than those approved for Gaspar Schetz. These sums largely reflected his claims. But his brokerage fees were cut back by two-thirds to a total of £1,204 (over £1.2 million today), with the result that he ended up owing the queen £2,667 12s. 8d., which he was obliged to refund to the exchequer.[26]

Cecil spared Gresham the worst of Winchester's reprisals, probably because his own financial dealings as Elizabeth's chief minister were not beyond reproach and he needed Thomas on side. The audit was largely finished by the time a complaint was lodged by a respected Antwerp merchant, Albrecht Jansen, who wrote in impeccable French to inform Elizabeth that Thomas had swindled him over the repayment of a loan of 29,800 thalers. Whereas Gresham was meant to repay the loan according to a previously fixed exchange rate, he had instead paid at a less favourable market rate.[27]

Although Jansen's complaint was inherently credible, Cecil dismissed it unheard. From now on, Gresham would enjoy a relatively clear run as the queen's banker until his retirement. The one major difference was that Elizabeth – probably on her lord treasurer's advice – intervened after the audit was over to reinstate the 13s. 4d. she had specified in her instructions of December 1558 for Thomas's *per diems* while in London.[28] With this modification, Gresham sought a royal pardon for any accounting irregularities for which he might have been responsible since Elizabeth's accession, which she eventually granted.[29]

But Gresham couldn't relax. The outbreak of Wars of Religion in France threatened to turn the existing European order upside down, proving just how prudent Cecil had been to insist on building up a stockpile of munitions at the Tower. There was much talk of revolts and assassinations, partly encouraged by the easy availability of the new wheel-lock pistol, one of the landmark technological innovations of the sixteenth century. Uniquely suited to political assassinations, this was a weapon that by the 1560s could be purchased legally almost anywhere in Europe. If loaded and primed ahead of use, it could be hidden inside clothing, then grabbed and discharged using only one hand. One of the earliest assassinations outside Italy using a handgun was that of the Mercer Robert Packington, a vocal supporter of the early reformers and a member of Parliament, who on Monday, 13 November 1536 was shot in Cheapside at four o'clock on an unusually misty morning as he crossed the street to attend mass in the Mercers' Chapel.[30]

As Elizabeth's diplomatic representative in Brussels, Thomas was constantly on his guard. So far, Philip II – although wary of Elizabeth's Protestant religious settlement and the support she might give to a new generation of militant Calvinists across the Channel – had been prepared to bide his time. Obstinate heretic though she was in his opinion, the Spanish ruler was anxious not to quarrel with his former sister-in-law.[31] In an effort to bolster the grip of the Catholic Church in the Netherlands, Philip had created several new bishoprics and archbishoprics, a pet project with him. Its unfortunate effect was to infringe on the rights of the existing clergy and upset the nobles and city magistrates by appearing to limit their power. Especially irksome to William of Orange and his friends was the promotion of Margaret of Parma's chief adviser, Granvelle, to the archbishopric of Mechelen. As an unpopular move, however, this paled into insignificance when Philip introduced the Inquisition into the Netherlands.

For the moment, most of the citizens of Antwerp were loyal Catholics – Calvinist preachers had as yet to make much impact on civic life. But while going about his business there, Thomas began to feel threatened as the general disquiet led to spasmodic outbreaks of xenophobia. The earlier furore over his exports of bullion had caused him to avoid walking the streets after dark.[32] Soon he was to sell his mansion known as 'St Franciscus' in the Lange Nieuwstraat and acquire a rural estate outside the city, which he kept for seven or eight years. His country estate is only known from a single, very fragile tax record once in a 'loose folder' in the Antwerp archives but no longer available to researchers. But he was already well-established in his new property by September 1563, when he wrote a letter 'from the suburbs of Antwerp'.[33]

The new turmoil in Europe quickly drew in Elizabeth. In the late summer of 1562, her favourite, Robert Dudley, persuaded her to come to the aid of the beleaguered French Protestants (Huguenots) at Le Havre, who were under siege from superior Catholic forces commanded by the duke of Guise. Gresham joined Cecil and Dudley in lobbying for the intervention, warning the queen that 'if Monsieur de Guise have the upper hand of the Protestants, that then the French king, the king of Spain, the pope, the duke of Savoy and those of that religion will set upon the queen's majesty only for religion's sake, whether she doth take part or not'.[34] In saying this, Gresham showed how far he had committed himself to Cecil's reading of international politics.

On 20 September, Elizabeth agreed terms with the Huguenot leaders by which she would supply them with 6,000 troops under the command of Dudley's elder brother, Ambrose, earl of Warwick, along with a loan of up to 140,000 French crowns of the sun (around £27,500 sterling). In return, she was granted Le Havre as a pledge until Calais was restored to her. For her part, she sought only to recover Calais; she was still smarting that Philip II in his eagerness to make peace at Cateau-Cambrésis in 1559 had written off her claim to the town. Beyond that, she meant to do little for the Huguenots. She was only too well aware of the risks Cecil had taken in Scotland in 1559–60 and of the danger of alienating the French Catholics and Philip II at the same time.

Once the decision to intervene was made, Gresham had to raise more loans and secure fresh supplies of munitions in Flanders or Germany. He was then to organise the transport of coffers containing some £20,000 in a variety of untraceable gold and silver coins, many of them French or Spanish, from the Tower to Portsmouth, before smuggling them into the war zone in Normandy.[35] All this was to be done secretly, not least because the duke of Guise was himself seeking credit of 200,000 crowns.[36]

Unfortunately, Warwick's campaign in 1562–3 was not just a military failure: it united the whole of French opinion against England. There were economic consequences too. The power vacuum created by the fighting encouraged English pirates to attack shipping in the Channel, especially off the coast of Flanders. By December 1563, Anglo-Spanish relations would deteriorate as a result of this piracy to the point where Margaret of Parma's government imposed an embargo on imports of certain English goods, swiftly followed by a complete embargo on trade.[37]

Elizabeth, lobbied by Cecil, retaliated by transferring all wool and cloth exports to the north German port town of Emden, where the ruler, Count John, was eager to offer his services. Here, though, Cecil put a foot wrong. Some 500 miles away from the major centres of supply and a sea journey of three days or more from England, Emden afforded an alternative point of entry into the markets of Germany and central Europe, but only considerable economies of scale could justify this circuitous route. Instead of listening to Gresham, who fully understood the workings of the cloth and money markets, Cecil and Elizabeth were overly influenced by the toadying views of the Governor of the Merchant Adventurers. John Marsh inspired instinctive trust but was principally an establishment figure, more lawyer than merchant, a member of a suspiciously large number of government committees and in no position to tell the queen anything she did not want to hear. Meanwhile Gresham's persistence in cautioning her against Emden led Elizabeth to relieve him of his diplomatic responsibilities, which she transferred to Dr Valentine Dale, a seasoned bureaucrat and expert on international and maritime law.[38]

What counted in Brussels, and to Philip, on the other hand, was Elizabeth's apparent inability or unwillingness to control the attacks on Flemish and Spanish shipping by English pirates. This was coupled with an obstructive attitude on the part of the English courts, which offered little or no redress to victims if they were foreigners.[39] Not to mention the English customs duties and various charges imposed on foreign merchants in the Anglo-Brabant trade.[40] Before he was replaced by Dale, Gresham tried to counter Margaret of Parma's protests at these outrages, but failed to satisfy her. In the absence of William of Orange, Gresham went to see the count of Egmont, a friend of William and a sympathetic member of the council of state in Brussels, but he too was adamant that Elizabeth was in the wrong, saying 'I cannot but marvel that the queen's ships should misuse the king's [i.e., Philip's] subjects'.[41]

By January 1564, Antwerp was in lockdown. As Richard Clough explained, with trade at a standstill the authorities feared an insurrection, since 'here is such misery within this town that the like hath not been seen'.[42] Street muggings and burglaries soared and a corn merchant's house was attacked by armed looters.[43] The city magistrates did their best to break the deadlock, sending a gift of wine to Gresham in the hope that he could broker an accord.[44] To their dismay, Elizabeth walked away from the negotiations just as Margaret of Parma was about to make concessions. By focusing not on events in Antwerp, but on the indignities suffered by English merchants in the ports of Spain, where they were subject to a campaign of harassment and ill-treatment, she took her eye off the ball.

Petitioned again by Antwerp's leaders who assumed he had more influence than he really did, Gresham assured them that he was actively seeking Cecil's aid, who was 'of all the lords of the privy council the most inclined to do you pleasure'.[45] Thomas then set out for home, and had arrived by the end of the month. His crossing from Dunkirk was frightening: his ship was closely shadowed by seven French warships and had to turn back, but he was in Dover before nightfall the next day after what he described as 'a very sore passage'.[46]

By the summer of 1564, Thomas had persuaded Cecil and Dudley to write soothingly to the magistrates – in a reluctant Cecil's case, three times. The gist of these letters was to urge the civic powers to lobby in Brussels (or even Madrid), rather than London, if the deadlock was to be broken.[47] This was disingenuous, as a large part of the problem was Elizabeth herself. Now almost thirty-one, she was coming of age as a ruler and was no longer the vulnerable twenty-five-year-old who had taken the throne on the death of her half-sister. She had chosen Emden as a transit port not for any sound commercial reasons, but on ideological grounds. The town was an important Protestant centre. She also hoped it would help her to cultivate those well-heeled German princes who, like the count of Mansfeld, she believed had money to burn and who could supply her on demand with the munitions and mercenaries she felt she needed.

The move of the wool and cloth fairs to Emden proved a disaster. On their arrival, the London merchants found they had been condemned to live and trade in a squalid, hostile town with few facilities and none whatever for dyeing or finishing their cloths. On 14 June 1564, they opened their new mart; by July it had collapsed. Meanwhile the Merchant Adventurers had surrendered their lease on their administrative headquarters in Antwerp. This raised fears that the disruption of trade might become permanent. Several now took the decision to abandon the Anglo-Brabant trade altogether, whatever the outcome of the negotiations with Brussels. They were only too well aware that neither Margaret of Parma nor Philip II was much troubled by any loss to the industry and economy of Brabant, despite the sufferings of its people. To make things worse, the winter of 1564–5 would prove to be one of the coldest of the sixteenth century. In Antwerp, grain became scarce and bread prices soared to unaffordable levels. In London, the ice froze on the Thames and people walked or skated across it.

On 29 December 1564, Elizabeth at last gave way, lifting the embargo with effect from New Year's Day and declaring that 'the intercourse of merchandise betwixt this realm and the said Low Countries shall ... continue free, open and as mutual as it was immediately before the late interchangeable stays and prohibitions thereof'.[48] Antwerp reopened to English shipping and, contrary to all expectations, the market bounced back: 'great quantities' of English broadcloths and kerseys were shipped over even before the departure of what was left of the regular cloth fleet. A peace conference was arranged to settle the outstanding differences between London and Brussels, but Gresham was not one of the delegates. He may well have predicted the slow pace and relative fruitlessness of such negotiations.[49]

For the time being, Thomas preferred to focus on the things he did best. While trade had been at a standstill, he had found something new and exciting to occupy him. Coinciding with the withdrawal of English troops from Normandy in 1563, Winchester and Cecil had begun sending him a slice of surplus tax receipts and the proceeds of sales of crown lands, with instructions to deploy the cash towards overseas loan redemption. The sums involved could often be surprisingly large: £3,500 or £4,000 here, £12,000 there.[50]

In this way – and by switching other essential borrowing to Lombard Street whenever an opportunity arose – Gresham had steadily wound down Elizabeth's foreign debts to a far more manageable £94,000 or so by the close of 1564.[51] It was a remarkable achievement given the difficulties he faced, and now he set himself another challenge. The lifting of the trade embargo was followed by a general easing of interest rates, accompanied by a rise in the value of pound sterling to a market high of around 23s. 4d. in Flemish currency.[52] This meant that, for the first time in Elizabeth's reign and without specific authorisation from her or Cecil, he could once again attempt something that had been a gleam in his eye for a decade.

Using the cash the privy council was now regularly sending him to make scheduled repayments at the older, less favourable rates, Gresham aimed to take advantage of the new, lower rates to slash foreign borrowing almost to zero as soon as he could manage it. Inevitably, funds from London tended to arrive in dribs and drabs. He was given no reliable income stream, but as a born dealer he knew how to turn what he received to best advantage. He had done the same thing twice before, in the closing months of Edward VI's reign and again in Mary I's reign.

From now on, Gresham would make overseas debt redemption his personal crusade. With the ideological rift between the Catholic and Protestant states in Europe threatening to grow wider by the day, he believed Elizabeth's sovereignty to be at stake. If a Protestant queen was to survive, she had to be solvent. If she *did* need to borrow at home or abroad, she must do so from a position of strength. And Thomas was determined to make this happen. He was about to extend his remit as Elizabeth's banker to uncharted waters.

A MERCHANT PRINCE

Just as in Antwerp Thomas Gresham turned his network of contacts into a private intelligence service, so he steadily built up close relationships with those at the nerve centre of power in London. Sir Thomas Parry, Elizabeth's cofferer, to whom Gresham previously reported almost as often as he did to Cecil, had suddenly fallen ill and died in December 1560. His departure left Cecil largely unchallenged. As the queen's secretary of state and chief minister, Cecil managed the flow of her correspondence, organised the meetings of her privy council, briefed her ambassadors and controlled her state papers, to the point where contemporaries later said of him: 'after climbing the ladder of success, he pulled it well out of everyone else's reach'.[1]

Cecil's only possible rival was Lord Robert Dudley, Elizabeth's favourite, and the only man she ever truly loved. He had the flashy, swashbuckling good looks she always found irresistible in a man, but any serious hopes he had of getting divorced and marrying the queen were scuppered when his wife, Amy Robsart, the daughter of a wealthy Norfolk landowner, was found dead at the foot of a small stone spiral staircase.[2] Suspicions pointed to Dudley. After weathering the scandal, he learned to work with Cecil, more or less as part of a team. Their styles and methods could be very different, but their aims had much in common. They both wanted to exclude Catholics from the succession and help the Flemish and Dutch Protestants resist direct Spanish rule.

Gresham's links to both men went back to Edward VI's reign. Cecil had been the duke of Northumberland's right-hand man in financial affairs. In Dudley's case, Thomas's connections were more personal. Two of his Norfolk cousins and several of his or his servants' friends or relatives were also Dudley's servants or Amy Robsart's relatives. In August 1560,

Gresham had written to Dudley, urging him to use his influence to help one of them secure lands in and around Wymondham in Norfolk 'for the stay of his living and for the better service of the queen's majesty in those parts'.[3] Perhaps most compellingly, Gresham would end up as one of Dudley's most important creditors besides the queen, doubtless advising him on his borrowing needs at several late-night suppers the two men shared.[4] Dudley then went on to sell lands in Norfolk to Gresham for a knockdown price, a common signal of obligation.[5]

One of the more obvious ways in which Thomas could win friends at court was by going out of his way to 'procure' from Antwerp, France, Germany, or as far away as Valladolid or Seville in Spain, all such goods or services as those in positions of power would thank him for. High priorities on Elizabeth's earlier shopping lists were an iron chest from Antwerp and a Turkish riding horse from Germany, along with quantities of silk stockings and 'collars' for her 'headpieces of silk'.

'Sir,' Gresham had advised Cecil in the spring of 1560, 'it may please you likewise to do my most humble commendations to my Lord Robert Dudley, and to declare unto him that the queen's majesty's Turkey horse doth begin to mend in his foot and body, which doubtless is one of the readiest horses that is in all Christendom and runs the best.'[6] Shortly afterwards, a scribbled postscript to Parry read, 'It may please you to show my Lord Robert that the queen's majesty's Turkey horse waxes a very fair beast, and with the queen's majesty's leave, I do intend to bring [it] home myself.'[7]

But before shipping the horse across the Channel, Thomas was obliged to nurse it, 'being six months in healing of a disease which he had'.[8] The total cost of veterinary care and transport came to £10 (over £10,000 in modern values), although naturally Thomas made sure every penny was added to his expenses as later submitted for Lord Treasurer Winchester's approval.[9] Gresham then briefed Parry,

> and whereas your honour would have a great iron chest bought for the queen's majesty, with a little key, I have sent you a key of the fairest chest that is to be had in all this town, if the key be not too big. If the queen's majesty will, I pray you I may know the length and I shall cause a chest to be made purposely.[10]

Six weeks later, he could confirm, 'I have sent you overland, to Dunkirk, the young curtal [i.e., small horse with its tail docked] I gave you with the queen's majesty's Turkey horse. As likewise I have sent you four dozen of the same black buttons you spake to me for, which costs you forty-eight shillings the dozen.'[11]

Suitable 'collars' for Elizabeth's silk headpieces were simple to source; not so, her silk stockings.[12] Gresham finally had to send to Spain for them, as he had before when making a gift of a pair to Edward VI. As he warned Dudley, 'I have made due search for silk hose for the queen's majesty, but here is none to be gotten. Therefore I have sent her highness's measure into Spain, and thereby to make twenty pairs according to her majesty's commandment in that behalf.'[13] The silk stockings were later delivered to the queen through Dudley, to whom one of the minor functionaries of the Merchant Adventurers was already carrying letters.[14] Perhaps not surprisingly, Gresham was then asked to get silk stockings for other courtiers or their wives. As he informed Cecil in another of his many postscripts, 'I have written into Spain for silk hose both for you and my lady your wife, to whom it may please you I may be remembered.'[15] Cecil, it seems, had insisted that his stockings be black. As Thomas confirmed when at last he tracked some down, 'I have sent you herewith two pair[s] of black silk hose and [a] pair for my lady your wife.'[16]

For Dudley, Gresham supplied gold canvas most likely for wall coverings, and for Cecil he went on to purchase six silver candlesticks, a clock, six velvet chairs and six more of Spanish leather, seven pieces of tapestry, various maps and plans, a hundred German handmade shirts and a wolfskin gown. Comestibles for Cecil's table included sausages from Bologna, hams, bacon and two wild boar ready cured and smoked in Antwerp. These were followed by whole shipments of expensive paving stones, slates for roofing, marble pillars and panels for wainscoting to fit out a gallery, five cases of glassware and nine 'hearths for chimneys', all destined for the ongoing construction works at the chief minister's ancestral seat near Stamford in Lincolnshire.[17]

After five years as her banker, it began to gnaw away at Gresham that, despite all his efforts to serve and please Elizabeth, she had neglected the promise she made to him on her accession, when she said that 'if I did her no other service than I had done to King Edward her brother and Queen Mary her sister, she would give me as much as ever both they did'. What especially rankled was her decision, after Winchester's most recent audit, to curtail his accustomed *per diems* of twenty shillings a day while he was in England, and reinstate the 13s. 4d. she had specified in her instructions of December 1558.[18] His confidence in her was unshaken, but on 3 October 1563 he dared to send her from Antwerp the most impertinent reminder she is likely to have received from any subject since her coronation day. He may well, by now, have come to regard himself psychologically as a merchant prince, even if there was as yet no real material sense that his rank had decisively shifted on the basis of his knighthood. If, however, by acting out this role he expected to raise his profile in the eyes of a ruler as touchy about status and her royal prerogative as Elizabeth, he had misread her character.

'It hath pleased your highness by your last instructions,' Thomas began, 'to abridge me of my diets of twenty shillings a day being in England, which I will assure your majesty doth not a little disquiet me, considering the service and travail that I have taken for your highness this five years.' As he set about jogging her memory, 'both in King Edward's time, your late brother, as also of Queen Mary, your late sister', he had always been allowed twenty shillings a day 'where so ever I went'. He then starkly rammed home the fact that her siblings had rewarded him with munificent grants of land 'to me and my heirs for ever', which she had failed as yet to do, despite, as he claimed, 'that you shall find that I have done your highness other manner of service, both of greater importance and of greater mass and charge, [in] all manner of ways, than I have done to your late brother and sister, put both their charge together'.

Not only that, he continued, but 'besides this, I am become lame in your majesty's service, and now wax old. In consideration whereof, I trust that your majesty will be no less beneficial unto me than your late brother and sister was [*sic*]; for so your majesty did promise me when I took this great charge upon me.'[19]

It was an extraordinary outburst, not helped by the fact that at the age of forty-four, Gresham was not old even by sixteenth-century standards, despite the pain in his damaged leg. His claims of age appear all the more exaggerated when one considers that Cecil was only a year or so younger, and he would have to continue in office for thirty-five more years, his pleas to be allowed to retire in his seventieth year brushed aside by the queen. As to Winchester, he was over seventy-five in 1563, but despite rapidly failing health would soldier on for another nine years.

In Gresham's defence, a thunderbolt from which he would never fully recover had struck him five months earlier. On 2 May 1563, his and Anne Ferneley's only child together, the now sixteen-year-old Richard, died suddenly at their Intwood estate. The household had fled there from an outbreak of plague in London. On 20 May, John Conyers, Gresham's servant and now Richard Clough's principal assistant, wrote to Sir Thomas Chaloner in Madrid:

> As [of] the first of this present [month] my master's son fell sick of the pleurisy and was presently let blood for the same ten hours together. So that as [of] the second of this present, he departed this world, of whose soul God have mercy. I assure your honour it was no small grief unto my master and to my lady for that they had no more children.[20]

Conyers went on to play down their grief, adding, 'But now, thanks be to God, they are all well satisfied, for that the will of God must be fulfilled.'[21] These words are almost certainly there for form's sake: both Catholics and Protestants considered it an affront to God's wisdom and providence to indulge too visibly in extended periods of deep mourning after the loss of close family members.

From Madrid, Chaloner replied, 'Your heavy news of the death of your master's son, I assure you, hath not a little grieved me for good Sir Thomas his sake.'[22] Independently, Chaloner's former deputy, the diplomat and inveterate gossip Henry Cobham, who also worked for Gresham, wrote to Chaloner from London on 14 May, 'Sir Thomas Gresham's only son is dead', although he did not know the cause.[23]

The death of his son triggered a shift in Gresham's attitude to life. He seemed to feel uneasy at the country home where the youth had died. Ferneley went further and positively refused to live there anymore. Thomas still owned the property a few months later, but disposed of it shortly afterwards.[24] He was to keep Ringshall, the Suffolk estate he would shortly inherit after his stepmother's death, but seems to have moved most of its contents to one of two new country estates he purchased, one at Mayfield in Sussex, the other at Osterley, near Brentford, in the parish of Heston in Middlesex, where he gained a licence to construct a deer park.[25] He was addressing letters to Cecil from Osterley as early as January and April 1564, so had clearly made his shift into the existing house there by then.[26]

It was mainly through what was to become the sheer opulence of Gresham's various properties that he would finally make the social leap to the life of a merchant prince. Even many noblemen and their wives could not afford a deer park, although it was Robert Dudley who stepped in to stock Gresham's with a gift of animals from his own estates at no cost. Almost certainly Ferneley welcomed these moves: a woman increasingly consumed by social ambition, she would soon be spending part of her summers at the spa at Buxton in Derbyshire to take the waters and mingle with the great and the good.[27] The hot springs there had been famous since Roman times for their curative powers. Dudley and other noblemen or their wives would make regular summer visits, giving the town a cosmopolitan flavour that appealed to Ferneley's desire to venture into a wider, more sophisticated world.

The next casualty in the family after young Richard Gresham would be Thomas's stepmother, Isabel, already seriously ill by the time she sent for her lawyer in April 1565 to make her will. Her funeral took place on 24 May, by which time she had made known her desire to be buried alongside her late husband in the church of St Lawrence Jewry, near her Milk Street home. She was Gresham's last link to his childhood and father, although the wording of her will made it clear that, like her daughter Christiana, Thomas's half-sister, she believed him to be avaricious.[28] She recognised his importance to the family by making generous bequests to him, and by appointing him as one of the overseers of her will with its princely benefactions to the Mercers' Company and to various charities in London, Oxford and Cambridge. And yet, she also made it an absolute provision that if Gresham made any attempt, 'by any way or means whatsoever', to contest, limit or otherwise interfere with the winding up of her estate, all bequests to him and his wife were to be instantly revoked and should 'utterly cease'.[29]

Isabel also made it a strict condition that Thomas was to refrain from touching any of her money or possessions before her will was proved. He was not permitted even to enter her house for a period of eight weeks after her death, such was her concern that he would try to take away some of her more valuable property or disrupt the work of her executors.

Even before these two deaths, Gresham had decided that it might be time for him and his wife to begin to live more luxuriously. Since recovering his position after the dismissal of Christopher Dauntsey early in Mary I's reign, he had begun investing much of his spare cash in land to supplement or augment the estates he had been granted. Most recently, he had purchased surplus properties from the earl of Arundel and the duke of Norfolk.[30] Other lands or manors he acquired by lease or purchase included Fawkener's fields, near Osterley, which had formerly been part of the estates of Syon abbey, along with a mixed bag of properties in Somerset, Surrey, Sussex, Yorkshire and elsewhere.[31]

As far back as November 1557, and then again in the months before he left London for Brussels in January 1560, Thomas had masterminded the purchase of a series of land parcels he then skilfully amalgamated to create the finest redevelopment site in London to come onto the market for many years. A large estate leading directly off Bishopsgate, irregularly shaped and stretching more or less as far back as the east side of Broad Street, it stood opposite his old mentor Antonio Buonvisi's former mansion, Crosby Place, and had a footprint of well over an acre.[32] Part of the site consisted of a large house and garden that had once belonged to Sir William Sharington, a notorious embezzler and currency fraudster. The other principal component was the house and garden formerly owned by Domenico Lomellini, a Genoese merchant who several times won money playing games of cards with Henry VIII.[33] To ensure his privacy, Gresham purchased a cluster of neighbouring properties only to demolish many of them.[34] With much of the site cleared by the autumn of 1561, he planned to create a magnificent brick and timber mansion to be known as 'Gresham House', and was soon spending vast sums on building works.

Once construction could commence, Gresham's craftsmen laboured six days a week.[35] Just possibly, the project may have been managed by Hendryk van Paesschen of Antwerp, a master mason who in 1561–5 also collaborated with the sculptor and designer Cornelis Floris on the Antwerp *stadhuis*, and would later oversee work on the Royal Exchange.[36] Stylistically, van Paesschen combined Flemish influences with Italian classicism, ornamented by the elaborate strapwork, imps and grotesque figures that were to become the distinctive Antwerp form of decoration.[37]

Despite the risks of spending money so fast, Thomas believed he could afford it. Rent rolls surviving from his East Anglian estates and other properties in Somerset, Sussex, Yorkshire, Durham, Derbyshire and Cambridgeshire from 1566 onwards show that his income from land alone in a good year ran to around £2,500 (over £2.5 million today).[38] On top were the profits, chiefly brokerage fees, of his banking deals. Clearly he believed this to be sufficient without engaging in some of the riskier speculations offered to investors at the time. When Sir John Hawkins sought investors in 1564 and 1567 for his infamous slave voyages from West Africa, for instance, Thomas did not subscribe. Many privy councillors and courtiers eagerly did so in the hope of large profits, notably Cecil and Dudley, along with several wealthy London merchants. Why Gresham had his doubts, and what they may have been, the sources do not tell us. It is impossible to guess his opinion as to the ethics of the trade.[39]

Gresham House, when finally it was completed in 1566, would be set around a large enclosed inner courtyard, well away from the noise and bustle of the street. Among its grandest features were two full-length Italianate loggias looking into the inner courtyard and two long galleries. A smaller outer courtyard connected the inner one to a gatehouse leading into Bishopsgate via a narrow passage. Adjacent to the west range of the court stood a large stable block with its own courtyard that could only be approached through an archway suitable for coaches leading off Broad Street. At the rear of the same range, at ground and first-floor levels, were eight identical almshouses with a gallery above, and facing south was a large walled garden.[40]

As to the contents of the house, they would be valued shortly after Thomas's death at £1,127.[41] We cannot be sure, but most likely they included several items belonging to his father, now inherited from his stepmother and described in her will. Among those for use in the hall, parlour and other living rooms were three large Turkish carpets, two more carpets specially woven with grasshoppers and another with a pelican, and sixteen cushions of various sizes, four of crimson satin, three of which were richly embroidered for use on window seats, and others for general use, some with the letter 'R'. For the bedchambers, Thomas inherited his father's 'state' bed of counterfeit cloth of gold and blue velvet, along with 'a counterpoint [i.e., counterpane] of fine imagery with grasshoppers' some 55 yards in length. These came accompanied by various other beds, bed curtains, coverlets, pillows and mattresses.[42]

Little is known about the Mayfield house, other than that the great hall measured 68 feet long by 38 wide.[43] Gresham seems to have furnished the property from scratch, reputedly spending an astronomical £7,553 (more than £7.5 million today) in the process.[44]

In the case of Osterley, he demolished the existing farm buildings and redeveloped the site over a period of ten years. The four corner turrets of the present eighteenth-century mansion, with their ogee moulding, almost certainly survive, suitably adapted, from Gresham's house. Not much is known for certain of its original architectural layout, other than that it featured an east-facing library and a private chapel, and remained largely untouched until comprehensively rebuilt for the Child family on the existing foundations by Robert Adam.

The only one of Gresham's buildings to survive more or less intact is the stable block at Osterley, now a National Trust café, which consists of a courtyard open on one side of two stories with semi-octagonal stair turrets in the angles. Built of red brick, with stone and plastered dressings, the structure retains many of its original features, although considerable alterations were made to its interior during Adam's remodelling.[45] Of a paper mill that Thomas converted from a corn mill on the river Brent on his Osterley estate there is now no trace, nor any indication that it ever produced much paper.[46]

From the spring of 1564 onwards, Gresham would make Osterley his principal country house. Set in a wooded park of 600 acres with ponds and little islands on which herons nested, it lay directly on the route Elizabeth regularly took on her way to or from her own favourite holiday haunt, Nonsuch Palace in Surrey. She lodged with the Greshams overnight in September 1564 and September 1565, and made a longer stay in January 1567.[47]

It was later said that during one of these visits Thomas had his bricklayers divide the front court of the half-finished mansion in two by a wall on Elizabeth's suggestion. Since a map of 1635 appears to depict a house built as an H or half-H, with a double courtyard in front, the story may contain a grain of truth. What sounds decidedly apocryphal is the claim that the work was done by candlelight in the middle of the night so as not to disturb the queen during the day with the noise of the workmen's carts.[48]

Furnishings at Osterley may partly have come from Intwood, and otherwise were bought new. Books and maps were brought from Antwerp for the library. And it seems that Gresham, like his factor Richard Clough, may have been more than merely a collector of books. At least three works were dedicated to him. Hugh Gough's *The offspring of the house of Ottomano* (1569), a translation of Bartolomej Georgijević's treatise on the Ottoman Turks, is clearly pitched as a book likely to appeal to an inveterate traveller.[49] Equally, Thomas Hacket's reprinting of *The treasury of Amadis of France* (1572), translated by Thomas Paynell, a 'how-to' guide to letter-writing, and in particular how to write ingratiatingly to those in power, might well have struck a chord.[50]

Of all the books dedicated to Gresham, however, it was Richard Verstegan's *The post for divers parts of the world* (1575) that he most likely kept on his desk.[51] Born plain Richard Rowlands in London, Verstegan was a Catholic who, in 1581, would flee to exile in Antwerp, where he reverted to his ancestral Dutch surname, but until then he was a well-respected goldsmith and cloth merchant. His book remains an invaluable gazetteer to the posts, roads, travel distances and different gold and silver coins in use all over sixteenth-century Europe. Published in a handy size, ideal for slipping inside the pocket of a gown, it was an indispensable merchant's *vade-mecum*.

Those living long-term at Gresham House, apart from Thomas himself, his wife Anne Ferneley, his illegitimate daughter, Anne, and a dozen or more of their servants, included Ferneley's now adult sons by her first marriage to William Read. No sooner was the building work completed than they both moved in, and once installed in their comfortable apartments, they stuck like clams. Thomas's irritation no doubt increased when his elder stepson, William, married Gertrude Paston, daughter of Sir William Paston of North Walsham in Norfolk and his wife Frances Clere, and she too came to live at Gresham House.[52]

Much of Gresham's exasperation probably stemmed from his stepsons' attitude that the world owed them a living. He may have come to see them as lazy freeloaders who ought to have made lucrative careers themselves, rather than see him obliged for ever to support them. Alternatively, he may have come to resent them after the death of his own son, not least since they – and especially William, the elder of the two – were their mother's pride and joy.

Gresham's cousin Cecily, the wife of Alessandro Buonvisi's former factor, Germain Cioll, also moved from her home, Crosby Place, across the street into Gresham House. By 1566, Cioll, no longer on Alessandro's staff but working for himself, was on the verge of insolvency, largely as a result of losses at sea and a run of bad debts. In 1567, he was forced into bankruptcy and compelled to sell Crosby Place – this despite having purchased the freehold barely six years earlier. With nowhere else to turn, Cecily, still only thirty-two and childless, sought Thomas's protection, which he willingly granted her.[53]

Intriguingly, Robert Dudley was another of Cecily's benefactors: he had once intervened to reimburse money owed to her by one of his servants.[54] But such relationships proved to be of only limited avail to Cioll himself. Despite Cioll having almost certainly first inducted the young, aspiring Gresham into the higher skills of Italian accountancy, then later directed him towards urgently needed sources of credit in Mary I's reign, Thomas refused to reciprocate. He was prepared to write to Cecil on his behalf. 'I am so bold,' he said, '[as] to send you a letter that my cousin Cioll hath written unto me, wherein I pray you, for my sake, as to help him to his money, if it be possible, in this his great necessity.'[55]

Asking Cecil to help Cioll was one thing; helping him himself was another. The most Thomas was prepared to do was to allow Cioll to move in with Cecily once the bailiffs had sequestered Crosby Place. Around 1573, it seems that Gresham would grant Cecily possession of one of the smaller properties on his Bishopsgate estate which he had purchased and not yet demolished, so she moved in there – but that was the extent of his generosity.[56] As he demonstrated with his sister-in-law Frances, whose annuity of £133 6s. 8d. he would later allow to fall into arrears, and his half-sister Christiana, who had stung him with her biting accusation of avarice, Thomas Gresham was never much of a family man if it cost him money.

ROYAL EXCHANGE

A s they approached their mid-forties, Renaissance rulers began to plan their legacy, and so did merchant princes. One of the many things Thomas Gresham would have discovered during his encounters abroad, if he had not already learned it at home, was that only those who commissioned some seriously good paintings or architecture during their lifetimes could be considered truly memorable. He might well have remembered from his studies at Gonville Hall the debate in classical literature about how to perpetuate one's fame. The question was, 'Which assures immortality more enduringly, a painting or a monument in stone?' Like Henry VIII when he had commissioned Hans Holbein the Younger to work on a large dynastic mural and associated panel paintings at Whitehall Palace, Gresham decided he would maximise his chances and have both.

Once the builders were at work at Gresham House and its brick and timber walls were rising above its foundations, Thomas took the first of a series of decisions in an evolving campaign to win lasting honour and reputation. He had long been an art connoisseur, who as early as the winter of 1544–5 had commissioned in Antwerp a mould-breaking full-length portrait of himself.

It was probably in 1563, while still active as Elizabeth's representative at Margaret of Parma's court in Brussels, that Gresham commissioned spectacular portraits of himself and Anne Ferneley from Anthonis Mor. (The usual date given for commissioning them is October 1564, when Mor was in Antwerp, making money from portraying 'les marchantz'. After Gresham left in January, however, he was not in Antwerp again for the whole of 1564, so could hardly have been painted then.) The finest, most technically accomplished portraitist in northern Europe, trained by the leading Netherlandish painter, Jan van Scorel, Mor had until very recently been Philip II's court artist and was now working independently. His distinctive style, which took elements from Titian and Giorgione as well as from the Flemish tradition of life painting, combined a genius for giving his sitters an appearance of authority that made people look up to them with an ability to create penetrating insights into their characters.

When giving Gresham his diplomatic credentials, Elizabeth had indicated that she would allow him to take Ferneley with him at government expense. In 1560, Ferneley had refused to go but by 1563 their relations had thawed. After the death of the couple's only son, Richard, in May that year, moreover, Ferneley had insisted on abandoning Intwood. So with Osterley not ready to receive her for another year, and with the plague still raging in London, it was an obvious choice for her to travel across the Channel with her husband. They took ship on 25 September, heading initially for Gresham's new house in the suburbs of Antwerp.[1] Whether the couple sat for their portraits in Antwerp or Brussels, we do not know, but either way, the most likely time of Mor's commission seems clear as the portraits could not have been done while the artist was working for Philip in Madrid.

Manifestly these remarkable images were painted from life. Infrared reflectography reveals the artist's underlying sketches, executed in black chalk. In Gresham's portrait, lines for the face, ear, eyes, nose and cheek can still be seen. The ruff on the collar is indicated by a quickly drawn line. Some light hatching indicates how contrasts of light and dark should be positioned, as on the forehead and knuckles. Ferneley's portrait has less by way of under-drawing and few lines are detectable in the face, cap, hands and clothing. Her cap and neckline were slightly adjusted by the artist, as were the folds in her sleeves and her chair's armrest. Small corrections can be seen to have been made by the artist to Gresham's hat and jacket while painting was in progress, while the fingers and thumb of Ferneley's right hand were slightly elongated.[2]

Thomas comes across as smooth and urbane. He seems more at ease than his wife, but his chin is determined and his pose is enigmatic. He wears an expensive black silk doublet and braided black cap and holds fine Spanish leather gloves. This is the look of a statesman and diplomat, as in many of Mor's other portraits. There are no signs of a merchant's mark or apparatus. Sitting upright on an x-frame chair like Mary I in Mor's portrait done for Philip II and now hanging in the Prado in Madrid, Thomas is the epitome of the merchant prince.

As to Ferneley, she looks somehow stiff in her chair as she stares out at us, fingering her gold chain. Her gown is of the most costly embroidered black silk and velvet, with a white silk partlet, square collar, wired Flemish hood and sleeves embellished with wrist ruffs. A pomander studded with pearls and maybe diamonds hangs loosely from her gold chain. Her three gold rings are set with an emerald, a cornelian and a sapphire respectively.

As to Gresham's monument in stone, it was probably in May 1563, while he and Ferneley were still at Intwood, mourning their dead son, that the mayor and aldermen of London first sent Lionel Duckett, a prominent silk merchant and up-and-coming city financier, 'to move Sir Thomas Gresham for and concerning his benevolence towards the making of a bourse and understanding his pleasure therein'.[3] The strong suggestion from the minute recording the decision is that, several months earlier, Gresham had floated the idea that he might one day fund the building of a bourse in London modelled on the one in Antwerp. Clearly, the idea did not arise wholly from the death of his son as is usually thought. In fact, proposals along almost identical lines had been made several times before in Henry VIII's reign by individual merchants or their livery companies, notably in 1518, 1521 and 1534. All of these had faltered, however.[4]

In 1538, during the final months of his mayoralty, Thomas's own father, Sir Richard Gresham, had written to Thomas Cromwell reminding him that he had lately shown him a well-ordered plan for just such a bourse to be built in Lombard Street. 'I do suppose,' he added, 'it will cost £2,000 and more, which shall be very beautiful to the city and also for the honour of our sovereign lord the king.'[5] Progress on that scheme had foundered too, chiefly because an inflexible private owner refused to sell the properties which the merchants had chosen as their preferred site. As a consequence, proposals for a bourse in Lombard Street fell into abeyance almost entirely for the next twenty years.[6]

In 1561, Richard Clough took up the cause in a letter written from Antwerp to Thomas Gresham. 'For indeed,' he declared, 'it is marvel that we have so good orders as we have ... considering what a city London is, and that in so many years they have not found the means to make a bourse, but must walk in the rain when it raineth, more like pedlars than merchants.' Clough held forth for over a page in this vein.[7]

Gresham was in no hurry: he took some twenty months to give Sir Lionel Duckett his considered response. On 4 January 1565, he at last sent Anthony Stringer, now his surveyor, to the mayor and aldermen with what looked like an unconditional offer to build a bourse at his own costs and charges, provided the city Corporation purchased and cleared a suitable site. An offer seemingly too good to refuse, it was quickly accepted. Four days later, after convening their various committees at an unprecedented speed, the city agreed that the bourse should be built on the site of certain houses standing between Lombard Street and the south side of Cornhill, the city's major east–west thoroughfare. Thomas, meanwhile, made it known that he meant 'to set such strangers [i.e., foreigners] to work on and about the making of the same bourse as to him shall be thought requisite and useful to be had for the accomplishment', to which end he sought the necessary work permits.[8]

Already, it seems, Gresham had it in mind to use a Flemish template and Flemish construction workers for his enterprise: his surveyor's earliest ground plan for the site survives in Cecil's archives on a large sheet of vellum, executed in pen and colour wash.[9] It shows a quadrangular courtyard with a columned arcade and two doorways, as well as two towers, each with a spiral staircase. From the outset, Thomas took his proposals forward in close consultation with Cecil, very much as he had during the general re-coinage at the beginning of Elizabeth's reign.

Once again the owner of the existing properties, in this instance the Merchant Taylors' Company, refused to sell, so an alternative site was selected, this time lying between the north side of Cornhill and Threadneedle Street, more or less directly opposite what is now the Bank of England. Much of it was owned by the dean and chapter of Canterbury, who were willing to sell. As the plot sizes must have been more or less the same for both sites, some 55 yards in length by 45 in breadth, the layout for the foundations as shown on Gresham's earlier ground plan did not need to be altered. The sum invested by the city on the purchase of freeholds was £2,208, but when the outstanding leases and sub-tenancies were bought out, eighty families rehoused and other fees and charges met, the total cost to the city climbed to £3,532 (over £3.5 million in modern values).[10]

From the evidence of Gresham's ground plan, it seems that he meant to replicate the main design features of the New Bourse at Antwerp, notably its spacious courtyard and upper storey complete with retail space for the sale of luxury goods, but in a more conspicuously classical style. To pull this off, he recruited the noted Hendryk van Paesschen of Antwerp as his master mason. Van Paesschen had been to Italy and his earliest works may have been some of the triumphal arches erected in Brussels

and Antwerp in 1549. He was very familiar with the main public buildings in Antwerp, not least from having overseen construction work on the
recently completed *stadhuis* there. Already it was clear that Gresham was
planning a building of an architectural grandeur that would be unrivalled
anywhere in London.

Before long the magistrates in Antwerp would be informed by
Hendryk's wife, Marie, that he was unable to appear before them, 'he of
necessity being in England, making and building there the bourse of the
merchants of London'.[11] And while the architectural drawings for Gresh-
am's Exchange are no longer extant, they were almost certainly made by
Cornelis Floris, with whom van Paesschen had worked on the *stadhuis*.
A passage in one of Clough's letters to Thomas clearly links their names.
As Clough explained, 'for the touch stone [i.e., hard black granite] you
send me [for], I can not write you answer by this my letter, for that both
Hendryk and Floris are both out of the town'.[12] It is just possible that
'Floris' here refers to Cornelis's brother, Frans, the painter and draught-
sman; however, the stylistic resemblance between the *stadhuis* and the
Royal Exchange makes this unlikely.[13]

Even before the existing properties on the site had been demolished
and the materials from the flattened houses sold or cleared, Gresham
began to backtrack. His philanthropy could only go so far. Suddenly, an
offer too good to refuse began to look suspiciously like one too good
to be true. At the outset it seemed as if he was genuinely seeking to use
his knowledge and experience to recalibrate the relationship between
Antwerp and London, building a bourse that could raise London's status
from a modest satellite of northern European trade to the metropolis.
Now he looked more interested in making money by renting out space in
a shopping mall.

On 7 January 1566, Sir William Garrard broke the news. One of the
wealthier elite who had abandoned Antwerp during the trade embargo of
1563–4 to invest in the slave trade, Garrard appeared before the mayor and
aldermen to explain that Gresham wanted to add cellars and vaults to the
Exchange, and to be unambiguously assured of his legal ownership of the
retail space in its upper storey 'to him and his heirs for ever'.[14]

Conscious of spiralling costs, Thomas was looking for ways to recoup
his hefty investment in building works from the future rents of around
a hundred small shops in the upper storey he was planning. The under-
ground vaults were to be for the use of the tenants as overflow retail space

and for the storage of their merchandise. Faced with his demands, the mayor and aldermen reluctantly agreed, with two provisos. First, Thomas should now solemnly promise to make over to the city the 'whole walk of [the] bourse [i.e., the central courtyard and its arcade]' where bankers, brokers, merchants and shipping insurers would be able to meet and make their deals. Secondly, the vaults he wanted were to be constructed 'so the doors be in the street side'.[15]

But this was just the beginning of the story. Disquiet intensified when Gresham made what, superficially, appeared to be a generous gesture rescinding much of what he had just asked for, but which, typically, had a sting in its tail. On 9 February, he promised that 'within one month next after the building and fully finishing of the bourse and bourse pawns [i.e., shops] and other buildings intended', he would, after all, legally assure to the city of London, should he die 'without issue of his body lawfully begotten', half the profits of the new Exchange *in its entirety* – shops, vaults and all – with the other half to the Mercers' Company, which was making a significant contribution to the cost of clearing the site. This conveyance, admittedly, was to take its full effect only after his and Anne Ferneley's deaths. But his co-investors, from then onwards, would reap their rewards in full, and in perpetuity.[16]

While Gresham's apparent change of tack delighted the members of the city Corporation, it marked, all the same, his first intimation to them that they were going to have to share the profits with the Mercers – assuming Thomas did what he said and gave either of them anything at all. And perhaps predictably, Thomas backtracked yet again: while he was willing to guarantee his building obligations by means of a recognisance of £5,000, he never did execute deeds which would have codified his gift of the new Exchange to the city and Mercers in anything approaching a mutually enforceable contract.[17]

Demolition work was completed by the end of May 1566, after which van Paesschen took possession of the site so that his men could 'fall in' with the foundations. Construction began on 7 June, when Thomas personally laid the first brick, watched by the city's elite, each of whom 'laid a piece of gold, which the workmen took up, and forthwith followed upon the same with great diligence'.[18] As has recently been observed, this 'propitious account' of the ceremony is decidedly sanitised.[19] Whether equipped with work permits or not, the men who gathered up the gold pieces were Flemings. The London bricklayers rose up in protest, and Gresham had an industrial dispute on his hands. There was picketing and a near-riot. At Gresham House later in the year, an unknown vandal defaced Thomas's coat of arms.

The city ended the quarrel by calling in the officers of the Bricklayers' Company, and then persuading Gresham to let local labourers have a fair share of the work. It was agreed that bricks would be sourced locally; Thomas would continue to import all of his ornamental stonework, marble pillars, paving stones and roofing slates from Antwerp, along with 40 tons of alabaster and much else, for which he already had a permit from Cecil.[20] Transporting ordinary bricks by river from the foundries at Battersea and oak beams from Suffolk or Hampshire was expensive enough for most London developers, but to ship entire boatloads of heavy masonry from Flanders was almost unbelievable to Gresham's fellow citizens, even the wealthiest of them. Only William Crow, the London bricklayers' unofficial shop steward, refused to stand in awe of such a feat. He was sent to prison to cool off 'for his very lewd demeanour towards Hendryk, the said Sir Thomas Gresham's chief workman there'.[21]

By the summer of 1567, Gresham was turning his mind to the finishing touches of the Exchange. On 17 August, Richard Clough reported, '[I have] received the pictures you write of, whereof I will cause the queen's majesty's to be made and will send you the rest back again with it so soon as it is done.'[22] A remark causing much later confusion to art historians, this meant that Thomas had sent his loyal factor either sketches or samples of the life-sized statues he meant to place around the inner façade of the courtyard at first-floor level, with the intention that the statue of Elizabeth alone should be sculpted at this stage. Clough, in particular, always described statues as 'pictures', such as when he informed Gresham in August 1566 that many of those 'pictures' shattered by the iconoclasts in Antwerp were images of saints, 10 feet high.[23]

According to the greatest Elizabethan expert on the city, the indefatigable annalist John Stow, Gresham's Exchange was finally covered with slate 'by the month of November in the year 1567 ... and shortly after fully finished'.[24] The main structure may well have been ready in time for Christmas 1567, since Gresham advised Cecil that, once the holidays were over, 'Hendryk, my workman', would go back to Antwerp, and not return until April.[25] 'Shortly after', on the other hand, is a very ambiguous phrase. A great deal of finishing off must have been needed, which may explain why the cartouche of one of the two earliest depictions of the Exchange by the doyen of Flemish engravers, Frans Hogenberg, gives '1569' as the completion date. Although themselves undated, these engravings were most likely first published in 1571.

No trace of Gresham's building survives today and little exists by way of contemporary description beyond Stow's observation that its brick and timber structure was roofed in slate, and the remarks of a visiting Frenchman, one 'L. Grenade'. He came to London in 1576 and put down his thoughts in a manuscript now in the Vatican Library. According to Grenade, merchants from all over Europe congregated together in different sections of the quadrangle and arcade from 11 a.m. to 12 noon, and again from 5 p.m. to 6 p.m. Estimated to be 80 paces long by 60 wide, the cobbled quadrangle was said to be large enough to hold 4,000 merchants. Grenade explains that because each nationality had its own part of the building, it was easy to locate foreign merchants and get business done. The Exchange was also a convenient place for the delivery of letters and messages, and an important hub for gathering news from abroad. Above the entrance on the south side, approached by steps off Cornhill, was a bell tower. A bell in its upper storey rang to alert the merchants to the times when the market opened, and again when business closed.[26]

Otherwise, the best depictions we have are Hogenberg's visual representations. Although somewhat idealised, these give more than a clue. Above and all around the arcade flanking the quadrangle was a large open gallery containing around a 120 or so boutique-sized shops, above which was an attic. A colonnade of marble Doric columns marked the boundary of the arcade, all supporting semicircular arches, each set with a plain keystone. The floor of the arcade beyond the colonnade was paved throughout with black and white marble, with a continuous stone bench set against the wall. Inside, a classical frieze of recumbent figures ran around the walls, perhaps cast from Gresham's 40 tons of alabaster. Along the colonnade, above each semicircular arch, was a niche with space for a statue of a king or emperor; only Elizabeth's statue was in place by the time the Exchange first opened for business and no more were purchased until a generation after Thomas's death.

Hogenberg gives a sense of the imposing classical double entrance to the Exchange on its south side, and of the bell tower, which had two projecting balconies and an open belfry. Surmounted by four ogee-shaped buttresses, it was crowned by a gigantic grasshopper. Other grasshoppers, either in lead or copper-gilt, were to be found clinging to any convenient perch: as finials at the ends of the roof ridges, on chimneys and on the attic dormers. A clock with face and hands was added in 1599.[27]

As to the first-floor open space that would shortly become England's earliest shopping mall, this was described by a German visitor in 1602 as 'a fine broad vaulted gallery, where may be bought almost everything a man may imagine by way of costly wares'.[28] Completely given over to retail outlets each approximately 7½ feet long and 5 feet wide, the Flemish-inspired design brought a cosmopolitan feel and offered a unique shopping experience to Londoners.[29]

Although Gresham had pledged that 'within one month next after the building and fully finishing of the bourse', he would make an outright grant of the entire buildings and profits of the new Exchange to the city and the Mercers' Company to take effect after his and his wife's deaths, it was a promise he did not even considering honouring until shortly before he died. If, however, his intended beneficiaries found that not everything could go their way, so did Thomas. He had always planned that his magnificent new edifice would be known by Londoners as 'the Bourse', or more affection-ately 'Gresham's Bourse', with his coat of arms prominently displayed over the entrance.[30] Instead, he received something of a put-down when, shortly after Christmas 1570, Elizabeth sent word that she would open it herself and rename it the 'Royal Exchange'. She meant to grant it a royal title, not as a favour to Gresham or to honour him, but to make it crystal clear to everyone, Englishmen and foreigners alike, that all matters of coinage and currency exchange in England were subject to her royal prerogative. They were not matters for a mere functionary like Gresham to claim as his own.

On the morning of 23 January 1571, the queen left Somerset House in the Strand where she had spent the night, attended 'with a great company and solemnity', and rode in her coach along Fleet Street, past St Paul's and into Cheapside. There, she would be greeted with loud cheers and great rejoicing by the citizens, 'since she had not entered the precincts of the city for two whole years on account of the plague'.[31] From Cheapside, she pro-gressed past the Stocks Market into Threadneedle Street, past the north side of the new Exchange, and on to Gresham House in Bishopsgate where Gresham and Anne Ferneley feasted her. She returned via Cornhill, so that she could enter the Exchange by its main entrance on the south side. After mounting the steps into the courtyard, she viewed 'every part thereof above the ground, especially the pawn [i.e., first-floor gallery], which was richly furnished with all sorts of the finest wares in the city'.[32]

A few hours later, once her curiosity was fully satisfied, she summoned a herald and a trumpeter, and – closely watched by the French ambassador and his guests – Gresham's bourse was 'proclaimed the Royal Exchange, and so to be called from henceforth, and not otherwise'. Now the royal arms would be emblazoned above the main entrance in Cornhill, with Gresham's squeezed in awkwardly at the side.[33]

At least Elizabeth's intervention yielded Gresham an unexpected dividend. Like many aspiring entrepreneurs who try something radically different in the retail sector, he had failed to lease more than a proportion of his floor space before her visit was announced, so that his gallery remained 'in a manner empty'. The moment she made her decision known, everything changed. On learning of her intentions, Thomas

> in his own person went twice in one day round about the upper pawn, and besought those few shopkeepers then present, that they would furnish and adorn with wares, and wax lights, as many shops as they either could or would, and they should have all those shops so furnished rent-free that year, which otherwise, at that time, was forty shillings a shop by the year.[34]

Almost instantly, Gresham secured enough takers to fill up his space, although if the shopkeepers thought they had a bargain, they would be sadly mistaken. Within two years, Thomas began hiking up the rents, so that within two or three more they would double to £4 10s. a year for every one of his shops. By then, he had attracted milliners, haberdashers, booksellers, goldsmiths and apothecaries selling everything from new and reconditioned armour, carpets, fine jewellery, glassware, books and musical instruments to mousetraps, bird cages, lanterns, shoe-horns and herbal remedies.[35]

Most disappointingly from Gresham's point of view, it would not be him but Cecil to whom Elizabeth, on 9 March 1575, would grant a royal patent as the 'keeper of the change, exchange and rechange in England and all the queen's dominions beyond the seas'. By this grant, Cecil gained an exclusive right to sell licences to merchants or brokers permitting them to engage in foreign exchange transactions either with the government or with one other. In addition, he was entitled to levy a small tax or duty on both buyer and seller for every financial instrument traded on the floor of the Royal Exchange, and to receive half of all forfeitures or penalties to the crown that were incurred on account of any prosecutions brought for illegal foreign exchange dealing.[36]

Naturally, Cecil promptly set about sub-licensing three London merchants, none of them Gresham, to perform these tasks as his agents in exchange for an annual rent. A subsequent royal proclamation restricted their charges by way of tax or duty to a maximum levy of 1½d. in the pound sterling imposed on each party to a transaction.[37] All the same, this meant that these three merchants are likely to have raked in at least half as much a year from their sub-licences as Gresham did from the rental income from his shops. How much was paid to Cecil is unknown, but receipts recorded by just one of the chief minister's agents covering a ten-month period in 1576–7 amounted to £71 13s. 10d. If that applied to all three agents, it would make their combined levies from fees and charges not less than £258 a year (more than £258,000 today).[38]

Gresham's Royal Exchange was to survive largely unchanged as the chief commercial focus of the city until it was destroyed during the Great Fire of London in 1666. But as the city and the Mercers' Company – both of whom had long memories where money was concerned – would shortly become aware, the project harboured the seeds of future conflict.

INTO THE BLACK

Throughout most of 1565, Thomas Gresham lived at Osterley or lodged with Richard Candeler in his London factor's office in Lombard Street, from where he could conveniently supervise his building works. While in the city, he made his bargains and negotiated foreign loans in his usual style, then left his Antwerp factor, Richard Clough, to follow his careful instructions. In May, Gresham advised Cecil that he was unable to meet him at Greenwich, where the chief minister was mulling over plans to open a silver mine in Cumberland, excusing himself on the grounds that he was entertaining 'divers of my kinsfolk' at Osterley.[1] Always he kept a tight rein on Clough, checking on the repayment and prolongation of the government's loans, and in particular closely monitoring fluctuations in interest rates.[2]

That year, once the trade embargo had been lifted and the markets reopened, turned out to be a record one for London's merchants in Antwerp. Normal trading with the Netherlands and Spain had resumed and the dearth of credit was suddenly replaced by a superfluity. Antwerp seemed to be swimming in cash. As Gresham informed Cecil in June, the advantage lay in checking the rates available in Germany and on Lombard Street too.[3] While Antwerp had been paralysed by the embargo, other markets had sprung up, notably in Hamburg, and Thomas found he could occasionally borrow more cheaply there. In any case, his policy of exploiting the strength of sterling after the general re-coinage, coupled with falling interest rates, meant that he had reduced Elizabeth's foreign debts to around £64,000 (over £64 million in modern values).[4] Government finances, overall, were for the first time modestly in surplus, as Cecil noted with obvious satisfaction in a series of private memos in May. From now on, it would be possible to send Gresham larger sums than before to expedite loan redemptions.[5]

During the winter of 1565–6, Elizabeth sought to speed up the negotiations in Bruges by appealing to Philip II to treat directly with her, ruler-to-ruler. She recalled Sir Thomas Chaloner as her ambassador in Madrid, sending in his place Dr John Mann with instructions to open the conversation. A prickly Oxford academic not well suited to the role, Mann landed at Bilbao on 17 March 1566 and reached Madrid on 3 April. Philip was too busy to see him, as he was supervising the planning and first phase of construction of his magnificent palace-monastery of San Lorenzo de El Escorial just outside the city, which he had designed to resemble Solomon's Temple. Only on 19 May could Mann secure an audience, after which it took the Spanish ruler until midsummer to respond to Elizabeth's request.[6]

While Gresham was awaiting news of Mann's mission, he spent the time on his own Spanish diplomacy, seeking to recover the losses he had sustained personally through overreaching himself in his ill-fated expedition to the fairs of Medina del Campo and Villalón in Mary I's reign, when several bankers had made themselves bankrupt owing him cash. In 1559, Elizabeth had capped these losses at £647, which Thomas had been obliged to reimburse.[7] Now, after years of searching, his agents in Spain, Edmond and Robert Hogan, assisted by Cecil's spy, William Fayre, who also worked for Chaloner and Gresham, had tracked down the offending parties and what a local bailiff believed to be their hidden assets. Hopeful of recovering half his loss by offering to write off the other half, Gresham sent his letters of attorney to Fayre, witnessed by Germain Cioll. 'I have thought good to commit this matter into your hands,' Thomas informed Fayre in a covering letter, 'and do send you herewith my procuration for the recovery thereof ... for I understand my said debtor[s] be sufficient to pay me.' Sadly for Thomas, they were not.[8]

By the summer of 1566, this setback paled into insignificance. Thomas was still in London, preparing to leave for his estate at Ringshall to select timber for his building projects, when Cecil received a highly disturbing letter from John Fitzwilliams, the Deputy Governor of the Merchant Adventurers, warning him that, since 24 June, Calvinist so-called 'hedge' preachers had been delivering open-air sermons to huge crowds in the fields outside Antwerp. Whipping up religious hysteria against Catholics and Lutherans alike, these preachers, several of whom had attracted hard-core radical supporters whom Richard Clough believed to be little more than thugs, were even agitating for violence.[9] Moreover, the euphoria following the successful restoration of trade had not been sustained: buyers for English cloths were suddenly few again. Fitzwilliams strongly advised that if the English merchants 'stayed [i.e., ceased] shipping for a time, in my simple opinion they should not do amiss'.[10]

By July, the numbers attending these impromptu Calvinist rallies had risen above 20,000, and their leaders began to demand the right to deliver sermons within the city walls.[11] A crisis loomed in Antwerp, made worse by severe shortages of bread following a disastrous harvest in 1565 and war in the Baltic region that hindered the usual imports of grain. To be on the safe side, Cecil and Lord Treasurer Winchester allocated Gresham £4,900 in cash from the exchequer 'for the provision of grain' from East Anglia, where the harvest had been plentiful.[12] Well aware of their hardship, Thomas offered the Antwerp magistrates a large shipment of wheat, barley and rye to relieve their distress, but the offer was refused: his proposed profit margin was just too exorbitant.[13]

During such difficult times, the poverty, crime and violence stirred earlier by the embargo returned. A rumour that the regent, Margaret of Parma, planned to send in troops to quell the preachers sparked an explosion. Eyewitness reports from Richard Clough, written over a six-week period beginning on 10 July 1566 and delivered to Thomas at Ringshall before he quickly forwarded them on to London, were to shock everyone who read them.[14]

In a series of graphic bulletins, one of which was marked 'haste, haste, haste, post-haste, haste' to avoid all ambiguity as to its urgency, Clough described how 'here hath been and is presently a marvellous stir, not only here, but throughout all the country'. Roving gangs of troublemakers incited the insurgents, and Clough presciently compared the events unfolding before his eyes to the outbreak of the struggle between the Huguenots and the Guises in 1562.[15] The rising in Antwerp, however, turned out to be far more of a populist insurrection. At Armentières near the French frontier it was ordered that 'no man should go to the sermon upon pain of hanging, whereupon on Sunday in the morning went out of the town to the sermon above 16,000 persons, all with their weapons in battle array'. After the sermon, they 'returned into the town, and went to the head bailiff's house, whom had taken one preacher prisoner two or three days before, and commanded him to deliver the prisoner, which he refused. Whereupon they went to the prison and brake it, and delivered the preacher, and so every man departed.'[16]

On 4 August 1566, Clough reported that the Calvinists were buying all the horses and weapons they could lay their hands on with money subscribed by members of their congregations. In Brussels, he added, Prince William of Orange had presented a petition to Margaret of Parma on behalf of the nobles, asking why it was that the Catholics were said to be raising mercenaries in Germany, but she refused to answer it. She 'feigneth sick' and 'hath sent away all her jewels and plate to Cologne, and would gladly be gone herself'.[17] Another bulletin from Clough, sent on the 11th, predicted ominously that blood would soon be spilt. 'And if there be once bloodshed, then the stir will begin. God be merciful unto them, and to us all, for and if they do once begin, it will be a bloody time.'[18]

It was this worrying report which caused Gresham to rush back from Suffolk to London. Even as Clough was putting pen to paper in Antwerp on the morning of the 21st, Thomas was packing his chest, ready to ride to Dover later in the week to take ship for Brabant.[19] He left London on the 23rd, accompanied by the faithful John Spritewell, only to receive, 'being within one mile of Rochester ... at twelve of the clock this night', Clough's final, most explicit bulletin, which had made its journey from Antwerp in a record two days.[20]

As Clough reported, on the evening of the 20th, 'all the churches, chapels and houses of religion [were] utterly defaced, and no kind of thing left whole within them, but broken and utterly destroyed'.[21] The iconoclasts did not spare Antwerp's chief jewel, the Church of Our Lady, with its prized altarpieces and sculptures, many by the acknowledged masters of the Flemish Renaissance. It did not seem to matter that a majority of these artworks had been paid for by the subscriptions of ordinary members of the guilds and crafts of the city and stood in the nave, or main body, of the church rather than in the chancel, and so could have been seen and enjoyed by everyone.

At five o'clock in the evening, said Clough, as the priests began to sing their plainsong, a group of rowdy hoodlums had bawled out Calvinist psalms. When rebuked and ordered to leave by the magistrates, they refused and were joined by reinforcements, who at about six o'clock 'brake up the choir, and went and visited all the books; whereof, as it is said, some they saved and the rest [they] utterly destroyed and broke'.

Next, they attacked 'the image of Our Lady, which had been carried about the town on Sunday last, and utterly defaced her and her chapel, and after the whole church, which was the costliest church in Europe, and have so spoiled it that they have not left a place to sit on in the church'. Some then went to the nearby parish churches, others to the monasteries and nunneries, 'and made such dispatch as, I think, the like was never done in one night, and not so much to be wondered at of the doing, but that so few people dared or could do so much'. 'After dark,' as Clough concluded, 'when I saw that all should be quiet, I, with above 10,000 more, went into the churches to see what stir was there'.

> Coming in to Our Lady church, it looked like a hell, where were above 10,000 torches burning, and such a noise as if heaven and earth had gone together, with falling of images and beating down of costly works; [in] such sort, that the spoil was so great that a man could not well pass through the church. So that, in fine, I cannot write you in ten sheets of paper the strange sight I saw there, organs and all, destroyed.[22]

On reading this litany of destruction, Thomas ordered Spritewell immediately back to London to take Clough's letter to Cecil, hastily scribbling a covering note, written 'at one of the clock after midnight'.[23] Naturally, it was less the iconoclasm that so alarmed Gresham as the prospect of a complete collapse of law and order in Antwerp, and therefore of trade and the bourse. As he warned the chief minister, 'it will alter all money matters, whereby I shall find no money for the payments of my bills of exchange'.[24]

Thomas's immediate problem, and the reason his presence was vital in Antwerp, was that the end of August was the critical date for repaying or prolonging a significant proportion of Elizabeth's outstanding foreign loans, and these were absolute cut-off points, otherwise the government would be in default and the value of sterling would plunge. Gresham had reduced the queen's immediate liability in this particular credit cycle to £34,386 in Flemish currency (around £30,000 sterling), but she and Cecil had also ordered him to borrow an extra £20,000.[25] As Clough's bulletins explained, it would be impossible to raise this level of credit in a market operating under siege, assuming it was functioning at all.

Frustratingly for Gresham, once he had found a ship, his sea crossing took him a full four days: he arrived in Antwerp at 5 p.m. on the afternoon of 29 August and was lucky to get inside the walls as 'there is great watch both of men of war and other, and the gates these two days hath been locked, no man to go out'.[26] Sooner than Clough had feared, though,

Thomas was able to get things working, prolonging the whole of Elizabeth's debts for six months and borrowing a further £13,700 in Flemish currency, mainly from south German bankers, chiefly Christopher Welser of Augsburg. But finding the rest of the extra £20,000 sterling she wanted was another matter – this despite Thomas organising lavish hospitality for her creditors, obviously at her expense.[27]

At first, Margaret of Parma offered concessions to the insurgents: for a very brief interval, she suspended the Inquisition and allowed the Calvinists to continue to preach freely in the fields. This defused the immediate crisis, but many wealthy merchants were fleeing the city, and as the news of the destruction began to spread, Philip II, closeted in Madrid, hardened his heart. Even before the full extent of the crisis became known there, his advisers made it plain, as Thomas informed Cecil, that he 'would have the churches made up again and would have mass sung and ... for every man to go to mass that would'. Worse, at least from the viewpoint of trade, no Englishman 'shall be suffered to come unto the town of Brussels, which maketh our Englishmen to provide for the packing of themselves and their goods away, as the most part of all other wealthy merchants here hath already done the like'.[28]

Elizabeth and Cecil closely monitored events. They were dumbstruck when Philip coolly and deliberately announced his decision to disown Margaret of Parma's concessions and reimpose the Inquisition, ordering the full force of canon law and the auto-da-fé to be turned against the Calvinists. Gresham was to become deeply embroiled in these menacing developments. On 2 September, William of Orange, fast emerging as the leader of the Protestant cause in the Netherlands, defied the regent, proclaiming an accord in Antwerp which granted Calvinists and Lutherans safe places for their worship and promised not to admit an outside garrison without the consent of the magistrates.

Gresham worried that it might not be enough. He had written the previous day to Cecil: 'I fear me this business doth now but begin, which here is much doubted [meaning "not doubted"] that it will grow to much slaughter without God's help.' He believed that Orange had genuinely meant to mediate in the interests of peace, but the Catholics would be suspicious of his motives. When they gathered their strength, they would exact their reprisals: 'whatsoever outward face he [Orange] showeth to the papists, he is in heart a right Protestant'.[29]

Two days later, Gresham was invited to dinner by Orange and his wife, 'who gave me very great entertainment'. Orange told him 'that now he had agreed with the Protestants', but Philip II 'would not be content with these our doings' and Gresham once again expressed his fears, 'which causeth me to think that this matter is not yet ended, but like to come to great mischief, and especially if the King of Spain may get the upper hand'.[30] Orange asked Gresham whether the English merchants were inclined to leave the town or not. Gresham replied that he had not heard such things, but to Cecil he was more candid. 'Your honour', he wistfully told him, 'shall do very well in time to consider some other realm and place for the utterance of our commodities that is made within our realm ... which in this brabbling time is one of the chiefest things your honour hath to look unto, considering in what terms this country doth now stand, in which is ready one [*sic*] to cut another's throat for matter of religion.'[31]

Gillis Hooftman, a wealthy Antwerp merchant and one of the queen's leading creditors who would soon be importuning Clough for repayment of what was owed to him, was another dinner guest. A staunch Calvinist, he asked Gresham, 'How think you, Mr Gresham, forasmuch as the queen's majesty and her realm is of this religion, think you that she giveth aid to our noblemen as she did in France for the religion's sake?' It was the $64,000 question. Wisely, Gresham answered, 'I was no counsellor, nor never dealt with such great matters.'[32] He was walking on eggshells. While Orange and his allies had no hesitation in asking for Elizabeth's unambiguous support for the Protestant cause, he was all too aware – both from Cecil's comments and his own observations – that she was hardly a willing ally of the Calvinists, whom she repeatedly infuriated with lectures on their duties of obedience to lawful princes and on the threats of insurgent republicanism.

Despite having raised little more than half of the new borrowing he sought, Gresham left Antwerp in mid-September. 'I have gone through all the money men by one practice or other and especially with all them which I was wont to deal withal,' he confided, 'of whom there was not a penny to be had.'[33] After returning the compliment by inviting Orange to a banquet at his country house along with William's wife, his brother and other relatives and friends, Thomas staged a bold theatrical display, carefully calculated to maintain confidence in his dark wizardry. Quite simply, he called on all his friends from the bourse and let them know 'that I have no more need of money, and that I have contented all of the creditors, which is most convenient for me so to do as the time now requireth'.[34]

Where salvaging his reputation was concerned, no lie was better than a big one.

With many of Antwerp's smaller bankers now declaring insolvency, was Thomas's banking career now over too? To the obvious irritation of his fellow Merchant Adventurers, Gresham was purposefully unavailable in Antwerp over the winter of 1566–7, while he attended to his own affairs in London. Elizabeth nonetheless instructed him to return in February 1567, when he was to discharge all her debts about to fall due for repayment or prolongation.[35]

On the face of it, the task was impossible, except Cecil in the end allowed Gresham to do much of it the easy way. Considering that the pound sterling was still strong and the queen had the funds, the chief minister decided that Thomas should travel accompanied by an armed escort and a chest full of 'gold current moneys', which he was to use 'to content and pay thereunto our creditors, as well such as ought to have payment this February as the others that ought to have payment in June'. 'Gold,' Cecil mused, 'will extend at the best value thereof in Antwerp.'[36] As a result, after converting his gold coins into Flemish currency, Gresham handed over to Elizabeth's creditors a total of £29,908 (around £25,670 sterling) 'in full payment of these debts' – an astonishing result, but one that in this instance owed nothing to his skills as a market manipulator.[37]

For all that, he could not escape the worsening political situation. Even before disembarking from his ship, Gresham found himself petitioned by the leaders of the Dutch reformed church, who blithely imagined he could persuade Elizabeth to lend her weight and her money to the Calvinist cause.[38] Meanwhile, all Europe was ablaze with news of the assassination at Kirk O'Field in Edinburgh of Henry, Lord Darnley, second husband of Mary queen of Scots. Thomas met William of Orange again, who introduced him to his close ally, Philippe de Montmorency, count of Hoorn, a member of the council of state in Brussels. What was happening in Scotland? they asked; and what steps would Elizabeth take to secure the safety of the Protestant state in England? All believed she should marry, and Orange drew Thomas into a discussion of the pros and cons of various candidates. The most credible of these was still the Archduke Charles, for whom Cecil had declared his support.[39] But Thomas had to be careful – his previous forays into this taboo topic had not served him well, and he knew that of all the subjects Orange raised with him, this – from an English perspective – was by far the most delicate.[40]

On 9 March 1567, Gresham heard from his spies that some 40,000 Protestants in Antwerp were prepared to die for their faith, while Margaret of Parma had mustered some 16,000 infantry and 3,000 cavalry, many of them Spanish-trained. He predicted there would soon be 'much slaughter'.[41] Shortly afterwards, he personally witnessed terrifying events that went some way to prove it. The regent's troops were now but a few leagues from the city, with orders to suppress the insurgency. The Calvinists, who felt their lives and their property were in peril, threatened a coup. Peace overtures were begun, once more brokered by Orange, but although the Calvinists were guaranteed a share in the defence of the city, they were heavily outnumbered.

Gresham praised Orange's efforts, reassuring Cecil that 'the prince very nobly hath travailed, both night and day, to keep this town from manslaughter and from despoil'.[42] But Orange could not stop the advance of the regent's forces. In fear, the Calvinists took up arms: Thomas found shelter on 13 March, when a pitched battle between Catholic troops and a large number of Calvinists took place at Oosterweel on the Scheldt, just a few miles from Antwerp. Despite commanding some 1,200 infantry, the Calvinists lacked cavalry support and were heavily outnumbered. After a five-hour onslaught, they were put to flight and this seemed to be a turning point. All over the Netherlands, Calvinist worship ceased. Towns that had defied Philip II hurried to make their peace, and many frightened Calvinists and their supporters fled into exile abroad.[43]

In Antwerp, there was uproar. Vast crowds of people of all nationalities and beliefs poured onto the streets, angry with both the regent and the Calvinists for the divisions they were causing. Gresham witnessed it all, reporting that the Lutherans stayed loyal to the magistrates and joined the Catholics in resisting the Calvinists, who unwisely regrouped with their artillery 'before the town house [Gresham's name for the *stadhuis*] and in Our Lady's churchyard, so that there was [*sic*] six men for one against the Calvinists, which they knew well enough'.[44] Once more the Calvinists were routed. After that, order was, for a short while, restored.

Gresham found this experience searing. He lost no time in making it clear to Cecil that Antwerp had become too dangerous for him, 'for that I saw never men so desperate, willing to fight'.[45] On top of this, he was increasingly dismayed by what he considered to be Elizabeth's failure to give him the rewards he felt were rightfully his.

Writing to her from Antwerp in September 1566, Thomas had again dropped the broadest of hints, appealing to her 'to have some consideration of my service whereby I may be the better able to serve you in my old days'.[46] Given the risks he knew he was facing, he was sorely vexed by the fact that all she ever seemed to have on her mind was a shopping list – most recently for another horse, silk scarves, yet more 'collars' and 'a sword set with diamonds'.[47] The last she had ordered during a stay at Lord Admiral Clinton's house at Sempringham in Lincolnshire during her summer progress earlier the same year, when Gresham had attended on her. As Thomas tetchily briefed Cecil, the sword 'at my coming to Antwerp' was sent to Frankfurt for safety 'by the reason of the great brabbling that was in Antwerp'. He would have to get it back from there, and until he did, the queen would have to wait.[48]

Thomas followed up by sending Cecil yet another comprehensive résumé of his services since 1551, and of the sums he had borrowed and repaid in Antwerp and on Lombard Street since Elizabeth's accession, declaring:

> And as this is the thirty-first journey of charge that I have passed the seas for her majesty ... and as her majesty did promise me by the faith of a queen in your presence when I took this great charge upon me, that if I did her but the service as I did to her sister and brother, or to one of them, she would give me as much land as them both did ... it may please her of her royal goodness now in mine old days to have the like consideration of my service as her brother and sister had.[49]

It still stuck in Gresham's throat that the promise she had made to him at Hatfield in 1558, when he had kissed her hand and she confirmed him in his post as government banker, had yet to be redeemed. To add insult to injury, rumours were rife that he was in Antwerp to hand over large sums to William of Orange and the Calvinists to raise an army, which made him vulnerable to arrest and imprisonment by the regent or Philip II's agents. 'Sir,' he confided to Cecil, 'I will assure your honour, this town is in [a] very hard case, and happy is the man that is out of it.'[50]

Back in London, Gresham heard from Clough that Philip, despite the victory of Margaret of Parma's troops at Oosterweel, had made up his mind to dismiss her and replace her as regent with the notoriously ruthless Fernando Álvarez de Toledo, duke of Alva. When that news broke, Thomas resolved that he would never himself return. Instead, he would direct the queen's affairs in Antwerp through Clough and his assistants. The best intelligence had it that Alva, Spain's toughest and most experienced general, was to be sent at the head of a newly recruited Spanish army of Flanders with orders to fuse the seventeen provinces of the Netherlands into a unitary state, and with Brussels as its capital.

On 22 August 1567, Alva made his grand processional entry into Brussels at the head of 12,000 crack troops. With that fatal turn of events, the game would completely change. No longer a series of relatively localised skirmishes over the rights of the Calvinists to preach or of the nobles to retain their privileges, it signalled the beginning of the full-scale revolt against Spain known as the Eighty Years' War or Dutch War of Independence. So began Elizabeth's cold war with Spain.

MARRYING OFF
A DAUGHTER

Over the winter of 1566–7, Gresham remained almost continuously at Gresham House to keep an eye on the building works at his new Exchange.[1] Now fully settled into the opulent surroundings of his city mansion, he became a topic of gossip for his flamboyant hospitality. Given Anne Ferneley's desire for social status this probably served to bring her and Thomas closer together. On her visits to Buxton, Ferneley rubbed shoulders with several of the nobility or their wives, striking up a familiarity with George Talbot, earl of Shrewsbury, the owner of the spa and much of the town. One of the richest landowners in England, the husband of the famous 'Bess of Hardwick' and the custodian of Mary queen of Scots for fifteen years, the earl was closer to Elizabeth, Cecil and just about the whole of privy council than most other noblemen besides Lord Hunsdon, the queen's cousin.

Privy councillors, nobles, fellow merchants and diplomats, including the French ambassador, regularly dined with the Greshams in Bishopsgate. Notable foreign guests included Odet de Coligny, cardinal de Châtillon, the recently excommunicated brother of two of the most prominent Huguenot leaders, who had fled to England to seek asylum and raise funds for the Protestants in the French Wars of Religion. Landing at Dover on 8 September 1568, de Coligny made his way to London, where a week later, on Cecil's instructions, Gresham greeted him as he disembarked from his barge at Tower wharf and escorted him to Gresham House. There he stayed for a week, until Elizabeth was ready to receive him.[2]

Through such hospitality, Thomas became better acquainted with his neighbours, who included several of London's elite. He already knew Alderman William Bond, the new owner of Crosby Place, purchased from the bankrupt Germain Cioll. Gresham and Bond had been on familiar terms since 1553, when they had joined a syndicate of investors in a pro-posed voyage to discover a north-eastern passage to China through the Arctic Ocean and the Bering Sea. Three ships had sailed from Tilbury in Essex, two of which foundered in the intense cold off the coast of northern Lapland, but a third, captained by Richard Chancellor, made it safely into the White Sea. The result was that Chancellor finally reached Moscow and was able to negotiate a trade agreement with the tsar, Ivan the Terrible. The Muscovy Company incorporated as a joint-stock enterprise, to which Mary I granted a royal charter in 1555.[3]

Now one of London's wealthiest grandees, Bond and his wife, Mar-garet, were parishioners at the church of St Helen's in Bishopsgate, as were Thomas and Anne Ferneley. Intriguingly, Bond was far less controlling a husband than Thomas: he regarded his wife very much as a partner in his business, which she went on to run singlehandedly for ten years after his death. A zealous Protestant, whose charitable bequests included twelve sermons 'for the edifying of well disposed people in the said parish church of [St] Helen upon twelve several Sundays', Margaret Bond would later be recorded in tax assessments as second only to Thomas as the richest resident in the parish.[4]

Another neighbour and familiar acquaintance was the retired dip-lomat Sir William Pickering, one of very few Londoners affluent enough to own his own coach pulled by two horses and once (highly implaus-ibly) mentioned as a possible husband for the young Queen Elizabeth.[5] His fine mansion, Pickering House, stood in the adjacent parish of St Andrew Undershaft, but he too worshipped regularly at St Helen's. As with Gresham, Pickering's career had taken off after encounters with John Dudley, duke of Northumberland. In the later years of Edward VI's reign, Pickering had been the resident English ambassador in France, and in the spring of 1558 Mary I sent him to represent her at Philip II's court in Brussels, while Thomas was in Antwerp. They had met several times and always found something new to talk about. At one rendezvous at Dunkirk, Gresham found Pickering 'sore sick' and 'in danger of his life' from the effects of a burning ague, but was unable to stay as long as he would have liked as he had money to carry back to Antwerp.[6]

Unlike Thomas, who kept his illegitimate daughter well out of sight and never once mentioned her in letters to Cecil or Dudley, Pick-ering treated his own natural daughter, Hester, as his legitimate heir. He would soon be leaning over backwards to write his will in such a way that, despite her birth and gender, she should receive a proper education and inherit the lion's share of his estate. Liberal-minded, cosmopolitan and extremely well-connected to writers, academics and artists as much as to Cecil and Dudley, Pickering appointed a group of powerful courtiers and other London citizens as his executors to make sure that Hester got her full entitlement.[7]

Gresham, on the other hand, tended only to befriend those who could profit him sooner or later. He could spot talent when he saw it, and the rising star he chose to be his new lawyer and confidant was Roger Manwood, the smartest, toughest barrister in London, who aroused the strongest of feelings for his alleged sharp practice in conveyancing.[8] Thomas had discovered him in 1564, when he tried him out as his advocate in the court of Chancery to see off the aggrieved tenants of Anne Ferneley's manor of Beccles. In response to Gresham's aggressive tactics when managing the Ferneley inheritance, the tenants had risen up in protest and brought a collective lawsuit against him, alleging that he falsely claimed to own large tracts of their common land.[9]

With Manwood by his side, Thomas defeated the tenants.[10] He could hardly lose, since Manwood appears to have denied his opponents access to the documents they sought to prove their case, although Thomas for once had to step out of the shadows in court proceedings and swear on oath to the truth of the assertions Manwood made on his behalf.[11] By way of thanks, Gresham urged Cecil 'to have my friend Mr Manwood in remembrance and the warrants for four bucks and one stag that heretofore I have molested you withal'. But it would be an uphill struggle, since Cecil harboured a growing antipathy for Manwood – they would regularly cross swords, notably after 1572, when Manwood secured advancement to the judiciary.[12] Rather than expressing his pleasure at Manwood's promotion, however, Gresham secretly asked Robert Dudley to block it: he would have been better suited if Manwood had been made one of Elizabeth's special counsel, as in that capacity he could continue to defend Thomas in court.[13]

Gresham always kept his religious beliefs almost entirely private, but after Elizabeth had ruled for almost a decade, he felt it safe enough to disclose his broad inclinations. To provide themselves with regular weekly sermons from someone they wanted to hear, twenty-four of the hundred or so parishioners of St Helen's joined forces to hire a special lecturer to preach on Sundays after the end of the regular services. Such lecturers were usually Calvinist in leaning, and it is likely Thomas shared these sympathies, since the churchwardens' accounts prove that his yearly contribution towards the salary of the lecturer was forty shillings, double that of Alderman Bond and a larger sum than subscribed by any other parishioner.[14]

Thomas then paid 6s. 8d. 'for his licence to eat flesh', which suggests that he refused to switch almost exclusively to a fish diet on Wednesdays, Fridays and Saturdays and during the forty days of Lent as an act of Parliament decreed. His payment was 'put into the poor men's box according to the statute'.[15] Such statutes and proclamations were, however, chiefly designed to protect the commercial interests of the fishing industry and were not overtly religious in intent.[16]

Whether or not Gresham was privy to the appointment, in 1570, of the twenty-five-year-old Luke Clapham as the new parish minister at St Helen's is unknown, but as Clapham was ordained by Edmund Grindal, an exile in the reformed city of Strasbourg in Mary's reign, he would have been at the cutting edge of Protestantism. As bishop of London, Grindal made it his mission to replace the 'dumb dogs' of the capital's pulpits with 'godly' preaching pastors of a staunchly Calvinist inclination. For this and his subsequent choices, Elizabeth would come to regard Grindal as a covert fifth columnist, and later an illicit and dangerous revolutionary. The mere fact that Thomas continued to worship at St Helen's once Clapham was in charge is a signal that he came to hold (or at least could readily tolerate) more advanced Protestant convictions.[17]

A final hint suggestive of Gresham's religious preferences came a century after his death, when the last complete edition of John Foxe's multi-volume Protestant martyrology and history of the church, the *Acts and monuments* (or 'Book of Martyrs'), appeared in 1684. Prefaced in its first volume by a brief biography of Foxe, the anonymous author explained that Gresham had always held Foxe 'in great account and estimation, being part of them such as had born the highest places of honour in the city'.[18] If the report is accurate, it thus placed Thomas alongside those like Cecil, who after Elizabeth's accession had been keen to see the first edition of this massive martyrology in print, and were prepared to offer financial support to help bring it about. Beyond this, the sources – notably Thomas's letters – are completely silent.

It was probably when Gresham returned to Antwerp for the last time in March 1567 that he commissioned duplicate portraits of himself to add to those already hung in his houses. Dendrochronology suggests that the wood for the panel support of one of these duplicates dates from at any time between 1546 and 1578. The usually suggested date is *c*.1565, but since Gresham appears to have aged considerably since he was painted by Anthonis Mor in 1563, a date of 1567 is more credible. Once more he seems to have searched out artists who, like Mor, had been trained by the leading Netherlandish painter, Jan van Scorel.[19] The two paintings are almost identical, but neither is a copy of the other. In each case, preliminary sketches lie beneath the paint surfaces in exactly the same places, but the paint-handling technique is different. This suggests that the portraits are from the same studio but by different artists.[20] Very likely Gresham's plan was to hang one version of this new portrait-type at Osterley, the other at Mayfield; one presumes the spectacular portraits of Thomas and his wife by Mor would have had pride of place in the great hall or in one of the long galleries at Gresham House.

Depicted three-quarter-length against a dark-brown background, Gresham assumes a commanding pose. Although portrayed more as a knight than a merchant, he lacks his coat of arms. Standing slightly to the left, he loosely fingers his purse with his right hand, while his left rests on the hilt of his sword. One of the main places where both artists made last-minute changes is in the hand on the purse. Originally, Thomas's hand tightly clenched the purse, but this was changed to a more relaxed posture. Such adjustments may well indicate Gresham's direct involvement, as he would have been well aware that clenched fingers over the purse had unwelcome associations with avarice.[21]

Gresham now appears well into middle age, though his beard and moustache have not yet turned grey. His face is tired and wrinkled; his brown eyes lack their usual sparkle. He seems to be losing some of his passion for life: he looks slightly unkempt, as if he no longer had time to visit his barber, yet his fashionable clothes advertise his wealth. He wears a black slashed silk doublet flecked with gold, a black velvet gown and a black cap. His cap and doublet are adorned with gold buttons, while the slashes in the doublet, anchored by a gold chain, open just wide enough to expose a gold-embroidered silk trim or lining.

The years 1568 and 1569 marked the beginning of the duke of Alva's reign of terror in the Netherlands. They were also the ones in which Gresham set himself the task of marrying off (and, in his eyes, making respectable) his daughter. Unlike his friend Pickering, who treated his natural daughter like any loving father would treat a child and who, by making her his unrestricted heir, left her free to marry the man of her choice, Thomas paid scant attention to young Anne's feelings. It seems that he wanted her off his hands as quickly and as cheaply as possible, arranging for her to be married as soon as the law allowed.

By canon law, a girl could be married as young as twelve, although most parents considered fifteen to be the absolute minimum.[22] Sixteen was relatively common, twenty-one relatively late. Thomas's manoeuvres to marry Anne off to one of the sons of Sir Nicholas Bacon, his erstwhile brother-in-law and guardian of his elder stepson, were to begin when she was no more than thirteen. The bridegroom was to be the twenty-three-year-old Nathaniel, Sir Nicholas's second son by his first wife, Jane Ferneley. Although Jane was dead and Sir Nicholas had married Anne Cooke, Cecil's sister-in-law, Thomas had taken care to keep up the connection, especially once Elizabeth made Sir Nicholas lord keeper of her great seal.

Educated under his father's, and perhaps more significantly his formidable stepmother's, watchful eyes, Nathaniel had studied for a year at Trinity College, Cambridge in 1561–2, before training as a lawyer at Gray's Inn.[23] Originally, the plan seems to have been that he should marry Thomasine, the daughter and sole heir of John Copledike of Kirby Cane in Norfolk. A recently discovered letter from Sir Nicholas to Nathaniel's elder brother, written in July 1568, suggests that a betrothal was not far away. Then things unexpectedly changed.[24] By April 1569, Sir Nicholas was searching for a different wife for his son. Gresham stepped in. On 29 June, a special dispensation was secured from Archbishop Matthew Parker of Canterbury, possibly on account of Anne's age. The wedding may also have been rushed, because the dispensation authorised it to take place without the reading of the customary church banns, and it could be held without regard to the dates or times of the year at which marriages were normally prohibited by canon law, including Septuagesima, Advent, the week after Easter or Rogationtide.[25]

Nathaniel and his young bride were married in July 1569.[26] The records of the arrangements, still tucked away in the archives, reveal just how devious Thomas could be where money was involved. Barely was Anne's dowry successfully negotiated, the marriage contract signed and sealed and the wedding over, than Nathaniel discovered to his dismay that the lands Thomas had promised the young couple were not given outright as he assumed they would be. These were the east Suffolk manor of Combs, near Stowmarket; the north Norfolk manors of Morston and Langham; and the east Norfolk manor of Hemsby with the parsonage there. Between them, they should have yielded the bride and bridegroom an annual income of some £280 a year (over £280,000 in modern values). Instead, shortly before the wedding, Gresham, assisted in legal matters by his new friend Roger Manwood, signed and sealed an indenture retaining a life interest in these properties, then promptly leased as many of them as he could to tenants, collecting large upfront premiums for himself, so that only correspondingly lower rents amounting to £100 were due to the Bacons, and even those were payable only at Gresham's discretion.[27]

At best, Thomas had misled the Bacons, at worst swindled them. It was this 'strange dealing', as Sir Nicholas euphemistically put it, that prompted him to say of Thomas, 'but this is not the first [time], for myself was as ill dealt withal in the beginning and worse. Where no good faith is kept, there ought to be no trust'. It turns out that a latent animosity between Gresham and the bridegroom's father went right back to the family's days in Basinghall Street, when Sir Nicholas had lodged there. As Sir Nicholas confided to his son-in-law, the lawyer Francis Wyndham, 'these merchants would never perform their promises when it came to the push'.[28]

When criticising Gresham, though, one had to tread warily, for Thomas, it seems, was quick to take offence. As Sir Nicholas advised his son, 'how so ever these things be, you must for a time endure it without finding any fault and to seek an humble and courteous manner by suit to recover that which in honesty and truth pertains to you'.[29] In an effort to steal a march on his father-in-law, Nathaniel asked his younger brother, Edward, to 'keep his ears open' in London and learn as much as possible to his advantage as he could. He also sought Francis Wyndham's assistance and prompted Sir Nicholas to speak again to Gresham about the disputed title and outstanding rents.[30]

So young was Nathaniel's bride, she was at first sent to Sir Nicholas's main house at Gorhambury, near St Albans, in Hertfordshire for six months or so. There, she was placed under Anne Cooke's tutelage. As Nathaniel declared, 'for it were good for me, better for my wife, and meet for us both so to be brought up as, hereafter, the one might have best liking of the other'.[31] But this transitional period was not merely to introduce Anne gradually to her new husband so that they would later be able to share a bed; it was also to provide her with the rudimentary literacy Gresham and Anne Ferneley had so shamefully neglected to give her.

Nathaniel later reflected in a letter to his stepmother:

Your ladyship knoweth how, being matched in marriage as I am, it stood me upon to have some care of the well bringing up of my wife, for these words of Erasmus are very true: 'It is better to be well educated than to be well born'. If she should have had the want of both, I had just cause to fear what might befall. Hereupon, being not able to remedy the one, I did as much as in me lay to provide for the other, and therefore I sought by all the means I could to have her placed with your ladyship.[32]

Since Anne Cooke and her sister Mildred were numbered among the most learned women of their generation, and both championed the cause of female education, one may assume that Cooke concurred.

Not that much could be done in six months. Of the surviving letters written by Nathaniel's young wife in the years immediately after their marriage, three at least were drafted by Nathaniel on her behalf. She needed help in setting down the words, and sometimes they went through more than one draft. The wording is plainly Anne's own: she dictated or imparted the gist, which he then wrote out for her to copy. When she wrote to her birth-mother, Winifred Dutton, she wrote as a child, revealing her youth and insecurity. She felt lonely and homesick in Norfolk and longed to see the woman who bore her. Later, anxious at the approaching birth of her own first child, she informed Dutton, 'I wish with all my heart my fortune were so good as to have you there.'[33]

Surprisingly, Nathaniel's letters make it clear that Gresham and Ferneley had at first strongly objected to the newly married Anne receiving Cooke's instruction or of her living in her house for a transitional period. Ostensibly, their fear was that Cooke would be too 'sharp' towards her. But it quickly emerged that much of what really troubled Gresham and his wife was the question of expense: who was going to pay for her board and lodging? As Nathaniel acknowledged in a letter to Ferneley, 'Madam ... in my talk had with your ladyship, I perceived you were not minded, if my wife were placed here, to be at any charge with her. I will undertake that shall be so, rather than any let [i.e., harm, disagreement] shall thereby grow.'[34]

At last the matter was resolved. The six months during which Nathaniel's bride went to live with Cooke at Gorhambury were to be at the Bacons' expense, 'though with much ado first, and those sticking most

who had least cause to stick at it'.[35] How far Ferneley's role in the affair
reflected her opinions rather than Gresham's own is impossible to judge.
The latter seems more likely, as over the next twenty years Nathaniel sometimes used his aunt as an intermediary and confidante in preference to his
stepmother and several times stayed or came to dine at Gresham House.
Nathaniel's links to Ferneley were not so cordial, however, that they could
not be soured by the question of his wife's property settlement, over which
he continued to smart.[36]

Ferneley's lack of concern for the welfare of Thomas's daughter may
be partly explained by the fact that she had her own personal difficulties to
cope with. Her beloved mother, Agnes Daundy, now in her mid-eighties
and extremely frail, fell mortally sick and made her will six weeks after
Nathaniel Bacon's wedding.[37] Ferneley had already lost her father, her elder
sister and her son, Richard, from her marriage to Thomas. She very much
wanted to visit her mother in Norwich before she died, where she had
moved from West Creeting to live closer to other family members. But
Ferneley was not permitted to travel: she had now become tantamount to
a prisoner herself, unable to leave Gresham House.

In June 1569, just a few days before Gresham sought a special dispensation to marry off his daughter, he and Ferneley received a most
unwelcome guest. Sent by the queen to live with them under house arrest,
their prisoner was the twenty-four-year-old Mary Grey, youngest sister of
the ill-fated Lady Jane Grey and a woman many Protestants believed had
a serious claim to the throne. To Elizabeth, everything the Greys represented was an abomination. Nothing made her more uneasy than talk of
her successor. In her mind, no one except herself and her siblings had ever
had a legitimate right to succeed.

Mary's offence, like that of her elder sister Katherine, had been to
fall in love and marry without Elizabeth's consent. When, in 1560, Katherine had secretly wed the earl of Hertford, the eldest son of the executed
duke of Somerset, the queen had sent her to the Tower, and even when
she finally released her, she kept her under house arrest. In desperation,
Katherine starved herself to death. Learning nothing from her fate, Mary
followed her example, marrying in 1565. Her husband was Thomas Keys,
the queen's serjeant-porter, a widowed commoner twice her age with six
or seven children.

If Mary nurtured hopes that the union might pass unremarked, she
was naïve. Elizabeth pounced on this unfortunate legatee of the Grey

dynasty with all the vitriol of which she was capable. Keys, who was almost 7 feet tall (Mary was said to be very short), was confined to a vermin-ridden cell in the Fleet prison. Only Cecil was willing to do what he could to relieve his fouler conditions.[38] Shortly before Christmas 1566, Keys was fed half a rib of roast beef for his dinner which, unknown to him, had been accidentally dropped into a form of insecticide used to cure mange in dogs and which no one else in the prison was willing to eat.[39] The physician, Dr Christopher Langton, whom by sheer coincidence Gresham had called in for the birth of his now dead son, Richard, was sent for. Langton was able to administer what Keys described as 'a physic to purge me ... which cost 8s. 6d'. It was a close shave, but within a week Keys was suffering no serious ill-effects.[40]

Gresham and his wife were Mary Grey's third custodians. That Elizabeth chose Thomas to take charge of her might indicate the queen's trust in him, but could equally well be regarded as a kind of punishment for the Greshams on account of their pushiness. The sheer responsibility, not to mention expense, of the task was daunting. It was also extraordinarily sensitive, not just in view of the queen's combative attitude to Mary and her clan. The problem was that Cecil, in the labyrinthine world of Elizabethan succession politics, had been an ardent, secret *supporter* of the Greys for the last fifteen years – and still was. Almost incredibly to modern eyes, Cecil still regarded Mary Grey as a viable successor to the throne if Elizabeth suddenly died, and a far preferable candidate to the Catholic Mary queen of Scots. So if the Greshams handled Mary too harshly, *he* would hold them to account.

Mary spent much of her time reading and praying to be released.[41] By May 1570, her husband had at last been freed from his torments in the Fleet and was no longer under guard. In a letter written from Sandgate Castle in Kent, he asked Archbishop Parker to intercede with the queen and privy council for him, 'that according to the laws of God I may live with my wife'.[42] Parker passed the letter on to Cecil, among whose papers it still remains. The queen did not relent, and one doubts whether Cecil ever plucked up the courage to show it to her; Elizabeth was still furious with him for his earlier efforts on behalf of Katherine and the earl of Hertford. Mary and Keys would never see each other again and Mary would be forced to stay on at Gresham House or Osterley.

If she was like a rabbit caught in a snare, however, so were the Greshams. They dared not leave Mary unsupervised, solely in the care of servants. Ferneley bore the brunt of the strain. On 20 September 1570, in a scribbled postscript in the margin of a letter to Cecil chiefly concerned with money matters, Gresham made an impassioned plea. 'Sir,' he wrote, 'I have written to my lord of Leicester to move the queen's majesty to the removing of my lady Mary Grey who hath been with me these fifteen months. I pray you to set your good helping hands for the removing of her, for that my wife would gladly ride into Norfolk to see her old mother who is ninety years of age and a very weak woman, not like to live long.'[43] But just as Mary's own appeals for release were callously brushed aside, so were Thomas's, and he was destined to repeat them time and time again.

Barely a month later, he put pen to paper no fewer than three more times. After reporting yet more financial dealings on the exchange and informing Cecil that his marble pillars for his Stamford gallery had finally arrived, Thomas explained that he would have visited him personally, but could not come to court as one of his servants at Osterley had contracted plague. So worried was he about contagion that he wanted 'the queen's majesty's leave to ride with my wife and household to my house at Mayfield in Sussex, thirty-five miles out of London'. But this presented a dilemma: he needed to 'know the queen's majesty's pleasure' about what he 'shall do with my lady Mary Grey'. Gresham was becoming desperate, since Ferneley was in outright revolt over the cuckoo in her nest. He pleaded with Cecil to urge Elizabeth to find Mary a new gaoler. But again, all was in vain.[44]

In January 1571, Mary still languished at Gresham House, the queen simply rejecting out of hand all Thomas's petitions to be rid of her – it was as if he and Ferneley were suddenly of no more importance to her than the kitchen maids or rat catchers in her palaces. There was certainly no way in which Elizabeth would consent to meet or greet Mary Grey or anyone connected to her. When Gresham and Ferneley feasted the queen at Gresham House on the day she opened the Royal Exchange, Mary was kept safely out of sight. No one had the nerve so much as to mention her existence.

Over the next few months, Gresham badgered Cecil six more times to help him to be rid of his prisoner, so repetitively that the words became something of a mantra.[45] For a moment, it looked as if he was victorious. On 19 July, he wrote to the chief minister from Gresham House, asking him to offer the queen 'my most humble thanks for the delivery of my lady Mary Grey, and for her great goodness always showed unto me'.[46] Alas the report that he was to be relieved of his charge was false. Thomas was now at his wits' end, not least as events abroad were by now approaching their point of no return.

THE END OF
ANTWERP

In the nine months after his grand processional entry into Brussels in August 1567, the duke of Alva oversaw a systematic purge of the Calvinist leaders and their protectors. As Thomas Dutton and Richard Clough briefed Gresham from their base in the Keizerstraat in Antwerp, he had invited the counts of Hoorn and Egmont to dinner within weeks of his arrival, only to have them arrested and imprisoned in the castle at Ghent.[1] On 5 June 1568, shortly after 11 a.m., they were executed.

The aspiring courtier Sir Henry Lee, stopping over in Antwerp on his way to Cologne, sent the news to Cecil. An art connoisseur who would one day rise to fame as 'queen's champion' in Elizabeth's Accession Day tilts and become chief impresario of the cult of Gloriana, Lee was visiting Anthonis Mor's studio, where he too sat for his portrait. A Calvinist sympathiser, he was appalled but unsurprised by the turn of events. 'The duke of Alva', he scribbled breathlessly, 'nowhat abstaineth from his first begun course, but with much cruelty to the utter dismaying of all this country proceedeth. On Tuesday last he began his execution[s], on which day in Brussels died twenty-two gentlemen; on Wednesday three, and as yesterday being Saturday, Count Egmont and Count Hoorn.'[2]

William of Orange was Alva's next intended victim. Suspecting a trap, William slipped across the frontier into Germany and was swiftly declared an outlaw. William's brother, Louis of Nassau, led a mass popular uprising in the north-eastern provinces of the Netherlands but he was defeated and Alva's troops now occupied these territories. In an attempt to make their causes interdependent, William forged an alliance with the Huguenots; alas on the resurgence of the French Wars of Religion, the deal collapsed.

Now permanently based at Gresham House or at one of his country estates, but as mesmerised as ever by a series of rapid upwards and downwards swings on the Antwerp bourse as reported to him by Richard Clough, Gresham constantly gathered intelligence from his network of spies and informers, passing on any news he thought valuable to Cecil or Robert Dudley.[3] Ever since he had appointed Francesco di Tomasso as his confidential courier, Gresham had always relied on his own trusted employees to deliver letters and important documents, even more so now that the diplomatic and commercial posts were regularly intercepted.[4] By being close at hand to the nerve-centre of power in London, Gresham was in a perfect position to offer advice whenever English interests appeared to be threatened. No one else had his knowledge of the markets or his links to those whose lives revolved around them.

Alva's purge threw Antwerp into chaos. A steady victory of the more conservative voices over the revolutionaries in the city had the effect of putting merchants who had supported the Calvinists out of business, and many Englishmen discovered to their horror that their debts would not be honoured by the sequestrators. But despite his onslaughts against the Calvinists, Alva sought to remain on good terms with Elizabeth at least for the moment. Fearful of disruptions to his sea route to Spain, he continued to seek English cooperation in repelling pirates and privateers from the Channel. Although it was Philip II's policy to avoid the sea route whenever possible, instead sending convoys of barges down the Rhine and the Scheldt and marching his troops over the Alps, he still relied heavily on the maritime line of communication. In fact, much of the day-to-day business of Don Guerau de Spes, the new Spanish ambassador in London, had so far concerned Channel piracy.[5]

In December 1568, the Channel took centre stage when a small flotilla of the fast-sailing Spanish vessels known as *zabras* heading from Santander to Antwerp was forced to seek shelter off the Cornish and Hampshire coasts. Besides wool and luxury goods, the vessels were carrying 155 chests of Spanish silver *reales*, of which three-quarters were intended to pay Alva's army of Flanders. Gresham, who later had his servants weigh part of the contents of these chests to gain a rough idea of their value, provisionally estimated that they were worth in the region of £80,000 sterling (over £80 million in modern values).[6] The ships had at first been scattered in the Bay of Biscay by a storm, and then again at the entrance to the Channel by Huguenot privateers. Their captains had been instructed at all costs to avoid entering a French port, leaving them no choice but to seek refuge in English waters. The nature of their cargo was known to the Genoese and

Lucchese merchants who had lent the money to Philip, and to a few other Italians in London who did not feel bound to keep the secret. As a result, the treasure and its value became a topic of feverish speculation.[7] Blockaded by the privateers, the Spanish vessels were forced to stay at anchor, but the largest treasure-ship lying at the entrance to Southampton Water was in imminent danger of attack.

Cecil decided to intervene. He instructed the local admiralty officials to ensure the safety of the cargoes by having them brought ashore. In an aide-mémoire written on 18 January 1569, by which time relations between England and Spain had turned frosty, Cecil maintained that the Spanish captains were only too happy that their goods were on English soil, even going so far as to help to unload them. Broadly, his line was that the treasure was to be landed as an act of Anglo-Spanish collaboration, to save it from the French.[8]

At first, his action caused far less perturbation to Alva or de Spes than it did to those London merchants who traded out of Spanish ports and feared confiscation of their goods. As feelings began to run high in the city, the Merchant Adventurers joined in to voice their concerns, beseeching Cecil not to provoke Philip II needlessly. So fearful were they of running risks anywhere in the Spanish king's empire that they convened a meeting to debate whether their next fleet of ships should sail for Antwerp. By forty votes to eighteen, they decided to accept the risks.

Then de Spes played his hand. He went to Whitehall Palace to seek an audience with Elizabeth. This was not instantly granted, from which he inferred that the chests of treasure were going to be retained as booty. He sent his secretary post-haste to Antwerp to urge Alva to take instant, drastic measures. This was a catastrophic error, as no final decision as to what to do with the money had been taken. A week later, de Spes was given an audience at which the queen told him she understood that the treasure, legally, belonged not to Philip but to merchants, although she did not yet know precisely who. He should know her mind in four days' time. Whatever her intentions, the tone of her remarks convinced de Spes that the money would not, after all, pay Alva's troops, but would be kept by the heretic English.[9]

Most likely Elizabeth's gut instinct was to return the chests of treasure to Santander in dribs and drabs to cause Alva maximum inconvenience and to remind Philip of his dependence on her goodwill. Cecil, if left to his own devices, would probably have taken advantage of the chance to write off the entire residue of Elizabeth's outstanding debts and avoid a fresh round of taxes. In the privy council the debate reached a stalemate during which the treasure would remain, unopened, in its chests. The stalemate was only broken when Alva, appalled by the lurid reports he had received from de Spes, ordered the arrest of all the English merchants then in Antwerp. Around 120 of the Merchant Adventurers were detained, their goods sequestered and the keys to their warehouses confiscated.[10]

The news reached London on 3 January 1569. In a letter marked 'Haste, haste, post-haste, with diligence', Lord Cobham, warden of the Cinque Ports, gave Cecil the latest intelligence. 'Since the sending of my last,' he reported, 'I have received advertisements that our merchants and their goods be stayed in Flanders.'[11] Shortly after midnight, the news was broken to the lord mayor, Thomas Rowe, by 'certain worthy English merchants' who arrived to see him 'very suddenly and very fearfully'. They had 'credible advertisements', they said, 'that all our English nation resident in Antwerp were arrested ... and be kept prisoners in the English House there and by the guard of a thousand men, and all their goods attached, and none of our nation whatsoever to depart upon pain of death'.[12]

Three days later, the mayor and sheriffs processed in their scarlet gowns to Cheapside to read out the queen's proclamation, ordering all subjects of the king of Spain to be arrested in retaliation, together with 'their goods, merchandises, ships and vessels', a proclamation also printed in French and sent to Brussels to be distributed there.[13] All of this would have delighted the worried London merchants. Together with the mayor, they had presented a 'remembrance' to Cecil, asking for just that: they had wanted all 'the bodies, ships and goods of all the subjects of the said king [to] be had under arrest and their bodies to be sequestered from their houses, counting-houses, books, warehouses and goods, and they themselves to be committed unto several and sure custody and keeping'.[14] This was the most damaging blow ever inflicted on the Anglo-Netherlands trade. The resulting standoff would last for almost five years.

Realising he had gone too far, Alva sent the lawyer Christophe d'Assonleville on a mission to England to reach a settlement. Voluble, assertive and emotional, d'Assonleville was the wrong man for the job. Lodged by the queen with Alderman Bond at Crosby Place, he was to be shadowed and kept closely under observation by Gresham at all times, not least during his visits to de Spes, who was now under house arrest, allegedly for his own safety.

Assiduously passing information back to Cecil, Gresham reported the
length of the meetings between de Spes and d'Assonleville, the very limited
(but already stale) intelligence he managed to extract from d'Assonleville
concerning Alva's plans for the Netherlands, along with his repeated
requests for an audience with Elizabeth.[15] Since Alva's envoy refused to
talk to anyone on the English side except the queen, his meetings with
privy councillors in late January and February ended in recriminations. In
particular, an after-dinner conference on 25 February, held at Sir Nicholas
Bacon's new London house near Charing Cross, took a wrong turn when
Gresham, never a born diplomat, plied d'Assonleville with arguments to
demonstrate the strength of the English bargaining position, while brag-
ging somewhat preposterously that Elizabeth could muster 50,000 men
whenever she wanted, and that 'she was better supplied with men-at-arms,
artillery, war vessels, munitions, victuals and warlike stores than any three
of the other European sovereigns together'.[16]

D'Assonleville took umbrage, and on 5 March set out for home
without waiting for Alva's authorisation. Gresham, meanwhile, was surprisingly relaxed about his own breach of protocol. Resigned to the effective
loss of Antwerp as northern Europe's chief money market, he advised Cecil
that the queen's foreign creditors could be repaid in Hamburg if necessary,
and that existing loans could be prolonged or new ones secured there too,
if it came to the worst.

Thomas would not come back fully into vision until 14 September,
by which time many, although far from all, of the chests containing Alva's
treasure had been taken to the Tower and opened. Amazed at their value,
Gresham was soon to be found supervising the assaying of the silver,
weighing it out in sacks and bags, and sealing them with the queen's seal
– not forgetting to have his servant remove silver worth 6s. sterling from
each bag as his cut.[17]

Unable to bear seeing so much money standing idle, he directed
Cecil's thoughts back towards his adventure in Mary I's reign, when he had
brought back silver *reales* from Spain to the value (after deduction of losses
and expenses) of £73,626 sterling. A proportion had been re-minted as
English coins, and that was his recommendation again. This time, however,
Thomas expressed his hope that most of the money could be coined in this
way. The economic benefits of increasing the quantity of good silver coin
in circulation aside, the government could make a quick, easy profit from
the margin to be gained by re-minting the under-valued *reales* in this sort

of quantity. It could, he believed, amount to at least £3,000 or £4,000 (£3–4 million in modern values).[18]

By then, Thomas had fresh intelligence for Cecil that definitively resolved the question of how to settle the legal ownership of the money in the government's favour. The uncertainty had first arisen when, at South-ampton, the captain of the largest treasure ship asked permission to open one of the chests in order to meet his expenses. Once done, 'divers manifest writings' were discovered 'to prove that the said treasure did appertain to certain merchants and was not the proper treasure of the king of Spain'.[19]

At this point a Genoese-born merchant who had taken up English citizenship, Benedetto Spinola, came to call on Thomas at Gresham House, introducing him to one Tommaso Ragio. According to Ragio, a fellow Genoese, the money had been borrowed partly from him, and he wanted his share returned. As the conversation unfolded, Gresham not only learned the identities of the other merchants who had advanced Philip his loans, he also worked out how much of the treasure belonged to Genoese bankers and how much to Spaniards. The final answer was that 2,371,414 silver *reales* belonged to the Genoese and only 835,290 *reales* to Spaniards.[20]

Elizabeth had already decided that the money belonging to Spaniards was to be seized to compensate English merchants for the loss of their property in the Netherlands and Spain. Now, as Gresham advised, all Cecil had to do was to persuade her to borrow the Genoese funds herself for a year or two. But he also aimed at a double whammy: the borrowed money would be re-minted into English coin at a handsome profit, but he would later repay the Genoese lenders in lower value Flemish pounds rather than in sterling, and at a rate 'as the exchange now goeth'. Such a ploy would be 'very profitable to her majesty'.[21]

Gresham's advice was accepted. From Spinola he arranged to borrow at a nil rate of interest, so strong was Elizabeth's bargaining position given that she already had all the money in hand – this provided a template for loans from the other merchants.[22] He then helped to oversee the process of re-coinage, which he advised Cecil could proceed at the rate of £1,000 sterling a day. When the closing account was rendered, it reported that out of a total of 3,276,012 silver *reales* handed over to the mint, 2,481,303 were turned into English coin worth £67,322 (over £67 million today), some 11,961 had been disbursed in costs and charges, leaving the rest in bullion whose value was assessed at £21,600.[23]

Alas, despite his optimistic predictions, it is a decidedly moot point how much profit Gresham actually made for Elizabeth. When it was time to repay the Genoese bankers their loans in Flemish pounds at a rate 'as the exchange now goeth', Thomas discovered that the currency markets had moved sharply against him, and he could only obtain 22s. 6d. in Flemish money for the pound sterling as opposed to the 25s. od. he was expecting. His gamble on the future strength of sterling had backfired, and he was forced to repay £65,455 sterling as against the £55,340 of his original calculation.[24]

In other words, the government, overall, made a paper loss of a staggering £10,115 sterling (over £10 million in modern values) compared with what Thomas had initially claimed Elizabeth would gain by his wheeling and dealing on the exchange. As with his earlier Spanish adventure, he failed to deliver on his promises.

Furthermore, the affair of the treasure-ships would have damaging political repercussions. In February and early March 1569, while the chests of treasure were still untouched and Gresham was still boasting to d'Assonleville that Elizabeth was better prepared militarily 'than any three of the other European sovereigns together', the notoriously hawkish de Spes was taken in by a plausible, but conspiratorial Florentine banker, Roberto Ridolfi, who had links to the pope and Mary queen of Scots. According to Ridolfi, Robert Dudley, fearful after Philip II extended Alva's reprisals to all English merchants in Spain, had accused Cecil of being the cause of most of the country's ills.[25] While such reports are extremely dubious, there was more substance to a plot involving Ridolfi, de Spes and a cabal of dissident Catholic nobles who felt marginalised by Cecil.[26] Forced by her enemies in Scotland to abdicate and imprisoned at Lochleven Castle, Mary escaped and fled across the Solway Firth to England in 1568, where her presence served to destabilise the delicate political balance. Rumours were rife of a letter from the pope urging her to marry the duke of Norfolk, England's premier peer, and then claim Elizabeth's throne.

The possibility of establishing a dependably Catholic succession should Elizabeth not marry was a powerful lure to the Catholic families of northern England, especially the Percys, earls of Northumberland, and Nevilles, earls of Westmorland. They had a relatively weak attachment to Elizabeth and nothing but disdain for those privy councillors they called 'upstarts', notably Cecil. On 26 October 1569, Northumberland and Westmorland were summoned to London. Instead, they began mustering their tenants, after which they rode with their followers to Durham and, on 14 November, raised the standard of revolt.[27]

So began the Northern Rising, the most serious rebellion since Henry VIII had begun suppressing the monasteries. Carrying the Cross and the banners of the Five Wounds of Christ, some 6,000 rebels marched into North Yorkshire, besieging Barnard Castle and celebrating the mass as they went. They claimed to be the protectors of the commonwealth, protesting that they wanted to save Elizabeth from a 'lawless faction of Machiavellians'. By this, they meant that they aimed to purge 'King Cecil' and his allies from the privy council and Parliament and replace them with good Catholic noblemen loyal to the queen.

Gresham was still too busy supervising the re-coining of Spanish *reales* in the Tower to worry much about disturbances in the north. But the turbulence of the religious climate must have impinged on his consciousness in August 1570, when he sat at the Guildhall as one of a group of special commissioners appointed to try John Felton, a notorious Catholic renegade. Felton's offence – for which he would be tortured and hung from the gallows – was to nail to the front door of the bishop of London's palace at Fulham a papal bull issued by Pius V, declaring Elizabeth to be excommunicated and deposed on the grounds that she was a heretic, a schismatic and a tyrant.[28]

The re-minting at the Tower completed and his accounts finally submitted to Cecil's scrutiny, Gresham's focus was on picking up the pieces after Philip's and Alva's reprisals had severed the Anglo-Brabant trade, seemingly for ever. By now, the attention of the Merchant Adventurers had switched exclusively to how Hamburg might evolve as an international transit port in place of Antwerp. A free, Lutheran city with ancient commercial links to London, it was to all practical purposes its own master, ruled by a mercantile oligarchy whose chief governors were the burgomasters and senate. It greatly helped that the Adventurers' representatives had already agreed a preferential trade accord with these leaders, valid for ten years. They had won the right to sell their wares in Hamburg to anyone they chose, and were not to be pursued in the courts there for faulty cloths after a period of three months. As long as they paid a modest local import duty, their goods were not to be subject to any other levy. What's more, Englishmen trading more generally in Hamburg were to be exempt from paying income tax, ground rent, wharf or anchorage fees, and they might use the great crane by the waterfront free of charge. It all seemed too good to be true.[29]

Such were Hamburg's apparently overwhelming commercial advantages that Cecil swiftly approved the Adventurers' choice. Emden was ruled out, as Alva had installed a garrison of Spanish troops at the stronghold of Delfzijl, commanding the Ems estuary. So confident was Cecil about the merits of the new transit port, he lost no time in poaching Richard Clough from Gresham and posting him to Hamburg to be the new Deputy Governor of the Merchant Adventurers there. Clough was to settle his affairs as soon as he could, then abandon Antwerp and Gresham's service for good.

Recently married to Katherine of Berain, a wealthy widow and heiress from Denbighshire in North Wales, Clough arrived in Hamburg with the cloth fleet on 23 May 1569, much against his will, accompanied by his wife, baby daughter, Anne, and an illegitimate son born to an 'Antwerp wife'.[30] He simply hated the place, which he considered unsafe.[31] The citizens he judged 'envious and beggarly both of goods and wits'. They claimed to be free 'under the emperor as they say upon themselves, but not so upon themselves that they are able to withstand by estimation the power of a prince, if they were put thereunto'.[32]

Clough's impressions would largely be confirmed by a memo Cecil received from one of his spies in January 1570. Upon reaching the city, the English found it in a state of disarray. Rumours abounded that the King of Denmark planned an assault, 'for he hath long threatened the same'. It was said the king had demanded protection money from the citizens 'towards the payment of his soldiers in his late wars with Sweden, which they refused to furnish ... And they have prohibited that none of their burghers or indwellers shall depart the town or send away any of his goods without consent of the lords, upon pain of life and goods'.[33]

For Gresham, however, the crucial issue for the future would be less the fortunes of the cloth trade than the ready availability of credit in Hamburg and his ability to roll over the residue of the queen's loans. Since Clough was no longer in Thomas's employment, their correspondence came to an abrupt end. Clough's kinsman and assistant, Thomas Dutton, still relatively young, also left for Hamburg, along with another of Gresham's servants, Thomas Denny, but they now worked exclusively for Clough, in whose house they lodged.[34] As Gresham's factor, Clough was replaced by his brother Hugh, who continued to supply Thomas with information from Antwerp when he could.[35]

Disappointingly, much of what the Hamburg civic powers had promised the Merchant Adventurers was indeed too good to be true. As a transit port, the city's principal drawbacks were the length of the crossing up the North Sea, which increased costs and travelling times; its relative isolation from the main trade routes through Germany and on to Italy; and the frequent icing over of the Elbe during the winter months, which disrupted traffic. Moreover, with Alva on the offensive, the English needed expensive royal navy protection to sail safely past the coast of the Netherlands, and for this they had to pay.

For Gresham, this meant that a vibrant financial market never took hold in Hamburg as it had in Antwerp. Several German banking firms opened smaller branches there, but the Italians were conspicuously absent. With his sore leg more troublesome than ever, travelling so far himself to open a new office would be too much for Gresham to contemplate. Instead, the time when he might need to wind down his European operations seemed to be approaching: from now on, he would set out to make London's wealthiest merchants and citizens his targets of first resort for borrowing, along with a few selected Italians, with whom he continued dealing long after the money from the Spanish treasure was repaid.

The manoeuvres required to achieve this decisive shift would mark Gresham's apogee as Elizabeth's banker. He had come a long way from when, in 1544, he and Stephen Vaughan had agonised over how to smuggle vast quantities of cash and bullion past the noses of the authorities in order to bring home the money needed for Henry VIII's last campaign in France. The switch to government borrowing chiefly from Londoners, with many of the contracts sealed with a handshake in the precincts of his own Royal Exchange, would signal the beginning of a new era, one in which bargains would be in sterling throughout and there would be far less need for Gresham's dark wizardry. For all that, if Thomas was feeling older and less physically agile, he was still mentally sharp and far from defeated. Could there still be one last glorious deal in him?

A GOLDEN GOODBYE

The years from 1569 to 1574 were extremely challenging for Gresham. The move of the Merchant Adventurers to Hamburg did not turn out well. Sales of the first shipment of cloths sent there in May 1569 were disappointing: only the cheapest, coarsest goods sold in any quantities. It would take two years for exports, especially of kerseys or worsteds, to creep up towards anything approaching the levels previously achieved in Antwerp.[1] Correspondingly, many of the high-quality wares once purchased at the Brabant fairs were less readily available in Hamburg. With the government's receipts from the customs in the port of London dropping by the day, Elizabeth found herself in desperate need of funds, despite the windfall of the bullion from the duke of Alva's treasure ships.[2]

Since Hamburg was largely unequipped to furnish the credit the government required, the privy council first raised cash by levying a large forced loan from all English subjects thought to be capable of payment. Of the wealthiest Londoners on the government's hit list, thirty-four, including Gresham, his aunt Lady Katherine (Sir John Gresham's widow) and Alderman William Bond, were put down for £100 each, and about 250 others for the lesser sum of £66.[3] In total, £14,800 was raised in the city by this unpopular method (over £14.8 million in modern values) and no interest was paid.[4]

Next, Cecil and Gresham, working together, turned to the Merchant Adventurers, thinking to repeat their success in the summer of 1560 when, in an emergency caused by the collapse of the negotiations with the count of Mansfeld, they had successfully extorted a loan of £60,000 sterling, payable in two tranches of £30,000 each.[5] That might have worked then, but the timing now was inopportune. If trade and customs revenues had shrunk temporarily, so had sales and therefore profits. In June 1569,

Richard Clough, installed as Cecil's resident agent in Hamburg, secured an offer of £6,444, but that was all the Adventurers said they could afford.[6] When, in July, Cecil demanded a larger sum, rejection was immediate.[7]

Tempers had cooled by November, and the Adventurers were persuaded to double their earlier offer; other merchants selling only wool pledged £4,200.[8] But these amounts were still far from enough. So desperate did Gresham become for credit, he briefly contemplated approaching old contacts in Antwerp, but it was too dangerous. As he warned Cecil, 'No man which keepeth any accounts there dare deal with the queen's majesty or with any of her subjects, because the king of Spain hath made a proclamation to the contrary, which I assure your honour is very straightly looked unto.'[9]

The time had come for a new, bolder approach. From this point onwards, Gresham would seek systematically to shift the burden for financing the government's borrowing requirement from Europe to the city of London. He had nurtured the idea in embryo since 1558–9, when it had underpinned his advice to Elizabeth and Cecil in two of his most famous memos.[10] The main difference now was that Thomas proposed to remove the element of coercion that had so conspicuously governed his and the privy council's earlier impositions on the merchants. His actions, as reflected in the small print of his agreements, show that he meant to do so by the straightforward expedients of offering them fair and highly competitive rates of interest, and of borrowing their cash and making repayments almost exclusively in sterling, so that the risks of serious losses (on either side) through rigged or fluctuating rates of exchange or other economic mishaps were stripped away.[11]

Gresham first signalled this way of thinking in a letter to Cecil, written from Gresham House on 14 August 1569 'at nine of the clock at night'. Echoing much of what he had thought and said earlier, Thomas repeated his mantra that the queen must free herself from reliance on foreign bankers. She 'should not use any strangers, but her own subjects'. For the first time he added what he would make his new leitmotif: Elizabeth, by financing her credit requirements exclusively at home, could prove to Philip II and all the other rulers of Europe 'what a prince of power she is'.[12] As he went on to explain, it all came down to basic issues of trust and familiarity. He knew, he said, from almost twenty years' experience in dealing 'for the credit of the queen's majesty beyond the seas' that when she borrowed at home, 'I found great honour to the prince as also great profit to the merchants and to the whole realm, whatsoever our merchants say to the contrary'.[13]

After receiving this letter, Cecil instructed Gresham to raise £20,000 in loans in London, a task Thomas quickly performed by taking up sums varying from between £1,100 and £2,100 from fourteen of the wealthiest citizens. Those lending included Sir Lionel Duckett, shortly to be elected mayor and knighted; Sir Roger Martin, another leading city notable, recently mayor; and Gresham's neighbour, Alderman William Bond. Yielding a total of £21,100 for the queen's coffers, these bargains were for a period of six months at an annualised interest rate just short of 13 per cent, plus a brokerage fee of 1 per cent, payable to Thomas.[14]

By charging a fee of 1 per cent, Gresham would eventually earn himself around £840 (worth over £840,000 today), because he successfully prolonged each of these loans on exactly the same terms no fewer than three times, with the interest compounded. Despite his grossly inflated charges, it was a virtuous circle, because the government got its money, while the merchants (according to Gresham's audited accounts) were repaid £28,689 after two years. Those staking £1,500 received £1,953, while those staking £2,000 got £2,603. Given that all these transactions were in sterling, and the money was safe and repayment prompt, the investors achieved more than satisfactory returns.[15]

As soon as the word got around, Thomas discovered that other wealthy Londoners were eager to enter the market.[16] Occasionally, he still found it necessary to borrow abroad.[17] Between 1570 and 1574, he took up a run of smaller loans of £1,000 or £1,500 in Hamburg or other north German towns. In 1570–1, he accepted an offer of 100,000 thalers (worth £25 million today) from merchants in Cologne, but the deal turned sour.[18] Conditions eased a little in the autumn of 1571, when cloth sales in Hamburg began to recover somewhat. Gresham stepped in instantly, borrowing £13,102 for a year.[19] Part of him, admittedly, always hankered after Antwerp. It had been his spiritual home for so many years, and for a while he nursed hopes that it might be possible one day to return there, if on a drastically reduced scale. But the omens were poor.[20]

On 18 March 1570, Gresham passed a milestone when his erstwhile factor, Richard Clough, who had loyally assisted him for twenty-five years, died in Hamburg of a lingering illness.[21] Only a week before, the city's magistrates had written to their counterparts in Lübeck, requesting them to send a physician to attend on him.[22] It was barely ten months since Clough had left Gresham's service to work for Cecil, and he still felt himself psychologically and emotionally bound to his old employer, whom he continued to call 'my master' until days before his death.

First among the legacies in Clough's will, written 'with mine own hand' on 20 September 1568, was the sum of £1,200 in Flemish pounds, due to Gresham 'by a bill in my box wherein my bills of debt are'. Other gifts included £20 sterling to Anne Ferneley 'to make her a pair of bracelets' and £10 to Thomas's illegitimate daughter. Then, in mid-February 1570, after Clough knew that his beloved wife Katherine of Berain was pregnant with their second daughter, he added no fewer than three codicils to his will. One provides a unique insight into his relationship with Gresham.[23]

As he dictated the passage to his notary from his sickbed,

> Whereas I, Richard Clough, of late did make a will and testament of a former date, sithens [i.e., since] which time I have sundry and often times been moved in my conscience, that whereas I did win and conquest certain sums of my goods in the time of my service under and with my master, Sir Thomas Gresham; therefore, for the true discharge and clearing of my conscience, I do freely give to my said master, Sir Thomas Gresham, all my moveable goods (all my lands excepted) to do his pleasure therewith, and refer it to his will whether that he will suffer my wife, children, and friends to enjoy them all, or any parcel thereof, according to my last will and testament, or no.

He then added pitifully,

> O my master, do unto my poor wife and children as you would I should do to yours, and if you were in the same case, for they have no father to trust unto but you; and thus I bid you, and my gracious lady, farewell till it please God to send us a merry meeting. Your old servant, Richard Clough.[24]

The implication is that Clough had, from time to time, embezzled small amounts of money from Thomas, for which, now facing death, he sought to make amends. History has been kind to Gresham, because a clerical note in the margin of the official register of the archbishop of Canterbury's probate court notes that, on 9 November 1570, he or his legal counsel formally renounced his claim to anything from Clough's estate arising from this codicil.[25] What history overlooks is that, three years later, Thomas went out of his way to apply for, and secure from Cecil, the public guardianship of Clough's two daughters and co-heirs.[26] As their duly appointed guardian, he was free to take over and manage a large estate in North Wales, including many acres planted with valuable timber, until they reached their age of majority. It is entirely possible that, as their guardian, Thomas preserved their inheritances intact, without the slightest hint of asset-stripping. Then again, he would have been the only man in the country to behave that way, since wardships were investments purchased from the crown and treated as such.[27]

Gresham and Ferneley, meanwhile, continued to wrestle with their role as gaolers to the unfortunate Mary Grey. Their prisoner's misery and depression were to be much increased after the sudden death of her husband, Thomas Keys. On 8 September 1571, Gresham asked Cecil for his advice on how to cope with this tragic event, for Mary had taken the news 'grievously'. Worse, she was begging him that Elizabeth would permit her 'to keep and bring up' her brood of stepchildren, a request Thomas was clearly immensely relieved the queen would indignantly refuse.

So anxious was Thomas not to put a foot wrong with Elizabeth where the Grey dynasty was concerned that he was reluctant to allow Mary even to wear 'any black mourning apparel' for her husband without asking Cecil's permission first.[28] And over the ensuing months he sent still more petitions for Mary's removal from Gresham House 'for the quietness of my poor wife'.[29]

Emboldened by her grief, Mary wrote to Cecil on 7 October from Osterley, calling herself 'Mary Keys', something she had never dared do before when all her letters were signed 'Mary Grey'. In a beautifully neat Italianate hand closely reminiscent of that of her eldest sister, Lady Jane, whose tutors she had shared, she entreated the chief minister, 'so much always my good lord in furthering my humble suit unto her majesty for her most gracious favour', to intercede for her. 'Seeing,' as she continued, 'God hath taken away the occasion of her majesty's justly conceived displeasure towards me', perhaps she would now 'pardon this my great fault committed against her majesty and receive me again unto favour.'[30]

But, as another flurry of letters testifies, forgiveness for Mary was not forthcoming, nor relief or respite for the disaffected Greshams. Thomas relayed to Cecil the suggestion that she might go to live with her stepfather, Adrian Stokes, in the backwoods of Leicestershire. This was eventually accepted.[31] Alas, the arrangements could not be settled for another whole year, during which time Gresham pleaded with ever-rising impatience to Cecil and Robert Dudley for her removal, 'which would be no small comfort and quietness to my poor wife and me, whom, as you know, hath been almost a prisoner in her own house for this three years'.[32]

To chivvy Gresham and Ferneley along, Elizabeth visited Osterley for two nights in July 1570 and overnight in June 1571.[33] She even at last redeemed, if in a decidedly backhanded way, her promise to Thomas on her accession that she would reward him with gifts of land.[34] Gresham had continued to solicit Cecil and Dudley shrilly on this sensitive subject, most recently in November 1568, when she had given the gnomic response that 'she is informed that I have purchased great matters about my house'. The implication was that she thought he was already quite wealthy enough.[35]

By her grants in May 1570 and January 1571, however, she gave Thomas properties in Isleworth and Twickenham close to Osterley, so close that many of them could be encompassed by his deer park – but their combined annual profits were no more than £27 7s. od. This was far from the generous grants he was given by the duke of Northumberland and Mary I, when he received lands annually yielding £363.[36]

In 1572, the queen finally allowed Gresham and Ferneley's prisoner to go free, but Mary Grey could not herself afford to leave. Writing in May from Gresham House, she complained that she was 'void of all friends' and had too little money. 'Miserable and wretched', as she depicted herself, she protested to Cecil that she had 'but four score pound a year of her majesty, of my own I have but twenty pound'.[37] She did not want to be a burden to her stepfather, who had to provide for his own family. Maddeningly we don't know how the matter was resolved, but Mary did manage to move to her stepfather's home in 1573 to the unconcealed jubilation of the Greshams: at last, they were rid of her. Some time afterwards she set up her own household in a house near Aldersgate in London, where she died on 20 April 1578.[38]

Thomas would reach another milestone in 1574, when Cecil armed him with sufficient cash to pay off the government's foreign debts in full. Once that was achieved and still smarting from the size of his land grant, he saw little further need to carry on working for Elizabeth. Now fifty-five, he had already begun to slacken off. His scourge, the marquis of Winchester, had died in 1572 and was replaced as lord treasurer by Cecil, whom Elizabeth raised to the peerage as Lord Burghley. As his successor as the queen's secretary of state, Cecil secured the appointment of his protégé, Sir Francis Walsingham.

Aged forty-five, twelve years younger than Cecil, Walsingham was another ardent Protestant with an almost messianic vision of Elizabeth's role in history. His world view had been shaped as the queen's resident ambassador in Paris in 1572, where he had witnessed the infamous St Bartholomew's Day Massacre, when thousands of Huguenots were slaughtered. Another investor in the Muscovy Company and by the summer of 1568 one of its leading officials, Walsingham had first met Gresham in the mid-1550s.[39]

Increasingly to be found relaxing at their country estates, Gresham and Ferneley were graced by further short visits from Elizabeth at Mayfield in the summer of 1573 and at Osterley in February 1574, April 1575 and May 1576.[40] Rarely now in attendance at court himself, Thomas still looked to Cecil and Robert Dudley to act as his chief protectors there. Only fragments of evidence survive as to the nature of Gresham's relationship with Dudley in these later years, but those that do suggest Dudley was by now heavily in debt to him.[41]

Ferneley was no slouch when it came to networking, either. In the summer of 1574, she made one of her trips to the spa at Buxton, where she was introduced to Cecil's elder son, Thomas. This connection she would later turn to the advantage of the elder of her two sons.[42] Gresham had no interest in the wider social world of Buxton himself, so Ferneley tended to go there on her own.

By this time, Gresham had made a firm decision to retire as Elizabeth's banker. On 3 May 1574, at his own request, the queen appointed a panel of commissioners, headed by Cecil and Dudley, to oversee the auditing of his final accounts and to get them approved and officially certified. This, of course, was no mere formality. Should he step back from his role without securing his official discharge, enrolled on parchment in the exchequer, he could potentially be investigated, and called to answer, at any unknown point in the future.[43]

To assist Cecil and Dudley, Elizabeth nominated Sir Francis Knollys, Sir Walter Mildmay and Walsingham, although this time the forensic work was done by their officials in the audit office.[44] It had been eleven years since Thomas had been forced to render his last accounts there, and to his utter horror, he discovered as the audit took its course that he was vulnerable to a whole raft of charges for disallowed payments and expenses.[45] For instance, his claim for a loan repayment of £6,900 to Paul van Dalle was struck out and the figure slashed to £2,803. Where he claimed £480 for New Year's gifts to the customs' officials of Brabant, this was cut to £200. An undocumented claim of £646 for rent was reduced to £300. Where Thomas asked for £200 for the annual expense of feasting the queen's creditors in Antwerp, this was completely disallowed. His claim of £2,000 for travel expenses to and from Antwerp for himself and eight servants was halved.[46]

Despite knowing from Winchester's previous audit that he was only meant to claim the full twenty shillings a day for his 'diets' when working abroad, Thomas had both continued to do so and also thrown in apparently unauthorised *per diems* of 5s. 4d. for four of his clerks. Here he was extremely fortunate: the auditors disputed only his claim for the clerks, which they halved, failing to spot that the queen had long ago restricted Gresham's *per diems* to 13s. 4d. when he was in London.[47] Finally, an exorbitant claim of another £1,000 for Gresham's riding charges and boat hire for journeys between his home and Elizabeth's court was cut by half.[48]

After toiling through a mountain of paperwork for the best part of a year, the auditors concluded that Thomas's account was £18,149 in deficit (over £18.1 million today). Ingeniously, Gresham managed to get this astronomical figure reduced to £10,883 15s. 4d. in the official report to the commissioners.[49] Now, only desperate measures could rescue him from such a huge shortfall. When his final, quite outrageous attempt to claim 'lost' interest at 12 per cent going back for ten years on any dormant cash balances in his account, the use of which he said 'he hath forborne', was indignantly rejected, bankruptcy stared him in the face.[50] What made things worse was that his usual point of contact in the exchequer, Robert Taylor – to whom even while the audit was in train Gresham would present one of his grasshopper rings – was unable to help him.[51] In debt himself and watching his back, Taylor was in the wrong department of the fiscal bureaucracy, concerned with cash payments, not auditing of accounts.

Gresham's old survival instincts kicked in. With the summer vacation of 1575 in the exchequer fast approaching, Elizabeth had gone on her most famous summer progress to Kenilworth Castle in Warwickshire, where she would be royally entertained by Dudley for nineteen days in July at eye-watering expense. On the pretence of needing it to check some figures over the holidays, Gresham contrived to borrow a duplicate set of enrolments containing the full entries of the accounts for which he was almost certain to be charged, then galloped off to Kenilworth. There, in collusion with Dudley and Cecil, whose spidery annotations as the new lord treasurer can be seen repeatedly on these documents, Thomas persuaded Elizabeth to write off the debt. How precisely he pulled this off will never be known. Failing fresh evidence, the assumption has to be that Cecil – the privy councillor closest to Gresham since 1558 – believed he might not survive the ensuing scandal himself if Thomas was declared insolvent. As to the scale of Gresham's deficit, all copies of his audited accounts now confirm it, besides the unprecedented manner of its discharge.[52]

And not only this. Thomas went further and on 12 August secured a royal pardon under the great seal of England that indemnified him in perpetuity for the charges the auditors had thrown into question.[53] Had he been forced to repay what they claimed he owed, he would have been ruined for the rest of his life. In this entire sorry business, scarcely any deceit or subterfuge had been used. What Gresham had invoked to persuade Elizabeth to write off his mammoth debt was straightforward cronyism. All those favours he had done for Cecil and Dudley over many years had finally paid off for him. What the auditors thought about it when they returned to work at the beginning of October we can only imagine.

Just once more, while Gresham was still alive, did the government seek to borrow abroad. In a revamped version of Gresham's aborted proposal for borrowing in Cologne, some entrepreneurial London merchants cooked up a scheme in 1575–6 to borrow £100,000 in cash and bullion from a syndicate of lenders at a suspiciously low interest rate of 5 per cent. The privy council then muscled in on the deal, proposing to borrow up to £200,000 directly from the syndicate at 6 per cent or less.[54]

In November 1575, Gresham sent Walsingham a long list of points to be considered in the negotiations and volunteered the services of Edmond Hogan, who had returned home from Spain with his brother Robert, for fear of arrest.[55] One of many issues raised by the Cologne scheme was the question of remittance, as there was little alternative to taking the money by road to Antwerp, and from there to London by sea. Thomas made it forcefully clear that this would require a passport from Philip II and all the necessary permits, not to mention insurance. In theory, all this would be possible. In August 1574, an uneasy rapprochement had been reached with Philip at Alva's request, whereby Anglo-Spanish trade was allowed to resume for the moment. Alva's aim was clearly to undermine the prospect of an accord between Elizabeth and William of Orange. More than Philip, the duke believed that a wedge must be driven between the English and the Calvinist rebels.[56]

Whether or not a deal in Cologne of the type proposed was possible, Gresham was adamant that he was no longer the person to handle it. He particularly declined to organise the coffering up and carriage across a potential war zone of such a large amount of cash. 'To deal with the assurance of the said money from Antwerp hither,' he declared, 'I am no kind of way able to do it by reason of my years will not permit it.'[57] Sure enough, it wasn't long before the proposals were abandoned.

Once the milestone of 1574 was passed and all Elizabeth's outstanding foreign loans were liquidated, she and Cecil pinched and scraped to accumulate a cash surplus. The hope was that they might do away with the need to borrow completely. From just over £100,000 by the mid-1570s, this surplus in the exchequer would climb to over £300,000 by 1585–6. Alas, Gresham's protégé, Robert Taylor, and a fellow teller in the receipt of the exchequer, Richard Stonley, were caught with their hands in the till and the surplus vanished. Cecil had his work cut out to hush up the scandal, and an even tougher job to find sufficient funds to re-equip coastal defences and the navy.

In 1588 the cold war with Spain burst into conflict.[58] Then, large-scale government borrowing in the city of London would again become essential, except that most of the cash was raised by 'imprest' or else in the shape of loans or benevolences secured by the mortgage of crown lands, with all the resulting acrimony.[59] It would take another dynasty and almost another century for government borrowing to be governed by most of the normal rules of commercial lending at market rates. Barely had Gresham achieved this fundamental advance in the approach to sovereign debt than its final implementation was put on hold.

ONE LAST
GLORIOUS DEAL?

In June 1576, rumours of a scandal broke in the servants' hall at Gresham House. It was still being talked about twenty years later when eyewitness testimony in the court of Star Chamber brought more of it to light. Long before then, the episode had blighted Anne Ferneley's feelings towards her husband. For two or three years, Gresham had taken Anne Hurst, a maidservant at Gresham House, as his secret mistress. Witnesses later testified how he 'had some familiar acquaintance' with her, until she became pregnant and things went awry. The result was an illegitimate son, or so Gresham believed, who had to be 'placed' and paid for.[1]

Compared with those of a fellow London merchant banker, the Genoese-born Horatio Palavicino, who served Cecil in the 1580s and 1590s, Gresham's sexual transgressions were modest. Palavicino retained a pimp, one Gilbert Pereman, of St Nicholas's Lane, whose job description was to 'fetch him harlots', and especially 'some maiden to abuse which had not been dealt withal before'. Palavicino took a particular fancy to a Venetian woman called Gianetta and an inexperienced teenager called Angel, the daughter of a fellow merchant. It was his fetish for under-age virgins that caused Palavicino to send his pimp as far as Guildford in Surrey when he was unable to find suitable prey in London.[2]

In Gresham's case, he seems to have needed some form of emotional outlet as much as the sexual relief now that he was no longer experiencing the buzz and the sizzle of trading daily in the exchange markets. Little doubt exists as to the intensity of his infatuation for Hurst. One party to the scandal spoke not just of Gresham's 'extraordinary familiarity' with this young woman, but 'of the love he bore to the said Anne'.[3] In an effort to cover up his infidelity, Thomas promptly married off the pregnant Hurst to one of his servants, John Markham, who had worked at Gresham House for some seven or eight years. He, together with the child and his mother, would become the recipients of a carefully worked out financial settlement.[4]

Edmond Hogan, Gresham's loyal and by now longest-serving factor, who around this time named his second son 'Gresham' in Thomas's honour, was one of those best placed to know.[5] He later testified in court that the settlement took the form of a package of 'certain annuities or yearly rents' granted for ninety-nine years, notably one of £30 and another of £100 (i.e., a fixed annual income of over £130,000 in modern values).[6] There was also much talk afterwards, although perhaps not so much at the time, of additional annuities worth £600 a year, which were to come into force only after Gresham and his wife's deaths. And to buy Markham's continued silence, Gresham had purportedly sealed an indenture awarding him a final one-off lump sum of £500, due on 1 February 1597 and enforceable by a penalty clause of £1,000 should Thomas or his heirs and executors fail to pay up.[7]

Eyewitness sworn testimony enables us to enter directly into Gresham House. Hogan well remembered a conversation with Thomas Manson, Gresham's footman, who told him that when the news of the pregnancy first leaked out in the servants' hall, Gresham took a ring off his finger and ordered Manson to show it to Dr Mowse, a notary at Doctors' Commons, with a request to come to him at once. Dr Mowse had refused, saying he would not attend on Gresham even if he gave him a fee of £100. Meanwhile, Anne Hurst anxiously watched and waited in the small outer courtyard of Gresham House near the gatehouse leading into Bishopsgate. She was there when Gresham called for his horse and rode off to see Dr Mowse, and she was still there when he returned with 'certain deeds or writings' for Markham and herself, witnessed by Manson, which he 'did deliver into the hands and lap of the said Anne Hurst', saying 'Here wench, take thee these things and God be with thee.'[8]

The encounter was observed from the gatehouse by Gresham's porter, John Gurnell. He remembered how Thomas, on his return from Dr Mowse's lodgings, had thrust 'three writings' into Hurst's apron. After Gresham had gone back towards his gallery, Hurst had turned to Gurnell, saying, 'Farewell John, now I will trouble you no more. I have that I would have.'[9] Further unconfirmed talk ensued among the servants of a bond or obligation, also witnessed by Manson, by which John Markham reached an agreement with Gresham 'in a penalty or sum of money' that he would marry Hurst 'by a certain day'. One Geoffrey Hosier, of the parish of St Martin's in the Fields, later swore that he had been a witness to it.[10] Whatever the truth of these later allegations, Manson at the time thought Markham had done rather well for himself. 'Well, Jack Markham,' he was reported as saying several times in the hearing of others, 'my hand is set as a witness to certain writings that my master hath given thee, which will one day make thee a gentleman.'[11]

Little did Thomas know that, for once, he had been duped. In the absence of DNA testing, there can be no absolute certainty about the child's paternity, but sworn testimony makes it virtually certain that the baby's true father was John Markham. All along, he – not Gresham – had been Anne Hurst's true love. She was sleeping with him at exactly the same time as she was sleeping with Thomas. Witnesses appearing for both Anne Ferneley and John Markham in the subsequent Star Chamber litigation contesting the validity of the annuities granted to the Markhams agreed on very little other than that John Markham *was* the real father of the child.

Witnesses deposing under oath included one of Thomas's land surveyors, William Gilbert. According to Gilbert's testimony, Hurst had privately confided in him, naming Markham as the baby's father. She 'confessed to him this deponent that the said Markham had gotten her with child and that she hoped to obtain the good will of the said Sir Thomas Gresham that the said John Markham should marry her'. Markham, too, 'did secretly declare unto him this deponent that the said John Markham was in love with one Anne Hurst, a maidservant in the house of the said Sir Thomas Gresham and that the said Markham the elder had gotten the same maidservant with child.'[12]

Gilbert's testimony was corroborated by Richard Charles, since 1572 or 1573 a gentleman usher at Gresham House, who also spoke on oath. 'The said Anne Hurst was with child when she dwelt with the said Sir Thomas Gresham,' he declared, 'and the report in Sir Thomas Gresham's service then was that the said John Markham was father of the said child, and this deponent saith that he is verily persuaded in his conscience that the said John Markham was the father of the said child, and he is moved so to be persuaded for that the said Markham himself confessed so much unto him this deponent.' Charles also reaffirmed that Gresham 'did cause the said Markham to marry with the said Anne Hurst', in the belief that *he* was the father.[13]

With an unambiguous hint of the opportunities John Markham felt had come his way for blackmail, he recounted to Gilbert how he planned a 'device'. He would go to Gresham, and 'although he knew the child was his own, yet he would tell Sir Thomas Gresham that he kept his bastard, and by God's blood, unless he would do something for him as he had promised, he would bring both the cow and the calf home unto his manger.'[14]

When Markham disclosed his willingness to name and shame Gresham in the hope of receiving more money, the surveyor urged him, 'What? thou wilt not deal so', to which Markham 'replied with an oath, and said he would.' Gilbert advised Markham that, in all these affairs, 'he were best to look before he did leap'. But Markham's threats paid off. Some months later, after Gilbert had returned from Suffolk and Norfolk 'and divers other places' where he had gone to see about Gresham's lands and rents, Markham said to him, 'I bless Sir Thomas, so as I said I would ... he hath given me £30 or £50 and pledged he would make me assurance of some lease or some thing other.'[15] It would be this money that enabled the Markhams to move out of Gresham House with their son to their own lodgings in East Smithfield, where Markham set himself up as a brewer.

Gresham's manipulability and susceptibility to blackmail where Markham was concerned contrasts strikingly with his more general reluctance to do public service. Although he acted three times as one of the Mercers' Company's wardens and attended the annual Mercers' supper when he could, he refused to take his turn in holding wider civic office.[16] Never would he allow his name to go forward for election as one of London's sheriffs or for the supreme position of mayor as his father, Sir Richard, and uncle, Sir John, had done. Like some others of his generation, he resented the expense of the lavish ceremonies, feasts and processions he would be expected to lay on during his term, which in the case of the mayoralty had cost his father some £2,000 or more. The fine for avoiding the office was £500, but Thomas had no intention even of paying that. Instead, he sought, and secured, letters of exemption from Elizabeth.[17]

And yet, despite this reticence, Gresham was as concerned as ever to maintain his standing in the eyes of his fellow citizens. In the late 1560s, when the Mercers' Company fell into severe financial straits, its leaders decided to erect statues of prominent deceased benefactors in their hall by way of an encouragement to others. They began with statues of Sir Richard Whittington, Sir Henry Colet, Sir William Estfeld and Sir James Yarford, all of whom had made substantial gifts to charitable causes in their wills.

Gresham, though, was the first living man to demand recognition in this way, even though he was still debating with himself how exactly he was going to settle the administration and profits of the Royal Exchange in his will. By the time his statue was erected, he had still not given the Corporation of London or the Mercers any clue as to his final intentions. Then, when his statue was made and put on display in Mercers' Hall, he complained that it was not sufficiently like him, and insisted that it must be redone 'to his contentation'.[18]

After his retirement, Gresham's relationships with his relatives and some employees fell under increasing strain. As devious as ever where rents and lands were at stake, he quarrelled once more with his son-in-law, Nathaniel Bacon, over the legal title to the Suffolk and Norfolk manors he had failed to transfer to him in his marriage settlement. Despite sage advice from his father, Sir Nicholas Bacon, Nathaniel gave some 'sharp speech' on the subject to Gresham at a meeting in London. There was something of a row, for which shortly afterwards Nathaniel felt compelled to write a grovelling apology. 'I only crave,' he told Gresham, 'if any offensive words over hastily passed me, that notwithstanding, you judge of me as of one who maketh more account of your favour than of any man's besides mine own father's.'[19]

Relations with the Bacons were to thaw considerably after Gresham heard he had a grandson. 'Well beloved son,' he wrote to Nathaniel the same day as he heard the news from Sir Nicholas, 'I am glad that it has pleased God to send my daughter a boy, but am sorry I cannot come to the christening ... I have asked my daughter to give her son a cup "to carouse in".' Unfortunately, the child died in infancy and this interlude of warmth with him.[20]

Gresham's health was now his usual reason for not venturing more than thirty or so miles from London. In November 1575, he gave his side of the story where his health was concerned to Sir Francis Walsingham, complaining that he was 'sixty-two years of age and blind and lame ... as likewise all my servants be dead and gone that I have brought up, saving one whose name is Edmond Hogan'.[21]

Some of this is untrue. When Gresham wrote this letter, his affair with Anne Hurst was in full flood, he was still only fifty-six and, although his sight had deteriorated somewhat, he was most definitely not blind and could write as well as ever, if somewhat more crabbily. But he was still deeply troubled by his leg injury, which had left him walking with a limp.[22]

More honest is Gresham's admission that his servants and contacts had largely moved on after his retirement. Once their career prospects were on the wane, they voted with their feet or in some cases were let go. It was most likely because of the sympathy shown by Anthony Stringer towards Nathaniel Bacon and his wife over their financial predicament that Thomas dismissed him and had all his goods seized.[23] John Saunders, another of Gresham's land agents suspected of over-familiarity with the Bacons, was also summoned to Thomas's counting-house, then sacked, although later reinstated at the earnest intercession of Sir Nicholas.[24]

Of Gresham's other servants, many either found new posts or retired themselves. Edmond Hogan was the notable exception, although his brother, Robert, moved seamlessly into Walsingham's service.[25] Not only was Walsingham the privy councillor to whom Gresham would largely report from now on, the new secretary-of-state had already intervened swiftly to take over Gresham's European intelligence networks.

Richard Candeler, Gresham's factor in Lombard Street, left in February 1575 to set up and run the Office or 'Chamber' of Assurances in the Royal Exchange. His duties were to make and register all insurances of any kind, so that underwriters could see the terms of current and past policies as a matter of public record.[26] Thomas Dutton and Thomas Denny were already in Cecil's service by the time Richard Clough had moved to Hamburg, and after Clough's death, Dutton retired to Isleworth.[27] Francesco di Tomasso, Gresham's confidential courier, had disappeared from the records by 1570. John Lawrence, Thomas's steward, and Thomas Manson were among the dozen or so stalwarts who stayed on at Gresham House, where they were joined by Philip Cely, who had replaced Stringer as one of Thomas's surveyors.[28]

A need for economy in Gresham's household may well have caused him actively to cut back on staff. When he retired, he stopped earning other than from the rents from his lands, the interest on his loans and the rents from the shops in the Royal Exchange. Scrutiny of the surviving income and expenditure accounts of his surveyors and receivers shows that Thomas had a blind spot where land management was concerned.[29] William Gilbert, his surveyor in Suffolk and Norfolk, and William Bacon (possibly a distant kinsman of Nathaniel or Sir Nicholas Bacon), a receiver or bailiff in Yorkshire and elsewhere, were among those who let him down, running up deficits and owing him large sums. By 1569, Gilbert owed him £305, rising to £588 by 1579, and Bacon owed £164.

Desperate for cash when word arrived in 1574 that Elizabeth was planning another visit to Osterley, Thomas ordered Gilbert 'that we should with all speed gather up as much money as we may get in and so to come to London'.[30]

Worse, the auditors in the exchequer began to unearth fresh debts that Thomas owed to the queen, items not discovered at the time of his final audit and dash to Kenilworth in July 1575. These were not covered by the royal pardon Gresham had secured, as its wording explicitly excluded all accounts or arrears of accounts or other monies overlooked or not disclosed during the audit. Such sums, declared the letters of pardon, 'shall be charged and paid by him'.[31]

By November 1576, these debts amounted to £5,883 (over £5.8 million in modern values). With something of a struggle, Gresham contrived to raise sufficient funds to repay all but £500 of this amount, but the whole eluded him, and on the 21st he concluded terms to defer payment of the balance for ten years, failing which he would incur a penalty of £600.[32] Now that he no longer had his 1 per cent brokerage fees and generous *per diems* to rely on, his income fell short of his expenditure. In brief, he was asset rich but cash poor. To increase his liquidity, he began selling numerous small and some larger parcels of land. This was the very thing his father, Sir Richard, had disinherited Thomas's elder brother, John, for doing.[33]

Confronted by growing financial pressure in the spring of 1577, Gresham put his pocket first and reputation second. Eager to bridge the widening shortfall in his income, he dreamed of one last glorious deal, using the contacts and experience he had acquired earlier in his career. With Hamburg proving a disappointment and the trade to Antwerp now closed despite a brief revival in 1573, the London merchants were actively seeking new markets for their exports, still overwhelmingly cloth, wool, tin, lead, iron and leather.[34]

To this end, the agents of the Muscovy Company were establishing an overland trade from Russia to Persia. Travelling factors were employed, who sold English cloth and other wares and brought back many of the spices and other merchandise which Antwerp had previously supplied. Since 1551, there had also been the beginnings of a trading relationship with Morocco (known then as 'Barbary'), where cloths were exchanged for sugar. Typically, the duke of Northumberland had helped to kick off the process. And to help drum up interest in strange overseas lands and peoples and in foreign trade, an English translation of Thomas More's

Utopia by Ralph Robinson, a clerk of the mint, was published, sponsored by a city haberdasher, George Tadlow, and dedicated to Cecil.

The figures for 1566–8 show that the expansion of trade into north Africa and the eastern Mediterranean was at first slow. The breakthrough came in 1570, when an unintended consequence of Pius V's bull declaring Elizabeth to be excommunicated and deposed triggered a major break-through. Since the bull declared all the queen's loyal subjects to be heretics, it freed them from the Catholic Church's strict embargo on (and puni-tive fines for) trading with infidels. Hence the English bid for a share of these lucrative markets, with an eye clearly fixed on Constantinople and the trade routes to Asia.[35]

Elizabeth laid down just one condition: she decided to ban the export of armaments to Morocco and to the Ottoman Turks, and assured the Portuguese ambassador that this aspect of the trade would be prohibited. The king of Portugal still claimed a monopoly of trade with Morocco and the Guinea coast, and was particularly vigilant over shipments of arms. In respect of Morocco, Elizabeth gave the ambassador a written undertaking. 'Her majesty', Cecil's draft of this unambiguous document declared, 'will give order that her subjects shall carry no armour to be delivered from their own possession to any in Barbary, upon pain of confiscation for all such goods as shall be laden within the ship or the value thereof.'[36] Quite apart from her unwillingness as a relatively weak Protestant sovereign to challenge the political and commercial power of Spain and Portugal, Elizabeth privately had her own objections on religious grounds to Christians arming Muslims.

Seeing fast, easy money to be had by defying this ban, what Gresham now planned to do was smuggle 195 tons of iron shot to Morocco, spe-cially calibrated in two different sizes to fit the types of cannon owned by the sultan, Muley Abd el-Malek, who in the summer of 1576 had deposed his nephew, Muley Abu Abdallah Mohammed II.[37] Assisted by Edmond Hogan, Gresham intended to barter the iron shot for a large consignment of top-quality saltpetre for which he already knew there was a willing cus-tomer. Walsingham and the privy council had expressed an urgent need for saltpetre, and were prepared to pay handsomely for it. Supplies in the arse-nals of the Tower and the naval dockyards were low, and Walsingham was lobbying the queen for the necessary funds. Soon he would have £20,000 (more than £20 million in modern values) to spend on saltpetre and gun-powder, and if the quality was good enough, he did not intend to enquire too closely where it came from.[38]

Gresham had been asked to purchase saltpetre in Hamburg or Danzig during the two years before his retirement, but had failed to locate enough of the requisite standard at the right price. Now Hogan showed a sample of some Moroccan saltpetre to Cecil and Ambrose, earl of Warwick, the master of the queen's ordnance, who heartily approved of it.[39]

In Gresham's mind, the crucial role of saltpetre in national defence, coupled with his own pressing need for cash, overrode any issues of defying the queen's ban on exporting arms to Muslim countries. By helping Walsingham obtain his saltpetre, he could claim he was merely being patriotic. Besides, saltpetre was something Thomas thought he knew about. Not only had he purchased and transported shipments from Antwerp or Hamburg several times in the past, he was something of a champion for holding large reserves. 'Sir,' he had advised Cecil in the spring of 1563 during Warwick's expedition to assist the beleaguered Huguenots at Le Havre, 'I assure you, £20,000 worth of saltpetre will stand her highness in better stead than the laying up of £100,000 in gold and treasure.'[40] In another letter he had urged, 'I would I were of that credit with the queen's majesty as I were able to persuade with her highness to make provision for the sum of £10,000 worth of saltpetre, by the reason there is no weapon so esteemed as the gun is.'[41]

In 1577, therefore, Gresham persuaded himself that supplying Walsingham with saltpetre of a higher quality and lower price than could be sourced in central Europe would be an act of public benefit, even if the arms deal with Muley Abd el-Malek had to be done clandestinely.[42] All the better that Gresham and Hogan, between them, would be likely to net a profit of more than £2,000 (over £2 million today) from this one transaction alone.

A key impediment to overcome was the Portuguese ambassador's surveillance. Hearing rumours of imminent smuggling, the ambassador's spies watched and waited, before catching some of Hogan's men red-handed at the port of Harwich in Essex. The ambassador immediately rode to alert Elizabeth, and on 5 March 1577, Hogan was summoned to appear before the privy council the next day to explain himself.[43]

It was a narrow squeak, but Hogan wriggled free by coming clean. Muley Abd el-Malek was now in touch with Gresham via Hogan. Thomas's reputation as a commercial fixer had reached Marrakesh, and with him overseeing the deal, the government's interest could be protected and secrecy preserved. On this basis, Cecil, Robert Dudley and Walsingham, all three, decided to turn a blind eye to any illegal activity if it meant that Thomas could obtain the saltpetre. Furthermore, as Hogan briefed Cecil in a signed deposition, if the bargain went ahead, the sultan had dropped broad hints that he would offer the London merchants special trading privileges, opening up Safi and Agadir as the transit ports for Christian goods travelling overland to Constantinople. The inference was that by arming his regime, the English might aspire to displace the Venetians and the Portuguese as the dominant trading partners in the eastern Mediterranean.[44]

Hogan, meanwhile, pitched himself as a quasi-ambassador to Morocco, who under Gresham's watchful eye could safely be sent there to seal an accord while making his own deals on the side. It was an alluring proposal – and it chimed with Elizabeth's own agenda. For if Walsingham wanted saltpetre, she wanted sugar. It was well known that, like most wealthy Londoners, she had an addiction to sugar and sweet confections, notably sugar comfits and marzipan, the proof of which were her blackened teeth.[45]

What resulted, therefore, was little short of a conspiracy between Gresham, Hogan and the privy council whereby Gresham and Hogan would discreetly trade armaments for saltpetre behind Elizabeth's back, but as the prelude to negotiating a major sugar deal. Gresham's role clearly emerges from previously unnoticed entries for 1577 in his 'Day Book', scribbled almost illegibly in his own handwriting across two separate folios at the back. Everyone who has so far studied the 'Day Book' has claimed Thomas ceased using it completely in July 1552. The trick is to decipher just over a page and a quarter's worth of densely written entries headed: 'Money laid out by me Thomas Gresham for the account of iron shot as followeth'.[46]

One intriguing entry is for twenty shillings paid by Gresham to the clerk of the privy council for the copying out of a letter to the sultan from the queen, and for sending Hogan his instructions, with the implication that Thomas had ghost-written both documents.[47] Other entries include payments 'to the widow Adams' for the hire of a house in Lewes in Sussex used for storing 195 tons of iron shot at 6d. per ton, and for its crating and subsequent freighting via the nearby port of Newhaven to the Isle of Wight to await collection by a larger transport ship, the *Galleon*, which Gresham had chartered in London for the onward voyage to Safi.

Since pirates continually preyed off shipping in the Strait of Gibraltar, the *Galleon* needed to be fully armed. A cannon salvaged in 2003–4 from the wreck of a late-Elizabethan merchant vessel in the Thames estuary was found to have a 'TG' insignia on the barrel as well as the moulded emblem of a grasshopper. The wreck, however, is neither that of the *Galleon*, nor is it of a ship ever owned or hired by Thomas. Seemingly the cannon had once been his, proving that he sometimes needed to supply his own weaponry when shipping cargoes into dangerous waters. Otherwise, twelve dendrochronological samples taken from the hull of the wreck indicate that the timbers were not felled until after 1574. What's more, the ship recovered in the Thames was carrying a particular type of bar iron, known as 'voyage iron' or 'slave iron', used as currency exchanged for slaves in the West African slave trade. Whoever owned the cargo on this ship was a slave trader, which Gresham was not. Clearly the cannon was sold on after his death.

Inevitably, several of the entries at the end of Gresham's 'Day Book' relate to the more unusual costs one would only expect to incur during a secret operation. Thus, the expenses of Hogan and his men included 'riding at night for the sailing of the ships at the Isle of Wight', payments to servants to buy their silence, bribes to customs officials, twenty shillings 'for the writing of a letter for the [privy] council to stay their hands', and so on.

Finally, Gresham noted payments for various gifts to be taken to Marrakesh for the sultan and his senior officials. Since Muley Abd el-Malek enjoyed western music and hunting ducks with dogs, Thomas made sure that his ship sailed with four English water spaniels and 'a great bass lute' on board. Evidently bass lutes were hard to come by at short notice, as Thomas had to persuade Robert Dudley to part with his and pay one 'Francis' his expenses for fetching it. Other purchases included a fine comb case with ivory combs and 'all necessary things for it bought of best', along with two 'great gilt bowls' weighing 60 ounces.[48]

After spending three weeks in Newhaven and Lewes, Hogan left Portsmouth for the Isle of Wight on 6 May 1577, where he arrived next day. All 195 tons of shot, or 19,023 individual cannon balls, had already been shipped there from Newhaven in specially made barrels on board two smaller coastal vessels Gresham had chartered.[49] When collecting the barrels from the Isle of Wight, his transport ship became overloaded: before it could begin its two-week voyage to Safi, no fewer than 543 cannon balls had to be taken off and forty were lost. (Gresham made a note in his 'Day Book' to remind himself to bill the shippers for the losses.)

Hogan successfully completed his mission. Once Muley Abd el-Malek was in possession of his iron shot, he kept to his side of the bargain. Hogan docked at Portsmouth three months later with a cargo of 15 tons of saltpetre. He even made considerable progress with what Elizabeth, rather than Walsingham, expected of him. After at least three sessions with the sultan, he negotiated future safe passage for the London merchants into Moroccan ports and territories, along with passports to sail freely with all their goods through the Strait of Gibraltar and onwards towards Constantinople. Muley Abd el-Malek also promised to remove many of the obstacles put in the way of English merchants in the sugar trade. In particular, he undertook to clamp down on a racket whereby the middlemen who controlled his sugar mills traded sugar futures for English cloth or cash, but then failed to deliver the sugar or return the cash.[50]

Gresham must have been euphoric. It seemed as if all his troubles were about to be resolved: a new career as an arms dealer in Morocco opened up for him. Alas, any such hopes would be dashed. Muley Abd el-Malek was dead within a year, killed (some said poisoned) on the battlefield of Alcázar. His successor, his brother Muley Ahmed al-Mansur, refused to allow any more saltpetre to be exported.[51] Thomas had pulled off his last glorious deal, and there would never be another.

A WIDOW'S PLIGHT

In the spring of 1575, Thomas Gresham at last turned his mind to the vexed question of the final dispositions he would make in his will. Now in his late fifties, he was suffering from a troublesome urinary problem. To cope with it, he devised his own medication, marked 'probatum est', which suggests that he or someone close to him found it effective. His formula speaks for itself: 'Take the snail that hath a shell, break off the shell off his back and slit him and take out his guts. Dry him at the fire, and make powder of him, and drink it with [a] posset made of white wine.'[1]

He consulted physicians, among them Christopher Langton, to whom he gave an annuity of £2.[2] Only a couple of years younger than Gresham, Dr Langton was still in practice despite his expulsion from the College of Physicians for breach of the statutes and sexual misconduct. Caught red-handed while disporting himself in bed with two young women, Langton's punishment was to ride on horseback through the streets of London on a market day, facing the animal's tail and wearing his velvet-lined gown of fine damask and his blue hood, to be ridiculed and pelted with rotten fruit and vegetables by the citizens.[3]

Telling no one person more of his intentions than each of them individually needed to know, Gresham set about tying up his property in such a way as to ensure that neither his wife nor any of his or her relations would be able to exercise any influence over the decisions he intended to make, now or in the future. He met his lawyer and principal conveyancer, Roger Manwood, at Gresham House on 22 April 1575 to settle some preliminary details in his little gallery off the outer courtyard leading into Bishopsgate. Then, on 20 May, he signed and sealed a quadripartite indenture, a lengthy document that put the vast majority of his lands into the hands of trustees, who would act for him in the present, and in the future for whichever beneficiaries he might eventually decide upon.[4]

Never before tracked down, the text of the quadripartite indenture lies buried in an exemplification of various records later certified into the court of exchequer. Rather touchingly, Thomas's main proposition in this lengthy document was that he still hoped to have a legitimate son, to whom much of his property would one day descend. A crucial passage made special provision should he die 'leaving his wife conceived with a man child then unborn'.[5]

On 4 and 5 July following, Gresham made his will – or rather two. For like that of his father, Sir Richard, Thomas's will was, in fact, two separate documents: one exclusively for his lands, the other for goods. Unlike his father, Thomas did not make the mistake of tacking on to his will of goods any last-minute alterations to his will of lands.[6] All the same, the way in which he laid down his bequests would become the cause of a protracted battle between Anne Ferneley, his aggrieved widow, and the rest of his beneficiaries, a struggle so vitriolic that it would eventually require an act of Parliament to pacify.[7]

Gresham's will of lands was explosive. He wrote it himself, he proudly declared, every single word, 'with my own hand, and to each of the eight leaves have subscribed my name, and to a label fixed thereunto all the eight leaves, [I] have set my seal with the grasshopper'. Assuming no living son was born to Thomas and his wife, the will's effect was to give Ferneley a life interest in the profits of all his lands and the Royal Exchange, but only just over half of these lands were granted outright 'to her and her heirs and assigns for ever'. The value of those such as Osterley and others in Suffolk, Norfolk and elsewhere that Ferneley gained outright amounted to a far smaller proportion of the total than she believed to be her due. In all other respects, Thomas's landed estate was to be governed by the trusts set out in the quadripartite indenture.[8]

Of those properties governed by trusts, the Royal Exchange, its site and profits, were to be shared equally by the Corporation of London and the Mercers' Company. There, too, was a gigantic sting in the tail, because in return for all this seeming wealth, the Corporation and the Mercers did not receive the Exchange as an unencumbered asset as they had been expecting. Instead, they were saddled with creating and administering in perpetuity a new institution of higher learning for Londoners to be called Gresham College. This they were to hold in trust as a permanent memorial to its founder. All the profits of the Exchange were to be dedicated to it, aside only from a few modest annual sums for the maintenance of Gresham's almshouses and for the relief of poor persons and prisoners in the city's gaols and hospitals – this last disposition was customary for London merchants of any substance making their wills.[9]

As to Gresham's estates in Sussex, chiefly his fine manor house at Mayfield and the lands around it, they were to go after Ferneley's death to his nephew by marriage, Sir Henry Neville of Billingbear in Berkshire. Neville had become Gresham's heir-at-law despite their relative lack of familiarity.[10] Neville's second wife, Elizabeth, the only child of Thomas's deceased elder brother, seems to have parted from her husband and was living at Gresham House when she fell ill and died in 1573. If Gresham indeed left Mayfield to the Neville branch of the family only out of a sense of duty, it might explain the monumental catch in his benefaction, which was that the Nevilles were expected to pay *all* of the feudal taxes assessed as due to the crown on Gresham's death for his *entire* estate, regardless of how much those might turn out to be.

Finally, Thomas used his will of goods to make a series of specific bequests to relatives and servants. Ferneley was to receive 'all my whole goods, as ready money, plate, jewels, chains of gold, with all my stock of sheep and other chattels that I have within the realm of England', except that she was also to be solely responsible for paying the whole of Gresham's fast-mounting debts, a point doubly stressed by its repetition in Thomas's will of lands. Bequests to servants ranged from £5 up to £40, with a number receiving small annuities. Several bequests to other relatives such as to the now-widowed Cecily Cioll and to Gresham's great-nieces were comparatively generous, ranging from £100 up to £500. No charitable bequests of any kind were made in the will of goods.[11]

Many parties to Gresham's settlement would find it sadly disappointing. Among them was the University of Cambridge, to which Thomas had promised a handsome benefaction, which he failed to honour. In March 1575, Richard Bridgewater, the university's orator, wrote to him twice in the hope of salvaging the offer and of heading off any intention Thomas might have formed of donating funds to Oxford or founding a new institution in London. On 8 April, the university wrote to Mildred Cooke, Cecil's wife, a patron of the university and like her sister, Lady Bacon, one of the most learned women of her generation, to see if she could help by jogging Gresham's memory. All was to no avail.[12]

Thomas did at least make good shortly before he died on his unfulfilled promises to his illegitimate daughter, Anne, and her husband,
Nathaniel Bacon. On 14 February 1579, he signed and sealed a charter of
release, granting them 'all such estate, title, interest, term, possession, claim
and demand whatsoever' in the Norfolk and Suffolk manors he had promised to grant them in their marriage settlement.[13] At last they had outright
ownership of the lands and the leases he had kept from them for so long.
This transformed their finances and their relationship with him.[14] Thereafter, Gresham wrote to his son-in-law no fewer than eight times during
a period of less than five months.[15] Up until then, Nathaniel had rarely
assisted his father-in-law. Now that friendly relations were restored, he
responded to a positive flood of requests to act as an intermediary, causing
Thomas to congratulate him on 'your carefulness in my causes'.[16]

The vast majority of Nathaniel's favours related to Gresham's urgent
need for money. By July 1579, Thomas was so short of cash that he urged
Nathaniel in an almost illegible postscript, 'Son, I trow you, besend away
all the money you can get.'[17] In September, he repeated the call when a land
sale for £1,000 in cash or (£1,200 on credit) suddenly came into prospect,
positively begging his son-in-law 'to send me your letters by a foot post, for
that I have great payments to make the 6th and the last [days] of October
next'.[18]

Gresham was desperately struggling to keep himself afloat, freely
admitting to Nathaniel that he was a seller of land and not a buyer, and that
he would consider any reasonable offers.[19] Despite earning what must have
amounted to a substantial profit from the sale of the Moroccan saltpetre
in 1577, he was strapped for cash. He had incurred further debts, chiefly as
a stockholder in Martin Frobisher's three disastrous voyages in 1576–8 in
search of a fast route to Asia through the north-west passage. The venture
had morphed into a mining expedition and had nothing to show for it
beyond 1,500 tons of useless mineral ore, quarried from a small island off
the coast of Baffin Island in north-eastern Canada. Gresham poured £470
(worth over £470,000 today) into this black hole. Ten years earlier, the
loss would scarcely have pricked him, but his fortunes had changed.[20]

On Saturday, 21 November 1579, between 6 p.m. and 7 p.m., Thomas
had just returned from the Royal Exchange to Gresham House when he
suffered a stroke. Aged no more than sixty, he 'suddenly fell down in his
kitchen, and being taken up was found speechless, and presently dead'.[21]
The funeral was held on 15 December at St Helen's Bishopsgate, where

Gresham characteristically had secured a prize burial spot by offering an endowment to build a steeple, but never made good on it.[22] His remains were interred in the erstwhile Nuns' Quire beneath a fine marble and alabaster tomb he had commissioned before he died. Of typical Flemish design, the fluted chest of the tomb may well have been carved in Antwerp, although Southwark, an expanding suburb of London on the south side of the Thames, is also possible. An increasing number of highly skilled Flemish and Dutch refugee sculptors had settled there, taking advantage of a wealthy and densely populated market.[23]

The tomb is lavishly decorated with strapwork and Mannerist armorial cartouches. One is directly adapted from a plate in a volume of prints produced in 1566 by Jacob Floris, a younger brother of Cornelis.[24] St Helen's survived the Great Fire of 1666 and German bombing in the Second World War, only to be severely damaged by the bombs of terrorists in 1992 and 1993. Gresham's shattered tomb had to be put back together piece by piece: it is no longer possible to see properly the downturned torches, signifying the extinction of life, held by two nude cherubs on the north side of the chest. Fortunately, a finely carved grasshopper, surmounting the knight's helm on the south side above Gresham's coat of arms, survived intact.

Barely was Gresham's funeral over than his creditors began knocking at Anne Ferneley's door. Traditionally, historians have depicted her as a black widow: greedy, litigious, happy to destroy or harass her opponents – and she could certainly be very quarrelsome. Much of her time was spent seeing lawyers and dealing with several dozen court cases. But she had her reasons: her late husband had left her with large debts she struggled to repay. Anne had little option but to enforce such rights as she had.[25]

The simple fact is that Thomas owed money left, right and centre. When, in July 1590, Ferneley's lawyers finally came to render something approaching a near-complete reckoning, it exceeded £23,030 (over £23 million in modern values) owed to thirty-five different lenders. The major creditors included several of the city's leading financiers, such as Sir Lionel Duckett, from whom Thomas had taken up commercial loans for the government in and after 1569, and who had personally lent him a total of £1,840 (worth more than £1.8 million today).[26] Other large creditors, more surprisingly, included Thomas's own former servants, Edmond Hogan, who had advanced £1,034, and Thomas Dutton, who had risked £1,323 of his life savings. Gresham's unpaid debts to the queen, meanwhile, were found to have climbed to £2,000, a figure exclusive of the outstanding balance of £500 arising from Thomas's earlier debt of £5,883.[27]

To fend off these creditors, Ferneley sprang into action just five weeks after her husband's funeral. In 2018, evidence surfaced in the often neglected Talbot Papers in Lambeth Palace Library to show that Ferneley, astonishingly, was seriously considering an offer to sell Gresham House, or possibly Osterley, to the earl of Shrewsbury, even though she only held Gresham House during her lifetime in trust for the Corporation of London and the Mercers' Company.[28] That she contemplated selling Gresham House can only mean that, almost from the moment of her husband's death, she had it in mind to attempt to overthrow his will. As to Shrewsbury, he was most definitely a credible purchaser. With him and his important friends on side, an act of Parliament to overturn Gresham's will so as to raise sufficient funds to satisfy his creditors would have seemed a viable proposition.

Unfortunately for Ferneley, the deal fell through within a few weeks or months. Shrewsbury, as he himself explained, could afford 'no such great thing considering that [sic] debts I owe'. Ferneley's asking price was much too high, with the result that the earl declared that he must 'be contented with old Coldharbour and Chelsea for the time'.[29] (Coldharbour was a riverside property south of Thames Street, close to Old Swan Street, once belonging to Lady Margaret Beaufort, Henry VII's mother.)

With negotiations with Shrewsbury at an end, Ferneley had to start selling land in earnest. Beginning by divesting herself of properties in Great and Little Walsingham and elsewhere in Norfolk granted by Edward VI, she continued by offering for sale many of the manors Gresham had purchased from the earl of Arundel in the same county, although (as with Shrewsbury) not all prospective buyers would meet her price.[30] Where debts to the crown were at stake, Cecil did his best to help her by restraining the exchequer's officials until, that is, Ferneley attempted to reduce the net cost to herself by transferring assets to the queen to which her title was disputed by third parties. Once she tried that, the chief minister seemed less sympathetic to her pleas for help.[31]

More mundanely, and occasionally vindictively, Ferneley refused to pay some of the smaller creditors, and simply waited for them to take legal action in the courts. She was especially vile to Frances Thwaites, to whom Gresham had granted an annuity of £133 6s. 8d. He had failed to keep up the payments in the last years of his life, but Ferneley refused to pay anything at all and a major row ensued. After several times unsuccessfully asking Ferneley for payment of both the annuity and arrears, on one occasion going personally to Gresham House to demand her money, Frances decided to sue in the court of Chancery, claiming that she had no alternative but to demand forfeiture of Gresham's recognisance of £1,333 guaranteeing payment. Unfortunately, she died before her case could be heard.[32]

Other smaller beneficiaries of Gresham's settlement fared no better. When Thomas Manson, his footman, came to Ferneley to seek payment of a legacy of £20 and an annuity of £10, she brushed him aside, claiming that her late husband's debts far exceeded his realisable assets, and that she had no means to satisfy any further demands. She paid some of his wages, but no more. It would be a whole ten years before Manson plucked up his courage and decided to sue.[33]

In Ferneley's defence, her late husband had completely shackled her financially. Around the time that her attempt to sell Gresham House or Osterley to Shrewsbury failed, a new threat arose. Richard Kingsmill, the chief prosecuting counsel in the court of Wards and Liveries, challenged the legality of Thomas's efforts to minimise the feudal taxes due on his death, to the considerable chagrin of his disgruntled heir-at-law, who was expected to pay them. No slouch himself when it came to money matters, Sir Henry Neville quickly came to see that he could only limit these costs by campaigning to have a sizeable proportion of them transferred to those parts of Gresham's estate that were to be enjoyed by Ferneley and the Corporation of London and the Mercers' Company.[34]

Ferneley, meanwhile, continued to seek ways to wriggle herself free of Gresham's settlement: she believed she had a right to far more than he had chosen to leave her. After the death of their only son together in 1563, she was well over fifty-five and there were no more children of their marriage. The 'man child then unborn' who played such a prominent role in Gresham's quadripartite indenture of May 1575, never materialised, which was hardly surprising.

What Gresham had spectacularly failed to do was provide for the long-term future of Ferneley's two sons by her first marriage, William and Richard Read. Despite assuming control of all her assets as his working capital when he had married her in 1544, including those properties in which she retained a life interest in trust for her sons, Thomas made no bequests to his stepsons or to William's wife, Gertrude Paston, or to their four children, Anne, Thomas, Francis and William. The lands Ferneley already held in trust for her sons in her own right would, admittedly, come to them on her death, but now that she had grandchildren, she no longer regarded those as anything like sufficient.

Ferneley knew she had to make provision for her descendants by her first marriage out of that portion of her late husband's estate which was left solely to her. Gresham's will fully allowed her to do this, but as the true extent of his debts slowly began to emerge, it became disturbingly clear that if she did so to the degree that she wished, she would no longer be able to live sufficiently in the style to which she believed herself entitled.

By March 1581, the upshot was that all the main contending parties to Gresham's estate came to agree with Ferneley that they had something to gain by joining forces to secure a private act of Parliament to overturn Thomas's will. In making this move, the Corporation's role was crucial. Anxious to secure statutory protection for the Royal Exchange, they paid all the customary fees due from those promoting private bills to the Speaker of the Commons, the clerk of the House and the serjeant, adding extras for the clerk's staff and for a certified copy of the act. They decided that members of the Mercers' Company should bear half these costs and duly extracted their share of the money from them.[35]

The resulting act was largely good news for the Nevilles, the Corporation and the Mercers, but a crushing defeat for Ferneley. Not only were the Nevilles confirmed in their rights to Mayfield and its linked estates, they were allowed to take possession with immediate effect and Sir Henry was exonerated from paying any of the feudal taxes outstanding on these and all of Gresham's other lands. The Corporation and the Mercers were confirmed in their ownership in equal shares of the Royal Exchange after Ferneley's death, subject to the conditions of trust laid down by Gresham. Thomas's creditors were also winners. The act required Ferneley to pay them in full within two years at the outside, failing which any unsatisfied creditor could complain to a high-powered panel of commissioners to include Walsingham, Sir Christopher Hatton and Sir Walter Mildmay.[36]

Ferneley's position was now much worse than before. Although she was confirmed in her rights to the residue of Gresham's estate, she would receive a large bill for feudal taxes and was for ever barred from making further claims on the lands settled on the Nevilles. Also, the panel of commissioners established by the act was given the right to sell as much of her share of her late husband's lands as they thought necessary to discharge his outstanding debts, whether she consented or not.

Her response was systematic non-cooperation. She gradually stopped paying the wages of her servants or reimbursing her tenants for repairs they made to her properties.[37] She delayed payment of the legacies to Gresham's great-nieces for several years, despite the enforcement powers of the commissioners appointed to hear complaints.[38] Correspondingly, she ruthlessly pursued through the courts her own debtors or those whom she believed to have infringed her manorial or other property rights.[39] She also set out to maximise the return from the assets she still controlled, determined to extract the most she could achieve in rents or charges from the shops in the Royal Exchange while she was still its principal beneficiary and before its site and profits passed irrevocably into the hands of the Corporation and Mercers.[40] She even refused to make essential structural repairs to the fabric of the Royal Exchange. When part of it collapsed, the privy council had to order her to do so, and yet she continued to haggle until it was agreed that the Corporation and the Mercers should share the costs with her.[41]

In the end, Ferneley was to discover that even her humblest servants could enforce their rights. Beginning in 1589, Thomas Manson sued for his legacy and the arrears of his annuity. The court of Chancery found in his favour and ordered Ferneley to bring his money personally into court. When she refused, a royal pursuivant was sent to Osterley to arrest her, only to be told that she was out. Ruled to be in 'wilful contempt' of the court, she used every legal trick to argue that a previous crime Manson was alleged to have committed disqualified him from payment.[42]

In February 1591, the new lord chancellor, Sir Christopher Hatton, decided enough was enough. He ordered Ferneley to pay what she owed or be arrested by a serjeant at arms and go to prison. Only then did she finally admit that she was beaten and Manson got what was rightfully his.[43]

To safeguard the interests of her descendants, Ferneley gradually began to transfer her assets to them. In March 1587, she made a handsome provision for her grandson, Thomas Read (eldest son of William Read), when he married Mildred Cecil, one of William Cecil's granddaughters. The marriage settlement took the form of a tripartite indenture, for which Ferneley's side of the conveyancing was done by Roger Booth, an experienced notary whom Gresham had used himself from time to time.[44] Most unusually, the arrangement was that Thomas Read, in consideration of the grant, would pay his grandmother £1,000 to assure to himself the immediate occupation of certain of her properties. Besides lands in Suffolk,

Norfolk and Yorkshire, these included Osterley with the mansion house and all its amenities, including the deer park – although, where Osterley was concerned, Ferneley took care to retain a life interest for herself, 'without impeachment of any manner of waste whatsoever'. Her decision was wise, as her profligate grandson had barely taken up his inheritance than he began selling chunks of it.[45]

As she approached her mid-seventies, Ferneley came to rely most heavily on the elder of her two sons, William Read, who continued to live much as before at Gresham House with his wife Gertrude Paston and their unmarried children. Her younger son, Richard, who stayed single, still lived there too. In 1586, Richard began to sell on to speculators some of his future interests in the lands his mother held in trust for him, notably the manor of West Bradenham in Norfolk. He was always short of money as neither he nor his brother ever seemed to think it necessary to do an honest day's work.[46]

It was Paston – commonly said to be as greedy and scheming a woman as could be found in the whole of London – who would first involve her mother-in-law in a clumsy attempt to buy back and destroy the valuable annuities Gresham had granted to his mistress, Anne Hurst, and her future husband, John Markham, when Hurst had first announced her pregnancy.[47] Already Paston had been denounced by the royal pursuivant in Thomas Manson's case to be a 'scoffer' and an impersonator after he had the misfortune to encounter her at Osterley. For some reason, she had pretended to be Ferneley – until she realised the pursuivant was there to make an arrest.

It would seem that Ferneley finally discovered the identity of Hurst and her now teenage son in 1590, when Paston and Thomas Read began offering John Markham money to buy back Gresham's deeds of annuity. Markham refused to sell, complaining that the price offered was too low, with the result that Read had him arrested and briefly thrown into prison on trumped-up treason charges. Read had better luck after Markham and his wife began borrowing on the deeds to support themselves. Once they got a taste for living beyond their means, they fell in with villains and forgers. Several forgeries were made that were designed to create even more generous annuities than Gresham had intended. Of these new deeds, a number were sold on. To give them an air of authenticity, they were sealed with a specially engraved grasshopper seal, complete with a motto of 'Love, Serve and Obey' as inscribed on the first of Thomas Gresham's portraits. The most convincing forgeries were manufactured by the same Roger Booth whom Ferneley had employed to draw up her grandson's marriage settlement.[48]

By the spring of 1595, the Markhams had played into Ferneley's hands. She sued for fraud and forgery in the court of Star Chamber and after eighteen months of battling to and fro, she finally won. So serious were the charges that she was assisted in the later stages of her case by Edward Coke, the queen's attorney-general, the most talented and fearsome legal advocate of his generation. In the course of witness testimony during what became one of the courtroom dramas of the century, the full details of Gresham's clandestine affair with Anne Hurst were laid out on public view.[49]

Hurst, though, was dead before the litigation ran its full course. John Markham quickly remarried a twenty-three-year-old woman called Helen, but when she learned of the extent of his crimes, she turned queen's evidence.[50]

Ferneley died at Osterley on 23 November 1596, the eve of the day on which the court of Star Chamber handed down its final decree.[51] On the 24th, Coke entered a motion, seeking to be allowed to complete the case solo on her behalf, which the judges allowed. Markham, Booth and their accomplices were heavily fined, made to stand on the pillory and imprisoned, and the forged deeds (and perhaps, inadvertently, some genuine ones too) were cancelled and annulled.[52] It was the end of an era.

GRESHAM COLLEGE

On 14 December 1596, in the middle of a freezing winter, Anne Ferneley's body was solemnly carried to the church of St Helen's, Bishopsgate, and laid to rest in her late husband's tomb with all the heraldic pomp and ceremony she had always believed she deserved.[1] The chief mourner was William Read, the elder of her two sons by her first marriage. He was supported by his wife, Gertrude, and their three surviving children. His younger brother, Richard, predeceased his mother, as did William's eldest son, Thomas.[2] Both died at Osterley in or about 1595, seemingly the victims of summer plague epidemics engulfing London and its suburbs for several years after 1593. Well over a tenth of the urban population died, and twice as many fell sick. Wealthy merchant families fled fifty miles or more, closing much of the city for business.

With Ferneley's passing, Thomas Gresham's plans for a new college for Londoners to be based at Gresham House and funded from the profits of the Royal Exchange at last came to fruition. In return for holding in trust half each of the site, shops and revenues of the Exchange in perpetuity, the Corporation of London and the Mercers' Company between them were to choose seven suitably qualified professors to give lectures in divinity, astronomy, music, geometry, law (meaning 'civil' or Roman law, and not English 'common' law as taught at London's inns of court where students trained to become barristers), physic (meaning medicine) and rhetoric. Each professor was to be paid £50 a year, half in March and half in October, a competitive salary comparable with a post at Oxford or Cambridge.

The seven subjects chosen by Gresham differed little from those already available at the established universities. In this respect, Thomas was no innovator and seems to have given little thought to culture or learning more generally. At Cambridge, students seeking a bachelor's degree would study rhetoric (interpreted to include classical literature, history, poetry and moral philosophy as well as communications skills) and logic, along with natural philosophy (mainly interpreted to mean arithmetic, geometry and astronomy). Music was treated as a subset of astronomy, approached from the viewpoint of 'sphaera mundi' or the celestial universe – the notion that a serene order presides over the earth, and that the heavens above revolve in a sublime harmony. Cambridge students seeking mainly professional qualifications could choose from more advanced, specialist degrees in theology, medicine and civil law, which were usually five-year courses.[3]

Administratively, however, Gresham College differed radically from Oxford and Cambridge. This is where Thomas's originality lay as a founder. Notably, the college's students were self-selecting. They might be merchants or their sons, craftsmen, artisans, apprentices, anyone engaged in a trade that would enrich both the city and the country and who felt they would benefit practically or intellectually from attending lectures. They were not required to matriculate, pay fees, eat compulsory dinners, fulfil a residence requirement or subscribe to the Thirty-Nine Articles of Religion (one of the chief doctrinal formularies of the late-Elizabethan and Jacobean Church along with the Book of Common Prayer).

In spite of these profound organisational differences, or possibly because of them, the leaders of the established universities feared that Gresham's new college could prove a serious rival by poaching their staff or benefactors. So fearful was Cambridge of an exodus of donors that Dr John Jegon, the vice-chancellor, embroiled Cecil in a crude attempt to block the Gresham trustees from selecting professors out of Cambridge's talent pool.[4] In the event, Jegon need not have worried, as there was no subsequent fall in the numbers of either lecturers or benefactors at the university.

Almost from the outset at Gresham's new college there were four terms, as at the inns of court, amounting to a total of 126 days. Everything was to be kept relatively informal: it was possible for students to attend one or two lectures then go back to their normal places of work or even travel abroad before attending more. There were no entrance requirements, no degrees or paper qualifications awarded and no written or oral examinations or assessments.[5]

To create housing for the seven professors and a lecture room, the

Corporation and Mercers were given Gresham House, its gardens, walks and appurtenances in trust. They were to 'have, hold or enjoy the same' for as long as they made sure that the seven professors were 'sufficiently learned to read the said seven lectures ... and daily to read the several lectures'. A final condition of appointment was that every professor had to stay single or else forfeit the position.[6]

In its early stages, Gresham College proved to be something of a nightmare for its trustees. Wisely, Gresham had not attempted to prescribe any specific curriculum in any of his chosen subjects, leaving this to the professors and to the trustees, but less prudently had failed to elaborate on how the new college was to be run, in particular whether it was to be self-governing or largely controlled by the trustees with the assistance of external assessors. In particular, Gresham had failed to lay down how many lectures were to be given by each individual professor and whether lectures were to be delivered in Latin as in the established universities or in English. The language question was crucial: while Latin was the *lingua franca* of the educated classes and lectures at Oxford and Cambridge were given in that tongue, the vast majority of the ordinary Londoners whom Gresham had in mind as his core student body would neither speak Latin nor wish to learn it, so would not benefit if the lectures were incomprehensible to them.

Once the trustees had taken possession of Gresham House, they began a process of selecting seven leading scholars to be the foundation professors, initially with no specific duties beyond 'daily to read the several lectures' as stated in Gresham's will. Fairly quickly, however, the trustees came to see the need for some form of governing rules or regulations. Two sets of 'ordinances' were drawn up in 1597 and 1598, laying out when, for how long, and in what languages the lectures were to be read; more controversially, advice or guidance was offered regarding the methods of lecturing to be adopted and in several instances specifying topics to be covered or avoided.[7]

Divinity was a uniquely sensitive area. Although Protestantism was well established in London by the mid-1590s, a new, highly conservative archbishop of Canterbury, John Whitgift, believed that puritan preachers posed a challenge to both Church and State. Ably assisted by the most zealous of his apparatchiks, his household chaplain Richard Bancroft, whom in 1597 he promoted to be bishop of London, Whitgift clamped down on anyone who failed to satisfy his new and more stringently devised criteria for religious orthodoxy. At the other end of the spectrum, a staunch minority of English people had stayed Catholic, despite the hefty monthly fines to which they could be subjected. Since the Ridolfi plot and Northern Rising, the country had lived through the Babington plot of 1586, the execution of the Catholic Mary queen of Scots and the defeat of the Spanish Armada. As a result, the privy council in 1591 agreed the texts of two of the harshest royal proclamations against Catholics of Elizabeth's reign. No longer were offenders merely to pay their fines for failing to attend church, they were to be locked up in prison as 'the abettors and maintainers of traitors'.[8]

At Cambridge, the authorities sought to limit the scope for religious controversy among theology students by focusing the curriculum as much as possible on biblical scholarship and history. Particular emphasis was placed on a crucial tenet of the Thirty-Nine Articles, namely that 'Holy Scripture containeth all things necessary to salvation'. Worried by the possibility of radical religious dissent at the new college, and especially cautious since Whitgift and Bancroft were based just a short distance away – Whitgift on the opposite bank of the Thames at Lambeth Palace and Bancroft at St Paul's – the Gresham trustees took an equally safe approach geared towards orthodoxy and conformity. They decided that the professor of divinity should devote his energies to upholding 'the truth of doctrine now established in the Church of England'. He was allowed to cite patristic or scholastic texts in his lectures, but only provided he did not 'impugn any doctrine, order, rite or ceremony received and allowed in the Church of England'.[9]

At first, the trustees specified that every professor should deliver three weekly lectures of one hour each, two in Latin, with a one-hour recapitulation in English. When the foundation professors rejected this workload as excessive, a compromise was agreed: two hours a week were to be allocated for the lectures in each subject. The professors would first lecture in Latin for one hour, and then repeat the same lecture in English. Exceptions were in law, where the professor was to deliver both lectures in Latin, with a fifteen-minute summary in English, and to deal only with practical subjects like wills, trusts, contracts, sale and purchase, ships and seamen. On a similar basis, half of every hour of the professor of music's lectures was to be devoted to 'practice by concert of voice or of instruments', rather than having a full hour on pure theory.

Further stipulations concerned the order of precedence among the professors, the entertaining of guests and dining arrangements. Disciplinary rules were laid down covering aspects of personal behaviour: dicing and cards were forbidden, although bowling and archery were allowed. Drunkenness, sexual or criminal offences or serious neglect of lecturing duties could result in dismissal. The professors were to reside at Gresham House during the terms in which lectures were given. Finally, and most threatening in the eyes of the new professors, independent external assessors would regularly inspect the college and report to the trustees.

In response to such attempts to impose rules and regulations on them, the professors had a devastatingly simple answer: most refused to sign them. Whereas the trustees maintained that schemes of governance were necessary since Gresham's will had so obviously failed to lay them down, the professors believed that they had a right to act autonomously and could lawfully dispute any set of rules presented to them by the trustees on the grounds that they were not in Gresham's will.

The standoff lasted from 1597 to 1600. The privy council got involved. There was talk of an appeal to the court of Star Chamber, but in the end no decision appears to have been reached there. The trustees suspended the professors' salaries for eighteen months, which only inflamed the dispute. In the end the privy council simply ordered the trustees to resume payment of salaries. The professors had won.[10]

In these early years, the trustees were in an unenviable position. On the plus side, lectures were being offered twice a week in each subject, even if the compromise over hours of work meant that, in most subjects, it was actually one hour a week in each language, so halving the amount of preparation time for the professors. On the minus side, Gresham's will, the provisions of which had been reinforced by the 1581 act of Parliament, had encumbered the trustees with a college they did not want, one that was imperfectly endowed and governed by a sadly deficient trust deed.[11] Although Gresham had handed over his fine London mansion to the new college with all its fixtures and amenities, he had not put aside any special funds for its operational costs and building repairs over and above the annual profits from the Royal Exchange.

And those profits were minimal to begin with. In order to maximise her income while she still had a life interest in the Exchange, Anne Ferneley had shamelessly renewed every one of Gresham's original twenty-one-year leases to the 120 or so retail outlets there as and when they began to expire in the early and middle years of the 1590s. Moreover, she renewed all of them at low rents in return for high upfront premiums. By doing this, she earned herself around £4,000 in cash (over £4 million in modern values).[12]

Alarm bells had begun to sound as early as 1595, when allegations were brought in the court of Chancery that Ferneley was attempting to sell reversions to leases in the Exchange that had not yet fully expired.[13] Then, two tenants with four different leases up for renewal petitioned the Mercers' Company, worried as to whether their tenancies would be respected after Ferneley's death. They received the answer that they would be permitted to enjoy the balance of the term of any lease she had lawfully granted to them. When, however, matters came fully to a head after Ferneley's death, the Gresham trustees sought to redress the deficiencies in their funding at the tenants' expense. First they asserted that all Ferneley's tenants had become tenants-at-will, which meant they lacked security of tenure or the right to sell or pass on their tenancies to their heirs. Next, they proposed rent increases of roughly £2 a year for every shop, plus an additional cash premium equivalent to six months' rent.[14]

The howls of protest reached the ears of the privy council. Already the tenants had complained about a variety of issues, including an apparent difference of approach between the Corporation and the Mercers over how best to handle some of these appeals. In entertaining such disputes, the privy council ran up against interventions from the disgruntled Reads, and itself acted somewhat arbitrarily, fed up with the amount of its time the affairs of Gresham College and the Exchange seemed to be consuming.[15]

The upshot was a compromise, dictated in 1599 by the privy council. The trustees granted no fewer than seventy-two new leases for the tenancies in the Exchange, some covering several shops or stalls. The average additional term of each lease was around seventeen years, to ensure that all the leases expired at the same time in 1616, when the trustees would be free to renegotiate terms with all their tenants.[16]

Another major hurdle faced by the trustees was the fact that William Read and his extended family were still living very comfortably rent free in Gresham House, and refused to leave – this just possibly because Cecily Cioll continued to be allowed to live in one of the associated properties on the estate until 1609. Until they did, their commodious apartments could not be turned over to the college's foundation professors. Since Read had effectively been disinherited by his stepfather, he was in no mood to compromise. Not even his wife's death in October 1605 would tempt him to quit.

Read claimed the benefit of a forty-year lease his mother granted him in January 1581 that also gave him rights in part of the Royal Exchange.[17] Ferneley had offered this lease to one Richard Wright at a modest annual rent of £6 13s. 4d. A few weeks later, it became clear that Wright was little more than a straw man, when she became a party to an assignment of this same lease to Read. From Wright's sworn testimony, it is clear that Ferneley deliberately contrived this lease to allocate a significant number of the finer rooms in Gresham House on the Bishopsgate side of the site to her son and his family before possession was lost on her death.[18] What neither she nor her elder son could have anticipated was the determination of the new professor of music, Dr John Bull, to move into his allocated space. Allotted some of Read's rooms for himself and his collection of musical instruments, Bull had the advantage of royal patronage on his side.[19]

To the irritation of the trustees, Elizabeth had foisted Bull on them. On 30 November 1596, just as they were considering other candidates for the music professorship, a letter from Whitehall Palace, written in peremptory terms, arrived at the Guildhall, informing the Corporation that the queen expected them to prefer her candidate to the professorship. This was despite the fact that Bull was a notorious Catholic and knew no Latin, which meant that the trustees would need to grant him a dispensation to lecture entirely in English.[20]

The trustees had already ordered Read to be evicted from the gallery and other prime space he was occupying before Bull arrived. He had promised to vacate 'such rooms as he detaineth from the lecturers', but had failed to do so. After taking legal advice, the trustees decided to intervene. They may have believed their case was so invincible that formalities were unnecessary. More likely, Bull, confident in his royal connections and right of occupation, insisted.[21]

Read's eviction began in July 1597, just a week or so before Bull was due to give his inaugural lecture, which had to be postponed. Under the supervision of the chamberlain of London, Thomas Wilford, who attended to protect the rights of the Corporation, the bailiffs and surveyors acting for the trustees recovered possession of Read's part of the mansion, after which a carpenter and a blacksmith fixed nails, a padlock, two hasps and a staple to the doors to prevent him from returning. Read complained to the court of Star Chamber, alleging riot and the unlawful seizure of chests containing 'evidences concerning his inheritance', armour and other 'household stuff'. To gain entry, he maintained, the bailiffs had chipped out a large hole in a solid brick wall dividing the hall of Gresham House from the rooms Read was occupying.[22]

Read's lawsuit, much of it frivolous, did not result in any reprisals against those he accused. On the other hand, even if the trustees had displaced him and his relatives from much of their space, they must have failed to do so completely, since they were still threatening him with eviction as late as 1618.[23]

By then, Bull had long resigned his professorship. In 1607, he became the first casualty of Gresham's rule that those appointed should all be single, after James I ordered him to marry one Elizabeth Walter of the Strand, aged about twenty-four, whom he had made pregnant.[24] Nor was the wayward musician ever likely to return at some future date, since in 1613 he was forced to flee to Antwerp after a spectacular sex scandal. Articles were filed against him in the court of High Commission, which accused him of multiple adulteries with his maidservants, usually committed shortly after dawn in the lower compartment of a truckle bed while his wife was asleep in the compartment above.[25]

Only in January 1621, when Read's lease from his mother was about to expire, were the trustees at last free of Ferneley's poison pill. It seems likely that, by then, Read was living at or near Osterley for much of his time, as later the same year he had to be carried 'ten miles' back to London in a horse litter to enter a plea in yet another of his interminable lawsuits. He died shortly afterwards, but even then it took the trustees until January 1624 to evict his relatives once and for all.[26]

By this time, the weary trustees had discovered the final flaw in Gresham's pet project. This was the extent to which the college would be regarded by powerful courtiers as a source of patronage for those whom they wished to reward with lifelong sinecures at someone else's expense. Elizabeth's nomination of Bull was just the first in a long run of abuses by the crown or privy councillors. Gresham College was ideal for patronage purposes: it was central, it provided comfortable housing, light duties and a very good salary.

At least Bull, whatever his moral failings, was a brilliant musician, the star pupil of the queen's favourite chapel composers, John Blitheman and William Byrd, and a virtuoso keyboard instrumentalist. His qualifications were incontestable, unlike those of several of the appointments later inflicted on the college, beginning with the various candidates preferred by Robert Cecil, the son and political heir of Elizabeth's long-standing chief

minister. No stranger to corruption in an age where greed, financial pecu-
lation and profiteering far exceeded anything imagined during Gresham's
lifetime, Cecil imposed nonentities on the college at every opportunity.[27]

It was Matthew Gwinne, the foundation professor of physic, and
Henry Briggs, the foundation professor of geometry, who rescued the
college's reputation during its first thirty or so years. A fine scholar and
a prolific writer of Latin and Italian poetry, Gwinne – a man very likely
known to William Shakespeare (see p. 235) – had famously encouraged
Fulke Greville to write the life of the Elizabethan soldier-poet Philip
Sidney and helped Greville to edit the 1590 edition of Sidney's *The Count-
ess of Pembroke's Arcadia*. As to Henry Briggs, he was to make significant
contributions towards the development of logarithms and the use of
scientific instruments, and his work on astronomy, geography and navi-
gation proved to be invaluable for ship owners and merchants. Under
his guidance, Gresham College came to offer an ideal rendezvous where
those engaged in scientific pursuits could meet with others who shared
their interests and exchange news concerning the latest experiments and
discoveries.[28]

After his departure in 1620 to take up the newly founded Saville
chair of geometry at Oxford, Briggs continued to play a crucial role as an
external adviser to the trustees. He was able to engineer several impressive scientific appointments, beginning in 1620 with Edmund Gunter as
professor of astronomy. It would be almost entirely due to Briggs, Gunter
and their protégés that Gresham College was able to offer regular weekly
lectures of the more practical, relevant type planned by its founder.[29]

During the Civil War, the college was used at various times as a store-
house, a prison and a garrison, and the turnover of personnel among the
trustees was rapid. Several of the professors, using their own patronage
connections, were able to bypass the college and their responsibilities.
In 1607, when the rules had been enforced, Matthew Gwinne had been
ejected from his professorship after marrying. In 1652, by contrast, Thomas
Horton, professor of divinity, an academic lightweight, kept his job by
shamelessly calling in favours. Most notoriously, William Petty, a professor
of music who found his true calling as an early economist and statistician,
used his connections to Henry Cromwell, Oliver's fourth son, to carve
out a fortune of £9,000 mapping confiscated lands in Ireland and acquire
18,000 acres for himself while still on the payroll at Gresham College.[30]

The college's decline would not pass unremarked. In 1647, an anonymous polemicist, calling himself 'Vitruvius', published a biting satire entitled *Sir Thomas Gresham, his ghost*.[31] A savage indictment of the college, written mainly in verse, it begins with an address to the 'impartial reader', deploring how far the professors had fallen short of their obligations as set out in Gresham's will. It continues when a group of sailors and artisans gather to complain how few lectures the professors deign to give and how little value they are to mariners or practical men. Such is their contempt for their audience, if anyone has the temerity to ask for more lectures, they will offer even fewer. So proud and pettifogging are they, 'they will do as they list', while the trustees, rather than reforming them, prefer to support them in their indolence.

The 'ghost' in reply gives a chilling verdict. 'How comes it then to pass,' he asks, 'that Gresham's will is thus perverted?' Declaring himself shocked and dismayed that his trust could be betrayed so blatantly, Gresham's fictional ghost suggests that his will be checked as he did not demand lectures in Latin, nor did he limit their number or when they should be given. If the trustees are unable to provide a remedy, then they should give the profits of the Royal Exchange to other, worthier charities.

On 28 November 1660, a remedy seemed to have been found. The inaugural meeting of what was shortly to become the Royal Society took place at Gresham College in the rooms of Lawrence Rooke, professor of geometry, following a lecture at the college by Christopher Wren, professor of astronomy. Attended by twelve people including Robert Boyle, this group of scientific doyens gained an institutional identity in 1662 when Charles II granted it a charter of incorporation. By late May 1663, 135 members had been elected. Alas, Gresham College and the Royal Society were separately run and mutually hostile from the outset, despite an overlap of key personnel in the shape of Wren and Robert Hooke. Far from providing the intellectual support needed to revive the college's flagging reputation, the Royal Society's leaders merely wanted a rent-free home with a meeting room, a library, an archive repository and laboratory space for their experiments until they could secure their own premises in 1711.[32]

Although Bishopsgate was almost entirely spared the ravages of the Great Fire of 1666, the Royal Exchange was burned to the ground, along with such other notable city landmarks as St Paul's, Bridewell hospital and Newgate prison. For several years, Gresham College had to be used as a temporary Exchange until a replacement could be finished on a slightly expanded site. Rebuilt at a cost of £80,000, the Second Royal Exchange would open its doors for financial business in September 1669, but it was another two years before the shops were ready to re-admit the tenants.

Along with the Bank of England, founded in July 1694 in Mercers' Hall, the Second Royal Exchange would help to make London the financial centre of the globe. Meanwhile, Gresham College had paid a heavy price for the over-intensive use of its space by the interlopers. Only in 1673 were its main courtyard, passages and galleries finally cleared of lingering tradesmen and the debris from their makeshift shops and overcrowded lavatories. When the college reopened, it was in a lamentable state. Some professors refused to lecture; others were absentees or had adapted or extended their lodgings in order to sublet them. Attendances dwindled to a handful even at Hooke's lectures. On several occasions no one at all came.[33]

By 1686, the city's auditors took exception to paying the professors' salaries on the grounds that most apart from Hooke gave few or no lectures and a number lived scandalous lives. Their enquiries revealed drunkenness, rampant subletting and a comprehensive neglect of duties. Between 1702 and 1704 the trustees made several attempts to have a bill passed through Parliament empowering them to demolish the old college and build a new, smaller one. Their intention was to use the profits from the land so released to replenish the college's finances, which had been in a parlous state since the building of the Second Royal Exchange.[34]

These initiatives all came to nothing. Far from Gresham's vision ending in triumph, it looked as though his college was gradually heading towards a slow, painful extinction.

GRESHAM ON
THE STAGE

In 1605 or 1606, Thomas Gresham was put on the London stage. The playwright was Thomas Heywood; the play Part II of *If you know not me, you know nobody*, which in its 1606 printing was subtitled *With the building of the Royal Exchange and the famous victory of Queen Elizabeth in the year 1588.*[1] Drawing on an earlier, apparently undeveloped script, the play overall is something of a hotch-potch, not least in its concluding scenes where Elizabeth, somewhat abruptly, is saved from a pistol-wielding assassin and goes on to defeat the Spanish Armada. Much of it, however, focuses on Gresham and especially his founding of the Royal Exchange. As the play's central protagonist, he appears at first sight to be idealised as a merchant prince – fabulously wealthy, wholly devoted to Elizabeth, ready to serve his country, charitable towards his fellow citizens. But Heywood's character is more layered than would first appear, his idiosyncratic text often recalling the real man.

Born a rector's son in Lincolnshire in about 1573 and matriculating at Emmanuel College, Cambridge in 1591, Heywood would have only been a child when Gresham died in 1579. His university career was cut short by his father's death, but by the middle of 1593 he had plunged himself into London's vibrant literary scene.[2] After first being associated with Philip Henslow's company, the 'Lord Admiral's Men', Heywood joined the earl of Worcester's players in about 1601. They in turn scooped the patronage of James I's wife, Anne of Denmark, in 1603, taking the title 'Queen Anne's Men'. The company moved between three theatres, the Boar's Head, the Rose and the Curtain, before finally finding a permanent home at the Red Bull in Clerkenwell in 1607.

Heywood and many members of his audience would thus have witnessed the furore created in 1595–6 by the sensational legal testimony in

Anne Ferneley's Star Chamber case against John Markham, which had all of London gossiping. Then came a new twist: in May 1605, even as Heywood's play was about to be staged and a whole year before print copies went on sale, Roger Booth, Markham's chief accomplice, began openly petitioning James I and Sir Robert Cecil. After serving nine years in prison, Booth was determined to get his revenge on Ferneley's descendants. In 1606, Ferneley's elder son, the recently knighted and indomitably litigious William Read, fought back. In a case that made legal history, he accused Booth and Markham of forging a whole new cache of deeds said to be made by Thomas Gresham.[3]

The case of *Read v. Booth and Markham* dragged on for three more years. After a full airing of the facts, the attorney-general finally referred the case to the court of King's Bench, where John Markham would be sent to the gallows for the alleged new forgeries and Booth would escape only by the skin of his teeth.[4]

Both parts of *If you know not me, you know nobody* were box office hits.[5] Part I of the sequence was entirely dedicated to a eulogistic study of Elizabeth's early years. Drawn mainly from the pages of John Foxe's classic Protestant martyrology, the *Acts and monuments*, it showed how the intrepid young daughter of Henry VIII and Anne Boleyn had managed to triumph against all adversities, including her half-sister's enmity, to mount the throne for which providence had destined her.[6]

Part II, written as a sequel, was no less flattering to the queen. The central prop of its story arc is the fame brought to her reign by the unrivalled fiscal genius of Thomas Gresham, and in particular his attempts to seal a monopolistic sugar deal with the sultan of Morocco that will make him as rich as Croesus if it works out. He knows the risks are high, but the profits will be commensurate. Evidently Thomas's efforts to camouflage the true nature of his and Edmond Hogan's shady dealings with Muley Abd el-Malek in 1577 had been successful.

As the drama approaches its climax, a couple of confidence tricksters and thieves get their comeuppance and Heywood sneaks in some of the bawdy brothel scenes that so delighted Jacobean audiences. One 'John Gresham', supposedly Thomas's reprobate nephew who claims his uncle cheated him out of his inheritance, cavorts with French prostitutes before wooing a rich widow who he hopes will free him from his creditors. She does agree to pay off his debts, but only on condition she does *not* have to marry him. (Although Thomas did not have a reprobate nephew, his feckless elder brother was called John, and there were more than enough disputes over debts and inheritance in the wider family circle for Heywood's cameos to strike a chord.)

The play opens with a Moroccan merchant and Gresham's factor singing Thomas's praises. He is described as 'a man of heedful providence / And one that by innate courtesy / Wins love from strangers'. He is 'a merchant of good estimate', one who is 'clear from avarice and base extortion'.[7] The two are discussing a proposed bargain by which, for a purchase price of £60,000 (over £60 million in modern values), Gresham would secure a monopoly of the sugar trade, which was bound to be eye-wateringly lucrative in view of the almost insatiable demand of the queen and the Londoners for everything sweet. When Gresham enters, the merchant presses him for an early answer to his offer, which he can take back to his own master. Gresham suggests he should 'taste a cup of wine' while he decides what to do, which gives him a chance to consult his factor.

Heywood uses their ensuing dialogue to provide what he believes will give his audience a more searching depiction of Thomas Gresham's true character. Despite an ongoing fury in late-Elizabethan and Jacobean London over the abuses of monopolies by courtiers and favoured merchants for private gain, Gresham and his factor spare no thought for the economic evils they provoke, which are condemned in Parliament and the courts.[8] Nor do they trouble themselves with any of the wider diplomatic or moral ramifications of Christians trading with Muslims, as Thomas conspicuously failed to do in 1577.[9] What concerns him most in the play is not the ethics or social utility of the deal, but its profit element – in particular, whether the deal was too risky: it was supposed to endure only for the lifetime of the reigning sultan.

Gresham's response is telling. He professes himself fully aware of the dangers, saying 'Let not the hope of gain / Draw thee to loss.'[10] Even the lure of huge returns does not entirely banish caution – until, that is, more pressing considerations take over. Of these, the one that really counts is what his fellow merchants in the city are saying about the deal and by inference his part in it. His factor's response is just what he had hoped for:

> 'Tis held your credit, and your country's honour,
> That being but a merchant of the city,
> And taken in a manner unprovided,
> You should upon a mere presumption

And naked promise, part with so much cash,
Which the best merchants both in Spain and France,
Denied to venture on.[11]

To hear of this acclaim from his fellow merchants, and to think of himself as venturing where the Spanish and French fear to tread, delights Heywood's Gresham. This is typical of the real man's braggadocio. Thomas had always been a swaggerer, eager to surround his dealings with an aura of Mephistophelian sorcery. He sought fame as the high priest of the market partly as a way of creating for himself an illusion of indispensability. Throughout his letters, be they to government ministers like the duke of Northumberland in Edward VI's reign or William Cecil in Elizabeth's, or to the monarchs themselves, there ran a constant thread: that it is he, and he alone, who could manage and manipulate the money markets to the government's advantage and for England's glory.

After the sugar deal is struck, Heywood's Gresham suffers two blows: his ships carrying the marble statues he had specially commissioned to grace the walls of the Royal Exchange are lost at sea, and the reigning sultan dies at the battle of Alcázar. As really happened in 1578, when Muley Abd el-Malek was killed, his successor was reluctant to renew his agreement, leaving Thomas stranded. In Heywood's play, the consequences are dire, as the new sultan refuses to return Gresham's money, sending him instead a present of 'a costly dagger and a pair of slippers'.

Gresham brushes such disasters aside. Appearances, after all, are what matters:

A dagger that's well,
A pair of slippers come unto my shoes,
What, thousand pound in sterling money,
And paid me all in slippers, then oboes play,
On slippers I'll dance all my care away:
Fit, fit, he had the just length of my foot.
You may report lords when you come to court,
You Gresham saw a pair of slippers wear
Cost thirty thousand pound.[12]

His show of defiance to such vast losses, which another character in the play says would have killed him had he faced them himself, is taken to a further level in the same scene. While Thomas is feasting the Russian ambassador at Gresham House in Bishopsgate, the envoy refuses to buy a pearl for £1,500 (worth over £1.5 million today), which Gresham himself goes on to purchase, only to order it to be crushed in a mortar and the powder mixed in a glass of wine to make a cordial.[13] He then toasts Queen Elizabeth:

> Instead of sugar, Gresham drinks this pearl
> Unto his queen and mistress: pledge it lords,
> Who ever saw a merchant bravelier fraught,
> In dearer slippers or a richer draught?[14]

His flamboyant gesture, he swiftly maintains, is made merely to signal how he scorns losses 'which cannot be regained', and not to flaunt his wealth. This might well have satisfied those moralists who condemned not wealth itself, but the love of it, were it not for the fact that most of Heywood's audience would have remembered that a single pearl costing £1,500 was worth half as much again as the spectacular 'tablet of diamonds with a great pearl pendant' that Anne of Denmark gave to Juan Fernández de Velasco, the constable of Castile, on his arrival in London in 1604 to celebrate the treaty marking an end to the Elizabethan war with Spain.[15]

Would the real Thomas Gresham have wasted so much cash on such a futile display of ostentation? Possibly he would – provided Elizabeth could be present to witness it – but Heywood's play also describes the founding of the Royal Exchange, which Gresham could not really afford, but which he saw as one of the keystones of his legacy. In the play, Thomas, who is caught in a storm on Lombard Street, fumes that London, a 'famous city', does not have a proper, enclosed meeting place for merchants where they will not be 'wet to the skin' every time it rains. As it is, he says, 'every shower of rain must trouble them':

> I'll have a roof built, and such a roof,
> That merchants and their wives, friend and their friends
> Shall walk underneath it as now in [St] Paul's.[16]

As in real life, Heywood's Gresham does not bear the costs involved alone. While he speaks of his hopes for the enterprise, a delegation arrives from the lord mayor and court of aldermen to tell him they have earmarked a site in Cornhill:

> The city at their charge
> Have bought the houses and the ground,
> And paid for both three thousand five hundred three and twenty
>   pound;
> Order is given the houses will be sold
> To any man will buy and remove them.[17]

Once the site had been cleared, everything was ready:

> The plot is also plained at the city's charges,
> And we in name of the whole citizens,
> Do come to give you full possession
> Of this our purchase, whereon to build a bourse,
> A place for merchants to assemble in,
> At your own charges.[18]

Heywood zooms in on Gresham's ability to draw others into his scheme, a point the playwright emphasises when Thomas suggests people copy him in giving rich rewards to the craftsmen who are putting up the building:

> This seventh of June we the first stone will lay
> Of our new bourse, give us some bricks.
> Here's a brick, here's a fair sovereign,
> Thus I begin, be it hereafter told
> I laid the first stone with a piece of gold.
> He that loves Gresham follow him in this,
> The gold we lay, due to the workmen is.[19]

Since others follow his example, Gresham's supposedly magnanimous gift turns out to look more philanthropic than it really was. And yet Heywood seems to have no detailed understanding of how Thomas failed to reimburse the Corporation of London or the Mercers' Company adequately for their investments in the real-life Exchange.

The play sees the origin of the Exchange developing from a dinner party Gresham attends to resolve a lawsuit he is defending against Sir Thomas Ramsey, one of London's wealthier aldermen and a merchant to whom the real Gresham owed £1,000 when he died.[20] The litigation in the play relates to a plot of land Ramsey was arranging to purchase until Gresham snatched it from under his nose. While at the dinner, Gresham is shown the portraits of notable city benefactors, such as Sir Richard Whittington, and is led to confront his own lack of charitable giving. Expressing his regret that he, and so many others, have died without leaving 'good to be remembered by', Thomas resolves to emulate and surpass the donors of the past:

> Why should not all of us being wealthy men,
> And by God's blessing only be raised; but
> Cast in our minds how we might them exceed
> In godly works, helping of them that need.[21]

After hearing out one of the other dinner guests, who says that such works are best begun while the giver is still alive in case their heirs or executors fail to carry out their wishes, Gresham vows to act at once, declaring 'The good I mean to do: these hands shall give.'[22]

The good is the Exchange. But Heywood's Gresham wants to do more than simply perform a noble deed; he seeks to win immortality for himself because of it. He wants the city to remember and 'speak of him for ever' and is overjoyed when, at the royal opening of his Exchange, Queen Elizabeth knights him for his services (Gresham was actually knighted in December 1559) and says that nowhere in London can be found 'a monument of greater beauty'. It is the earl of Sussex, though, who voices emphatically what Gresham aspires to by way of recognition: 'This Gresham's work of stone / Will live to him when I am dead and gone.'[23]

While covering the Exchange in some depth in his play, Heywood says little of Gresham College, which is mentioned only in passing:

> And lords so please you but to see my school,
> Of the seven learned liberal sciences,
> Which I have founded here near Bishopsgate,
> I will conduct you. I will make it lords
> An university within itself
> And give it from my revenues maintenance.[24]

****

What makes Heywood's portrait of Gresham ultimately unsatisfying is its almost complete inability to conjure up any sense of Thomas's inner world. Heywood was simply not up to the task. And yet, is there another, more tantalising possibility? Did William Shakespeare have Gresham at least at the back of his mind when he and his most likely collaborator, Thomas Middleton, scripted *Timon of Athens*? A far subtler, more layered drama, the play is the only known attempt by any writer in Elizabethan or early Jacobean London to represent the interior world of an acknowledged plutocrat and supremely successful patron, who – when his wealth is lost and he is driven into poverty by his creditors – flees into misanthropic isolation.

No one is suggesting a simplistic, direct analogy between Gresham and Timon: that is never how Shakespeare worked. In any case, *Timon of Athens* was left unfinished with several awkward loose ends. Infrequently performed (and rarely successfully), the play can only be regarded as a dramatic experiment or work in progress. Timon is an exceedingly rich Athenian citizen who enjoys bestowing extravagant gifts on those he convinces himself are his friends: he throws lavish banquets; he willingly pays off a debt to release a man he knows from a debtor's prison; he gives a valuable horse to someone who admires it.[25] Since Gresham never sought to buy friendship as such, the comparison can never be exact.

On the other hand, Gresham – like the great Jakob Fugger before him, if on a much smaller canvas – believed his great wealth gave him a near-autonomy and the ability to do things his way. Timon is just like this, and when he loses his wealth and hears his creditors hammering on the door, he loses what defines him, for poverty strips out his inner being and who he is. In this respect, the psychology of a supremely wealthy man brought low is likely to be common to both Timon and Gresham.

Probably written about 1606–7, *Timon* was squeezed in at the last moment to the 1623 first folio edition of Shakespeare's *Comedies, histories and tragedies, published according to the true original copies*, but no grounds exist for thinking it was performed then.[26] Most likely Shakespeare first stumbled upon a plot for Timon's story while researching *Antony and Cleopatra* (1607), since Plutarch, a rich source for Shakespeare, whose *Lives* had been translated from the original Greek by Thomas North in 1579, gives a brief account of Timon's life when he relates Antony's. A pithy dialogue entitled 'Timon the Misanthrope' by the second-century Greek satirist Lucian of Samosata also lies behind the play, a work well known in a Latin translation to anyone who, like Shakespeare, had a grammar-school education.[27]

Although aged only fifteen when Gresham died in 1579, Shakespeare was well established in London as an actor and playwright by the time Thomas's reputation first came under public scrutiny in Anne Ferneley's Star Chamber litigation. If he did not already fully understand it from his extensive reading of classical literature, Shakespeare would have seen at first hand that the fame of allegedly great men could rest on shaky foundations.

Shakespeare was living in Bishopsgate Ward not far from Gresham House throughout the winter of 1596–7, when Ferneley died and was buried, and when the whole sorry saga of Gresham's will, the forgeries of John Markham and Roger Booth and the quarrels and litigation surrounding the establishment of Gresham College were first the talk of the city.[28] He very likely knew Matthew Gwinne, the foundation professor of physic at Gresham College, or heard reports of him from the Italian author, translator and lexicographer John Florio, with whom the playwright shared the patronage of the earls of Southampton and Pembroke. Gwinne was Florio's collaborator on his great English edition of Montaigne's essays, published in 1603.[29] In the preface to his work on Montaigne, Florio lamented that 'Master Doctor Gwinne' was not better known as a luminary of letters in his own right.[30] Florio's friendship with Gwinne is fully documented – apart from several encounters in Oxford, the great Neapolitan philosopher, poet and spy Giordano Bruno saw them in conversation at the door of the French embassy in Salisbury Court, off Fleet Street. If Shakespeare met Gwinne through his association with Florio, he would have learned a great deal about Thomas Gresham.[31]

Shakespeare's play uniquely combines tragedy and urban satire. His Timon character genuinely believes that the beneficiaries of his largesse will be only too ready to help him should the need arise. When his fortunes decline, however, and his creditors demand their money, he finds that his so-called friends only have excuses. As the shrewd philosopher, Apemantus, succinctly states:

> I should fear those that dance before me now
> Would one day stamp upon me. 'T has been done,
> Men shut their doors against a setting sun.[32]

With only his faithful steward remaining, Timon leaves his house to make his solitary home, Lear-like, in a cave in the forest, eating roots to survive, and rails against everything and everyone other than his steward. When inadvertently he finds gold while digging for food, he spurns it, now that he understands its true value. He dies while still in the forest, cursing the world and refusing to help anyone in it ever again.

Outwardly, the facts of Timon's story bear little resemblance to Thomas Gresham's. Most obviously, Timon gets his thrills from giving and the sense of power it provides, exulting in the glow of what he truly believes is the adoration, and gratitude, of his 'friends'. That he might spark a burgeoning resentment amongst those continually beholden to him – even if they greedily accept whatever he gives them – is not something he considers until poverty strikes and their fickleness is starkly revealed.

And yet, some hauntingly resonant echoes pervade Shakespeare's characterisation of Timon's scenes in the forest. Timon's dark night of the soul once his debts strip his identity away could so easily have been Gresham's experience. Had Thomas lived even just a few years longer, he too, like his unfortunate widow, would have suffered the extreme humiliation of attempting to sell Gresham House or Osterley to George Talbot, earl of Shrewsbury, to pay down debt, along with the shame of seeing his reputation dragged through the courts as his creditors, one by one, came to sue for their money.

A REPUTATION
ESTABLISHED

After its trustees failed to win parliamentary approval in 1704 for a move to smaller, more economical accommodation, Gresham College staggered on from crisis to crisis.[1] Its general state of dilapidation was impossible to remedy given a significant fall in profits from the Second Royal Exchange. Tenants in the retail trade there faced cutthroat competition from rivals in nearby Cheapside, in Covent Garden or in the New Exchange on the Strand, where shops were larger, rents lower and leases shorter, as well as from a proliferation of boutique outlets for the sale of chocolate and exotic groceries.[2]

Many brokers, agents and money men also now preferred to meet in taverns or coffee houses, or else to adapt private houses for business purposes rather than continuing to meet in the open courtyard or covered walks at the Exchange. The modern stockmarket originated in about 1680 at Jonathan's Coffee House in Exchange Alley, a narrow passage linking Cornhill and Lombard Street, where dealers traded government securities. Shipping and insurance services became centred on Lloyd's Coffee House on Tower Street in 1686, and from 1691 on Lombard Street, although Lloyd's underwriters did take up some of the spare capacity in the Exchange in 1774.[3]

In 1768, in a catastrophically inept bargain, the trustees sold the site of Gresham College to the crown for a fixed annuity of £500. In its place, a new Excise Office was erected. To compensate the professors for their loss of amenities, the act of Parliament authorising the sale doubled their salaries to £100 and allowed them to marry.[4] To enable the work of the college to continue, the trustees allocated space for a lecture room and a library over the south entrance of the Royal Exchange. Thinly attended lectures continued to be delivered there until, on the night of 10 February

1838, fire once more razed the Exchange to the ground.[5] It would take until September 1840, and much ferocious infighting, before a recommendation to rebuild more or less on the same site, but with considerably improved road access, from designs by Sir William Tite, was finally approved.[6]

In 1839, J. W. Burgon published what for almost a century served as the classic two-volume *Life and times of Sir Thomas Gresham*. Arising out of a prize essay publicly read at the Mansion House in 1836, Burgon's life was for its date quite remarkable in the extent of its archival investigations. Its author had taken considerable pains to transcribe, usually accurately, much of Gresham's voluminous correspondence in the State Paper Office. But the bulk of the Tudor financial records, notably Thomas's 'Day Book', the many documents relating to the official auditing of his accounts and his notebook covering some of his more controversial activities in Mary I's reign, eluded him, as did the most important material relating to Gresham's private life.

For all its monumental learning, Burgon's work is flawed by the same excesses of fawning admiration and nationalist hubris that Lytton Strachey in *Eminent Victorians* would come to despise and debunk. Gresham, Burgon concluded, died at the age of sixty 'with unsullied honour and integrity, one of the most illustrious names of which our metropolis can boast ... By the skill with which he contrived to control the exchange with foreign countries, he may be considered to have laid the foundations of England's commercial greatness'. He was 'a true patriot': a man 'acute in counsel, prompt in judgement and energetic in action', a loyal husband and father 'beloved in private life and honoured in his public station'.

On Monday, 28 October 1844, Queen Victoria came to open the Third Royal Exchange, which at its eastern end was surmounted by a campanile with a freshly gilded grasshopper on top, perhaps the only surviving relic of Gresham's original Exchange. That autumn day was one of celebration, an official public holiday. By 10 a.m., the crowds were standing eight or ten deep on each side of St James's Park. Thousands more thronged the streets and vantage points of the processional route: Trafalgar Square, Charing Cross, the Strand, Fleet Street, Ludgate Hill, St Paul's churchyard, Cheapside, Mansion House and finally the new Exchange itself. Enterprising shopkeepers replaced their usual window displays with raised seats, which they rented to those who could afford them. Official stands had been hastily erected by government carpenters a few days before.[7]

The queen left Buckingham Palace in the elaborately gilded and carved state coach, pulled by eight perfectly matched cream horses and escorted by yeomen of the guard. Dressed in a shimmering white satin and silver tissue gown and with a diamond tiara at the front of her hair, the twenty-five-year-old Victoria sat beside her husband, Prince Albert, who looked resplendent in the scarlet uniform of the Honourable Artillery Company. A secondary line of carriages conveyed the queen's mother, her uncle and key political figures like Sir Robert Peel (prime minister), Henry Goulburn (chancellor of the exchequer), William Gladstone (president of the board of trade), and everyone's favourite, the duke of Wellington.

Foreign ambassadors, including those from Belgium, the Netherlands, Austria, Bavaria, Portugal, Russia, the United States, Denmark, Venezuela, Mexico and Turkey, were there. So too were officials from the Corporation of London and the Mercers' Company in their scarlet and maroon gowns – amongst them one Mr William Gresham, a descendant of the Gresham clan.

Just over an hour after she had left Buckingham Palace, Victoria reached the great western portico, the main entrance of the new Exchange, ascended the grand staircase and made her way to a suite known as Lloyd's Rooms. Four long tables were already laid out in one of these rooms – a huge chamber measuring 98 feet long by 40 feet wide known as the Subscribers' Room. At the far end of the space was a much smaller cross table, where the queen and her most honoured guests would eat.

But before the banquet could begin, Victoria passed through into a much smaller room leading off the Subscribers' Room, where a throne of crimson velvet and gold on a raised dais was ready. From there, she listened to the address read by the city's recorder or chief legal official. In his speech, the recorder explained that the Exchange was not merely dedicated to the 'commerce of the world' but also to Sir Thomas Gresham, 'that eminent citizen and benefactor of his kind'. He had planned and constructed the First Exchange 'at his own charge', and had constantly at the forefront of his mind 'the relief of indigence and the advancement of literature and science'.[8]

When Victoria returned to the Subscribers' Room and grace had been said, the banquet began. Sitting on a gilded, silk-embroidered Louis XIV-style chair, Victoria ate at her cross table with her husband, mother, uncle and a handful of other guests. She had not, however, come merely to preside over a banquet, but to open the Exchange. When the meal was over, she retraced her steps through the Subscribers' Room and down the grand staircase to the inner courtyard, where she performed her crucial task: officially to open and name the new building. 'It is my royal will and pleasure,' she declared, 'that this building be hereafter called the Royal Exchange.' It was Gresham's apotheosis: he would have loved every minute of it.

Alas, the glory days of the Third Royal Exchange proved to be short-lived. By the close of the nineteenth century, other specialist exchanges had developed and the building was no longer London's preeminent commercial symbol. In 1928, even its most stalwart occupant, Lloyd's, moved out.[9] In 1971, a reporter for the *Illustrated London News* described it as a 'white elephant', its cavernous structure in a shocking state of disrepair.[10] Although, after extensive renovations, there was a brief period of trading again in the 1980s, when the London International Financial Futures Exchange moved in, this did not continue. Finally, in 2001, there was remodelling yet again, and the Exchange became what it is today: a showpiece for restaurants and boutique shopping. Currently occupying 51,000 square feet of luxury retail space, the Exchange houses internationally known names such as Boodles, Tiffany and Co. and Fortnum and Mason. In that sense at least, Gresham's plan for commercial activity on the site remains alive.

The opening of the Third Exchange by Queen Victoria had a coda. Three days later, the *Times* reported that the ancient Catte (or 'Ketton') Street, near the Guildhall, was to be renamed Gresham Street, 'the end houses labelled accordingly'. This was despite its lack of any obvious connection with Sir Thomas Gresham beyond the fact that a passage off it had once led to the backdoor of his childhood home and he had briefly rented, then purchased, John Abbot's house on this street from the Mercers' Company, before moving to Lombard Street and, later, Gresham House.[11]

As to Gresham College, the fire which destroyed the Second Royal Exchange gave it a fresh lease of life. For a short time, lectures were delivered at the London Institution. But with the publication of Burgon's biography and the decision to build a new Exchange, the rediscovery of Gresham's name, reputation and founding aims pushed the Corporation and the Mercers' Company into constructing a new college building. Land was purchased in 1842 at the south-west corner of Basinghall Street and Gresham Street and the building was opened by the lord mayor in a well-attended ceremony on the afternoon of 2 November 1843.[12] Costing £7,000, it came complete with an upstairs lecture theatre and a library.

Heraldic stained glass adorned the windows, and the lecture theatre, semi-circular in shape and fitted with benches rising one above the other, had seating for 204 with another 130 in the gallery.[13]

Yet the problems of the past were far from over, as an anonymous contributor to *All the year round*, a British weekly magazine founded and owned by Charles Dickens, bore witness in 1860. This contributor, almost certainly Dickens himself, had decided to attend a Latin lecture at the new college, to be given by the professor of rhetoric.

> I presented myself at the Gresham College. A pleasant faced beadle, gorgeous in blue broadcloth and gold, and with the beaver-iest hat I had ever seen – a cocked-hat bound with lace like the Captain's in Black-Eyed Susan – was standing in the hall, and to him I addressed myself, asking where the lecture was given. 'In the theatre upstairs, sir. Come at one, and you'll hear it in English.' 'Isn't it given in Latin at twelve?' 'Lor' bless you, not unless there's three people present, and *there never is*! I give 'em five minutes, but they never come! Pity, ain't it?'[14]

Until 1876, lectures were still to be delivered in Latin and English during the four law terms according to the protocol agreed by the foundation professors and the trustees, but not at other times in the year. Then, when Lord Selborne was master of the Mercers' Company, the professors themselves volunteered improvements. Among the proposals accepted were that all the professors should deliver no fewer than twelve lectures in English only, each to be of not less than one hour's duration. The lectures were to be given at three different periods in the year, and during these three periods the professors should deliver a course of four lectures each week.[15]

After these changes, attendances at lectures soared so dramatically that on the eve of the First World War, the Basinghall Street site had to be redeveloped and extended by half. The Mercers and the Corporation provided the necessary £50,000, of which £20,800 was towards the cost of acquiring some adjoining property. The scheme was approved in 1911, the foundation stones being laid on 24 July 1912. The new lecture hall, lined throughout with oak, was to be 68 feet by 40 feet, seating almost 500 people, with rooms above to use as offices. The official opening took place on 15 December 1913, when the lord mayor and sheriffs presided.[16]

Barely three months after the onset of the Second World War, though, the lectures were suspended and the building put to a variety of different uses for government departments, for concerts, even for a police dance. After the War, the lectures started up again, but so did the che-quered history of the college. After several ill-fated attempts to merge it with parts of City University, the Basinghall Street site was leased to the Bank of New Zealand in 1983 at a rent of around £32 per square foot. The lectures resumed in an inaccessible Level 12 of Frobisher Crescent in the Barbican with a few special lectures in the Guildhall, but this arrangement did not work and could not last.[17]

In 1991, Gresham College moved to the appropriately historic setting of Barnard's Inn in Holborn, after which a steady recovery began. Three additional professorships of commerce, environment and information technology were established between 1984 and 2015. Visiting professors are now also regularly appointed, besides a large number of single-lecture speakers. The college has lately added a new dimension to itself as a 'virtual' centre for higher learning. Whereas by 2017 some 18,000 people were attending its lectures and special events annually, its wider online audi-ence exceeded 3 million. So, if in today's global world the Royal Exchange bears little resemblance to what Sir Thomas Gresham had envisaged some four and a half centuries ago, that criticism can no longer be levelled at the college.

As the 500th anniversary of his birth approaches, the Victorian view of Gresham's life and career largely inspired by Burgon's biography becomes impossible to sustain. Something subtler is needed. A revolution-ary man in his own sphere not least through his sheer lack of interest in the religious controversies of his age, Gresham came very close to being a financial mastermind, but – like the duke of Northumberland in Edward VI's reign with whom he so clearly struck up a rapport – he was something of a maverick in business and life. His guiding hand at the helm helped to keep England safely afloat in some of the most turbulent of times, but he followed his own rules and did things his own way. He made his greatest discovery as early as the closing years of Mary I's reign, which was that bankers and money markets could hold monarchs and sovereign govern-ments to ransom, just as much as the reverse.

True, this was a discovery as yet far more readily applicable to England than to the Habsburg empire or Catholic Spain. Unlike Eliza-beth I's monarchy, Philip II's was too big to fail. Spain could always find fresh credit from somewhere, usually the Genoese, despite Castile's fiscal system several times reaching the point where it was unable to support its vast machinery of debt servicing, which was never less than 50 per cent of ordinary revenues. Unafraid to render unvarnished expositions of his economic beliefs to his employers and to demand corresponding rewards for his services, Gresham's interventions make him, in a very real sense, a harbinger of a world to come: one in which national sovereignty is answerable to the machinations of the market, to whose imperatives crowned and elected heads alike would eventually learn to bow.

Given such a massive imbalance in the power structures of early modern Europe, Gresham had the wisdom after Elizabeth's accession to see that the burden for financing the crown's borrowing requirement should be shifted as far and as soon as possible from the riskier, more expensive credit markets of northern Europe to the safer, cheaper ones of the city of London, which she might also better control. As he explained to William Cecil, by securing government credit exclusively at home, Elizabeth could prove to Philip II and all the other rulers of Europe 'what a prince of power she is'.

Gresham's ability to memorise and recall the minutiae of his many thousands of business deals over his lifetime was truly remarkable. Even when his leg injury became a daily affliction, he continued to juggle a multitude of transactions. Communication skills were never his strongest suit, and yet his head for figures was unequalled in his day. One feels that, if alive after 1839 and a railway enthusiast, he would have been able, and positively eager, to memorise and show off his knowledge of every successive volume of Bradshaw's *Railway timetables*. His obsession with fast, easy returns in Edward's reign led to his almost unhinged proposal to Northumberland that a state-controlled monopoly for the sale of lead should be enforced by capital punishment. And yet, it was his unrivalled know-how, more of it (one suspects) communicated verbally than in writing to those in power, that helped to underpin the general re-coinage of 1560–1, which did so much to restore the strength of sterling at home and abroad, and which put English trade and the domestic economy back on a solid footing.

He had plenty of wobbles along the way. When a credit crunch in Antwerp knocked him for six in September 1561, he had to beg for a government bailout. Moreover, his crowning achievement, to end Elizabeth's dependence on foreign loans by finding credit exclusively at home, could only be fully realised in 1567 after he was first allowed to pay down her foreign debt the easy way, redeeming her outstanding loans with substantial cash surpluses accumulated by Cecil in the exchequer.

As Stephen Vaughan's understudy in the last years of Henry VIII's reign, and then as government banker to three successive Tudor monarchs, Gresham was keen to please, always thinking laterally and yet playing his luck like a gambler. He certainly had his triumphs in the 1550s. In the closing months of Edward's reign, he took advantage of a period of radical market adjustment to halve the government's foreign debt, a breath-taking feat he repeated in Mary's reign. Twice, though, he conspicuously failed to deliver the profits he promised. His Spanish adventure in Mary's reign involved a superhuman effort, but is shrouded in smoke and mirrors and almost certainly ended in an embarrassing loss. In the case of the Genoese treasure in Elizabeth's reign, he took a huge bet on the future strength of sterling, only to find he had made a costly mistake.

As Elizabeth's chief financial agent, and for a while part-time ambassador to the court of Margaret of Parma in Brussels, Thomas was a loyal servant, in many ways bewitched by the young queen on whom he attended at Sempringham during her summer progress in 1566. In these years, he became closely linked through ties of mutual dependence, and later cronyism, to Cecil and to the queen's favourite, Lord Robert Dudley, for whom he secured luxury items or building materials abroad and to whom, in Dudley's case, he lent money or stood surety for debts. Increasingly at his ease in the corridors of power, Thomas could delude himself into thinking he had a special relationship with rulers as proud and astute as Philip II or Elizabeth. But by advising Elizabeth several times on her marriage, he showed he was susceptible to hubris.

As a merchant in his own right, Thomas was highly successful, but unusual. He was the only known merchant of his day to muddle up his personal and professional spending quite so cavalierly in his surviving business accounts, and to write off his gambling debts against his profits from trade. Obviously he found trading purely as a merchant far too limiting, and was quick to reinvent himself as government banker in 1549 when the cloth trade was gripped by a severe recession. He returned to trade only while he was briefly out of favour early in Mary's reign and again after his retirement when, desperate for ready cash, he believed he could pull off one last glorious deal by smuggling 195 tons of iron shot to Morocco, despite Elizabeth's ban on trading in armaments with Muslims.

Making deals was Gresham's raison d'être. A man who clearly found it difficult to build lasting relationships even with members of his own family, he found the emotional outlets he needed in his work. To flourish, he needed to be on the trading floor of the bourse. A compulsive trader, he was exhilarated by the sheer cut and thrust of the markets. He had his finger on their pulse. He knew every Flemish, south German or Italian merchant operating in Antwerp or London who mattered, living and breathing exchange rates as if he were a walking ticker board. Like the house of Fugger before him, he built up his own postal system, his personal network of spies and informers, revelling in his news and intelligence networks and in the contacts he had assiduously cultivated (and often bribed) over many years. He learned how to play off banker against banker, politician against politician, balancing the repayment of one loan by negotiating another.

Far from being a self-made man, Gresham was born into one of the wealthiest mercantile dynasties in London, with a father and uncle whose names already opened doors into the commercial world. But he learned his trade the hard way as an apprentice, rather than obtaining his city privileges by right of birth. Even his fiercest critic would have to admit he was a grafter. Restless by temperament as much as duty, he went back and forth to Antwerp and beyond around 120 times, braving the seas in small vessels with rudimentary navigational equipment and with no prospect of rescue should the ship run into difficulties through storms or enemy or pirate attacks. Only when his terrifying experiences in Antwerp after the battle of Oosterweel in 1567 made it clear to him that not even William of Orange would be able to broker peace between Philip II and the Calvinists, and that Antwerp was finished for good as a preeminent commercial hub, did he finally settle down at Gresham House.

He had some amazing experiences. He was one of the very last people to see Thomas Becket's gold-plated shrine and shattered skull, and yet strangely he never mentioned it once in his letters. He seems barely to have been aware of the extent to which he stood at the crossroads of the old world of saints, relics and miracles and the new world of trade, markets and consumerism. A man who allowed the theological controversies of his age to pass him by almost entirely, he kept his personal views on religion to himself, conforming to the norms of whatever regime was in power, and only latterly giving a signal of his convictions by making payments to support a lecturer with radical religious sympathies to preach at his local parish church.

On the minus side, Thomas was an unashamed self-publicist, and there were very few dealings that came free of a catch or a sting in the tail for his fellow merchants, family members, the Corporation of London or the Mercers' Company. He was a master schemer, healthily free of ideological preconceptions, and yet so many of his 'devices' and experiments for obtaining loans or making profits on the exchange markets reeked of the innovative power of skulduggery.

Gresham's timely, mud-spattered appearance before Elizabeth at Hatfield after a mad dash from Antwerp in November 1558 was a stroke of pure theatrical genius. But he could several times complain to her, in writing, of her lack of generosity towards him compared to her half-brother and half-sister, using unbelievably impertinent language. No one spoke to Elizabeth in the way Gresham did in his letter of 3 October 1563. After expressing 'not a little disquiet' at her treatment of him, and pointedly reminding her that her siblings had rewarded him with munificent grants of lands, Thomas was lucky not to find his career brought to a premature end. The fact that she received his letter in stony silence should have sounded alarm bells for him. After she read it, not even Cecil or Dudley could rescue his hopes for grants of land.

As to how he made much of his money other than from market trading on his own account, the tricks of his trade included inflating his brokerage fees; charging as much for rolling over a loan as for negotiating it in the first place, and then charging compound interest on the accumulating balance; charging interest at 12 per cent on any unpaid expenses or fees; and presuming that his *per diem* allowances were higher than those currently authorised, then waiting to see if anyone noticed. He would also account to the marquis of Winchester or Cecil's auditors in Flemish pounds when it suited him, rather than in sterling, which enabled him to widen his margins fractionally. It took them years to track down just the more blatant discrepancies.

Gresham was nothing like as wealthy as he sought to appear. Despite Elizabeth pardoning him the astronomical shortfall of £10,883 15s. 4d. (over £10.8 million in modern values) in his accounts when he retired as her banker, he died asset rich but cash poor. Heavily in debt and frantically selling off land, he left Ferneley to fend off his many creditors. Even what he saw as his lasting memorials, Gresham College and the Royal Exchange, were not what they seemed, each requiring considerable financial input from the Corporation and the Mercers. His near-contemporary,

the investor and money-lender Thomas Sutton showed what true philanthropy meant when he left over £60,000 (more than £60 million today)
to endow a London hospital, a benefaction dwarfing the Royal Exchange
and Gresham College several times over.

Appearances mattered hugely to him. Gresham House and Osterley,
which came complete with a deer park, were more like royal palaces than
the homes of the comfortable middle classes. By his patronage of fashionable artists to depict himself and his wife, by his lavish hospitality and by
entertaining Elizabeth several times at one or other of his houses, he rein-
vented himself as a merchant prince. The only member of his livery guild
to insist on having a statue of himself made in his own lifetime, he greatly
cared about how he was viewed by his contemporaries and how his legacy
would reflect upon him.

Gresham's relationship with his wife, Anne Ferneley, was no romantic
idyll. He married her for her money, admittedly a fairly common event in
the sixteenth century, when wealthy widows were much prized as brides
by younger men. From the outset, however, Ferneley had cause to feel
aggrieved at her husband's appropriation of the lands in which she held a
life interest in trust for her sons by her first marriage. Her first husband had
treated her more as a business partner and equal than as a Tudor wife, and
she had come to the marriage free of debt herself, bringing with her much
of her late husband's working capital. This Thomas promptly invested in
his own business, and yet, when he died, he left her burdened by a mountain of debts. What particularly irked her was that she wanted to provide
for her sons and grandchildren from her first marriage, and was massively
hampered by their exclusion from Thomas's will.

By the standards of the age, Gresham's affairs with Winifred Dutton
and Anne Hurst were relatively venial transgressions, despite the church's
teaching. We should perhaps regard them with cool objectivity. On the
other hand, his betrayal of their marriage vows insulted Ferneley's pride,
while his infatuation with Hurst led to scandal in the court of Star Chamber
when his dirty washing was hung out for all to see. Her husband's infidelity
with Winifred Dutton was almost certainly the reason Ferneley declined
to accompany Thomas to Antwerp in 1559, after Elizabeth made him her
diplomatic representative in Brussels.

And if Gresham's marriage was troubled, his treatment of his relatives
belies the Victorian image of him as 'beloved in private life'. His uncle,
Sir John Gresham, raged at him for his betrayal of his fellow merchants

when he forced them into one-sided bargains with the crown. No love was lost between Thomas and his elder brother, John, whom he fought in the court of Chancery over their father's will of lands. Relations with his sister-in-law were better, but Thomas went on to short-change her over the payment of her annuity in her hour of need. His half-sister, Christiana, sued him in the court of Chancery for his meanness to another sibling's loyal servants, describing him as 'avaricious, and one that only looketh to [his] singular profit'. He even cheated his illegitimate daughter and her future husband over their marriage settlement, only pangs of conscience shortly before his death causing him to relent.[18]

Gresham was heartbroken by the death in 1563 of his only legitimate son, Richard. It was a blow from which he never fully recovered. His gnawing sense of loss was undoubtedly one of the things which propelled him into building the Royal Exchange: if he could not have a legitimate son and heir, then his legacy would be a magnificent monument instead. Then, when Elizabeth sent word that she would grant the Exchange a royal title to assert her prerogative over all matters of coinage and currency exchange, so that the Exchange would never be known as 'Gresham's Bourse', Thomas began to turn his mind to the foundation of a new college for Londoners that would forever bear his name. How sincere a champion of education he really was is hard to tell. As the founder of Gresham College, he saw himself as one, and yet he never once mentioned his ideas in any of his letters. He even refused to educate his own daughter, then quibbled over costs when the Bacons took over the responsibility.

Unlike his near neighbour and fellow parishioner at St Helen's Bishopsgate, the wealthy retired diplomat Sir William Pickering, Thomas saw illegitimacy and gender as an insuperable barrier: by his values, it seems to have counted for little that he had a daughter and believed himself (even if mistakenly) to be the father of a natural son. He settled annuities on Anne Hurst, her husband and her child when he thought he was the father – handsomely enough, he believed, to buy their silence. And yet, he could not bring himself to alter his will and make the child one of his heirs, instead shuffling him off the stage. By sixteenth-century norms, this was unusual. Even popes acknowledged their 'nephews'. Cardinal Wolsey, too, had first educated then made a handsome provision for his son, Thomas Winter. So did Henry VIII with his illegitimate son, Henry Fitzroy.

In the end, Gresham's legacy is less the degree to which he helped to make the city of London the embryonic hub of the international financial services industry than his grasp of elementary monetary theory and the paramount importance of exchange markets. As he advised Mary I's privy council, 'As the exchange is the chiefest thing that eats out all princes and all men that use it to the impoverishment of a whole realm, so being looked unto, it is the most profitablest [*sic*] and beneficial matter for the queen's majesty for the wealth of her realm that can be devised by the wit of man.'[19]

In 1857, Henry Dunning MacLeod proclaimed Thomas to be the inventor of 'Gresham's law', usually expressed by the phrase 'bad money drives out good money'. Robert Mundell, who won a Nobel Prize for economics, has interpreted this rather differently. 'The catchy phrase, "bad money drives out good", he maintained in 1998, 'is not a correct statement of Gresham's Law nor is it a correct empirical assertion. Throughout history, the opposite has been the case. The laws of competition and efficiency ensure that "good money drives out bad."'[20] Another way of conceptualising this rule might be to say that 'cheap money drives out dear money only if they must be exchanged for the same price'.[21]

In her final speech to Parliament on 22 November 1990, Margaret Thatcher powerfully presented her case against the existence of a European central bank.

> The point of that kind of Europe with a central bank is no democracy, taking powers away from every single Parliament, and having a single currency, a monetary policy and interest rates which take all political power away from us. As my right hon[ourable] friend the member for Blaby [Nigel Lawson] said in his first speech after the proposal for a single currency was made, a single currency is about the politics of Europe, it is about a federal Europe by the back door.[22]

Thatcher fully understood that those who control interest rates, monetary policy and the currency will, rightly or wrongly, also dictate the future of Europe. Had Thomas Gresham lived in the twenty-first century, this would have rung true to him. In the final analysis, it is the real 'Gresham's law' and we are still living with his legacy.

THE BIRTH DATE OF THOMAS GRESHAM

The matter of Thomas Gresham's birth date is not straightforward. By far the most convincing hypothesis is that he was born in 1519 at his father's house in Milk Street, to the north of Cheapside and within a few yards of London's Guildhall. No parish registers exist for St Lawrence Jewry, his London parish, before 1539, and no registers were ordered to be kept before 1538. No baptismal record exists, and Gresham only gave his age once again during his lifetime, in a letter to Sir Francis Walsingham, written in 1575, when he falsely claimed to be sixty-two in order to justify his approaching retirement.[1]

The inscription '1544 / Thomas Gresham / 26' on the full-length painting now in the possession of the Mercers' Company might seem to contradict the hypothesis, but the opposite is the case. Since we now know that Gresham's portrait was so conspicuously a celebration of life events culminating in the final days of 1544, it follows that the painting must have been completed in 1545, but with the symbolic date '1544' put on it. We need this information, because the age Gresham gives himself in the inscription, '26', if stated in 1545 rather than 1544, means that he was almost certainly born in 1519.

Several modern writers, encouraged by the inscription on the painting but unaware of the entry in the Mercers' Acts of Court concerning Gresham's admission to the livery of the 'pewcke' on 17 December 1544, have confidently given 1518 as his birth year: this is not entirely to be ruled out, as Thomas had an elder brother John, who was said by a panel of jurors to be thirty-four in 1551. Sixteenth-century jurors' verdicts on age, however, were notoriously unreliable.[2] And an old Gresham family pedigree, last seen in 1757 when it was partially printed and which in all other respects can be proved to be accurate, gives birth dates of 1519 for Thomas and 1518 for John. That pedigree, then, meshes perfectly with the new information about the life events celebrated in the painting.[3]

NOTES AND REFERENCES

Chapter 1: Seeds of ambition

1. NA, SP 1/135, fo. 244.
2. NA, SP 1/136, fos 30–31.
3. *Pilgrimages to Saint Mary of Walsingham and Saint Thomas of Canterbury*, ed. J. G. Nichols (London, 1849), pp. 55–6.
4. *Pilgrimages to Saint Mary of Walsingham and Saint Thomas of Canterbury*, pp. 118–20.
5. J. B. Martin, *The grasshopper in Lombard Street* (London, 1892), p. 5.
6. The seal first appears on a letter to John Paston, dated 16 October 1456. BL, Additional MS 43488, fo. 10; J. Baker, *The men of law, 1440–1550*, 2 vols, Selden Society Supplementary Series, no. 18 (London, 2012), I, pp. 779–80.
7. I. Blanchard, 'Sir Thomas Gresham', *ODNB*. See also his article 'Sir Thomas Gresham, *c.*1518–1579', in *The Royal Exchange*, ed. A. Saunders, London Topographical Society, no. 152 (London, 1997), pp. 11–19.
8. NA, PROB 11/19.
9. NA, PROB 11/48.
10. NA, C/24/16.
11. In his will, dated 1538, Worsopp described Isabel and Richard Gresham's daughters, Christiana and Elizabeth, as 'my cousins'. NA, PROB 11/27.
12. NA, PROB 11/27; J. Stow, *Survey of London*, ed. H. B. Wheatley (London, 1970), p. 249.
13. NA, C 24/25; NA, PROB 11/27; NA, PROB 11/48.
14. *LP*, II, ii, p. 1487 (no document number); *LP*, II, ii, appendix 62.
15. T. P. Campbell, *Henry VIII and the art of majesty: tapestries at the Tudor court* (London, 2007), pp. 157–61, 195–8.
16. M. F. J. McDonnell, *Notes and queries*, 195 (1950), pp. 454–6.
17. *Admissions to Gonville and Caius College in the University of Cambridge, March 1558–9 to January 1678–9*, ed. J. Venn and S. C. Venn (Cambridge 1977), pp. xiv–xv. See also S. Alford, *London's triumph: merchant adventurers and the Tudor city* (London, 2017), pp. 54–5.
18. Gonville and Caius College Archives, 'Indentures for Audit', unlisted documents covering the years 1531–1536.

19. *Biographical history of Gonville and Caius College, 1349–1897*, ed. J. Venn, 3 vols (Cambridge, 1897–1901), I, pp. 17–18, 19, 20–21, 22, 28; *Annals of Gonville and Caius College*, ed. J. Venn (Cambridge, 1904), p. 29; NA, SP 12/75, no. 54.

20. NA, C 1/636/50–2; William Roper, *The lyfe of Sir Thomas Moore knighte*, ed. E. V. Hitchcock, Early English Text Society, Original Series, no. 197 (London, 1935), pp. 60–63; John Guy, *A daughter's love: Thomas and Margaret More* (London, 2008), pp. 59, 60–63, 66, 77, 115–16, 203–4, 224.

21. The fraternity which afterwards became the Mercers' Company was under the protection of St Thomas Becket. The present-day Mercers' Hall in Cheapside still stands on the site of Becket's birthplace.

22. NA, SP 68/12, fo. 36.

23. The assertion that Gresham was a student at Gray's Inn seems to rest on the fact that he was commemorated in an armorial window there, but the window (now lost) had to date from no earlier than 1559, since records show that it described him as 'miles' or knight. If he was a member at all, it was an honorific admission between 1559 and before the Pensions Books of the inn begin in 1567. See Baker, *Men of law*, I, pp. 35, 780–81.

24. For evidence of Gresham's Italian expertise, see NA, SP 69/10, no. 585; NA, SP 70/16, no. 143.

25. *The Lisle Letters*, ed. M. St Clare Byrne, 6 vols (1981), IV, no. 1071.

26. NA, SP 1/133, fo. 38.

27. NA, SP 68/12, fo. 39v.

28. NA, E 36/256, fo. 66v; NA, KB 8/11/1, 3; *Miscellaneous writings and letters of Thomas Cranmer*, ed. J. E. Cox (London, 1846), pp. 258–9.

29. A. F. Sutton, *The mercery of London: trade, goods and people* (Aldershot, 2005), pp. 394–6.

30. NA, SP 1/135, fo. 244.

31. G. D. Ramsay, 'The Wiltshire woollen industry, chiefly in the sixteenth and early seventeenth centuries', Oxford DPhil (Oxford, 1939), Appendix B.

32. NA, SP 1/242, fo. 97; NA, C 66/695, no. 28; *LP*, XIII, ii, no. 671; *LP*, XIV, ii, appendix no. 42; Sotheby's sale of 15 July 2014, lot 401; *Valor ecclesiasticus*, ed. J. Caley and J. Hunter, 6 vols (London, 1810–34), V, pp. 253–4.

33. NA, SP 1/155, fo. 25v.

34. *LP*, XV, no. 850 (p. 422).

35. NA, PROB 11/30.

36. NA, PROB 11/30.

37. MC, Acts of Court, 1527–60, fo. 186.

38. The portrait currently hangs in Mercers' Hall. Its provenance can be traced back to Hoxne Abbey, one of Thomas Gresham's Suffolk properties. I gratefully acknowledge the help and kindness of Dr Charlotte Bolland of the National Portrait Gallery, who talked me in depth through the painting and allowed me to examine it at close quarters in the NPG studio while it was on temporary loan.

39. Written tests of pigment analysis, infrared reflectography, x-radiography and dendrochronology conducted at the NPG in 2007–8 all point to Antwerp and to

an artist whose brushwork was broader in approach than the more enamelled look of the portraits attributed to William Scrots. Alterations to the under-drawing beneath the paint surface show that the eyebrows and the bridge of the sitter's nose were changed by the artist as he went along. So were the left of the legs – the black of a former leg can still be seen beneath the pale paint of the floor tiles. At a late stage in the painting, the artist repainted the gloves held in Gresham's right hand as a folded V-shape, drawing the eye directly downwards to the skull.

40. *The book of the courtier*, ed. and trans. L. E. Opdycke (New York, 1901), p. 103.

41. *Vertue 'note books'*, ed. H. Jenkinson, A. J. Watson, H. Hake and others, Walpole Society, nos 18, 20, 22, 24, 26, 30; 6 vols (London, 1930–55), I, p. 119; IV, pp. 16, 115.

42. I owe this invaluable information to Dr Bolland.

Chapter 2: Antwerp

1. O. de Smedt, *De Engelse natie te Antwerpen in de 16ᵉ eeuw*, 2 vols (Antwerp, 1950–54); H. van der Wee, *The growth of the Antwerp market and the European economy*, 3 vols (The Hague, 1963); G. Marnef, *Antwerp in the age of reformation, 1550–1577* (London, 1996); I. Blanchard, *The international economy in the 'age of discoveries', 1470–1570* (Stuttgart, 2009); I. Blanchard, 'English royal borrowing at Antwerp, 1544–1564', in *Finances publiques et finances privées au bas moyen âge*, ed. M. Boone (Leuven, 1996), pp. 57–73; R. Ehrenberg, *Capital and finance in the age of the Renaissance* (New York, 1928); S. Alford, *London's triumph: merchant adventurers and the Tudor city* (London, 2017), pp. 39–51.

2. D. Ewing, 'Marketing art in Antwerp, 1460–1560: Our Lady's *pand*', *Art Bulletin*, 72 (1990), pp. 558–84.

3. FelixArchief, N#2077, fos 5–7v.

4. J. Wegg, *Antwerp, 1477–1559* (London, 1916), pp. 133–5.

5. I. Archer, 'Sir Thomas Gresham's London', Special lecture, 27 May 1997, Mansion House (London, 1997), pp. 1–3; G. D. Ramsay, 'The Wiltshire woollen industry, chiefly in the sixteenth and early seventeenth centuries', Oxford DPhil (Oxford, 1939), Appendix B; D. Oldroyd, 'John Johnson's letters', *Accounting Historians Journal*, 25 (1998), p. 60.

6. O. Gelderblom, *Cities of commerce: the institutional foundation of international trade in the Low Countries, 1250–1650* (Oxford, 2013), p. 31.

7. E. M. Carus-Wilson, *Medieval merchant venturers* (London, 1967), pp. 143–82; G. D. Ramsay, 'A saint in the city: Thomas More at Mercers' Hall', *EHR*, 97 (1982), pp. 269–88; G. D. Ramsay, *The city of London in international politics at the accession of Elizabeth Tudor* (Manchester, 1975), pp. 22–8.

8. 13 Elizabeth, c. 8.

9. *Religione e instituzioni religiose nell'economia Europea, 1000–1800*, ed. F. Ammannati (Florence, 2012), p. 169; Ehrenberg, *Capital and finance*, pp. 233–72 (where the wrong date is given); Blanchard, *International economy*, pp. 251–60.

10. NA, SP 1/135, fo. 244.

11. *LP*, XV, no. 264.

12. *LP*, XV, no. 448.

13. *LP*, XVIII, i, nos 731, 743.

14. BL, Cotton MS, Otho E.X, fo. 44 (damaged by fire); NA, SP 70/64, nos 1123, 1124, 1125.

15. NA, SP 70/64, no. 1158.

16. NA, SP 70/64, no. 1158.

17. BL, Cotton MS, Otho E.X, fo. 44; NA, E 351/18.

18. Passports, otherwise known as 'safe-conducts', first seem to have been introduced in the fifteenth century, probably during the Hundred Years' War. Issued mainly to diplomats, merchants or their factors, by foreign governments, they authorised a person to travel to, from, or through a foreign country, usually under defined restrictions of time and purpose and often carrying merchandise.

19. M. Girouard, *Cities and people: a social and architectural history* (New Haven and London, 1985), pp. 140–41.

20. Marnef, *Antwerp in the age of reformation*, p. 23.

21. NA, SP 68/12, no. 670.

22. G. Marnef, 'Protestant conversions in an age of Catholic Reformation: the case of sixteenth-century Antwerp', in *The Low Countries as a crossroads of religious beliefs*, ed. A.-J. Gelderblom, J. L. de Jong, M. van Vaeck (Leiden, 2004), p. 33.

23. C. E. Challis, 'Currency', in *The Royal Exchange*, ed. A. Saunders, London Topographical Society, no. 152 (London, 1997), pp. 68–9.

24. *LP*, XIX, i, no. 733; R. Verstegan, *The post for divers partes of the world* (London, 1576), p. 86; Ehrenberg, *Capital and finance*, p. 17; W. A. Shaw, *The history of currency, 1252–1894* (London, 1895), pp. 345–8, 356, 358.

25. H. Buckley, 'Sir Thomas Gresham and the foreign exchanges', *Economic Journal*, 34 (1924), p. 590.

26. *LP*, XVIII, i, no. 731.

27. D. Potter, *Henry VIII and Francis I: the final conflict, 1540–47* (Leiden, 2011), pp. 260–62.

28. C. E. Challis, *The Tudor coinage* (Manchester, 1978), pp. 248–55; L. Ling-Fan, 'Bullion, bills and arbitrage: exchange markets in fourteenth to seventeenth century Europe', London School of Economics PhD (London, 2012), pp. 85–94; Potter, *Henry VIII and Francis I*, pp. 248–55.

29. *LP*, XIX, i, no. 725; Potter, *Henry VIII and Francis I*, pp. 251–2, 254–5.

30. NA, SP 1/208, fos 185–86v, 192.

31. NA, SP 1/208, fos 183–84v.

32. P. Ramsey, 'Credit instruments', in *The Royal Exchange*, ed. Saunders, pp. 72–3; Buckley, 'Sir Thomas Gresham and the Foreign Exchanges', pp. 589–601; P. Spufford, *Handbook of medieval exchange* (London, 1986), pp. xxx–liii.

33. *LP*, XIX, i, no. 630; Ehrenberg, *Capital and finance*, pp. 158–60; Wegg, *Antwerp*, pp. 297–8.

34. *LP*, XX, ii, nos 551, 552.

35. *LP*, XX, ii, no. 262.

36. *LP*, XX, ii, nos 559, 564, 566; *LP*, XXI, ii, no. 1044; NA, SP 1/220, fo. 80.

37. *LP*, XX, ii, no. 272.
38. NA, SP 1/208, fos 192–3v.
39. *LP*, XXI, i, no. 1322.
40. NA, SP 1/220, fo. 80.
41. *APC, 1542–1547*, p. 488.

Chapter 3: Trade and domesticity

1. The house was described in a document of 1548 as 'the messuage and shops, cellars, solars, chambers, entries, buildings and curtileges' situated on the eastern side of Milk Street, and 'a warehouse and a long chamber above it, and a cellar and coal house beneath it, and a long entry and door called "le backdoor", opening out into the king's highway opposite the Guildhall'. See *CPR, 1548–1549*, p. 55.
2. NA, E 179/144/123, fos 6, 22.
3. *Two Tudor subsidy assessment rolls for the city of London, 1541 and 1582*, ed. R. G. Lang, London Record Society, no. 29 (London, 1993), no. 68.
4. NA, PROB 11/30.
5. MC, Gresham Journal, entry no. 2297. The total rent due is from entry no. 768. For a full description of Gresham's accounts and many details on which this chapter partly relies, see J. Newman, 'Thomas Gresham, private person rather than public figure', *History teaching review year book*, VII (1993), pp. 13–21.
6. MC, Acts of Court, 1527–69, fos 156v, 215v, 222v.
7. The deposition of Richard Damser in NA, C 24/16 strongly suggests that he was at Lincoln's Inn and is probably the 'John Gresham' identified as his cousin in J. Baker, *The men of law, 1440–1550*, 2 vols, Selden Society Supplementary Series, no. 18 (London, 2012), I, p. 780.
8. MC, Gresham Journal, entry no. 2371.
9. Newman, 'Thomas Gresham, private person', p. 19.
10. NA, PROB 11/30; Newman, 'Thomas Gresham, private person', pp. 15–16.
11. NA, SP 12/105, no. 69.
12. NA, PROB 11/30; MC, Gresham Journal, entry no. 768.
13. Gresham's Journal was purchased by Maggs Ltd for £800 at auction in Diss, Norfolk, in 1952. It is now in the Mercers' Company archives. For evaluation, see J. O. Winjum, 'The journal of Sir Thomas Gresham', *The accounting review*, 46 (1971), pp. 149–55; P. Ramsey, 'Some Tudor merchants' accounts', in *Studies in the history of accounting*, ed. A. G. Littleton and B. S. Yamey (London, 1956), pp. 185–201.
14. L. Pacioli, *Somma de aritmetica, geometria, proporzioni, e proporzionalità* (Venice, 1494). See also *Ancient double-entry bookkeeping: Luca Pacioli's treatise (AD 1494)*, ed. J. B. Geijsbeek (Denver: Colorado, 1914), pp. 32–81.
15. J. Y. Christoffels, *Nouvelle instruction et remonstration de la tres excellente science du livre de compte* (Antwerp, 1543). Bibliothèque royale, Brussels, ref. LP/5050/A; BL, C.31.h.25; Médiathèque municipale François Mitterrand, Poitiers, ref. CR/140.

16. C. Gordon, 'The first English books on bookkeeping', in *Studies of the history of accounting*, pp. 202–4; E. Stevelinck, 'Qui peut avoir traduit en anglais le premier livre de comptabilité paru en français?', *De gulden passer: bulletin van de vereeniging der Antwerpsche bibliophielen*, 70 (1992), pp. 69–85.

17. BL, Lansdowne MS 110, no. 59; G. Schanz, *Englische Handelspolitik*, 2 vols (Leipzig, 1881), II, pp. 1–156; P. Ramsey, 'Overseas trade in the reign of Henry VII: the evidence of customs accounts', *EcHR*, New Series, 6 (1953), pp. 173–82.

18. E. M. Carus-Wilson, *Medieval merchant venturers* (London, 1967), pp. xv–xxxiv; F. J. Fisher, 'Commercial trends and policy in sixteenth-century England', *EcHR*, 10 (1940), pp. 95–117.

19. MC, Gresham Journal, entry nos 535, 1011, 1012, 1810, 4348.

20. MC, Gresham Journal, entry no. 2793; NA, E 101/347/16; Longleat MSS, Thynne papers, I, fo. 246; I. Blanchard, 'Sir Thomas Gresham, c.1518–1579', in *The Royal Exchange*, ed. A. Saunders, London Topographical Society, no. 152 (London, 1997), p. 13.

21. MC, Gresham Journal, entry nos 535, 1011–12.

22. MC, Gresham Journal, entry no. 4348.

23. MC, Gresham Journal, entry no. 4531.

24. MC, Gresham Journal, entry no. 1577.

25. MC, Gresham Journal, entry no. 768.

26. N. Moore and S. Bakewell, 'Christopher Langton', *ODNB*.

27. MC, Gresham Journal, entry nos 1408, 1436. See also below, Chapter 19.

28. MC, Gresham Journal, entry nos 1545, 1613.

29. M. E. Bratchel, 'Alien merchant communities in London, 1500–1550', Cambridge PhD (Cambridge, 1975), pp. 31–272; R. Ehrenberg, *Capital and finance in the age of the Renaissance* (New York, 1928), pp. 199–200.

30. Bratchel, 'Alien merchant communities in London, 1500–1550', pp. 168–380. See also his articles: 'Regulation and group-consciousness in the later history of London's Italian merchant colonies', *JEEH*, 9 (1980), pp. 585–610; 'Italian merchant organization and business relationships in early Tudor London', *JEEH*, 7 (1978), pp. 5–32; 'Alien merchant colonies in 16th century England', *Journal of Medieval and Renaissance Studies*, 14 (1984), pp. 39–62.

31. *Two Tudor subsidy assessment rolls*, no. 31.

32. M. E. Bratchel, 'Germain Cioll, sixteenth-century London merchant: a biographical note', *BIHR*, 56 (1983), pp. 113–15.

33. MC, Gresham Journal, entry no. 1499.

34. MC, Gresham Journal, entry nos 2250–53, 2255–9, 2262; J. Oldland, 'The allocation of merchant capital in early Tudor London', *EcHR*, New Series, 63 (2010), pp. 1070–71; P. Ramsey, 'Two early Tudor cloth merchants: Sir Thomas Kitson and Sir Thomas Gresham', in *Produzione e consume dei panni de lana*, ed. M. Spallanzam (Florence, 1976), pp. 385–9; Ramsey, 'Some Tudor merchants' accounts', in *Studies in the history of accounting*, ed. Littleton and Yamey, pp. 195–6; A. F. Sutton, *The mercery of London: trade, goods and people* (Aldershot, 2005), p. 470.

35. Newman, 'Thomas Gresham, private person', pp. 17–19. For Thomas's fur-lined gowns, see Lettenhove, IV, p. 382

36. MC, Gresham Journal, entry no. 1466.

37. Longleat MSS, Thynne papers, I, fo. 243; Newman, 'Thomas Gresham, private person', pp. 17, 20.

38. MC, Gresham Journal, entry nos 489–90, 3288.

39. NA, PROB 11/30.

40. NA, C 2/Eliz/G1/57; C 3/29/109; C 3/234/1; C 33/52, fos 184v–5. See also below, Chapter 15.

41. MC, Gresham Journal, entry nos 2294–5.

42. MC, Gresham Journal, entry no. 2141.

43. E.g. MC, Gresham Journal, entry no. 3291.

Chapter 4: Risks and rewards

1. NA, SP 10/8, no. 4.

2. *APC, 1547–1550*, pp. 7–8, 67–74; E. W. Ives, 'Henry VIII's will: a forensic conundrum', *HJ*, 35 (1992), pp. 779–804.

3. SP 10/15, nos 11, 73; R. B. Outhwaite, 'The trials of foreign borrowing: the English crown and the Antwerp money market in the mid-sixteenth century', *EcHR*, New Series, 19 (1966), pp. 289–305; I. Blanchard, 'English royal borrowing at Antwerp, 1544–1564', in *Finances publiques et finances privées au bas moyen âge*, ed. M. Boone (Leuven, 1996), pp. 65–7.

4. *Literary remains of King Edward VI*, ed. J. G. Nichols, 2 vols (London, 1857), II, pp. 303, 355, 423.

5. Blanchard, 'English royal borrowing', p. 67.

6. C. E. Challis, *The Tudor coinage* (Manchester, 1978), pp. 95–9.

7. SP 68/4, no. 193.

8. Longleat MSS, Thynne papers, I, fo. 24.

9. NA, SP 68/3, no. 142. For interest rates, see L. Ling-Fan, 'Bullion, bills and arbitrage: exchange markets in fourteenth to seventeenth century Europe', London School of Economics PhD (London, 2012), pp. 109–112.

10. NA, SP 83/3, no. 142.

11. NA, SP 68/3, nos 139, 146, 147, 148, 150, 153, 154, 155, 156, 161, 163, 164, 166.

12. *LP*, IV, ii, no. 4662.

13. R. Ehrenberg, *Capital and finance in the age of the Renaissance* (New York, 1928), pp. 153–4.

14. Longleat MSS, Thynne papers, I, fo. 245; NA. SP 68/3, no. 148.

15. Longleat MSS, Thynne papers, I, fo. 245.

16. NA, SP 68/3, no. 171.

17. Longleat MSS, Thynne papers, I, fo. 246.

18. BL, Cotton MS, Otho E.X, fo. 43.

19. *Literary remains of King Edward VI,* I, pp. clxii–clxiv; BL, Cotton MS, Vespasian F.XIII, fo. 273; BL, Cotton MS, Vespasian D.XVIII, fos 1–82; BL, Cotton MS, Nero C.X, fos 84–93v.

20. S. Alford, *Kingship and politics in the reign of Edward VI* (Cambridge, 2002), pp. 156–70.

21. MC, Acts of Court, 1527–69, fo. 239v. The reserved rent was bought out from the crown at 20 years' purchase, and Gresham reimbursed that sum. This rent had fallen due to the crown by the Chantries Act of 1547. For the house, see A. F. Sutton, *The mercery of London: trade, goods and people* (Aldershot, 2005), pp. 169, 375.

22. NA, E 34/4; Blanchard, 'English royal borrowing', p. 67.

23. NA, E 34/4; *APC, 1550–1552,* p. 26.

24. NA, SP 68/9A, p. 146 (Sir John Mason's letter book).

25. NA, E 34/4; *Literary remains of King Edward VI,* II, p. 315.

26. *APC, 1550–1552,* p. 228.

27. *APC, 1550–1552,* p. 224; *APC, 1552–1554,* p. 164; NA, E 101/546/19.

28. *APC, 1550–1552,* pp. 243, 244–5, 287, 310–11, 312, 507, 510–11.

29. *APC, 1550–1552,* p. 252.

30. *APC, 1550–1552,* p. 452.

31. BL, Cotton MS, Otho E.X, fo. 43.

Chapter 5: A family quarrel

1. MC, Gresham Journal, frontispiece.

2. MC, Acts of Court, 1527–60, fos 222, 229.

3. These unsorted, unlisted court depositions can be found in NA, C 24/16, C 24/25, and much of this chapter relies on them. Unfortunately, some of the witnesses' statements are now muddled up in these boxes.

4. A. F. Sutton, *The mercery of London: trade, goods and people, 1130–1578* (Aldershot, 2005), p. 398.

5. NA, C 24/25 (deposition of Thomas Stephen).

6. MC, Gresham Journal, entry no. 5468.

7. NA, C 24/16.

8. That John Gresham was heavily in debt is shown by a bond to his father in the sum of £3,000, which under certain conditions Sir Richard offered to release. See NA, PROB 11/32.

9. NA, C 24/16.

10. NA, C 24/16.

11. NA, C 24/16 (witnesses examined 'ex parte Thomas Gresham', especially depositions of Sir Rowland Hill and John Hall); see also NA, C 24/25 for further corroboration.

12. NA, C 54/463, no. 24 (will of lands); NA, PROB 11/32 (will of goods).

13. NA, C 24/16

14. MC, Gresham Journal, entry nos 4635, 5056, 5392, 5464, 5468.

15. MC, Gresham Journal, entry no. 5056.

16. BL, Cotton MS, Julius B.IX, fo. 34v.

17. Longleat MSS, Thynne papers, I, fo. 24; MC, Gresham Journal, entry nos 3290, 3292, 3772, 4939; J. Newman, 'Thomas Gresham, private person rather than public figure', *History teaching review year book*, VII (1993), p. 19.

18. Longleat MSS, Thynne papers, I, fos 243, 246; MC, Gresham Journal, entry nos 1011, 1012, 1810, 3290, 3292, 3772, 4939.

19. NA, C 24/16.

20. NA, C 24/25.

21. NA, PROB 11/35.

22. Longleat MSS, Thynne papers, I, fo. 250.

23. Longleat MSS, Thynne papers, I, fo. 250.

24. BL, Cotton MS, Otho E.X, fos 43–4.

25. BL, Cotton MS, Otho E.X, fos 43–4.

26. MC, typescript list of Thomas Gresham's apprentices.

27. *APC, 1552–1554*, pp. 152, 218–19, 229.

28. J. Stow, *Annales, or, a generall chronicle of England ... continued and augmented with matters forraigne and domestique, ancient and moderne, unto the end of this present yeere, 1631*, 2 vols (London, 1631), II, p. 867.

29. NA, SP 69/7, no. 430; NA, SP 69/3, nos 162, 163; I. Blanchard, 'Richard Clough', *ODNB*; I. Blanchard, 'Sir Thomas Gresham', in *The Royal Exchange*, ed. A. Saunders, London Topographical Society, no. 152 (London, 1997), p. 14.

30. Hatfield MSS, CP 201/103.

31. R. Gwyndaf Jones, 'Sir Richard Clough of Denbigh, c.1530–1570', *Transactions of the Denbighshire historical society*, 20 (1971), pp. 72–5.

32. MC, Gresham Journal, entry nos 315, 416, 419, 487, 488, 537, 539, 2086, 2134, 2277, 2372; Newman, 'Thomas Gresham, private person', p. 20.

33. Newman, 'Thomas Gresham, private person', p. 19.

34. P. Ramsey, 'Some Tudor merchants' accounts', in *Studies in the history of accounting*, ed. A. G. Littleton and B. S. Yamey (London, 1956), pp. 195–6.

35. Newman, 'Thomas Gresham, private person', p. 17.

36. MC, Gresham Journal, entry nos 136, 137, 298, 1768, 1855, 1860, 2384, 2550, 3101, 3183, 3184, 3189, 3291; Newman, 'Thomas Gresham, private person', p. 17.

37. *Ancient double-entry bookkeeping: Luca Pacioli's treatise (AD 1494)*, ed. J. B. Geijsbeek (Denver: Colorado, 1914), pp. 60–61.

Chapter 6: The wheel of fortune

1. *TRP*, I, nos 372, 379.

2. C. E. Challis, *The Tudor coinage* (Manchester, 1978), pp. 105–12, and appendix 2; C. E. Challis and C. J. Harrison, 'A contemporary estimate of the production of silver and gold coinage in England, 1542–1556', *EHR*, 88 (1973), pp. 821–35; L. Ling-Fan, 'Bullion, bills and arbitrage: exchange markets in fourteenth to seventeenth century Europe', London School of Economics PhD (London, 2012),

pp. 85–9; D. Oldroyd, 'John Johnson's letters', *Accounting Historians Journal*, 25 (1998), p. 67.

3.	*The report of the royal commission of 1552*, ed. W. C. Richardson (Morgantown, West VA, 1974), pp. xxiii–xxix; MC, Gresham Journal, unnumbered, unfoliated entry.

4.	BL, Lansdowne MS, 1236, no. 13.

5.	*Literary remains of King Edward VI*, ed. J. G. Nichols, 2 vols (London, 1857), II, pp. 412–13; *APC, 1552–1554*, pp. 27, 58; NA, E 34/4; BL, Cotton MS, Galba B.XII, fos 209–14; BL, Cotton MS, Galba C.X, fos 102–5. These Cotton MSS, damaged in the fire of 1731, contain two separated parts of the same letter of 21 August 1552, but fortunately a full transcript of much of it had already been made. See *Ecclesiastical memorials*, ed. J. Strype, 4 vols (Oxford, 1822), II, ii, pp. 484–9.

6.	BL, Cotton MS, Galba B.XII, fos 209–12v.

7.	BL, Cotton MS, Otho E.X, fos 43–4.

8.	BL, Cotton MS, Galba B.XII, fos 209–12v; *Ecclesiastical memorials*, ed. Strype, II, ii, pp. 484–9.

9.	BL, Cotton MS, Galba B.XII, fos 209–14; *Ecclesiastical memorials*, ed. Strype, II, ii, pp. 484–9.

10.	BL, Cotton MS, Galba B.XII, fos 209–14; *Ecclesiastical memorials*, ed. Strype, II, ii, pp. 484–9.

11.	BL, Cotton MS, Galba B.XII, fos 209–14; *Ecclesiastical memorials*, ed. Strype, II, ii, pp. 484–9; Hatfield MSS, CP 201/103.

12.	R. Ehrenberg, *Capital and finance in the age of the Renaissance* (New York, 1928), pp. 65–72.

13.	33 Henry VIII, c. 7; 2&3 Edward VI, c. 37; *TRP*, I, no. 285.

14.	BL, Cotton MS, Galba B.XII, fos 210v–14; *Ecclesiastical memorials*, ed. Strype, II, ii, pp. 484–9.

15.	E. J. Hamilton, 'Imports of American gold and silver into Spain, 1503–1660', *Quarterly journal of economics*, 43 (1929), pp. 436–72.

16.	I. Blanchard, 'English royal borrowing at Antwerp, 1544–1564', in *Finances publiques et finances privées au bas moyen âge*, ed. M. Boone (Leuven, 1996), pp. 60–63, 67–8.

17.	Haynes, pp. 126–8.

18.	*APC, 1552–1554*, p. 169.

19.	NA, SP 10/15, no. 13; *APC, 1552–1554*, p. 169; *Literary remains of King Edward VI*, p. 460 (where the amount lent by the merchants is wrongly said to be £40,000).

20.	Hatfield MSS, CP 1/118; NA, SP 68/12, nos 647, 653, 655, 670; NA, SP 10/18, no. 24. See also, BL, Cotton MS, Otho E.X, fos 43–4. See also R. de Roover, *Gresham on foreign exchange* (Cambridge, Mass., 1949), pp. 220–22.

21.	NA, SP 10/18, no. 24.

22.	Hatfield MSS, CP 1/118; NA, SP 68/12, no. 653; see above Chapter 2.

23.	I. Archer, 'Sir Thomas Gresham's London', Special lecture, 27 May 1997, Mansion House (London, 1997), p. 4.

24. *APC, 1550–1552*, pp. 441–2, 453, 460, 464–5; NA, SP 68/12, no. 655; NA, SP 69/13, no. 800; 'Information of Thomas Gresham, mercer, touching the fall of the exchange, 1558'. See n. 1 to Chapter 9, and G. D. Ramsay, *The city of London in international politics at the accession of Elizabeth Tudor* (Manchester, 1975), pp. 61–6.
25. *APC, 1550–1552*, pp. 487–9.
26. NA, SP 10/18, no. 24.
27. NA, SP 68/12, nos 655, 656, 658.
28. E.g. NA, SP 68/12, nos 653, 656, 658.
29. NA, SP 68/12, no. 653.

Chapter 7: Smoke and mirrors

1. NA, SP 10/18, no. 11.
2. Inner Temple, London, Petyt MS 538.47, fo. 317; J. Guy, *The children of Henry VIII* (Oxford, 2013), pp. 142–9.
3. Urging on Cecil was Sir William Herbert, earl of Pembroke, who was spending lavishly and may well have been indebted to Gresham. See NA, SP 10/15, no. 5.
4. *CPR, 1553*, p. 240; *CPR, 1554*, pp. 260–61.
5. BL, Cotton MS, Titus B.II, fos 374–9; BL, Lansdowne MS 104, no. 1.
6. NA, E 34/4; BL, Cotton MS, Otho E.X, fos 43–4; *Ecclesiastical memorials*, ed. J. Strype, 4 vols (Oxford, 1822), II, i, pp. 544–5.
7. BL, Cotton MS, Otho E.X, fo. 44.
8. BL, Cotton MS, Otho E.X, fo. 44.
9. LMA, JB/002–003; NA, C 142/121/117.
10. For Cioll's age, see NA, C 24/16.
11. https://familysearch.org/ark:/61903/1:1:V5KS–MJP, 'German Syolle' and 'Sissely Gresham', 20 Jan. 1554, parish of St Michael Bassishaw, London.
12. NA, E 351/18; *CPR, 1557–1558*, p. 13.
13. BL, Cotton MS, Titus B.II, fo. 376.
14. NA, E 101/520/14A (unfoliated); NA, PROB 11/48.
15. NA, SP 70/30, no. 378 (fo. 18v).
16. See also *Ambassades de Messieurs de Noailles en Angleterre*, ed. R. Vertot, 5 vols (Paris, 1763), II, pp. 245, 247.
17. NA, SP 70/12, no. 389.
18. I. Blanchard, 'English royal borrowing at Antwerp, 1544–1564', in *Finances publiques et finances privées au bas moyen âge*, ed. M. Boone (Leuven, 1996), p. 68.
19. NA, SP 69/2, nos 77, 83, 98.
20. NA, SP 69/2, no. 104.
21. NA, SP 69/2, nos 87, 99, 89, 90, 98, 99, 103, 104, 105.
22. NA, SP 69/2, no. 103.
23. Guy, *The children of Henry VIII*, p. 49.
24. M. Keynes, 'The aching head and increasing blindness of Queen Mary I', *Journal of medical biography*, 8 (2008), pp. 106–108.

25. D. M. Loades, 'Philip II and the English', in *Felipe II (1598–1988). Europa dividida: la monarquía católica de Felipe II,* ed. J. M. Millán, 2 vols (Madrid, 1998), II, pp. 485–6.

26. *The diary of Henry Machyn, citizen and merchant-taylor of London, from A.D. 1550 to A.D. 1563,* ed. J. G. Nichols, Camden Society, Old Series, no. 42 (1848), p. 67.

27. *Diary of Henry Machyn,* ed. Nichols, p. 69.

28. NA, SP 69/3, no. 135.

29. NA, SP 69/3, no. 135.

30. M. Grice-Hutchinson, *The school of Salamanca: readings in Spanish monetary theory, 1544–1605* (Oxford, 1952), pp. 11–12, 107–108.

31. C. E. Challis, *The Tudor coinage* (Manchester, 1978), pp. 112–15.

32. NA, SP 69/3, no. 133; NA, E 351/18 (for the rent).

33. NA, SP 69/3, nos 130, 133, 135, 142, 146, 156, 162; NA, AO 1/1670/497; NA, E 351/2080.

34. Blanchard, 'English royal borrowing at Antwerp, 1544–1564', p. 69.

35. NA, SP 69/6, no. 319.

36. Gresham's notebook is NA, E 101/520/14A (unfoliated). For the other sources, notably transcriptions of legal testimony in the Spanish courts, see the notes below, and to Chapter 10.

37. NA, E 351/18.

38. NA, E 351/18.

39. *APC, 1554–1556,* pp. 34, 35, 71. See also NA, SP 69/4, no. 226.

40. NA, E 159/339, rot. 29–42. I am most grateful to Professor Glyn Parry for drawing these entries to my attention.

41. Grice-Hutchinson, *The school of Salamanca,* pp. 3–4.

42. NA, E 101/324/27; NA, E 159/339, rot. 29–42; NA, SP 69/5, no. 297.

43. NA, SP 69/5, no. 297.

44. NA, SP 69/5, no. 297; NA, E 351/18; NA, E 159/339, rot. 29–42.

45. NA, E 351/18.

46. NA, E 351/18.

47. NA, E 101/520/14A.

48. G. Redworth, 'Philip I of England, embezzlement and the quantity theory of money', *EcHR,* New Series, 55 (2002), p. 249; Challis, *The Tudor coinage,* pp. 112–13.

49. NA, E 351/18; *CPR, 1553–1554,* p. 176; NA, SP 69/7, no. 429.

50. NA, SP 69/3, no. 156.

51. Blanchard, 'English royal borrowing at Antwerp, 1544–1564', p. 69.

52. NA, SP 69/7, nos 420, 429, 430, 438; NA, E 351/18.

53. NA, SP 69/6, no. 354.

54. NA, SP 69/7, no. 428.

55. See below, Chapter 15.

56. BL, Lansdowne MS 118, fo. 72r–v.

57. NA, SP 69/2, no. 104.

58. NA, SP 69/2, no. 111.

59. NA, SP 69/7, no. 438.

Chapter 8: Regime change

1. A. F. Sutton, *The mercery of London: trade, goods and people* (Aldershot, 2005), pp. 398–9.
2. J. Stow, *A survey of the cities of London and Westminster*, 2 vols (London, 1720), I, pp. 258–9; NA, PROB 11/38.
3. NA, PROB 11/38.
4. *Illustrations of the manners and expenses of ancient times in England, in the fifteenth, sixteenth, and seventeenth centuries*, ed. J. Nichols (London, 1797), appendix, pp. 7, 12, 21, 24.
5. *CPR, 1555–1557*, pp. 152–4; BL, Additional Charter 16336.
6. NA, E 314/46; *CPR, 1569–1572*, p. 421. See also below, Chapters 13, 18.
7. NA, SP 69/8, nos 474, 475 (I–II); *APC, 1554–1556*, p. 321.
8. R. Ehrenberg, *Capital and finance in the age of the Renaissance* (New York, 1928), pp. 114–17.
9. NA, SP 70/15, no. 127.
10. *CPR, 1553–1554*, p. 176; *CPR, 1557–1558*, p. 193; NA, SP 70/15, no. 127.
11. NA, E 351/18 (the figures in this document were given in Flemish pounds, and I have converted them to sterling).
12. NA, E 351/18; NA, E 159/339, rot. 29–42.
13. NA, E 159/339, rot. 29–42; NA, E 159/341, *recorda*, Hilary term, 2 Eliz.
14. NA, SP 69/12, nos 751, 755.
15. NA, SP 69/12, no. 733.
16. *CSPSp, 1554–1558*, nos 420, 421.
17. NA, SP 69/12, nos 751, 755, 756, 758, 759, 766, 775, 779, 788, 845.
18. NA, SP 69/13, nos 797, 801.
19. NA, E 351/18; NA, SP 69/12, nos 751, 756, 758, 759, 775, 779.
20. *CPR, 1557–1558*, p. 13; NA, SP 69/12, nos 788, 789, 844; NA, SP 12/1, no. 45.
21. J. R. Taylor, 'Nathaniel Bacon: an Elizabethan squire, his family and household, and their impact upon the local community', UEA PhD (Norwich, 1989), pp. 104–12. The likely date of the affair and Anne's date of birth are calculated backwards from the date and circumstances of her marriage: see below, Chapter 15.
22. NA, C 24/12.
23. NA, SP 69/13, nos 833, 845. Gresham's letter of 17 October, written from Dunkirk, to Mary is lost, but referred to in SP 69/13, no. 845.
24. NA, SP 69/13, no. 839.
25. NA, SP 69/13, no. 845.
26. 'The count of Feria's despatch to Philip II of 14 November 1558', ed. M. J. Rodríguez-Salgado and S. Adams, *Camden Society*, 4th Series, 29 (1984), p. 331.
27. NA, SP 12/1, fos 3, 5.
28. NA, SP 70/15, no. 134; NA, SP 70/64, no. 1126.

29. NA, E 351/26; NA, SP 70/1, no. 74; NA, SP 70/2, nos 118, 124; NA, SP 70/3, no.
     165; NA, SP 70/5, nos 440, 516; NA, SP 70/16, no. 179; NA, SP 70/21, no. 533;
     NA, SP 70/147, Pt. 1, fos 101–2 (no number); NA, SP 12/6, no. 16; NA, SP 70/64,
     no. 1126; NA, SP 70/21, no. 535.

30. NA, 70/2, nos 118, 119; NA, SP 70/3, no. 165; NA, SP 70/5, no. 440; NA, SP
     70/9, no. 199; NA, SP 12/4, no. 10; Lettenhove, I, pp. 478–9.

Chapter 9: Gresham's law

1.   'Information of Thomas Gresham, mercer, touching the fall of the exchange,
     1558'. My source is a copy of the transcript made by Dr G. D. Ramsay, purportedly
     from 'Lord Burghley's papers, Longleat'. I have been unable to track down this
     document in the archives at Longleat, but a closely related version from an
     eighteenth-century transcript can be found as appendix 21 in J. Burgon, *The life
     and times of Sir Thomas Gresham*, 2 vols (London, 1839), I, pp. 483–6. I am most
     grateful to Dr Nigel Ramsay for allowing me to photocopy this and many more of
     his father's transcripts of Gresham's correspondence.

2.   'Information of Thomas Gresham, mercer, touching the fall of the exchange, 1558'.

3.   NA, SP 70/3, no. 167.

4.   NA, SP 70/3, no. 167.

5.   NA, SP 70/3, no. 167. See also NA, SP 70/2, no. 124 for an earlier intimation of
     the same approach in a 'remembrance' for Cecil.

6.   NA, SP 70/3, no. 167.

7.   NA, SP 70/3, no. 167.

8.   NA, SP 70/3, no. 167.

9.   E. J. Hamilton, 'Imports of American gold and silver into Spain, 1503–1660',
     Quarterly journal of economics, 43 (1929), pp. 436–72.

10. NA, SP 70/3, no. 167.

11. 'Information of Thomas Gresham, mercer, touching the fall of the exchange, 1558'.
     See also NA, SP 70/15, no. 134; NA, SP 70/16, nos 155, 156; NA, SP 12/12, no. 58.

12. NA, SP 70/11, no. 355.

13. R. B. Outhwaite, 'The trials of foreign borrowing: the English crown and the
     Antwerp money market in the mid-sixteenth century', *EcHR*, New Series, 19
     (1966), pp. 289–305.

14. NA, SP 70/8, no. 52.

15. NA, SP 70/17, no. 192.

16. NA, SP 70/17, no. 192. The document has systematic marginal annotations,
     probably in Parry's hand, but is endorsed by Cecil 'for borrowing of money'.

17. NA, SP 70/17, no. 192.

18. NA, SP 70/17, no. 192.

19. NA, E 351/26.

20. 'Information of Thomas Gresham, mercer, touching the fall of the exchange, 1558';
     NA, SP 70/15, no. 134; NA, SP 70/16, nos 155, 156; NA, SP 12/12, no. 58.

21. C. E. Challis, *The Tudor coinage* (Manchester, 1978), pp. 96–121, and appendix 2. See also C. E. Challis and C. J. Harrison, 'A contemporary estimate of the production of silver and gold coinage in England, 1542–1556', *EHR*, 88 (1973), pp. 821–35.

22. *CPR, 1558–1560*, pp. 66–7.

23. Hatfield MSS, CP 153/60; D. G. Borden and I. D. Brown, 'The milled coinage of Elizabeth I', *British numismatic journal*, 53 (1984), pp. 108–32.

24. *Merry Wives of Windsor*, I, i, 147–51. See also J. Evans, 'A numismatic question raised by Shakespeare', *Numismatic chronicle and journal of the Royal Numismatic Society*, 4th series, 5 (1905), pp. 307–14.

25. NA, SP 70/15, no. 134.

26. NA, SP 70/16, nos 155, 156; L. Ling-Fan, 'Bullion, bills and arbitrage: exchange markets in fourteenth to seventeenth century Europe', London School of Economics PhD (London, 2012), pp. 86–90.

27. NA, SP 70/16, no. 155.

28. NA, SP 12/12, no. 43 (and enclosure); J. Burgon, 'On the amelioration of the coinage, 1560', *Numismatic chronicle*, 2 (1840), pp. 12–17; Challis, *The Tudor coinage*, pp. 120–21.

29. NA, SP 12/12, no. 58; SP 12/14, nos 55, 57.

30. *TRP*, II, no. 471.

31. *TRP*, II, nos 472, 473, 487; C. E. Challis, 'Spanish bullion and monetary inflation in England in the later sixteenth century', *Journal of European economic history*, 4 (1975), pp. 383–4.

32. *The diary of Henry Machyn, citizen and merchant-taylor of London, from A.D. 1550 to A.D. 1563*, ed. J. G. Nichols, Camden Society, Old Series, no. 42 (1848), pp. 262–3.

33. Hatfield MSS, CP 153/60; Borden and Brown, 'The milled coinage of Elizabeth I', pp. 108–10.

34. *TRP*, II, no. 487; Borden and Brown, 'The milled coinage of Elizabeth I', pp. 108–10.

35. NA, SP 12/77, no. 4; Challis, *The Tudor coinage*, pp. 121–7; C. Read, 'Profits on the recoinage of 1560–1', *EcHR*, Old Series, 6 (1936), pp. 186–93.

36. H. D. McLeod, *The history of economics* (London, 1896), pp. 38–9, quoting his 1857 essay on the topic. See also R. de Roover, *Gresham on foreign exchange* (Cambridge, Mass., 1949), pp. 91–4.

37. 'Information of Thomas Gresham, mercer, touching the fall of the exchange, 1558'; NA, SP 70/3, no. 167; de Roover, *Gresham on foreign exchange*, pp. 91–2. See also below, Chapter 23.

38. T. W. Balch, 'The law of Oresme, Copernicus and Gresham', *Proceedings of the American Philosophical Society*, 47 (1908), pp. 18–29.

39. De Roover, *Gresham on foreign exchange*, pp. 226–7, 303–5.

40. De Roover, *Gresham on foreign exchange*, pp. 290–309; NA, SP 12/106, no. 6; HEH, Ellesmere MS 2229; BL, Sloane MS 3493; University of London, Senate House, MS 27, fos 27–36; M. Dewar, 'The memorandum "For the understanding

of the exchange": its authorship and dating', *EcHR*, New Series, 17, (1965),
pp. 476–87; D. R. Fusfeld and R. de Roover, 'On the authorship and dating
of "For the understanding of the exchange"', *EcHR*, New Series, 20, (1967),
pp. 145–52; C. E. Challis, 'On the authorship and dating of the memorandum
"For the understanding of the exchange"', *BIHR*, 56 (1983), pp. 34–45; T. H.
Lloyd, 'Early Elizabethan investigations into exchange and the value of sterling,
1558–1568', *EcHR*, New Series, 53 (2000), pp. 60–83.

41. Fusfeld and de Roover, 'On the authorship and dating of "For the understanding
    of the exchange"', p. 145.

42. De Roover, *Gresham on foreign exchange*, pp. 303–5; Fusfeld and de Roover, 'On
    the authorship and dating of "For the understanding of the exchange"', pp. 150–51.

43. See Chapter 6.

44. Fusfeld and de Roover, 'On the authorship and dating of "For the understanding
    of the exchange"', pp. 150–51.

45. HMC, *3rd report* (London, 1874), p. 230; *Tudor economic documents*, ed. R. H.
    Tawney and E. Power, 3 vols (London, 1924), III, p. 346. For the friendship, see
    NA, SP 70/28, no. 267.

46. *CPR, 1563–1566*, pp. 31–2; *Tudor economic documents*, ed. Tawney and Power, III,
    pp. 346–59 (esp. p. 356). See also BL, Harleian MS 660, fos 107–13v (transcripts of
    Ralph Starkey).

Chapter 10: Shifting tides

1. NA, SP 70/9, no. 194.
2. See Chapter 8.
3. NA, E 159/341, *recorda*, Hilary term, 2 Eliz.
4. NA, E 101/324/27; NA, E 159/339, rot. 29–42.
5. NA, E 351/26.
6. P. Génard, 'La maison de Thomas Gresham à Anvers en 1559', *Bulletin des archives
   d'Anvers*, II (1865), pp. 292–3; F. Donnet, *Coup d'oeil sur l'histoire financière
   d'Anvers au cours des siècles* (Antwerp, 1927), p. 133; O. de Smedt, *De Engelse natie te
   Antwerpen in de 16ᵉ eeuw*, 2 vols (Antwerp, 1950–54), II, p. 13.
7. NA, SP 70/11, no. 345.
8. NA, SP 70/11, no. 301; Haynes, pp. 236–7.
9. J. Guy, *'My heart is my own': the life of Mary, queen of Scots* (London, 2004),
   pp. 95–106.
10. NA, SP 70/9, no. 194.
11. NA, SP 70/12, no. 390.
12. NA, SP 70/11, no. 345.
13. NA, SP 70/11, no. 345.
14. NA, SP 70/12, no. 390.
15. BL, Cotton MS, Caligula B.X, fos 82v–5v.
16. NA, SP 12/12, no. 6.
17. NA, SP 70/10, no. 270; NA, SP 12/12, no. 65; NA, SP 70/15, no. 103.

18. NA, SP 70/14, no. 43.
19. NA, SP 70/10, no. 270; NA, SP 70/13, no. 473; NA, SP 70/14, no. 54; NA SP 70/15, no. 120.
20. NA, SP 70/14, no. 43; NA, SP 70/15, no. 134.
21. NA, SP 70/14, no. 43.
22. Teulet, I, pp. 467–77, 533–6.
23. NA, SP 70/13, nos 469, 470, 473.
24. NA, SP 70/13, no. 502.
25. There are nine surviving Gresham rings in private and public collections, seven bearing the device of a grasshopper in green enamel. D. Scarisbrick, *Tudor and Stuart jewellery* (London, 1995), pp. 31–3; N. Awais-Dean, 'A gem in the archives', *Jewellery history today* (Autumn 2013), pp. 7–8; See also https://collections. vam.ac.uk/item/O119787/the-lee-ring-ring-unknown; https://collections. museumoflondon.org.uk/online/object/118780.html.
26. NA, SP 70/13, no. 517; NA, SP/14, nos 26, 43, 64, 66; NA, SP 70/15, no. 127; SP 70/19, no. 362.
27. NA, SP 70/14, nos 43, 48.
28. NA, E 159/339, rot. 29–42.
29. NA, SP 70/15, nos 120, 134. For the relationship, see their father's will: NA, PROB 11/31.
30. NA, SP 70/15, no. 127.
31. NA, SP 70/14, no. 43.
32. NA, SP 70/8, no. 6.
33. NA, SP 70/14, no. 43.
34. A. F. Sutton, *The mercery of London: trade, goods and people* (Aldershot, 2005), pp. 395, 487–8.
35. MC, Acts of Court, 1527–69, fos 326v–27.
36. The gift of the cup is mentioned in Clough's codicil will, see NA, PROB 11/52.
37. NA, SP 70/15, nos 103, 134; NA, SP 70/16, nos 143, 152; NA, SP 70/17, no. 223.
38. NA, SP 70/17, no. 223.
39. MC, Acts of Court, 1527–69, fos 326v–27.
40. MC, Acts of Court, 1527–69, fos 326v–27.
41. NA, SP 70/17, nos 241, 242; NA, E 351/541, fo. 18v.
42. NA, SP 70/17, no. 191.
43. NA, SP 70/17, no. 241.
44. NA, SP 70/17, no. 241.
45. NA, SP 70/17, nos 242, 243.
46. NA, SP 70/17, nos 191, 241.
47. NA, SP 70/17, no. 242; L. Ling-Fan, 'Bullion, bills and arbitrage: exchange markets in fourteenth to seventeenth century Europe', London School of Economics PhD (London, 2012), p. 278.
48. NA, SP 70/8, no. 52.

49. *CSPSp, 1558–1567*, p. 67; *Queen Elizabeth and some foreigners*, ed. V. von Klarwill (London, 1928), pp. 113–15; S. Doran, *Monarchy and matrimony: the courtships of Elizabeth I* (London, 1996), pp. 26–30.
50. NA, SP 70/14, no. 74.
51. NA, SP 70/15, no. 83.
52. NA, SP 70/15, nos 103, 127.

Chapter 11: New threats and dangers

1. NA, SP 70/19, no. 362.
2. NA, SP 70/23, no. 652.
3. NA, SP 70/91, no. 1023.
4. NA, SP 12/80, no. 14.
5. NA, SP 12/85, no. 65.
6. NA, SP 70/23, no. 619; NA, SP 70/25, no. 66; NA, SP 12/18, no. 17.
7. BL, Lansdowne MS 4, no. 38; NA, SP 70/23, no. 619.
8. NA, SP 70/28, no. 267.
9. Gresham's audited accounts for 1563–1574 show that he kept a 'Book of Exchange' recording his foreign exchange dealings, and to this he repeatedly refers, but it does not now survive. See NA, AO 1/5/1; NA, AO 1/5/2.
10. NA, PROB 11/53.
11. NA, PROB 11/30; BL, Additional Charter 16336.
12. NA, SP 70/15, no. 120; NA, SP 70/16, no. 143. See also NA, SP 70/35, no. 693.
13. NA, PROB 11/62; NA, C 2/Eliz/G7/7; Berkshire RO, MS D/EN/F4.
14. Longleat MSS, Thynne papers, I, fo. 250. See above, Chapter 5.
15. NA, C 2/Eliz/G7/7; J. Ward, *The lives of the professors of Gresham College* (London, 1740), appendix 6. See also below, Chapter 19.
16. BL, Additional MS 35830, fo. 197; NA, SP 70/30, no. 377. See also NA, SP 70/30, no. 384; NA, SP 12/21, no. 60.
17. BL, Additional MS 35830, fo. 197.
18. R. Ehrenberg, *Capital and finance in the age of the Renaissance* (New York, 1928), pp. 119–20, 250.
19. BL, Additional MS 35830, fo. 197.
20. NA, SP 70/30, no. 377.
21. BL, Additional MS 35830, fo. 197; NA, SP 70/28, no. 231; NA, SP 70/30, nos 377, 378.
22. NA, SP 70/5, no. 440 (fos 126–27v); NA, SP 70/21, no. 533. For Winchester's growing suspicions, see NA, SP 70/15, nos 134, 127.
23. NA, SP 70/15, no. 99 (dated 12 June 1560, covering deals from 1–15 May). The total sum borrowed by Gresham for the crown was 462,417 guilders, to which should be added brokerage of 4,624 guilders and interest of 28,020 guilders; thus to be paid back in November and December there was due 495,061 guilders, or £82,510 in Flemish money. Of this, Gresham's cut in brokerage and interest combined was 4,901 guilders. These calculations were made by Dr George Ramsay. I am indebted

to Dr Nigel Ramsay for access to his father's unpublished papers. The true costs of brokerage ranged between ½d. and 1½d. per £1. See Gresham's audited (enrolled) accounts for 1563/4–1574 in E 159/369, *recorda*, Mich. term, 17 Eliz.

24. *CPR, 1560–1563*, pp. 36–7, 237.

25. NA, SP 70/1, no. 74; NA, SP 70/64, nos 1123, 1124, 1125; NA, E 351/26.

26. NA, E 351/26.

27. NA, SP 70/33, no. 546.

28. NA, SP 70/64, nos 1123, 1124, 1125; NA, SP 70/1, no. 74.

29. *CPR, 1560–1563*, p. 265.

30. L. Jardine, *The awful end of Prince William the Silent* (London, 2005), pp. 77–85; C. Whibley, *The triumphant reigne of kyng Henry the VIII* [an edition of Edward Hall's *Chronicle*], 2 vols (London, 1904), II, pp. 278–9; A. F. Sutton, *The mercery of London: trade, goods and people* (Aldershot, 2005), pp. 386–7; *The House of Commons, 1509–1558*, ed. S. T. Bindoff, 3 vols (London, 1982), III, pp. 48–9.

31. NA, SP 70/4, no. 358.

32. NA, SP 70/12, no. 390. See Chapter 10.

33. NA, SP 70/63, no. 1118; O. de Smedt, *De Engelse natie te Antwerpen in de 16ᵉ eeuw*, 2 vols (Antwerp, 1950–54), II, p. 13.

34. NA, SP 70/40, no. 358.

35. NA, E 351/33. See also NA, SP 70/40, no. 334; NA, SP 70/53, nos 440, 468.

36. NA, SP 70/40, nos 376, 407.

37. NA, SP 70/67, no. 8; Lettenhove, III, pp. 634–6.

38. G. D. Ramsay, *The city of London in international politics at the accession of Elizabeth Tudor* (Manchester, 1975), pp. 232–44. See also the valuable critique of Ramsay's argument by C. Wilson, 'Reviews', *EcHR*, New Series, 29 (1976), pp. 504–6.

39. NA, SP 70/67, nos 11, 42.

40. AGR, MS Audience 368/3, fos 279–86.

41. NA, SP 70/67, no. 11. See also NA, SP 70/67, no. 42.

42. Lettenhove, III, p. 636.

43. Lettenhove, III, pp. 636, 668–9.

44. NA, SP 70/67, no. 22.

45. G. Marnef, 'Gresham and Antwerp', Gresham College lecture, 18 June 2008 (London, 2008), p. 9; FelixArchief, PK#1055 (unfoliated).

46. NA, SP 70/67, no. 72.

47. FelixArchief, PK#1055 (unfoliated); NA, SP 70/72, no. 385; NA, SP 70/73, no. 466.

48. FelixArchief, PK#1055 (unfoliated).

49. See below, Chapter 14.

50. NA, AO 1/5/1; BL, Egerton MS 2790, fos 72–3.

51. NA, AO 1/5/1; NA, AO 1/5/2.

52. NA, AO 1/5/2; NA, E 159/360, *recorda*, Mich. term, 17 Eliz. My warm thanks to Professor Glyn Parry for the E 159 reference.

Chapter 12: A merchant prince

1. *The diary of Baron Waldstein*, ed. C. W. Groos (London, 1981), p. 111.
2. C. Skidmore, *Death and the Virgin* (London, 2010), pp. 203–306, 377–8.
3. *Household accounts and disbursement books of Robert Dudley, earl of Leicester, 1558–61, 1584–86*, ed. S. Adams, Camden Society, 5th Series, 6 (1995), pp. 461, 470, 476. See also pp. 40, 65, 73, 77, 110, 139, 158, 165, 479. NA, PROB 11/31 (will of Robert Hogan, the elder); Longleat MSS, Dudley papers, I, fo. 155; M. J. Armstrong, *The history and antiquities of the county of Norfolk*, 10 vols (Norwich, 1781), X, pp. 75–7; J. Burgon, *The life and times of Sir Thomas Gresham*, 2 vols (London, 1839), II, appendix 29.
4. *Household accounts and disbursement books of Robert Dudley, earl of Leicester*, ed. Adams, p. 110.
5. *Household accounts and disbursement books of Robert Dudley, earl of Leicester*, ed. Adams, p. 73; *CPR, 1563–1566*, p. 262 (no. 1266).
6. NA, SP 70/14, no. 43.
7. NA, SP 70/15, no. 103.
8. NA, E 351/26.
9. NA, E 351/26.
10. NA, SP 70/16, no. 143.
11. NA, SP 70/86, no. 575; NA, SP 70/17, no. 223.
12. Longleat MSS, Dudley papers, I, fo. 155.
13. Longleat MSS, Dudley papers, I, fo. 155.
14. *Household accounts and disbursement books of Robert Dudley, earl of Leicester*, ed. Adams, p. 158.
15. NA, SP 70/13, no. 517.
16. NA, SP 70/14, no. 26.
17. NA, SP 70/8, no. 38; NA, SP 70/14, no. 74; NA, SP 70/28, no. 267; NA, SP 70/29, nos 307, 336; NA, SP 70/30, nos 378, 483; NA, SP 70/84, no. 429; NA, SP 70/86, no. 566; NA, SP 12/20, no. 43; NA, SP 12/74, no. 11; NA, SP 15/14, fo. 17; Lettenhove, IV, pp. 368, 379, 390–91; *Household accounts and disbursement books of Robert Dudley, earl of Leicester*, ed. Adams, p. 65.
18. NA, SP 70/64, nos 1123, 1124, 1125; NA, SP 70/1, no. 74. See above, Chapter 11.
19. NA, SP 70/64, no. 1123.
20. NA, SP 70/57, no. 702.
21. NA, SP 70/57, no. 702.
22. NA, SP 70/56, no. 676. The letter is dated '14 May', but a docquet note shows that this is an error for 'June'.
23. NA, SP 70/56, no. 673.
24. NA, SP 70/65, no. 1212.
25. *CPR, 1563–1566*, pp. 249–50; *CPR, 1566–1569*, p. 104.
26. NA, SP 70/67, no. 97; NA, SP 70/77, no. 912.
27. *Bath MSS*, V, pp. 20–1. Ferneley's familiarity with the Talbots, earls of Shrewsbury, suggests that she was a regular visitor to Buxton. See LPL, MS 3198, fo. 3; LPL, MS 3199, fo. 361; LPL, MS 3206, fo. 1001.

28.   See above, Chapter 5.

29.   NA, PROB 11/48.

30.   *CPR, 1558–1560*, pp. 10–11, 129, 374.

31.   NA, SP 70/77, no. 912; *CPR, 1563–1566*, pp. 249–50, 268, 512–13.

32.   Site measurements are taken from those specified in 8 Geo. III, c.32, the act of Parliament of 1768 whereby Gresham College was allowed to sell the site and buildings so that a new Excise Office could be built there. For a rough contemporary plan, see Ralph Agas's map of early modern London, now best viewed at https://mapoflondon.uvic.ca/agas.htm.

33.   *CPR, 1557–1558*, p. 329; *CPR, 1558–1560*, p. 377.

34.   *CPR, 1566–1569*, p. 257.

35.   J. Stow, *Survey of London*, ed. H. B. Wheatley (London, 1970), p. 156.

36.   J. Schofield, *Medieval London houses* (New Haven and London, 1995), p. 244, n. 108.

37.   M. Girouard, *Elizabethan architecture: its rise and fall, 1540–1640* (New Haven and London, 2009), pp. 167–9.

38.   BL, Additional Charter 16336; *An exact copy of the last will and testament, of Sir Thomas Gresham, kt. To which are added, an abridgement of an Act of Parliament, passed in the twenty third of Q. Elizabeth, A.D. 1581, for the better performing the last will of Sir Thomas Gresham, kt.* (London, 1724), pp. 27–31.

39.   BL, Lansdowne MS 6, no. 13; R. Pollitt, 'John Hawkins's troublesome voyages: merchants, bureaucrats and the origin of the slave trade', *JBS*, 12 (1973), pp. 26–40.

40.   Some information concerning the little gallery where Gresham received visitors can be worked out from incidental details in NA, E 163/14/7. For the exterior design, one is heavily dependent on the engraving by George Vertue, c.1739. See also Stow, *Survey of London*, ed. Wheatley, p. 159.

41.   *Biographia britannica: or, the lives of the most eminent persons who have flourished in Great Britain and Ireland*, ed. H. Brougham, J. Campbell, W. Harris and others, 6 vols (London, 1757), IV, p. 2388.

42.   NA, PROB 11/48.

43.   Nichols, I, p. 333.

44.   *Biographia britannica*, ed. Brougham, Campbell, Harris and others, p. 2388.

45.   Information from Robert Adam's plans and drawings, preserved at Osterley and owned by the National Trust. See also *A history of the county of Middlesex*, ed. C. R. Elrington and others, Victoria County History, 11 vols (London, 1962), III, pp. 100–3.

46.   NA, E 134/26 Eliz/Trin2.

47.   J. Norden, *Speculum Britanniae. The first parte [of] an historicall, & chorographicall discription of Middlesex* (London, 1593), p. 37; NA, E 351/541.

48.   T. Fuller, *The Worthies of England*, ed. P. A. Nuttall, 3 vols (London, 1840), II, p. 313.

49.   *STC*, no. 11746.

50.   *STC*, no. 545.

51.   *STC*, no. 21360.

52. NA, STAC 5/G7/30. The chronology, necessarily approximate, is worked out from East Riding of Yorkshire RO, MS DDCC/133/7.

53. M. E. Bratchel, 'Germain Cioll, sixteenth-century London merchant: a biographical note', *BIHR*, 56 (1983), pp. 114–15. See also NA, C 3/34/65; NA, C 3/198/78; NA, SP 70/83, nos 178, 229.

54. *Household accounts and disbursement books of Robert Dudley, earl of Leicester*, ed. Adams, p. 88.

55. NA, SP 70/83, no. 178. See also NA, SP 70/83, no. 229.

56. NA, PROB 11/56 (will of Robert Smith).

Chapter 13: Royal Exchange

1. NA, SP 70/62, no. 1034; NA, SP 70/63, no. 1118.

2. Rijksmuseum, Amsterdam, accessions SK-A-3118, SK-A-3119. Purchased by Catherine the Great in 1779, these companion paintings were on display at the Hermitage after 1838, where they hung in the German School Gallery. In 1931, they were sold by the former Soviet Union as part of a deal enabling Lenin to secure foreign currency. They had been subject to a fairly brutal restoration by Alexander Sidorov in 1872, when Ferneley's portrait was transferred from wood panels to canvas. Gresham's portrait must have been more stable as his was only cradled. A full conservation programme was undertaken by the Rijksmuseum in 2007. The yellowed varnish layers and discoloured over-painting were removed, paint damage retouched and new varnish applied. See M. van de Laar, D. de Haan and others, 'From wood to canvas: Anthonis Mor, portraits of Sir Thomas Gresham and Anne Ferneley', *Rijksmuseum bulletin*, 58, (2010), pp. 246–65.

3. LMA, COL/CA/01/01/013, fo. 237.

4. J. Imray, 'The origins of the Royal Exchange', in *The Royal Exchange*, ed. A. Saunders, London Topographical Society, no. 152 (London, 1997), pp. 20–23.

5. BL, Cotton MS, Otho E.X, fo. 45 (damaged by fire); G. Schanz, *Englische Handelspolitik*, 2 vols (Leipzig, 1881), II, pp. 632–3.

6. Imray, 'Origins of the Royal Exchange', in *The Royal Exchange*, ed. Saunders, pp. 23–6.

7. BL, Lansdowne MS 5, no. 27 (quotation from fos 95v–6).

8. LMA, COL/CA/01/01/015, fos 403–6v.

9. A. Saunders, 'The building of the Exchange', in *The Royal Exchange*, ed. Saunders, pp. 37–8.

10. J. Stow, *Survey of London*, ed. H. B. Wheatley (London, 1970), p. 173. Imray, 'Origins of the Royal Exchange', in *The Royal Exchange*, ed. Saunders, pp. 28–33.

11. FelixArchief, CERT #28, fo. 34; Saunders, 'The building of the Exchange', in *The Royal Exchange*, ed. Saunders, p. 40.

12. Lettenhove, IV, p. 394. See also M. Girouard, *Elizabethan architecture: its rise and fall, 1540–1640* (New Haven and London, 2009), pp. 169–70.

13. Girouard, *Elizabethan architecture*, p. 474, n. 87.

14. LMA, COL/CA/01/01/015, fo. 511; Imray, 'Origins of the Royal Exchange', in *The Royal Exchange*, ed. Saunders, pp. 33–4.

15. LMA, COL/CA/01/01/015, fo. 511. The eventual number of shops was 112. See MC, Acts of Court, 1596–1629, fo. 14v. See I. R. Adamson, 'Benjamin Jonson "of Gresham College": three pregnant words and their progeny explored', unpublished typescript. I am hugely indebted to Dr Adamson for his kindness in lending me a copy of this and other works relating chiefly to Gresham College and Sir Thomas's will, published and unpublished, and for allowing me to draw upon them.

16. LMA, COL/CC/01/01/019, fo. 12.

17. Adamson, 'Benjamin Jonson "of Gresham College"'.

18. Stow, *Survey of London*, ed. Wheatley, p. 173.

19. Saunders, 'The building of the Exchange', in *The Royal Exchange*, ed. Saunders, p. 39.

20. Lettenhove, IV, p. 327; Lettenhove, V, pp. 10, 15–16; NA, SP 70/89, no. 910; NA, SP 12/74, no. 19; LMA, COL/CA/01/01/016, fo. 61v.

21. LMA, COL/CA/01/01/016, fo. 61v.

22. NA, SP 70/93, no. 1253.

23. Lettenhove, IV, p. 343.

24. Stow, *Survey of London*, ed. Wheatley, p. 173.

25. NA, SP 15/13, no. 116.

26. L. Grenade, *'Les Singularitez de Londres, 1576'*, in *The Royal Exchange*, ed. Saunders, pp. 48–9.

27. Saunders, 'The building of the Exchange', in *The Royal Exchange*, ed. Saunders, pp. 41–2; S. Alford, *London's triumph: merchant adventurers and the Tudor city* (London, 2017), pp. 108–10.

28. 'Diary of the journey of Philip Julius, Duke of Stettin-Pomerania, through England in the year 1602', ed. G. von Bülow and W. Powell, *TRHS*, New Series, 6 (1892), p. 11. See also *The diary of Baron Waldstein*, ed. G. W. Groos (London, 1981), p. 175.

29. Saunders, 'The building of the Exchange', in *The Royal Exchange*, ed. Saunders, pp. 40–3.

30. A. Saunders, 'Reconstructing London: Sir Thomas Gresham and Bishopsgate', in *Sir Thomas Gresham and Gresham College*, ed. F. Ames-Lewis (Aldershot, 1999), p. 6; *Correspondance diplomatique de Bertrand de Salignac de La Mothe-Fénélon, ambassadeur de France en Angleterre de 1568 à 1575*, ed. A. Teulet, 7 vols (Paris and London, 1838–40), III, p. 443.

31. *Correspondance diplomatique de Bertrand de Salignac de La Mothe-Fénélon*, ed. Teulet, III, p. 443; Stow, *Survey of London*, ed. Wheatley, p. 173; *Reports from the lost notebooks of Sir James Dyer*, ed. J. H. Baker, Selden Society, no. 109, 2 vols (London, 1994), I, p. 195; R. Holinshed, *The first volume of the chronicles of England, Scotland and Ireland* (London, 1577), p. 1857.

32. *Correspondance diplomatique de Bertrand de Salignac de La Mothe-Fénélon*, ed. Teulet, III, pp. 443, 450–51; Stow, *Survey of London*, ed. Wheatley, p. 173; *Reports from the lost notebooks of Sir James Dyer*, ed. Baker, I, p. 195.

33. Stow, *Survey of London*, ed. Wheatley, p. 173. For the positioning of the royal arms, see Hogenberg's engraving of the exterior view from Cornhill: BM, Prints and Drawings, ref. 1880,1113.3670.

34. J. Stow, *Annales, or, a generall chronicle of England ... continued and augmented with matters forraigne and domestique, ancient and moderne, unto the end of this present yeere, 1631*, 2 vols (London, 1631), II, pp. 868–9.

35. Stow, *Annales, or, a generall chronicle of England*, II, pp. 868–9; NA, C 2/Eliz/ M8/20.

36. *CPR, 1572–1575*, no. 2971.

37. *TRP*, II, no. 618.

38. NA, SP 12/114, no. 52.

Chapter 14: Into the black

1. NA, SP 70/78, no. 990; NA, SP 12/36, nos 58, 59, 62.

2. NA, SP 70/78, nos 954, 990, 1001.

3. NA, SP 70/78, no. 1001.

4. NA, AO 1/5/1; NA, AO 1/5/2; NA, E 351/31. See above, Chapter 11.

5. NA, SP 12/36, nos 53, 54, 55.

6. *CSPF, 1566–1568*, nos 112, 202, 284, 400, 529, 588, 615, 652.

7. See above, Chapters 7, 10.

8. NA, SP 70/82, nos 63, 75; NA, SP 12/39, no. 20.

9. Lettenhove, IV, pp. 308–11.

10. NA, SP 78/88, no. 745.

11. G. Marnef, *Antwerp in the age of reformation, 1550–1577* (London, 1996), pp. 88–105.

12. NA, AO 1/5/2.

13. NA, SP 70/81, no. 1337; Lettenhove, IV, pp. 260–61.

14. Lettenhove, IV, pp. 313–15, 327–9, 331–2, 333–6, 337–9, 341–4.

15. Lettenhove, IV, pp. 313–15.

16. Lettenhove, IV, p. 314,

17. NA, SP 70/85, no. 502; Lettenhove, IV, pp. 331–2.

18. Lettenhove, IV, p. 334.

19. NA, SP 70/85, no. 533.

20. NA, SP 70/85, no. 543.

21. Lettenhove, IV, pp. 337–9.

22. Lettenhove, IV, pp. 337–9.

23. NA, SP 70/85, no. 543.

24. NA, SP 70/85, no. 543.

25. NA, SP 70/85, nos 533, 537; NA, AO 1/5/2.

26. NA, SP 70/86, no. 566.

27. NA, SP 70/86, nos 566, 575, 576; NA, AO 1/5/2.

28. NA, SP 70/86, no. 566.

29. NA, SP 70/86, no. 566.

30. NA, SP 70/86, no. 576.
31. NA, SP 70/86, no. 576.
32. NA, SP 70/86, no. 576.
33. NA, SP 70/86, no. 576.
34. NA, SP 70/86, nos 576, 593.
35. NA, SP 70/88, nos 745, 787, 780, 787; BL, Egerton MS 2790, fos 73v–4v.
36. BL, Lansdowne MS 102, no. 69. These emergency funds appear to have come from some sort of slush fund held in the queen's privy coffers or jewel house.
37. NA, AO 1/5/2.
38. NA, SP 70/88, no. 746.
39. Haynes, p. 444.
40. NA, SP 70/89, no. 811.
41. NA, SP 70/89, no. 811.
42. NA, SP 70/104B, no. 2222.
43. NA, SP 70/89, nos 817, 821; G. Parker, *Imprudent king: a new life of Philip II* (London and New Haven, 2014), p. 151.
44. NA, SP 70/104B, no. 2222.
45. NA. SP 70/104B, no. 2222.
46. NA, SP 70/86, no. 575.
47. BL, Egerton MS 2790, fo. 74; NA, SP 70/91, no. 1023.
48. NA, SP 70/91, no. 1023.
49. NA, SP 70/86, no. 576.
50. NA, SP 70/89, no. 811.

Chapter 15: Marrying off a daughter

1. NA, SP 70/86, no. 616; NA, SP 70/87, nos 655, 679, 690; NA, SP 70/89, no. 759.
2. NA, SP 12/47, nos 67, 70; NA, AO 1/5/1; Hatfield MSS, CP 4/113, 114; *CSPSp, 1568–1579*, no. 242; J. Stow, *Annales, or, a generall chronicle of England ... continued and augmented with matters forraigne and domestique, ancient and moderne, unto the end of this present yeere, 1631*, 2 vols (London, 1631), II, p. 662.
3. NA, SP 15/7, no. 39.
4. NA, PROB 11/58; NA, PROB 11/73; NA, E 179/145/252, fos 152–4.
5. NA, PROB 11/57.
6. NA, SP 69/12, nos 755, 756, 766, 779; NA, SP 69/13, no. 839.
7. NA, PROB 11/57.
8. J. Baker, *The men of law, 1440–1550*, 2 vols, Selden Society Supplementary Series, no. 18 (London, 2012), II, pp. 1057–8.
9. NA, C 3/29/109.
10. Gresham's victory can be inferred from later court proceedings, see NA, C 2/Eliz/G1/57; C 33/52, fos 184v–5.
11. Gresham's taking of the oath is noted at the top of his answer to the tenants, see NA, C 3/29/109.

12. NA, SP 70/84, no. 416. For Manwood's humiliation before the privy council at Greenwich in 1592, largely at Cecil's hands, see BL, Additional MS 48025, fo. 111.

13. Longleat MSS, Dudley papers, II, fo. 91.

14. LMA, P69/HEL/B/004/MS06836, fo. 26.

15. LMA, P69/HEL/B/004/MS06836, fo. 23.

16. 5 Elizabeth I, c. 5.

17. For Clapham as minister of St Helen's, see PROB 11/56 (will of Robert Smith). For his age and ordination, see http://db.theclergydatabase.org.uk/jsp/search/index.jsp, person ID: 40038.

18. John Foxe, *Acts and monuments of matters most special and memorable, happening in the church with an universal history of the same: wherein is set forth at large, the whole race and course of the church, from the primitive age to these later times of ours*, 3 vols (London, 1684), I, sig. [c6v].

19. One version hangs in Mercers' Hall; the other is in the NPG, reference NPG 352. I gratefully acknowledge the help of Dr Charlotte Bolland, who talked me through the painting in depth and provided access to conservation reports.

20. C. Bolland, 'Pictorial catalogue', in *Painting in Britain, 1500–1630*, ed. T. Cooper, A. Burnstock, M. Howard and E. Town (Oxford, 2015), pp. 57–9.

21. T. Cooper, *Citizen portraits: portrait painting and the urban elite of Tudor and Jacobean England and Wales* (New Haven and London, 2012), p. 52.

22. H. Swinburne, *A treatise of spousals or matrimonial contracts* (London, 1686), pp. 40–1, 47–8, 56–7.

23. *NBS*, I, pp. xv–xviii.

24. *Letters from Redgrave Hall: the Bacon family, 1340–1744*, ed. D. MacCulloch, Suffolk Records Society, no. 50 (Woodbridge, 2007), nos 36, 41.

25. G. W. G. Leveson Gower, *Genealogy of the family of Gresham* (London, 1883), p. 20.

26. *NBS*, I, pp. 10–12.

27. *NBS*, I, pp. xxxvii–xxxviii, 35–41, 47–9; *An exact copy of the last will and testament of Sir Thomas Gresham* (London, 1724), p. 31; *CPR, 1569–1572*, p. 136. Sir Nicholas Bacon also initially retained a life estate in lands he settled on Nathaniel and his wife: the difference is he did not grant leases to tenants on the eve of the wedding. See *NBS*, I, pp. xxxvii–xxxviii; *CPR, 1569–1572*, p. 136.

28. *NBS*, I, pp. 44, 37–8. See J. R. Taylor, 'Nathaniel Bacon: an Elizabethan squire, his family and household, and their impact upon the local community', UEA PhD (Norwich, 1989), pp. 104–9.

29. *NBS*, I, p. 44.

30. *NBS*, I, pp. 37–9, 40–3, 47–8; Taylor, 'Nathaniel Bacon: an Elizabethan squire, his family and household', pp. 84–5, 95, 105.

31. *NBS*, I, pp. 10–12, 22–3, 25; Taylor, 'Nathaniel Bacon: an Elizabethan squire, his family and household', p. 101.

32. *NBS*, I, pp. 22–3.

33. *NBS*, I, pp. 25–6, 75, 78; Taylor, 'Nathaniel Bacon: an Elizabethan squire, his family and household', pp. 111–12.

34. *NBS*, I, p. 12.
35. *NBS*, I, pp. 10–11, 12, 22–3.
36. Taylor, 'Nathaniel Bacon: an Elizabethan squire, his family and household', pp. 107–9.
37. NA, PROB 11/54; NA, SP 12/73, no. 66.
38. NA, SP 12/41, no. 47 (fos 125–6).
39. NA, SP 12/41, no. 47/1 (fo. 127r–v).
40. NA, SP 12/41, no. 47/1 (fo. 127r–v).
41. An inventory of Mary Grey's books is NA, SP 12/124, no. 19.
42. NA, SP 12/69, nos 17, 17/1.
43. NA, SP 12/73, no. 66.
44. NA, SP 12/74, nos 11, 14, 19.
45. NA, SP 12/77, no. 62; NA, SP 12/80, no. 14; NA, SP 70/119, no. 1296; SP 12/81, nos 5, 36, 38.
46. NA, SP 12/80, no. 5.

Chapter 16: The end of Antwerp

1. NA, SP 70/94, nos 1332, 1333.
2. NA, SP 70/104B, no. 2237; Lettenhove, V, p. 112.
3. NA, SP 70/96, no. 1530.
4. Lettenhove, V, pp. 163–4.
5. G. D. Ramsay, *The queen's merchants and the revolt of the Netherlands* (Manchester, 1986), pp. 73–80; G. Parker, *The army of Flanders and the Spanish road, 1567–1659* (Cambridge, 1972), pp. 57–70.
6. BL, Lansdowne MS 12, no. 11. See also NA, SP 70/119, no. 1296; NA, SP 70/120, no. 1309; NA, SP 12/81, no. 5.
7. Ramsay, *The queen's merchants and the revolt of the Netherlands*, pp. 85–94; C. Read, 'Queen Elizabeth's seizure of the duke of Alva's pay-ships', *JMH*, 5 (1933), pp. 443–64.
8. Lettenhove, V, pp. 253–62; Ramsay, *The queen's merchants and the revolt of the Netherlands*, pp. 92–111.
9. *CSPSp, 1568–1579*, nos 67–71; Read, 'Queen Elizabeth's seizure of the duke of Alva's pay-ships', pp. 448–9.
10. Lettenhove, V, pp. 235–6, 253–62; Ramsay, *The queen's merchants and the revolt of the Netherlands*, pp. 97–8.
11. Lettenhove, V, p. 209.
12. Lettenhove, V, p. 211.
13. *TRP*, II, no. 556; AGR, MS Audience 368/3, fos 330–39.
14. Lettenhove, V, pp. 218–19.
15. Lettenhove, V, pp. 288, 299.
16. Lettenhove, V, pp. 340–52; *CSPSp, 1568–1579*, no. 86.
17. NA, SP 12/60, nos 28, 29; BL, Lansdowne MS 12, no. 11.

18. BL, Lansdowne MS 12, no. 8. See also NA, SP 70/119, no. 1296; NA, SP 70/120, no. 1309; NA, SP 12/67, no. 33; NA, SP 12/81, no. 5; Read, 'Queen Elizabeth's seizure of the duke of Alva's pay-ships', pp. 457–8.

19. Lettenhove, V, p. 255.

20. BL, Lansdowne MS 12, no. 8; NA, SP 70/119, no. 1296; NA, SP 70/120, no. 1309.

21. BL Lansdowne MS 12, no. 8; NA, SP 70/119, no. 1296.

22. NA, AO 1/5/1 (where figures are stated in Flemish currency).

23. NA, SP 70/119, no. 1298.

24. NA, SP 70/119, no. 1296; NA, AO 1/5/1; NA, E 351/31. See also Read, 'Queen Elizabeth's seizure of the duke of Alva's pay-ships', p. 457, n. 45.

25. Lettenhove V, pp. 307–8.

26. *Correspondance diplomatique de Bertrand de Salignac de La Mothe-Fénélon, ambassadeur de France en Angleterre de 1568 à 1575*, ed. A. Teulet, 7 vols (Paris and London, 1838–40), I, pp. 233–7, 258–62.

27. *The rising in the north: the 1569 rebellion*, ed. C. Sharp (Durham, 1975), pp. 7–18.

28. NA, KB 8/41.

29. Ramsay, *The queen's merchants and the revolt of the Netherlands*, pp. 116–46.

30. Ramsay, *The queen's merchants and the revolt of the Netherlands*, pp. 130–32; T. Pennant, *The journey to Snowdon*, 2nd edn, 2 vols (London, 1784), II, i, p. 26.

31. Clough's arrival in Hamburg is documented by NA, SP 70/107, no. 255; also by a loan for £6,444 sterling he took up from the cloth merchants for the queen, see NA, AO 1/5/2.

32. BL, Cotton MS, Galba B.XI, fos 264–79.

33. NA, SP 70/100, no. 491; Ramsay, *The queen's merchants and the revolt of the Netherlands*, pp. 128–38; A. F. Sutton, *The mercery of London: trade, goods and people* (Aldershot, 2005), p. 436.

34. NA, PROB 11/52, where Dutton and Denny both witnessed Clough's will. For the death of Richard Clough, see below, Chapter 17.

35. NA, SP 70/113, no. 756. The relationship of Richard and Hugh Clough is established by Richard's first will, see NA, PROB 11/52.

Chapter 17: A golden goodbye

1.   G. D. Ramsay, *The queen's merchants and the revolt of the Netherlands* (Manchester, 1986), pp. 131–3.

2.   For Gresham's predictions on this point, see BL, Lansdowne MS 12, no. 8.

3.   NA, SP 12/49, no. 87.

4.   Hatfield MSS, CP 4/113–14; NA, AO 1/5/2.

5.   See above, Chapter 10.

6.   NA, AO 1/5/2.

7.   BL, Lansdowne MS 12, no. 10; A. F. Sutton, *The mercery of London: trade, goods and people* (Aldershot, 2005), p. 436.

8.   NA, AO 1/5/2.

9.   NA, SP 12/74, no. 19.

10. NA, SP 70/3, no. 167; 'Information of Thomas Gresham, mercer, touching the fall of the exchange, 1558'. See n. 1 to Chapter 9.

11. BL, Lansdowne MS 12, fos 28–9v (item not numbered); NA, SP 12/73, no. 44; NA, AO 1/5/1; NA, AO 1/5/2; Hatfield MSS, CP 4/113–14.

12. BL, Lansdowne MS 12, no. 8.

13. BL, Lansdowne MS 12, no. 8.

14. BL, Lansdowne MS 12, fos 28–9v (item not numbered); BL, Lansdowne MS 102, no. 83; NA, AO 1/5/2; NA, E 159/369.

15. NA, AO 1/5/1; NA, SP 12/86, no. 56. There are minor discrepancies in the figures given by these sources, but in all significant aspects they agree.

16. NA, SP 12/73, no. 44; NA, AO 1/5/2.

17. NA, SP 12/74, no. 15.

18. NA, SP 12/74, nos 15, 19; NA, SP 12/77, nos 2, 30.

19. NA, AO 1/5/2.

20. NA, SP 12/74, no. 15; NA, SP 12/77, nos 61–2.

21. NA, PROB 11/52. Clough's date of death, hitherto unknown, is established by *CPR, 1572–1575*, p. 164.

22. J. Burgon, *The life and times of Sir Thomas Gresham*, 2 vols (London, 1839), II, pp. 357–8. The document cited there is believed to have been destroyed by allied bombing in the Second World War.

23. NA, PROB 11/52.

24. NA, PROB 11/52.

25. NA, PROB 11/52.

26. *CPR, 1572–1575*, p. 164.

27. For the outright assertion that the bulk of the inheritance due to Clough's co-heirs was diverted to Gresham, see T. Pennant, *The journey to Snowdon*, 2nd edn, 2 vols (London, 1784), II, i, pp. 24–6. The suggestion there, however, is that this was achieved by a deed of survivorship.

28. NA, SP 12/81, no. 12.

29. NA, SP 12/81, no. 36; NA, SP 12/83, no. 20; NA, SP 12/85, nos 1, 65.

30. NA, SP 12/81, no. 37.

31. NA, SP 12/81, no. 54.

32. Longleat MSS, Dudley papers, II, fo. 91.

33. NA, E 351/541.

34. See above, Chapter 8.

35. BL, Additional MS 19398, fo. 73.

36. *CPR, 1569–1572*, pp. 47, 253.

37. NA, SP 12/86, no. 49.

38. S. Doran, 'Mary Grey', *ODNB*.

39. NA, SP 15/7, no. 39.

40. NA, E 351/541.

41. NA, LR 9/117.

42. *Bath MSS*, V, pp. 20–1.

43. *CPR, 1572–1575*, p. 377; NA, E 351/31.

44. NA, AO 1/5/2.

45. NA, AO 1/5/2; NA, E 351/31.

46. NA, AO 1/5/2.

47. See above, Chapter 11.

48. NA, AO 1/5/2; NA, E 351/31.

49. NA, AO 1/5/1; NA, AO 1/5/2; NA, E 351/31.

50. NA, AO 1/5/1.

51. For Taylor's ring, see D. Scarisbrick, *Tudor and Stuart jewellery* (London, 1995), pp. 31–3; N. Awais-Dean, 'A gem in the archives', *Jewellery history today* (Autumn 2013), pp. 7–8.

52. NA, AO 1/5/1; NA, AO 1/5/2; NA, E 351/31; NA, E 351/32. For a more conspiratorial account of this episode, see H. Hall, *Society in the Elizabethan Age* (London, 1888), pp. 65–8, 161–2.

53. *CPR, 1572–1575*, p. 550.

54. R. B. Outhwaite, 'Royal borrowing in the reign of Elizabeth I: the aftermath of Antwerp', *EcHR*, New Series, 86 (1971), pp. 251–63.

55. NA, SP 12/105, no. 69.

56. Ramsay, *The queen's merchants and the revolt of the Netherlands*, pp. 177–8.

57. NA, SP 12/105, no. 69.

58. J. Guy, *Tudor England* (Oxford, 1988), pp. 394–5.

59. Outhwaite, 'Royal borrowing in the reign of Elizabeth I: the aftermath of Antwerp', pp. 259–63.

Chapter 18: One last glorious deal?

1. NA, STAC 5/G31/20; NA, STAC 5/G21/27; NA, STAC 5/G2/21; NA, STAC 5/G40/21; NA, STAC 5/G24/3; NA, STAC 5/G7/6; NA, STAC 5/G31/39; NA, STAC 5/G23/23; NA, STAC 5/G36/18; NA, STAC 5/G29/18; NA, STAC 5/G25/6; NA, STAC 5/G18/5; NA, STAC 5/G19/5; NA, STAC 5/G21/32; NA, STAC 5/G11/29; NA, STAC 5/G8/23; NA, STAC 5/G24/25; NA, STAC 5/G34/34; NA, STAC 5/G27/25; NA, STAC 5/G6/28; NA, STAC 5/G6/40; NA, STAC 5/G7/30; NA, STAC 5/G7/27; NA, STAC 5/G35/26. See also, NA, SP 12/261, no. 46; NA, STAC 5/M38/3. Some, but far from all, of these documents are discussed by M. Pelling, 'Failed transmission: Sir Thomas Gresham, reproduction and the background to Gresham's professorship of physic', in *Sir Thomas Gresham and Gresham College*, ed. F. Ames-Lewis (Aldershot, 1999), pp. 56–60. See also below, Chapter 19.

2. LMA, CLC/275/MS33011/003, fo. 377r-v (microfilm), entries for 16 March 1579.

3. NA, STAC 5/G21/32.

4. It is just possible that Markham was related to the Gresham family. Paul Gresham of Little Walsingham, Sir Thomas's first cousin once removed and another of Sir Richard Gresham's executors, had married Elizabeth, daughter to Jerome (or possibly Jeremiah) Markham of Houghton in Nottinghamshire.

5. For the naming of 'Gresham' Hogan, see NA, PROB 11/114.

6. NA, STAC 5/G25/6; NA, STAC 5/G21/32.

7. NA, STAC 5/G25/6; NA, STAC 5/G21/32; NA, SP 12/261, no. 46.

8. NA, STAC 5/G34/34; NA, STAC 5/G25/6.

9. NA, STAC 5/G36/18.

10. NA, STAC 5/G11/29.

11. NA, STAC 5/G36/18.

12. NA, STAC 5/G21/32 (examined *ex parte* Anne Ferneley).

13. NA, STAC 5/G18/5 (examined *ex parte* John Markham).

14. NA, STAC 5/G21/32.

15. NA, STAC 5/G21/32.

16. *Queen Elizabeth I and her times*, ed. T. Wright, 2 vols (London, 1838), II, p. 62.

17. LMA, COL/CC/01/01/018, fo. 137; G. D. Ramsay, *The city of London in international politics at the accession of Elizabeth Tudor* (Manchester, 1975), pp. 35–6.

18. A. F. Sutton, *The mercery of London: trade, goods and people* (Aldershot, 2005), pp. 506–7.

19. *NBS*, I, pp. 64–5.

20. *NBS*, I, p. 254; J. R. Taylor, 'Nathaniel Bacon: an Elizabethan squire, his family and household, and their impact upon the local community', UEA PhD (Norwich, 1989), p. 74.

21. NA, SP 12/105, no. 69.

22. *NBS*, I, p. 85.

23. *NBS*, I, p. 100; Taylor, 'Nathaniel Bacon: an Elizabethan squire, his family and household', p. 105.

24. *NBS*, I, pp. 137–8, 184. See also *NBS*, I, pp. 7, 106, 109, 116–17, 117–18, 130–31, 164.

25. NA, SP 70/116, no. 1017 (fos 31–2).

26. *CPR, 1572–1575*, p. 510 (where the correct date is established); T. Sibbett, 'Early insurance and the Royal Exchange', in *The Royal Exchange*, ed. Saunders, pp. 78–9.

27. NA, PROB 11/83.

28. NA, STAC 5/G34/34; NA, STAC 5/G25/6; NA, STAC 5/G21/32; NA, PROB 11/61.

29. BL, Additional Charter 16336.

30. BL, Additional MS 70948, fos 62–3; BL, Additional Charter 16336; *NBS*, I, pp. 130–31.

31. *CPR, 1572–1575*, p. 550.

32. NA, E 159/396, rot. 202. My thanks to Professor Glyn Parry for this reference.

33. *NBS*, II, pp. 89–91, 108–10; *CPR, 1572–1575*, p. 390; *CPR, 1575–1578*, pp. 31, 131, 143, 144, 247, 267, 357, 461, 464, 509; NA, E 210/10486.

34. G. D. Ramsay, *The queen's merchants and the revolt of the Netherlands* (Manchester, 1986), pp. 174–82; L. Stone, 'Elizabethan overseas trade', *EcHR*, New Series, 2 (1949), pp. 30–58.

35. T. S. Willan, *Studies in Elizabethan foreign trade* (Manchester, 1959), pp. 4–5, 10–11, 98–106, 107–37; L. Jardine, 'Gloriana rules the waves: or, the advantage of being excommunicated (and a woman)', *TRHS*, Sixth Series, 14 (2004),

pp. 209–22; S. Skilliter, 'William Harborne and the trade with Turkey: a documentary study of the first Anglo-Ottoman relations', Oxford PhD (1977), pp. 23–4.

36. BL, Cotton MS, Nero B.I, fos 126–7 (formerly fos 167–8).

37. Gresham's deal has a backstory. Hogan's agent in Hamburg, John Williams, had previously arranged it with Muley Abu Abdallah Mohammed II. Samples of iron shot had been sent to Morocco 'for the proof' and the green light given for purchase, but Muley Mohammed had been toppled before delivery of the main cargo could be made. Muley Abd el-Malek had revived the transaction. See *APC, 1575–1577*, pp. 282–3; de Castries, I, pp. 199–205; Willan, *Studies in Elizabethan foreign trade*, pp. 118–20, 143–4; G. K. Waite, 'Reimagining religious identity: the Moor in Dutch and English pamphlets, 1550–1620', *Renaissance quarterly*, 66 (2013), pp. 1250–295. For details of the iron shot, see MC, Gresham Journal, unnumbered entries at the back.

38. NA, SP 12/115, nos 7, 8.

39. NA, SP 71/12, fos 1–3. For Warwick's role in the ordnance office and the difficulties of acquiring or manufacturing saltpetre, see NA, SP 12/91, no. 44; NA, SP 12/106, no. 41; NA, SP 12/139, no. 1; SP 15/24, no. 50.

40. NA, SP 70/53, no. 468.

41. NA, SP 70/53, no. 440.

42. A docquet note on NA, SP 71/12, fo. 2v shows that on or shortly after 6 March 1577, privy councillors became aware that Hogan's plan was to exchange saltpetre at least in part for iron shot. The problem was how to keep this information secret from the queen.

43. NA, SP 89/1, fo. 29r–v; de Castries, I, pp. 195–6, 203.

44. NA, SP 71/12, fos 1–3; de Castries, I, pp. 199–205.

45. J. Guy, *Elizabeth: the forgotten years* (London, 2016), pp. 16, 42, 148, 158, 240, 293, 378.

46. MC, Gresham Journal, unnumbered entries.

47. For Hogan's instructions, see de Castries, I, pp. 211–13. Naturally, the document nowhere mentions trading armaments for saltpetre. Nor does Hogan's report to the queen from Morocco, see de Castries, I, pp. 225–7.

48. MC, Gresham Journal, unnumbered entries. See also de Castries, I, pp. 239–49.

49. MC, Gresham Journal, unnumbered entries.

50. NA, SP 71/12, fos 1–3; de Castries, I, pp. 225–7, 239–49; R. Hakluyt, *The principal navigations, voyages, traffiques and discoveries of the English nation*, 2 vols in 1 (London, 1599), II, pp. 64–7; Willan, *Studies in Elizabethan foreign trade*, pp. 146–54.

51. *CSPSp, 1568–1579*, p. 679.

Chapter 19: A widow's plight

1. BL, Sloane MS 1759, fo. 4.

2. M. Pelling, 'Failed transmission: Sir Thomas Gresham, reproduction and the background to Gresham's professorship of physic', in *Sir Thomas Gresham and Gresham College*, ed. F. Ames-Lewis (Aldershot, 1999), p. 53.

3. *The diary of Henry Machyn, citizen and merchant-taylor of London, from A.D. 1550 to A.D. 1563*, ed. J. G. Nichols, Camden Society, Old Series, no. 42 (1848), p. 309.

4. The indenture of 20 May 1575 had at least two precursors, one signed and sealed on 1 September 1570, the second on 4 September 1571, using different trustees. Both would later come into contention. See NA, E 163/14/7; *CPR, 1569–1572*, p. 65; J. Ward, *The lives of the professors of Gresham College* (London, 1740), appendix 6.

5. NA, E 163/14/7.

6. NA, E 163/14/7; NA, PROB 11/61.

7. I. R. Adamson, 'Benjamin Jonson "of Gresham College": three pregnant words and their progeny explored', unpublished typescript. I am extremely grateful to Dr Adamson for supplying me with a typescript of this long and important article and allowing me to draw upon it.

8. NA, E 163/14/7; NA, PROB 11/61. See also *An exact copy of the last will and testament, of Sir Thomas Gresham, kt. To which are added, an abridgement of an Act of Parliament, passed in the twenty third of Q. Elizabeth, A.D. 1581, for the better performing the last will of Sir Thomas Gresham, kt.* (London, 1724), pp. 27–31 (where some of the arithmetic on p. 31 is in error, but the base figures are correct).

9. NA, E 163/14/7; NA, PROB 11/61. See below, Chapter 20.

10. The only reference in all of Gresham's letters to Neville is in one of 27 May 1565, written from Osterley, when Thomas informed Cecil: 'I have here my cousin, Sir Harry Neville, and divers of my kinsfolk, but God willing upon Wednesday I will give my attendance upon you.' NA, SP 70/78, no. 990.

11. NA, PROB 11/61.

12. J. Burgon, *The life and times of Sir Thomas Gresham*, 2 vols (London, 1839), II, pp. 435–6; Ward, *Lives of the professors of Gresham College*, appendix 3.

13. BL, Additional Charter 76333.

14. *An exact copy of the last will and testament, of Sir Thomas Gresham, kt.*, p. 31. See above, Chapter 15.

15. BL, Additional MS 70947, fos 32–3; *NBS*, II, pp. 89–91, 100, 105–6, 108–10, 110–11, 115; J. R. Taylor, 'Nathaniel Bacon: an Elizabethan squire, his family and household, and their impact upon the local community', UEA PhD (Norwich, 1989), pp. 105–6.

16. *NBS*, II, p. 108.

17. BL, Additional MS 70948, fos 32–3.

18. *NBS*, II, pp. 108–9, 110.

19. *NBS*, II, p. 110.

20. HEH, HM 715; NA, SP 12/119, no. 30; NA, SP 12/126, no. 32; NA, SP 12/124, no. 2; NA, SP 12/130, no. 35. See also *APC, 1577–1578*, p. 415. Not only had Gresham invested personally in these ill-fated ventures, he had given a personal guarantee of £250 to cover a shortfall in the queen's own substantial contributions. Fortunately, Elizabeth was so convinced that Frobisher had been onto a winner, she changed

her mind and paid for her shares in full, leaving Thomas breathing a hearty sigh of
relief. See NA, E 159/372, rot. 230. My thanks to Professor Parry for this reference.

21.   R. Holinshed, *The third volume of chronicles beginning at duke William the
      Norman, commonly called the conqueror* (London, 1587), p. 1310.

22.   J. Stow, *Survey of London*, ed. H. B. Wheatley (London, 1970), pp. 154–5. Stow's
      report appears to be confirmed by the absence of any payment in the St Helen's
      churchwardens' accounts for the 'grave and knell' of Sir Thomas Gresham, whereas
      other funerals had to be paid for. See LMA, P69/HEL/B/004/MS06836, fos
      29–31, where the details of funeral charges should have appeared.

23.   J. Edis, 'The Tottenham school of masons, *c.*1567–*c.*1618', De Montfort PhD thesis
      (Leicester, 2000), pp. 26–7.

24.   A. Wells-Cole, *Art and decoration in Elizabethan and Jacobean England* (New
      Haven and London, 1997), pp. 54–5.

25.   In reconstructing these years in the remainder of this chapter, I have greatly
      benefited from the work of Dr Adamson cited above.

26.   The reckoning was made by Ferneley's lawyer, Edward Coke, during the course of
      one of her lawsuits: NA, C 3/227/49. See also NA, SP 12/151, no. 9. For Duckett,
      see also NA, C 78/107, no. 4; and above, Chapter 17.

27.   NA, C 3/227/49. The outstanding £500 from the debt of £5,883 was settled in 1591
      by William Read by composition; see above Chapter 18 and NA, E 159/414, rot.
      114. I owe this reference to the kindness of Professor Parry.

28.   LPL, MS 3206, fo. 1001; LPL, MS 3198, fo. 3. My thanks to Dr Alan Bryson for
      pointing me towards the Talbot Papers.

29.   LPL, MS 3198, fo. 3.

30.   F. Blomefield, *An essay towards a topographical history of the county of Norfolk*, 5
      vols (Fersfield, 1739–75), V, pp. 834, 1040, 1145; M. J. Armstrong, *The history and
      antiquities of the county of Norfolk*, 10 vols (Norwich, 1781), X, pp. 15, 34, 75–7, 115.

31.   NA, SP 46/32, fo. 266; NA, SP 46/33, fo. 222; NA, SP 46/34, fo. 200; NA, SP
      46/37, fo. 141; Adamson, 'Benjamin Jonson "of Gresham College"'.

32.   NA, C 2/Eliz/G7/7; NA, PROB 11/62. In her will, Frances left instructions to
      her son-in-law, Sir Henry Neville, to continue the lawsuit and split the proceeds
      equally between her grandchildren. Unfortunately for Neville's children, the act of
      Parliament of 1581 simply cancelled the recognisance and the payments due under
      it in consideration of the larger transfer to Neville of the manor of Mayfield and its
      associated estates. See Adamson, 'Benjamin Jonson "of Gresham College"'.

33.   NA, C 78/81, no. 18; NA, C 33/81, fo. 445; NA, C 33/82, fo. 451.

34.   For a transcript of proceedings in the court of Wards and Liveries, see NA,
      E 163/14/7. Kingsmill also believed he had identified a series of legal flaws in
      Gresham's quadripartite indenture of May 1575. They sprang from his belief that
      Gresham's earlier indentures of 1 September 1570 and 4 September 1571 had not
      been completely revoked and extinguished. See also Adamson, 'Benjamin Jonson
      "of Gresham College"'.

35. *APC, 1581–2*, pp. 82–3; G. R. Elton, *The Parliament of England, 1559–1581* (Cambridge, 1986), pp. 78, 80; Adamson, 'Benjamin Jonson "of Gresham College"'.

36. Ward, *Lives of the professors of Gresham College*, appendix 6.

37. NA, C 2/Eliz/G5/59; NA, C 2/Eliz/E1/26.

38. See, for instance, *APC, 1585–7*, p. 164; *APC, 1587–8*, pp. 352, 360, 378–9; *APC, 1588*, pp. 9, 46, 56; *APC, 1588–9*, pp. 160, 172; NA, SP 12/224, no. 40.

39. NA, STAC 5/G3/8; NA, STAC 5/G4/30; NA, STAC 5/G5/2; NA, C 2/Eliz/ G15/26; NA, C 2/Eliz/G11/28; NA, C 2/Eliz/G13/40; NA, C 2/Eliz/G14/13; *APC, 1588*, pp. 332–3; *The first part of the reports of Sir George Croke, kt.* (London, 1669), p. 506.

40. See Chapter 20.

41. *APC, 1581–2*, pp. 82–3; NA, SP 12/187, no. 77; LMA, COL/CA/01/01/023, fos 270, 312. See also Adamson, 'Benjamin Jonson "of Gresham College"'.

42. NA, C 78/81, no. 18; NA, C 33/79, fo. 833; NA, C 33/80, fo. 831; NA, C 33/81, fos 16v, 115, 183, 204, 279, 293, 445; NA, C 33/82, fos 17, 119, 193, 211, 289, 304, 451; NA, E 128/2/4.

43. NA, C 33/81, fo. 445; NA, C 33/82, fo. 451.

44. East Riding of Yorkshire RO, MS DDCC/133/7; NA, STAC 5/G34/34.

45. East Riding of Yorkshire RO, MS DDCC/133/7; NA, C 2/Eliz/S27/14.

46. *The reports of Sir Edward Coke, kt.*, 13 vols (London, 1777), II, Part 3, p. 86.

47. NA, STAC 5/G7/30; NA, STAC 5/G21/32; NA, SP 12/261, no. 46; NA, C 33/81, fo. 16v.

48. NA, SP 12/261, no. 46; NA, STAC 5/G2/21; NA, STAC 5/G21/32; NA, STAC 5/ G21/27; NA, STAC 5/G7/30; NA, STAC 5/G31/39; NA, STAC 5/G40/21; NA, STAC 5/M38/3. See also M. Pelling, 'Failed transmission: Sir Thomas Gresham, reproduction and the background to Gresham's professorship of physic', in *Sir Thomas Gresham and Gresham College*, ed. F. Ames-Lewis (Aldershot, 1999), pp. 56–60.

49. NA, STAC 5/G31/20; NA, STAC 5/G21/27; NA, STAC 5/G2/21; NA, STAC 5/ G40/21; NA, STAC 5/G24/3; NA, STAC 5/G7/6; NA, STAC 5/G31/39; NA, STAC 5/G23/23; NA, STAC 5/G36/18; NA, STAC 5/G29/18; NA, STAC 5/ G25/6; NA, STAC 5/G18/5; NA, STAC 5/G19/5; NA, STAC 5/G21/32; NA, STAC 5/G11/29; NA, STAC 5/G8/23; NA, STAC 5/G24/25; NA, STAC 5/ G34/34; NA, STAC 5/G27/25; NA, STAC 5/G6/28; NA, STAC 5/G6/40; NA, STAC 5/G7/30; NA, STAC 5/G7/27; NA, STAC 5/G35/26. For the decrees in the case, see J. Hawarde, *Les reportes des cases in camera stellata, 1593 to 1609*, ed. W. P. Baildon (London, 1894), pp. 22, 26–7, 29, 64–6, 94.

50. NA, STAC 5/G2/21.

51. *The annals of St Helen's Bishopsgate, London*, ed. J. E. Cox (London, 1876), p. 285.

52. For full records of the final punishments in 1596, see Hawarde, *Les reportes des cases*, ed. Baildon, pp. 64–6, 94; NA, E 159/412, rot. 286. Punishments handed down after the opening round of litigation in 1595 can be seen in NA, E 159/410, rot. 178. Initially, Booth secured a pardon, see NA, SP 12/254, no. 76; NA, SP

12/255, no. 4; NA, E 159/410, rot. 167. But this was overridden in 1596. My thanks to Professor Glyn Parry for the references to documents in E 159.

Chapter 20: Gresham College

1. G. W. G. Leveson Gower, *Genealogy of the family of Gresham* (London, 1883), p. 11.
2. By 1597, William Read had inherited all his younger brother's lands as remainder-man in accordance with their father's will. For Thomas Read's death, see *The annals of St Helen's Bishopsgate, London*, ed. J. E. Cox (London, 1876), p. 285.
3. C. N. L. Brooke, D. R. Leader, V. Morgan et al., *A history of the University of Cambridge*, 4 vols (1988–2004), II, pp. 437–12, 511–16. Students qualified in civil law were able to practise in the Court of Admiralty, which presided over maritime and mercantile cases with a foreign element. Civil lawyers were based at Doctors' Commons in London, along with ecclesiastical lawyers.
4. *Annals of the Reformation*, ed. J. Strype (4 vols, London, 1824), IV, p. 376.
5. I am heavily indebted in this chapter to I. R. Adamson, 'The foundation and early history of Gresham College, London, 1596–1704', unpublished PhD (Cambridge, 1975); I. R. Adamson, 'The administration of Gresham College and its fluctuating fortunes as a scientific institution in the seventeenth century', *History of education*, 9 (1980), pp. 13–25; I. R. Adamson, 'The Royal Society and Gresham College, 1660–1711', *Notes and records of the Royal Society of London*, 33 (1978), pp. 1–21; I. R. Adamson, 'Benjamin Jonson "of Gresham College": three pregnant words and their progeny explored', unpublished typescript. I am extremely grateful to Dr Adamson for supplying me with copies of all of these important works and for allowing me to draw upon them. See also J. Ward, *The lives of the professors of Gresham College* (London, 1740), especially its valuable appendices.
6. NA, PROB 11/61.
7. Adamson, 'The foundation and early history of Gresham College', pp. 42–7, 258–74; Adamson, 'The administration of Gresham College and its fluctuating fortunes', pp. 15–17.
8. *TRP*, III, nos 738–9.
9. Adamson, 'The foundation and early history of Gresham College', pp. 44–5.
10. Adamson, 'The foundation and early history of Gresham College', pp. 47–56; Adamson, 'The administration of Gresham College and its fluctuating fortunes', pp. 15–17.
11. Adamson, 'The foundation and early history of Gresham College', pp. 43–7; Adamson, 'The administration of Gresham College and its fluctuating fortunes', p. 16.
12. Adamson, 'Benjamin Jonson "of Gresham College"'.
13. NA, C 2/Eliz/M8/20.
14. Adamson, 'Benjamin Jonson "of Gresham College"'.
15. *APC, 1596–1597*, p. 488; *APC, 1599–1600*, p. 408; *APC, 1600–1601*, p. 283; Adamson, 'Benjamin Jonson "of Gresham College"'.

16. LMA, COL/CA/01/01/026, fos 357, 361–2, 371–3, 390v, 422, 461–2; Adamson, 'Benjamin Jonson "of Gresham College".

17. Adamson, 'Benjamin Jonson "of Gresham College".

18. NA, STAC 5/R27/24.

19. For the musical instruments, see NA, STAC 5/R11/22.

20. NA, SP 38/4 (not numbered).

21. Adamson, 'Benjamin Jonson "of Gresham College".

22. NA, STAC 5/R11/22; NA, STAC 5/R18/25; NA, STAC 5/R27/24; NA, STAC 5/R36/22.

23. Adamson, 'Benjamin Jonson "of Gresham College". For a suggestion that Read was partially displaced, see the evidence of Edmond Hogan and Richard Wright in NA, STAC 5/R27/24.

24. P. Chappell, *A portrait of John Bull* (Hereford, 1970), p. 14.

25. HMC, *Report on the manuscripts of the Marquis of Downshire*, 4 vols (London, 1924–42), IV, pp. 270–71.

26. Adamson, 'Benjamin Jonson "of Gresham College"; *Annals of St Helen's Bishopsgate, London*, ed. J. E. Cox, p. 285. A possible funeral date for William Read is 23 October 1621, see *The register of St. Lawrence Jewry, London, 1538–1676*, ed. A. W. Hughes Clarke, Harleian Society, no. 70 (London, 1940–41), p. 142. A run of certificates of residence for tax purposes suggests that Read was partly living (or preferred to be taxed) in Middlesex in and after 1604. See NA, E 115/322/ 6, 120; NA, E 115/332/82; NA, E 115/327/141; NA, E 115/328/107.

27. Adamson, 'The foundation and early history of Gresham College', pp. 79–82.

28. W. Kaunzner, 'Henry Briggs', *ODNB*; F. R. Johnson, 'Gresham College: precursor of the Royal Society', *Journal of the history of ideas*, 1 (1940), pp. 413–38.

29. Adamson, 'The foundation and early history of Gresham College', pp. 79–97; Adamson, 'The administration of Gresham College and its fluctuating fortunes', pp. 17–22; Johnson, 'Gresham College: precursor of the Royal Society', pp. 427–37.

30. HMC, *Report on the manuscripts of the duke of Buccleuch and Queensbury, preserved at Montagu House, Whitehall*, 3 vols (London, 1899–1926), I, p. 60; T. Barnard, 'Sir William Petty', *ODNB*; Adamson, 'The administration of Gresham College and its fluctuating fortunes', p. 22.

31. *Sir Thomas Gresham, his ghost* (London, 1647), pp. 1–8.

32. Adamson, 'The Royal Society and Gresham College, 1660–1711', pp. 1–15.

33. A. Saunders, 'The second Exchange', in *The Royal Exchange*, ed. Saunders, pp. 121–35; Adamson, 'The foundation and early history of Gresham College', pp. 221–3; Adamson, 'The administration of Gresham College and its fluctuating fortunes', pp. 23–4; Adamson, 'The Royal Society and Gresham College, 1660–1711', p. 6; R. Chartres and D. Vermont, *A brief history of Gresham College, 1597–1997* (London, 1998), pp. 33–5.

34. Adamson, 'The foundation and early history of Gresham College', pp. 227–42; Adamson, 'The administration of Gresham College and its fluctuating fortunes', pp. 24–5; Adamson, 'The Royal Society and Gresham College, 1660–1711', p. 9.

See also *The case of the petitioners against the professors of Gresham College* (London, 1706), pp. 1–3.

Chapter 21: Gresham on the stage

1.   *STC*, no. 13336. For another account of Gresham's literary legacy, chiefly relating to the foundation of the Royal Exchange, see J. Gasper, 'The literary legend of Sir Thomas Gresham', in *The Royal Exchange*, ed. Saunders, pp. 99–107.
2.   D. Kathman, 'Thomas Heywood', *ODNB*.
3.   NA, STAC 8/245/21; Hatfield MSS, CP Petitions, nos 1130, 1365, 1869, 1870. For the dates when print copies of each part of the play were entered into the Stationers' Company register, see notes in *STC*, I, p. 582. My thanks to Professor Glyn Parry for the references to the Hatfield MSS.
4.   W. Hudson, *A treatise of the court of Star Chamber*, in *Collectanea juridica*, ed. F. Hargrave, 2 vols (London, 1792), II, pp. 65, 168, 214, 236; *The reports of Sir Edward Coke, kt.*, 13 vols (London, 1777), VI, Part 13, pp. 428–39; *English reports*, ed. F. Pollock et al, 176 vols (London, 1900–30), LXXVII, pp. 1446–7; HMC, *3rd report* (London, 1874), pp. 56–7.
5.   Eight separate printings of the first part of the play and four of the second are known, although the number of stage performances of each part is unknown, as are their venues.
6.   *STC*, no. 13328.
7.   *STC*, no. 13336, sig. A2.
8.   J. Guy, *Elizabeth: the forgotten years* (London, 2016), pp. 352–6, 360–61, 393.
9.   See Chapter 18.
10. *STC*, no. 13336, sig. A2v.
11. *STC*, no. 13336, sig. A3.
12. *STC*, no. 13336, sig. F2–2v.
13. *STC*, no. 13336, sigs. Fv–F2v.
14. *STC*, no. 13336, sig. F2v.
15. NA, SP 38/7 (warrant dated 6 Sept. 1604). See also C. W. Crupi, 'Reading nascent capitalism in Part II of Thomas Heywood's *If you know not me, you know nobody*', *Texas studies in literature and language*, 46 (2004), pp. 296–323.
16. *STC*, no. 13336, sig. C1–C1v.
17. *STC*, no. 13336, sig. E1v.
18. *STC*, no. 13336, sig. E1v.
19. *STC*, no. 13336, sig. E1v–E2.
20. NA, C 3/227/49.
21. *STC*, no. 13336, sigs. C4–D1.
22. *STC*, no. 13336, sig. D1v.
23. *STC*, no. 13336, sig. H1–H1v.
24. *STC*, no. 13336, sigs F2v–F3.
25. *Timon of Athens*, I, i, 106; I, ii, 216.
26. *Timon of Athens*, ed. A. B. Dawson and G. E. Minton (London, 2008), p. 10.

27. *Timon of Athens*, ed. Dawson and Minton, pp. 12–27, 341–400.

28. S. Schoenbaum, *William Shakespeare: a compact documentary life* (Oxford, 1987), pp. 221–3.

29. I. Wright, 'Matthew Gwinne', *ODNB*; C. Hill, *The intellectual origins of the English revolution – revisited* (Oxford, 1997), p. 47. My thanks to Dr Ian Adamson, who is working on the connections between Gwinne, Florio and Shakespeare, for a steer on this complicated question.

30. *STC*, no. 18041, sig. A3.

31. F. A. Yates, 'John Florio at the French embassy', *Modern language review*, 24 (1929), pp. 16–36; J. Bossy, *Giordano Bruno and the embassy affair* (New Haven and London, 1991), pp. 39, 42, 107; D. O'Connor, 'John Florio', *ODNB*; R. Ellrodt, 'Self-consciousness in Montaigne and Shakespeare', *Shakespeare survey*, 28 (1975), pp. 37–50; A. Harmon, 'How great was Shakespeare's debt to Montaigne?', *Proceedings of the Modern Language Association*, 57 (1942), pp. 988–1008; *Shakespeare International Yearbook, 6: Shakespeare and Montaigne Revisited*, ed. P. Holbrook (Aldershot, 2006), pp. 5–21.

32. *Timon of Athens*, I, ii, 142–4.

Chapter 22: A reputation established

1. I. R. Adamson, 'The Royal Society and Gresham College, 1660–1711', *Notes and records of the Royal Society of London*, 33 (1978), pp. 14–15.

2. L. L. Peck, *Consuming splendour: society and culture in seventeenth-century England* (Cambridge, 2005), pp. 46–60, 346–59.

3. J. Brewer, *The pleasures of the imagination: English culture in the eighteenth century* (London, 2013), pp. 37–48; D. Keene, 'The setting of the Royal Exchange', in *The Royal Exchange*, ed. Saunders, pp. 253–71.

4. 8 George III, c.32.

5. J. Watney, *An account of the mistery of mercers in the city of London*, 2 vols (London, 1914), I, pp. 109–10.

6. M. H. Port, 'Destruction, competition and rebuilding: the Royal Exchange, 1838–1884', in *The Royal Exchange*, ed. Saunders, pp. 279–305.

7. A. Saunders, 'Opening of the Royal Exchange by Queen Victoria', in *The Royal Exchange*, ed. Saunders, pp. 306–10; *Illustrated London news* (2 Nov. 1844), pp. 275–82; the *Times*, issue 18,753 (28 Oct. 1844), p. 5; the *Times*, issue 18,754 (29 Oct. 1844), pp. 4–6. My ensuing description relies on these sources unless otherwise indicated.

8. *Illustrated London news* (2 Nov. 1844), pp. 281–2.

9. C. Christmas, 'Decline and redevelopment of the Third Royal Exchange', in *The Royal Exchange*, ed. Saunders, pp. 401–15.

10. *Illustrated London news* (30 Jan. 1971), p. 14.

11. The *Times*, issue 18,756 (31 Oct. 1844), p. 7.

12. The *Times*, issue 18,444 (3 Nov. 1843), p. 4.

13.   The *Times*, issue 39,511 (17 Feb. 1911), p. 8; C. Dickens (attrib.), 'Lecture in Basinghall Street', *All the year round*, 3 (July 1860), pp. 301–3; R. Chartres and D. Vermont, *A brief history of Gresham College, 1597–1997* (London, 1998), p. 48.

14.   Dickens (attrib.), 'Lecture in Basinghall Street', p. 302.

15.   Watney, *An account of the mistery of mercers in the city of London*, I, pp. 112–13.

16.   The *Times*, issue 39,511 (17 Feb. 1911), p. 6; the *Times*, issue 39,960 (25 July 1912), p. 3; the *Times*, issue 40,396 (16 Dec. 1913), p. 6; Watney, *An account of the mistery of mercers in the city of London*, I, p. 113.

17.   The *Times*, issue 61,650 (20 Sept. 1983), p. 28; the *Times*, issue 61,765 (23 Feb. 1984), p. 22; the *Times*, issue 62,184 (8 July 1985), p. 25; Chartres and Vermont, *A brief history of Gresham College, 1597–1997*, pp. 57–69.

18.   It should be noted that a case in the court of Chancery, 'Thomas Gresham Esq. *v* Sir Henry Woodhouse', in which the plaintiff sought relief against a charge of usury and the litigation involved properties in London in which an estate for life was held by one 'Dame Cecily Gresham', had nothing to do with either Sir Thomas Gresham or with Cecily Cioll. These litigants were, in fact, members of a different branch of the Gresham clan. See NA, C 2/Eliz/G2/14.

19.   NA, SP 69/7, no. 438.

20.   R. Mundell, 'Uses and abuses of Gresham's law in the history of money', *Zagreb journal of economics*, 2 (1998), pp. 3–28. The quotation is from p. 26.

21.   M. Mainelli, 'Sir Thomas Gresham: Tudor, trader, shipper, spy and the ladies of Dulwich', version dated 1 June 2015, http://www.mainelli.org/?p=551.

22.   *Hansard*, 22 Nov.1990, House of Commons, 181, cols 445–53. The quotation is from col. 451.

Appendix: The birth date of Thomas Gresham

1.   NA, SP 12/105, no. 69.

2.   NA, C 142/93/50.

3.   *Biographia britannica: or, the lives of the most eminent persons who have flourished in Great Britain and Ireland*, ed. H. Brougham, J. Campbell, W. Harris and others, 6 vols (London, 1757), IV, pp. 2372–3, 2375–6, 2378, and notes A (p. 2372) and C (p. 2376). See also J. Ward, *The lives of the professors of Gresham College* (London, 1740), appendix 5.

INDEX

TG refers to Thomas Gresham throughout
Captions for colour plates are indicated by *pl*.

A

Abd el-Malek, Muley, 200, 201, 203, 204, 228, 230

accounting, 16th century, 35 *see also* Pacioli, Luca; double-entry bookkeeping

Allen, Sir John, 113

Al-Mansur, Muley Ahmed, 204

Alva, Fernando Álvarez de Toledo, duke of, 160–61, 166, 173, 174, 176, 191–2

Anglo-Netherlands trade, 19–23, 35–6, 46, 125–6, 128, 151, 152–3, 176, 180

Anna of Saxony, 119

Anne, Queen, 227, 231

Anne of Cleves, 15

Antwerp: Gresham family business in, 9, 11; art work in, 19; population, 20; rise as commercial hub of Europe, 19–20; port and harbour, 20–21; credit market consolidated at, 23; New Bourse, 25, 142, *pl.*; decline as commercial centre, 109, 120–21, 177; Spanish Inquisition, 124; embargo on English trade, 126–7; rise of Calvinism, 152–5; Calvinist purge, 174

Aristophanes, *The Frogs*, 103

Armentières, 153

Atkyns, Thomas, 55, 57

B

Babington Plot (1586), 219

Bacon, Nathaniel, 167–70, 197, 208

Bacon, Sir Nicholas, 34, 41, 76, 119–20, 167, 168

Bacon, William, 198

Bancroft, Richard, bishop of London, 218, 219

Bank of England, 226

Barnard Castle, 180

Beccles, Suffolk, 42, 164

Becket, Thomas, 7–8, 22, 245

Bekinsaw, Dr John, 14

Bendlowes, William, 34, 60

Bergen-op-Zoom, 19, 21, 22, 23, 70, 77

Berney, Robert, 34, 38, 59

bills of exchange, 28–9, 38

Blitheman, John, 223

Bond, Alderman William, 162–3, 165, 176, 183, 185

Bond, Margaret, 163

Booth, Roger, 213, 215, 228, 235

Boulogne, 27

Boyle, Robert, 225

Brabant fairs, 21–2, 70–71, 99, 127

Bradshaw, Henry, 56

Bradshaw, Thomas, 34, 35, 62

Bricklayers' Company, 146

Bridgewater, Richard, 207

Briggs, Henry, 224
Brocket Hall, Hertfordshire, 93
Bruno, Giordano, 235
Bull, Dr John, 222–3
Buonvisi, Alessandro, 76, 91
Buonvisi, Antonio, 39, 75–6
Buonvisi, Benedetto, 39
Buonvisi family (bankers), 28, 39, 91
Burgon, J. W., *Life and times of Sir Thomas Gresham* (1839), 238
Buxton, Derbyshire, 134, 162, 189
Byrd, William, 223

C
Calais: English loss of, 89, 108, 124; trading gateway to Europe, 27
Calvinism, in the Netherlands, 152–9, 173
Cambridge University, 6, 11–12, 13, 207, 217
Candeler, Richard, 88, 151, 198
Candeler, Thomas, 88
Carew, Sir Nicholas, 14
Cateau-Cambrésis, treaty of (1559), 108, 113, 124
Catholic persecution, 180, 219
Cecil, Mildred, 213
Cecil, Robert (*later* 1st earl of Salisbury), 223–4
Cecil, Thomas (*later* Lord Burghley, 1st earl of Exeter), 189
Cecil, William, 1st baron Burghley: under Edward VI, 65; and merchant loans, 70; Mary dismisses from Privy Council, 76; obscurity during Mary's reign, 85; chief minister to Elizabeth I, 4–5, 93–4, 129; TG's advice to, 96–7; and restoration of the currency, 100; and military defence, 109–10, 119; audits of TG's accounts, 122, 191; provides TG with funds, 127, 153; transfers English trade to Emden, Germany, 125; invests in the slave trade, 136; consulted over the Royal Exchange, 143; granted patent for

change and exchange, 149–50; and Roger Manwood, 164; supporter of the Grey family, 171, 187; and Spanish treasure ships, 175, 179; created lord treasurer and Lord Burghley, 188; and TG's illegal arms trade, 201–2; *pl.*
Cely, Philip, 198
Chaloner, Sir Thomas, 106–7, 108, 133, 152
Chancellor, Richard, 163
chantry properties, 46
Charles, Archduke, 116, 158
Charles, Richard, 195
Charles II, 225
Charles V, Holy Roman Emperor, 23, 26, 28, 60, 73, 79, 84
Cioll, Cecily (*née* Gresham), 76, 138–9, 207, 221
'Cioll, Germain' (Germin di Ciolo), 39–40, 76, 91, 138–9, 152
Clapham, Luke, 165
Clifton, William, 41
'clipped coin', 26
cloth trade, 19, 21, 22–3, 32, 35–6, 46, 72, 125–7, 153, 180–81, 183–4, 185, 199
Clough, Hugh, 181
Clough, Richard: background, 59–60; TG's factor in Antwerp, 59, 61, 84, 88, 108, 126, 151–5, 174; and TG's deal with the count of Mansfeld, 111, 114; and the Royal Exchange, 142, 144, 146; Cecil's agent in Hamburg, 181, 184; death and will, 185–7
Cobham, Henry, 133
coinage: 'clipped coin', 26; debasement of, 27–8, 64–5, 103; 'permission' or 'valued' money, 97, 100, 102, 112; re-minted from Spanish *reales*, 79–80, 177–8, 180; restoration of, 99–102
Coke, Edward, 215
Colet, Sir Henry, 196
Coligny, Odet de, cardinal de Châtillon, 162
Collège de Calvi, Paris, 13
Cologne, Germany, 185, 191

Conyers, John, 133
Cooke, Anne, 76, 167, 168–9
Cooke, Mildred, 169, 207
Copeland, William, 9
Copernicus, Nicholas, 103
Copledike, John, 167
Corporation of London: and Gresham
    College, 206, 216, 218, 222, 240, 241;
    and the Royal Exchange, 143, 145, 197,
    221, 232, 239; and TG's estate, 206, 212,
    213
Cranmer, Thomas, archbishop of
    Canterbury, 14, 44, 50
Cromwell, Henry, 224
Cromwell, Thomas, 2, 14, 23, 53
Crow, William, 146
currency debasements, 27–8, 45–6, 51,
    64–5

D
Dale, Valentine, 125
Dalle, Paul van, 94, 190
Damsell, William, 45–52
Damser, Richard, 56
Darcy, Thomas, 76
Darnley, Henry Stuart, Lord, 158
d'Assonleville, Christophe, 176–7
Daundy, Agnes, 15, 170
Dauntsey, Christopher, 77
Denny, Thomas, 181, 198
di Ciolo, Germin *see* 'Cioll, Germain'
Dickens, Charles, 241
double-entry bookkeeping, 35, 40, 62
Ducci, Gasparo, 60
Duckett, Lionel, 142, 185, 209
Dudley, Lord Guildford, 74
Dudley, Lord Robert (*later* 1st earl of
    Leicester): and Elizabeth I, 116; invests
    in the slave trade, 136; support for
    Cecily Gresham, 138; support for the
    Huguenots, 124; and TG's illegal arms
    trade, 201–2, 203; TG's relationship
    with, 5, 129–30, 133, 189; first wife's
    death, 129; and William Cecil, 129; *pl.*

Dürer, Albrecht, 21
Dutch War of Independence, 161
Dutton, Thomas, 88, 92, 181, 198, 209
Dutton, Winifred (mistress of TG), 92,
    169, 247

E
Edinburgh, treaty of (1560), 113
Edward IV, 72
Edward VI, 44, 50, 51, 65, 74
Egmont, count of, 126, 173
Eighty Years' War (Dutch War of
    Independence), 161
El Escorial, Real Monasterio de San
    Lorenzo de, 152
Elizabeth I: succeeds to the throne, 93;
    reliance on William Cecil, 65; retains
    TG as government banker, 4–5, 93–4;
    visits the Tower mints, 102; shuns TG's
    invitation to Mercers' Hall, 113–14;
    reprimands TG for negligence, 115; and
    marriage, 116–17, 158; relations with
    Lord Robert Dudley, 116; letter to TG,
    118; lifts trade embargo with Antwerp,
    127; transfers English trade to Emden,
    Germany, 125, 126–7; visits TG at
    Osterley, 137, 188, 189; names and opens
    the Royal Exchange, 148–9; grants
    lands to TG, 188; excommunication
    (1570), 200; bans sale of armaments
    to Morocco, 200; love of sugar, 202;
    promotion of Dr John Bull, 222
Elyot, John, 34, 36, 60, 81
Emden, Germany, 125, 126–7, 181
Erasmus, Desiderius, 8, 12
Estfeld, Sir William, 196

F
Fayre, William, 152
Felton, John, 180
Ferdinand I, Holy Roman Emperor, 107
Feria, Count of, 93
Ferneley, Anne (*later* Gresham): first
    marriage to William Read, the elder,

15; second marriage to TG, 4, 15–16, 120; in Antwerp, 24, 34, 59; affairs managed by TG, 42–3, 61–3, 247; and TG's illegitimate daughter, 92, 169–70; remains in London, 107–8; death of her son Richard, 133; takes waters at Buxton, 134, 162, 189; portrait by Anthonis Mor, 140–42, *pl.*; and TG's estate, 206, 207, 209–13, 220–22; case against John Markham, 215, 228, 235; death, 215; funeral, 216

Ferneley, Jane, 34, 76, 167

Ferneley, William, 15, 37, 42–3

Field of Cloth of Gold, 11

Fitzwilliam, Sir William, 15

Fitzwilliams, John, 115, 152, 153

Florio, John, 235

Floris, Cornelis, 135, 144

Floris, Jacob, 209

Fountains Abbey, Yorkshire, 15

Foxe, John, *Acts and monuments* ('Book of Martyrs'), 165, 228

Francis II, King of France, 108

Franco-Habsburg war, 26, 49, 67, 108

Frescobaldi (Florentine bankers), 39

Frobisher, Martin, 208

Fugger (German bankers), 50, 51, 61, 68, 90, 101, 121

Fugger, Anton, 61, 66, 80, 90, 121

Fugger, Hans Jakob, 121

Fugger, Jakob, 60, 68, 234

G

Galleon (transport ship), 202–3

Garrard, Sir William, 144

Gasparo Ducci of Pistoia, 29

Georgijevic, Barolomej, 137

Gerbridge, John, 107

Gilbert, William, 195, 196, 198–9

Gladstone, William, 239

Gonnell, William, 12

Gonville Hall, Cambridge, 11–12

Gough, Hugh, *The offspring of the house of Ottomano* (1569), 137

Goulburn, Henry, 239

Granvelle, Antoine Perrenot de, 107

grasshopper badge or crest, 9, 111, 147, 203, 209, 214, 238, *pl.*

Great Fire of London (1666), 150, 225

Gresham, Anne (daughter, *later* Bacon), 92, 138, 166–70, 208

Gresham, Anne *see* Ferneley, Anne (*later* Gresham)

Gresham, Audrey (mother, *née* Lynne), 9

Gresham, Christiana (half-sister, *later* Thynne), 9, 55, 57–8, 120, 139, 248

Gresham, Elizabeth (half-sister), 9, 55, 57–8

Gresham, Isabel (stepmother, *née* Worsopp), 9–10, 54

Gresham, James, 9

Gresham, John (brother), 9, 33, 54–6, 120, 248

Gresham, Lady Katherine (aunt), 87, 183

Gresham, Richard (son), 37–8, 62, 119, 132–3, 248

Gresham, Sir John (uncle): TG apprenticed to, 4, 13, 14; arranges for TG to convey cash for Henry VIII, 29–30; lord mayor of London, 33; under Edward VI, 45; quarrel with Joachim Höchstetter, 48; and Sir Richard Gresham's will, 54; trading ventures, 60; and TG's scheme for merchant loans, 71, 247–8; death and inheritance, 86–8

Gresham, Sir Richard (father): background and career, 4, 9–11; elected master of the Mercers' Company, 14; lord mayor of London (1537–8), 7, 14; purchases Fountains Abbey, 15; London property of, 33; and Joachim Höchstetter, 48; death, 53–4; dispute over will, 54–6; on plans for a London bourse, 142

Gresham, Thomas: birth, 2, 8, 251–2; family background, 9–10; childhood and education, 10, 11–14;

apprenticeship, 13; enters family business, 14; visits Thomas Becket's shrine at Canterbury, 7–8, 15, 23; marriage to Anne Ferneley, 15; promoted to liveryman in the Mercers' Company, 16; commissions self-portrait (1544), 16–18, *pl.*; member of the Merchant Adventurers, 22; first government business, 23–4; at the Antwerp exchange, 24–5; transports cash for Henry VIII, 30; moves to Basinghall Street, 32–3; journal ('Day Book'), 34–6, 38, 40, 41, 42, 56, 62, 119, 202, 203, 238; accounting skills, 35, 40; trading activities, 35–7; early exchange transactions, 38; attempt to oust William Damsell, 48–9; finds favour with the duke of Northumberland, 49; moves to Catte Street, 50; appointed government banker to Edward VI, 52; dispute over father's will, 54–6; moves household to Antwerp (1551–3), 59; buys house in Lombard Street, 59; management of wife's inheritance, 61–3, 164; tasked by Northumberland to reduce government debt, 66–7; manipulates Antwerp currency market, 67, 69–70, 73; recommends English lead monopoly, 68–9; switches government borrowing to merchant loans, 70–72, 73, 83, 96–7, 98–9, 114–15, 182, 184–5; lobbies to revoke privileges of the Hanseatic League, 72–3; granted lands by Edward VI, 75; regains position under Queen Mary, 76–8; operates unlicensed forge, 80; Spanish venture to raise money, 79–85, 90, 107; avoidance of religious controversy, 84, 164–5; granted lands by Queen Mary at knock-down price, 88; investigated over Spanish venture, 90; raises loans for war with France, 90–91; illegitimate daughter, 92, 166–70; reappointed government banker

to Elizabeth I, 93–4; diplomatic role in Brussels, 94, 106–7, 108, 123, 125–6; financial advice to Elizabeth I, 95–8; urges Elizabeth to restore debased currency, 99–102; receives knighthood, 106; purchases house in Antwerp, 107–8, *pl.*; supplies credit and munitions to Elizabeth, 109–16; threats to his safety in Antwerp, 110, 124; elected upper warden of the Mercers' Company, 113; invites Elizabeth to Mercers' Company annual supper, 113; reprimanded by Elizabeth, 115; recommends Elizabeth marry Archduke Charles, 116–17; leg injury and lameness, 118, 197; accounts audited, 121–3; reduces overseas debts, 126–7, 151; relations with Lord Robert Dudley, 129–30; 'procurement' of luxury goods, 130–31, 160; letters of complaint to Elizabeth, 131–2, 159–60; death of his son, 132–3; purchases estate at Osterley, 133, 134–5, 136–7; builds Gresham House, 135–6; books dedicated to, 137–8; commissions portrait by Anthonis Mor, 140–42, *pl.*; builds the Royal Exchange, 142–50, *pl.*; in Antwerp during Calvinist crisis, 154–60; leaves Antwerp for good, 160–61; hospitality of, 162–3; commissions self-portrait (?1567), 165–6, *pl.*; forced to host Lady Mary Grey, 170–72, 187–8; and Spanish treasure ships, 174, 177–9; guardianship of Richard Clough's daughters, 187; Elizabeth grants lands to, 188; pays government foreign debts in full, 188; audit of final accounts, 189–91, 199; appeals to Elizabeth to write off debts, 190–91; supposed illegitimate son, 193–5; statue erected in the Mercers' Company, 196–7; indebtedness, 199, 208, 209, 246; trades arms illegally to Morocco, 200–204; provisions of will, 205–8, 220; death and funeral, 208–9;

portrayed in Thomas Heywood's play, 227–34; and arguably in Shakespeare's *Timon of Athens*, 234–6; legacy, 242–5

character & characteristics: bribes and gift giving, 40–41, 53, 87–8, 110–12; communication skills, 3; compulsive dealing, 85, 246; deviousness, 2–3, 167–8, 197; family relations, 139, 197, 247–8; gambling, 33; grasshopper badge or crest, 9; information network, 111–12, 129, 174, 198; language skills, 4, 13; marriage and family life, 5, 62, 247; mercantilist view of economics, 98, 249; obsessiveness, 3; philanthropic projects, 5; religious beliefs, 164–5; reluctance to do public service, 196; self-importance, 2, 230; self-publicist, 246; sharp practices, 4, 246; style of dress, 40; unethical dealing, 200–201, 229

Gresham, William (descendant), 239

Gresham, William (uncle), 9

Gresham College: provisions for in TG's will, 206, 220–22; TG's plans for, 216–17; administration, 217–20; used for patronage purposes, 223–4; distinguished professors of, 224; satire on (1647), 225; and the Royal Society, 225; decline of, 224–6; during the Civil War, 224; site sold to the crown (1768), 237; operates from Second Royal Exchange, 237–8; new building in Basinghall Street(1842), 240–42; moves to Barnard's Inn, Holborn (1991), 242; *pl.*

Gresham House: building of, 135–6; family members living at, 138, 214; Elizabeth I visits, 148; TG's hospitality at, 162; Lady Mary Grey imprisoned in, 170, 172, 187; Anne Ferneley's attempt to sell, 210, 211; *see also* Gresham College

Gresham Street, 240

'Gresham's Law', 2–3, 102–3, 249

Greville, Fulke, 224

Grey, Lady Jane, 74–5

Grey, Lady Katherine, 170

Grey, Lady Mary, 170–72, 187–8

Grindal, Edmund, bishop of London (*later* archbishop of York) 165

Guicciardini, Lodovico, 25

guilds or livery companies, origins of, 12–13

Guise, duke of, 124–5

Gunter, Edmund, 224

Gurnell, John, 194

Gwinne, Matthew, 224, 235

H

Hacket, Thomas, 137

Hamburg, Merchant Adventurers move to, 151, 180–82, 183

Hanseatic League, 32, 72–3, 95–6

Harpsfield, Dr Nicholas, 86–7

Hatfield, 4, 93, 246

Hatton, Sir Christopher, 212, 213

Hawkins, Sir John, 135

Helfenstein, George von, 116

Henry VIII: succeeds (1509), 10; dissolution of the monasteries, 14–15; captures Boulogne (1544), 27; debases the coinage, 27–8; borrows money in Antwerp, 28–9; employs Frescobaldi (bankers), 39; death, 44; attended Midsummer Watch at Mercers' Hall, 113; illegitimate son of, 248

Heywood, Thomas, *If you know not me, you know nobody* (play, 1605/6), 227–34

Höchstetter, Joachim, 48

Hogan, Edmond: apprentice to TG, 34; TG's factor in Spain, 60, 81, 82, 88, 90, 107, 112, 152, 191; testifies in Ferneley's case against Markham, 194; loyalty to TG, 197–8; and TG's illegal arms trade, 200–202; TG's creditor, 209

Hogan, Robert, 112, 152, 191, 198

Hogenberg, Frans, 147, *pl.*

Holbein, Hans, the Younger, 140
Hooftman, Gillis, 157
Hooke, Robert, 225, 226
Hoorn, Philippe de Montmorency, count of, 158, 173
Horton, Thomas, 224
Hosier, Geoffrey, 195
Huguenots, 124, 173, 189
Hundred Years War (1337–1453), 3
Hungarian copper market, 68
Hunsdon, Lord, 162
Hurst, Anne (mistress of TG), 193–5, 214–15, 247, 248

I
Iñiguez, Juan, 81
Italian banking families, 39
Ivan the Terrible, 163

J
James V of Scotland, 7
Jansen, Albrecht, 123
Jegon, Dr John, 217

K
Katherine of Berain, 181, 186
Keck, Hans, 111
Kenilworth Castle, 190–91
Keys, Thomas, 170–71, 187
Kingsmill, Richard, 211
Knollys, Sir Francis, 104, 122, 189

L
Langton, Christopher, 37–8, 171, 205
Lawrence, John, 198
Le Havre, 124
lead trade, 36, 68–9
Lee, Edward, archbishop of York, 37
Lee, Sir Henry, 173
Lee, Sir Richard, 111
Leigh, Sir John, 76, 87–8
Leigh, Sir Thomas, 10, 76
Lixhalls, Andreas, 121
Lomellini, Domenico, 135

London International Financial Futures Exchange, 240
Louis of Nassau, 173
Lucian of Samosata, 234
Luther, Martin, 1, 12
Lutherans, 159
Lyster, John, 56

M
MacLeod, Henry Dunning, 2, 102, 249
Madrid, 94, 98, 121
Mann, Dr John, 152
Mansfeld, Herzog Christoph Albrecht, count of, 111, 114
Manson, Thomas, 194, 195, 198, 211, 213
Manwood, Roger, 164, 168, 205
Margaret of Parma: appointed regent in the Netherlands, 106; TG's diplomatic relations with, 108, 111, 112; and Anglo-Brabant trade, 126, 127; and the Calvinist crisis, 153, 154, 156, 159; *pl.*
Marie de Guise, 7, 108–9, 113
Markham, John, 193–6, 214–15, 228, 235
Marsh, John, 125
Martin, Sir Roger, 185
Mary, Queen: assumes the crown, 75; marries Philip of Spain, 78–9; persecution of Protestants, 84; pseudo-pregnancies, 84, 92; death, 92–3
Mary, queen of Scots, 108, 179, 219
Mary of Hungary, 27, 28, 61, 79, 84
Mason, Sir John, 51
Maximilian I, Holy Roman Emperor, 39
Mayfield House, 136, 172, 189, 207, 212
'Memorandum of Exchange' (1560s), 103–4
Mercers' Company: elects Sir Richard Gresham as master, 14; erects statue of Thomas Gresham, 196–7; and Gresham College, 216, 221, 240, 241; and the Merchant Adventurers, 22; promotes TG to liveryman, 16; and the Royal Exchange, 145, 239; and TG's will, 206–7, 212

Merchant Adventurers: exclusive rights of trade in the Netherlands, 22; and merchant loans, 115, 119; move to Hamburg, 180, 183; and the Spanish treasure ships, 175, 176; surrenders lease on Antwerp headquarters, 127; TG lobbies for over Hanseatic League, 72
Merchant Taylors' Company, 143
Mestrelle, Eloy, 100–102
Middleton, John, 9
Middleton, Thomas, 234
Mildmay, Sir Walter, 65, 90, 100, 122, 189, 212
Montreuil, Madame de, 7
Mor, Anthonis, 140–42, 173
More, Sir Thomas, 12, 39; *Utopia*, 1, 199–200
Morocco, English trade with, 199–204
Mundell, Robert, 249
Muscovy Company, 163, 189, 199

N
Negrón, Octaviano de, 81
Netherlands: Calvinism, 152–9; duke of Alva's regency, 160–61, 166, 173, 174; embargo on English trade, 125; Spanish Inquisition, 124; *see also* Anglo-Netherlands trade; Antwerp
Neville, Sir Henry, 207, 211, 212
Neville family, 179
New Bourse, Antwerp, 25, 143
New World bullion, 60, 69, 90, 98
Nonsuch Palace, Surrey, 137
Northern Rising (1569), 179–80, 219
Northumberland, John Dudley, 1st duke of (*formerly* earl of Warwick): lord president of Edward VI's council, 49–52, 64–5; currency devaluation, 64–5; promotes TG's career, 51–2, 65; and merchant loans, 70; revokes privileges of Hanseatic League, 72–3; and Lady Jane Grey, 74–5; executed, 75

O
Oosterweel, Netherlands, 159
Oresme, Nicholas, bishop of Lisieux, 2–3, 103
Ortels, Abraham, 61
Osterley House and deer park, 134, 136–7, 188, 189, 214

P
Pacioli, Luca, 35, 62–3
Packington, Robert, 123
Paesschen, Hendryk van, 135, 143–4, 145, 146
Paget, Sir William, 44
Palavicino, Horatio, 193
Parker, Matthew, archbishop of Canterbury, 167, 171
Parry, Sir Thomas, 99, 100, 114, 115, 116, 129
Paston, Gertrude, 138, 211, 214, 216
Paston, Sir William, 138
Paynell, Thomas, 137
Peckham, Edmund, 70
Peel, Sir Robert, 239
Percy family, 179
Pereman, Gilbert, 193
Petty, William, 224
Philip, duke of Burgundy, 19
Philip II of Spain: marries Queen Mary, 78–9; succeeds as king of Spain, 84; declares bankruptcy, 89–90, 121; war with France, 91, 92; returns to Spain, 94; rule in the Netherlands, 123–4; relations with Elizabeth I, 152; and Calvinist rising in the Netherlands, 156; appoints duke of Alva as regent of the Netherlands, 160
Pickering, Hester, 163–4
Pickering, Sir William, 163–4, 248
piracy, English, 125, 174
Pius V, Pope, 200
Plantin, Christopher, 61
Plutarch, *Lives*, 234
Pole, Cardinal Reginald, 84, 93

Pole, Sir Geoffrey, 14
population of towns and cities, 16th
 century, 20
Portugal, 200
Prayer Book, 50, 64

R
Radcliffe, Ralph, 34
Ragio, Tommaso, 178
Ramsey, Sir Thomas, 232–3
Read, Richard (stepson), 34, 119, 138, 211,
 214, 216
Read, Thomas, 213, 214, 216
Read, William, the elder, 4, 15, 32–3
Read, William, the younger (stepson), 34,
 119, 138, 211, 214, 216, 221–3, 228
Recorde, Robert, 37
Ridolfi, Roberto, 179
Rightwise, John, 11
Robinson, Ralph, 200
Robsart, Amy, 129
Rooke, Lawrence, 225
Roover, Raymond de, 103
Rowe, Thomas, 176
Royal Exchange: TG builds, 142–8, *pl*.;
 Elizabeth I names and opens, 148–50;
 in TG's will, 206–7; Anne Ferneley's
 management of, 213, 220–21; destroyed
 in Great Fire (1666), 225; *see also*
 Second Royal Exchange; Third Royal
 Exchange
Royal Society, 225

S
saltpetre, 27, 91, 119, 200–204
Saunders, John, 198
Savoy, Emmanuel Philibert, duke of, 91
Schetz, Erasmus, 47
Schetz, Gaspar, 60–61, 66, 80, 112
Schetz, Melchior, 44, 61, 64
Scorel, Jan van, 140, 166
Scotland, Protestant revolution in,
 108–13
Second Royal Exchange, 225–6, 237–8

Seville, Spain, 60
Seymour, Edward *see* Somerset, Edward
 Seymour, 1st duke of
Seymour, Jane, 113
Shakespeare, William, 224; *The Merry
 Wives of Windsor*, 101; *Timon of Athens*,
 234
Sharington, Sir William, 135
Shrewsbury, George Talbot, 6th earl of,
 162, 210, 236
Sidney, Philip, 224
Siegmund, archduke of Tyrol, 68
silver mining industry, 69–70
slave trade, 135–6
Somerset, Edward Seymour, 1st duke of
 (*formerly* earl of Hertford), 44–51
Southwood, William, 54
Spain: and New World trade, 60; TG's
 venture in, 79–85, 90, 107, 152; treasure
 ships seized by Elizabeth (1568), 174–9;
 war with England, 192
Spanish Armada (1588), 219
Spanish Inquisition, 124, 156
Spes, Don Guerau de, 174, 175, 177, 179
Spinola, Benedetto, 178
Spritewell, John, 60, 81, 82, 88, 154, 155
St Bartholomew's Day Massacre (1572),
 189
St Bavo's fair, Antwerp, 21, 115
St Helen's Bishopsgate, 6, 163, 164–5,
 208–9, 216, *pl*.
St Paul's School, 11
St Quentin, siege of (1557), 89
Star Chamber, 56, 193, 195, 215, 222
Stephen, Thomas (priest), 53
Steward, Augustine, 34, 46, 119
Stokes, Adrian, 187
Stonley, Richard, 192
Stow, John, 146
Stringer, Anthony, 88, 142, 198
Suffolk, Frances Brandon, duchess of,
 74
sugar trade, 202, 204, 228–9

T

Tadlow, George, 200
Talbot Papers, 210
Taverner, Richard, 12
Taylor, Robert, 190, 192
Thatcher, Margaret, 249
Third Royal Exchange, 238–40
Thirty-Nine Articles, 217, 219
Thomas, William, 50
Throckmorton, Nicholas, 112
Thwaites, Frances, 54, 120, 210–11
Thynne, Sir John, 57
tin trade, 36
Tite, Sir William, 238
Tomasso, Francesco di, 60, 174, 198
Treasury of Amadis of France, The (1572), 137
Tucher, Lazarus, 47, 60, 66, 77, 94, 109, 121

U

usury, 12, 23, 29, 89, 292 n.18
Uvedale, William, 87

V

Vaughan, Stephen, 28, 29–30, 36
Verstegan, Richard, *The post for divers parts of the world* (1575), 137–8
Vertue, George, 18
Victoria, Queen, 238–40

W

Waad, Armagil, 41
Walsingham, Sir Francis, 189, 191, 197, 198, 200–202, 212
Walter, Elizabeth, 223

Wars of Religion, 123, 124–5
Wars of the Roses (1455–1485), 3
Warwick, Ambrose Dudley, 1st earl of, 124–5
Welser, Christopher, 156
West Bradenham, Norfolk, 42
Whitgift, John, archbishop of Canterbury, 218, 219
Whittington, Sir Richard ('Dick'), 32, 196
Wilford, Thomas, 222
William, Prince of Orange, 119, 124, 154, 156–7, 159, 173, 191, *pl.*
Winchester, William Paulet, 1st marquis of: attends annual Mercers' supper, 114; audits TG's accounts, 90, 107, 121–2; on financial commission (1564), 104; length of service, 132; and merchant loans, 119; provides TG with funds, 127, 153; and wardship of William Uvedale, 87
Winter, Thomas, 248
woad trade, 36–7
Wohlstadt, Daniel, 101
Wolsey, Cardinal Thomas, 11, 248
wool trade, 35–6, 125, 127, 199
Worsopp, John, 10
Wotton, Sir Edward, 28
Wren, Christopher, 225
Wright, Richard, 222
Wriothesley, Sir Thomas, 29
Wyatt, Sir Thomas, 23–4, 75
Wyndham, Francis, 168

Y

Yarford, Sir James, 196
Ympyn Christoffels, Jan, 35